BRITAIN'S HABITATS

A Guide to the Wildlife Habitats of Britain and Ireland

SOPHIE LAKE, DURWYN LILEY,
ROBERT STILL & ANDY SWASH

WILD*Guides*

PRINCETON
press.princeton.edu

Published by Princeton University Press,
41 William Street, Princeton, New Jersey 08540
In the United Kingdom: Princeton University Press, 6 Oxford Street,
Woodstock, Oxfordshire OX20 1TW
nathist.press.princeton.edu

British Library Cataloging-in-Publication Data is available

Library of Congress Control Number 2014947358
ISBN 978-0-691-15855-6

Production and design by **WILD**Guides Ltd., Old Basing, Hampshire UK.

Printed in China

10 9 8 7 6 5 4 3 2 1

CONTENTS

PREFACE

There is a wide diversity of wildlife habitats in Britain and Ireland, ranging from dynamic coastal habitats to remote rocky mountains. They include ancient woodlands, flower-rich grasslands, extensive heathlands, a variety of wetlands and standing and flowing water. In fact, the habitats of Britain and Ireland can be categorised into 64 different types. The aim of this book is to enable you to recognise these different habitats when out and about in the countryside, to understand more about their ecology and conservation, and to appreciate the rich variety of plant and animals species they support.

The diversity of habitats found in Britain and Ireland is a consequence of both the varied geology and climate of these islands and the actions of humans. Almost all of our habitats are 'semi-natural', having evolved from natural habitats through human intervention (usually in prehistoric times), and have been maintained by humans for thousands of years. A tiny handful of ravine woodlands, inaccessible mountain ledges, unstable cliffs and shifting foreshores are near-natural, although not entirely unaffected by human activities. Such habitats are important because they are places where natural processes function more or less unhindered and where an element of wilderness still persists. However, semi-natural habitats can be just as important and support very diverse or specialist suites of species, for which they are greatly valued. These species are adapted to relatively open or disturbed conditions, and were probably present within natural clearings, wetlands and in coastal situations when woodland still covered much of Britain and Ireland, expanding into deforested areas in the Neolithic period, around 6,000 years ago. Some of these semi-natural habitats are ancient, and are cherished for their cultural and historical significance as well as their wildlife.

This book provides contextual information on the pressures that habitats are experiencing and indicates what is needed to prevent and reverse ongoing degradation and ensure the species to which they are home can flourish. As each human generation becomes accustomed to a progressively impoverished natural environment, it loses sight of the biological richness that previous generations took for granted, a phenomenon that has been called 'shifting baseline syndrome' and which results in the gradual diminution of society's understanding of how rich in wildlife our countryside could be. This book is intended to show how diverse and exciting our habitats can be and what makes them so worth caring about and caring for.

Some semi-natural habitats such as lowland meadows (TOP RIGHT, **Kingcombe, Dorset**) are pastoral in feel, a reminder of a time when our agricultural practices were more accommodating of wildlife; others, such as Upland Dry Heath and Caledonian Forest (CENTRE RIGHT, **Ryvoan Pass, Cairngorms**), are wilder in aspect and less obviously influenced by humans. Machair (BELOW, **South Uist, Outer Hebrides**) is a unique habitat found only on the coasts of north-west Scotland and western Ireland. Ravine woodlands (BOTTOM, **Thirlmere, Lake District**), are perhaps amongst the most natural of our habitats.

INTRODUCTION

Habitats are the places where plants and animals live. They are characterised by distinctive combinations of plant and animal communities and their physical environment. This makes it possible to identify individual types of habitat, which is useful in understanding where different species are likely to be found and what their needs are – crucial information for protecting wildlife. Habitats are also valued in their own right as the diverse products of interactions between plants and animals and their environment. For this reason, nature conservation legislation affords protection to habitat types as well as to species.

It is fairly easy to separate habitats into broad categories such as woodland, heathland, grassland, wetland and freshwater and many people are familiar with these terms. Yet within each of these categories there is a wide variety of different habitat types. These habitat types have been classified under a range of different systems (see *page 20*)

Some habitats will not fit easily into any one of the accounts given in this book – they might be transitional between different habitats, or a particular local expression of a habitat. For example, this site in Connemara supports a curious patchwork of Machair and Lowland Dry Heath.

that have been designed for a variety of purposes, and are in some cases very technical. This book provides a clear description of each of the wildlife habitats that are likely to be encountered in Britain and Ireland, enabling them to be recognised with confidence. For each habitat type, information is provided on its distribution and extent in Britain and Ireland, its ecology, origins and the way it has developed, and the conservation issues. These 'habitat accounts' also indicate the key features and species to look out for and the best times of year to visit.

Although most habitats can be recognised quite readily, it is important to remember that they are variable, and that transitions between the different types are common. These transitions (sometimes called 'ecotones') may support species typical of both habitats as well as other species that are particularly adapted to the transitional conditions. Sometimes habitats occur in easily distinguishable and often extensive patches with clear boundaries, but in other instances the transition is much more gradual and there is no distinct boundary. In some environments, or under particular management regimes, a variety of different habitat types and transitions between them can be found together in a distinctive combination which can, itself, be considered as a unique habitat. For example, Soft Cliff often contains a mosaic of grassland, wetland and scrub habitats, and Wood Pasture is a combination of woodland and grassland.

The Habitats of Britain and Ireland

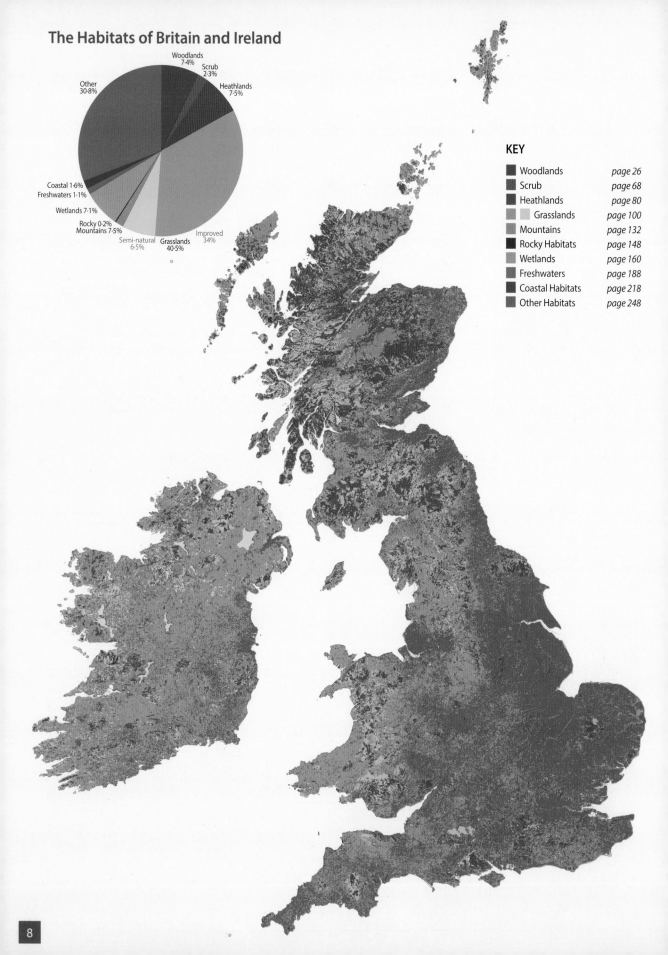

Pie chart:
- Woodlands 7·4%
- Scrub 2·3%
- Heathlands 7·5%
- Improved 34%
- Grasslands 40·5%
  - Semi-natural 6·5%
- Mountains 7·5%
- Rocky 0·2%
- Wetlands 7·1%
- Freshwaters 1·1%
- Coastal 1·6%
- Other 30·8%

KEY

	Woodlands	*page 26*
	Scrub	*page 68*
	Heathlands	*page 80*
	Grasslands	*page 100*
	Mountains	*page 132*
	Rocky Habitats	*page 148*
	Wetlands	*page 160*
	Freshwaters	*page 188*
	Coastal Habitats	*page 218*
	Other Habitats	*page 248*

ABOVE: **Frenchman's Creek, Helford River, Cornwall**. Here the boundary between the different habitats types (**Mudflat** and **Woodland**) is clearly defined. BELOW: In this view of the **Lake District** several different habitat types can be seen, including **Scree** (A), **Rocky Slope** (B), **Upland Acid Grassland** (C), **Bracken** (D), **Mixed Scrub** (E) and **Atlantic Oak Wood** (F). Individual habitat patches are straightforward to identify, but the edges are in some cases transitional, with one habitat type blending into another.

TYPES OF HABITAT

When trying to decide on a name for a habitat there is an impressive array of terms to choose from. Whilst some are broad and overarching (*e.g.* 'freshwaters'), others are very precise (*e.g.* 'Hard oligo-mesotrophic waters with benthic vegetation of *Chara* spp.'). The titles given to the habitat types included in this book err towards the more specific end of the spectrum as these are generally more informative. Full accounts are given for 64 main habitat types that fall within the broad habitat categories of woodlands, scrub, heathlands, grasslands, mountains, rocky habitats, wetlands, freshwaters, coastal habitats and 'other habitats', the latter being a catch-all for anything that did not fit comfortably elsewhere. Summary accounts are provided for a further nine rare habitats (five types of heathland and four types of freshwater lake).

Although most of the habitats covered in this book are recognised as UK Priority Habitats (see *Habitat Classification page 20*), even if their names may vary slightly, there are a few exceptions. This is either because, although not considered a priority for nature conservation, it is still a distinctive semi-natural habitat of some interest for wildlife (e.g. Upland Rush Pasture), or because it is in some way considered to be unique (e.g. Atlantic Hazel Wood). In order to provide a more logical classification from the point of view of identifying habitats in the field, some habitats have not been included within the same broad category that applies to UK Priority Habitats. For example, Calaminarian Grassland and Purple Moor-grass and Rush Pasture are within the grassland section of this book, although they are considered under 'inland rock' and 'fen, marsh and swamp' respectively as part of the UK Priority Habitat classification system. In addition, for ease of reference, most mountain habitats have been grouped together.

Woodland habitats are those dominated by trees. They include our most structurally diverse and natural-seeming habitats, although almost all are a product of the long-term interaction between people and nature.

Scrub includes habitats dominated by shrub species. Hedgerow and Bracken are included within this category, as they are in many ways ecologically similar.

Heathland includes open habitats dominated by dwarf-shrubs such as heathers, Bilberry and Crowberry. Most is semi-natural, a consequence of traditional agricultural practices carried out on poor soils.

Grassland habitats are those dominated by grasses and herbs. Some meadows are enclosed as fields, other grasslands form open landscapes, particularly in the uplands and on downland. Most would eventually revert to woodland without management.

Mountain habitats are found above about 700 m and are primarily influenced by environmental conditions; they are some of our most natural habitats.

Rocky habitats are exposed vegetated rock. Although very typical of mountains, they are also found in the uplands, and even at sea level (although this category does not include maritime cliffs).

Wetlands are a very diverse group of habitats predominantly influenced by the presence of freshwater. Most are transitional, but some have reached an equilibrium due to the wet nature of our climate or ongoing management.

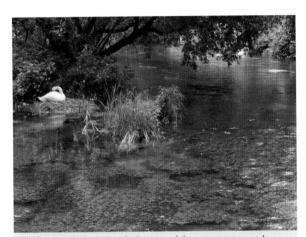

Freshwater habitats include rivers, lakes, streams, ponds and canals; all have open water, which can be either standing or flowing.

Coastal habitats include muddy, sandy and rocky shoreline habitats from the intertidal zone to the point inland where the maritime influence is no longer overriding.

Other habitats include those that are most strongly influenced by humans but can nevertheless still be rich in species, such as Brownfield and Arable.

FACTORS INFLUENCING HABITATS

The habitats we see today owe their origins to a complex range of interacting factors, including geology, geography, topography, climate and the influence of humans.

Geology and soils

Britain and Ireland have an incredibly varied geology, which is reflected in the diversity of habitats present and is unusual in such a relatively small area. The bedrock is fundamental in shaping the landscape and habitats present, although in some places its influence is softened by superficial deposits. These are derived through weathering (over geological time scales) or are transported by the wind (as in the case of Sand Dune and Machair), or by glaciers and their melt-waters. Such glacial drift covers much of Britain and Ireland, excluding the south of England. Soil nutrient status and acidity/alkalinity are also key factors in determining the type of habitats present. In some cases,

soils can also disguise the character of the bedrock, but the two are usually closely related as soils are derived from weathered rock. The decomposition of vegetation, leaching (whereby soluble substances are carried down through the soil by rainwater and become unobtainable to plants) and climate also influence the soil. On well-drained soils that developed under woodland, leaching is not a strong factor, and the soil, known as brown earth, contains plenty of organic matter incorporated by the activities of earthworms. In colder and wetter climates, leaching is more pronounced, leading to nutrient-poor soils. Where waterlogging occurs, anaerobic gleys form and are widespread in the uplands where they support moorland habitats. Waterlogging can also lead to the formation of peat and wetland habitats. On limestone, the strongly calcareous influence of the bedrock is too pronounced to be leached out and thin, slightly alkaline, free-draining soils (known as rendzinas) support distinctive calcareous grassland habitats.

Rock type

Igneous rocks such as granite and basalt are formed from molten magma and are usually very hard. They include both volcanic rock (formed by eruptions) and intrusive rock, which is formed deep in the earth's crust. Patchily distributed, these rocks are slow to erode and form the hard cliffs of Lundy and Strumble Head, Snowdon, parts of the Lake District, Arthur's Seat in Edinburgh, the highest peaks in Scotland and the tors of Dartmoor.

Sedimentary rocks dominate across most of England and much of Wales and central Ireland. They are ancient sediments laid down by rivers or on the sea bed, and include limestone, sandstone and shale.

Metamorphic rocks are secondary rocks, generated from either igneous or sedimentary rocks through heat and or pressure, deep within the earth's crust. Limestone metamorphoses into marble, and shale into schist or slate. Metamorphic rocks dominate in the Highlands of Scotland, Tyrone, Londonderry and Donegal.

KEY

SEDIMENTARY ROCKS
- Eocene, Oligocene, Pliocene and marine Pleistocene
- Cretaceous
- Jurassic
- Triassic
- Permian
- Carboniferous
- Devonian
- Silurian
- Ordovician
- Cambrian
- Late Precambrian

METAMORPHIC ROCKS
- Lower Palaeozoic and Proterozoic
- Early Precambrian

IGNEOUS ROCKS
- Intrusive
- Volcanic

1 Cul Mor, Assynt. These dramatic peaks are relics of a great sheet of Precambrian sandstone laid down on top of ancient metamorphic gneiss well over 2,000 million years old. Much of the landscape is characterised by Upland Wet Heath and Blanket Bog with mountain habitats found on the peaks.

2 Meall nan Tarmachan, near Ben Lawers, Perthshire. Rock formed from sands, muds and limestones deposited in an ancient sea *ca.* 600 million years ago was subsequently subjected to intense heat and pressure. The resulting metamorphic schists are renowned for their Upland Calcareous Grassland and mountain habitats.

3 Weeting Heath, Norfolk, is found in a gently rolling chalk landscape that has been overlain with wind-blown sands of glacial origins and supports stripes and patchworks of Lowland Dry Acid Grassland and Lowland Calcareous Grassland.

4 Woolbeding Common, West Sussex, overlies Greensand, a type of greenish sandstone laid down in the Cretaceous period. The area supports Lowland Dry Heath, Lowland Wet Heath and Wood Pasture, and secondary woodland including Lowland Dry Oak and Birch Wood.

5 Stonehill Down, Purbeck. This quarry was used to excavate chalk, a soft limestone formed in the Cretaceous (less than 100 million years ago) when this area was bathed in a warm, shallow sea. It supports Lowland Calcareous Grassland with Ash-dominated Lowland Mixed Oak and Ash Wood on the northern flank.

6 Igneous granite outcrops such as Haytor on Dartmoor, Devon are distinctive landmarks formed of hard rocks created around 300 million years ago. They are surrounded by heathland and grassland habitats with Blanket Bog.

7 Exmoor, Somerset/Devon. The relief is gentle compared to that of the Breacon Beacons (similarly formed of Old Red Sandstone) as the glaciers did not reach this far south in the Pleistocene. Exmoor is characterised by Upland Dry Heath, Upland Wet Heath, Blanket Bog and Atlantic Oak Wood.

8 The Burren, Co. Clare, has extensive exposures of Carboniferous Limestone, which formed as sediments in a tropical sea from approximately 350 million years ago and support Limestone Pavement, calcareous grasslands and a form of Atlantic Hazel Wood.

9 The Lake District hills are geologically varied and are composed of differently aged rocks, including volcanic rocks; sedimentary sandstones, siltstones, mudstones and limestone; and granite. They support a variety of upland habitats.

Climate, topography and geography

Britain and Ireland have an oceanic climate with relatively small differences between the summer and winter temperatures. The moderating influence of the Atlantic Ocean means that the climate is much milder than that of other places at comparable latitudes (*i.e.* those receiving a similar amount of solar radiation, such as Mongolia), and this shapes the habitats present. However, the climate varies across Britain and Ireland and this is reflected in the types of habitat that can be found in different areas. Oceanic western woodlands receive five times as much rainfall as their south-eastern counterparts, and are characterised by the abundance and diversity of moisture-loving mosses and liverworts (bryophytes). The wind-whipped Hebrides support unique coastal grassland heavily influenced by blown sand. Vast areas of the cool, wet north are blanketed in peatland habitats, while the continental climate of Breckland in East Anglia supports steppe-like grasslands and parched limestone grassland in the south can support Mediterranean plants.

Humans

Humans have had a profound impact on the habitats of Britain and Ireland since adopting a settled agricultural existence in the Neolithic period, when the process of woodland clearance became widespread (see timeline on *page 16*). Seven thousand years later the area of woodland had been reduced by more than 95%. During the intervening millennia, open semi-natural habitats came to dominate the landscape as a consequence of agricultural and associated practices. The relative amounts of semi-natural habitat fluctuated through the ages, but it was when these practices began to change radically in the second half of the 20th century that a staggering proportion of habitats was lost to agricultural intensification, afforestation and development. Habitat destruction has now slowed significantly (but not ceased), and deliberate re-creation and restoration is taking place. However, habitats are continuing to deteriorate due, for example, to climate change, pollution, inappropriate management and the affects of habitat fragmentation.

This map shows upland areas of Britain and Ireland defined by climate, soils and altitude. Habitats change in character at about 300 m above sea level, although in more exposed situations the transition can be much lower. Temperature falls around 0·6°C for every 100 m increase in altitude, so only cold-tolerant species are found at higher altitudes. Topography can also accentuate climatic conditions and increase the variety of species and habitats found at different extremes. Corries on the glaciated north and east-facing slopes of mountains support rare montane habitats requiring moist, cool, sheltered conditions; in contrast, warm south-facing well-drained slopes in the south can support Mediterranean species near the limit of their range.

KEY

▲ Peak over 900 m
⬛ Uplands

LEFT: Rainfall averages 3,200 mm per year in the higher areas of the Lake District and feeds innumerable small streams.
RIGHT: In Breckland, an average of 600 mm of rain falls per year and the drought-prone sandy soils support a sparse grassy sward.

Climate varies across Britain and Ireland according to latitude, the influence of the Atlantic Ocean and the prevailing south-westerly winds. Western areas are milder, wetter and windier, and show smaller differences in daily and seasonal temperatures. Eastern areas are drier with more extreme temperatures. The south of England can be influenced by the warm air mass from the continent, while northern Scotland is exposed to the polar air mass resulting in a 10–15 °C difference in temperature.

KEY
Mean January minimum temperature (°C)
1981–2011

7
5
4
3
2
1
0
−1
−2
−3
−4

KEY
Mean August maximum temperature (°C)
1981–2011

25
23
21
19
17
15
13
11
9

KEY
Mean Annuall Rainfall (mm)
1981–2011

4,140
3,740
3,380
3,020
2,660
2,300
1,940
1,580
1,220
860
500

Climate change

The climate of Britain and Ireland has changed dramatically in the past and is changing rapidly now. Current predictions suggest that summer temperatures will rise and summer rainfall decrease (particularly in the south), winter rainfall will increase and there will be an increase in sea-level rise and extreme weather events. Habitats have adapted to climate change in the past, but the unprecedented rate and scale of change and the degree of fragmentation of many habitats makes climate change one of the biggest challenges for conservation today. Habitats are likely to alter as climatic conditions become unsuitable for some existing species, and climate change may exacerbate the impacts of other factors such as atmospheric pollution or pathogens. However, new species for which conditions become suitable will arrive. Coastal habitats in particular will be impacted by rising sea levels. Action is needed to increase the resilience of habitats by reducing other pressures, by improving habitat management and by ensuring there is space for habitats and species to change in their distribution.

YEAR	EVENT
BC	
108000	Start of Devensian/Midlandian Glacial period (ice covers much of Ireland and Britain, north of a line from South Wales to The Wash)
24800	**Modern people arrive in Britain and Ireland (a peninsula of Eurasia)**
10000	Ireland separated from Britain. Woolly Mammoth and Woolly Rhinocerous extinct
9500	Climate warms at end of Devensian/Midlandian Glacial period; tundra-type vegetation; **significant movement of people into Britain**
8000	**Movement of people into Ireland**
7000	Scots Pine arrives in north-west Scotland
6000	Britain separated from European mainland
5000	Warmer, more oceanic climate; rain-fed bogs start to form
4000	Woodland reaches fullest extend
3000	Woodland clearance starts by Neolithic peoples using stone axes and ring-barking. First evidence of coppicing; Stonehenge and Newgrange built
1500	**First field systems in permanent clearings**
1000	Auroch extinct in Britain and Ireland
500	**Copper mined; use of metal tools expands woodland clearings, heathlands become established**
AD	
1000	
2000	

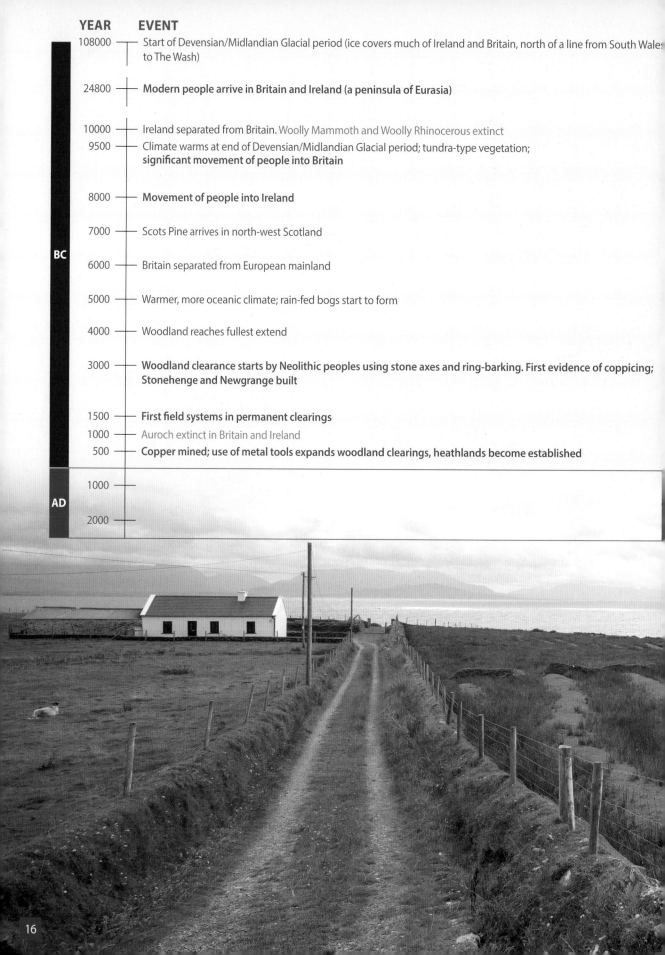

YEAR	EVENT
AD	
43	Start of Roman Britain, roads, drainage (*e.g.* Fens)
500	British human population 1·5 million
1086	Normans: 15% of England wooded; medieval open-field farming; Rabbit introduced
1349	Black Death, widespread abandonment of agricultural land
1564	First canal (Exeter)
1614	British human population 4 million
1621	Wolf extinct
1637	Start of major drainage works in Fens
1707	Jethro Tull invents seed drill; agricultural revolution about to start
1760	Industrial revolution, increase in use of fossil fuels, atmospheric pollution
1761	Enclosure Acts: loss of open field systems in Ireland and England
1792	'Year of the Sheep': Highland Clearances in Scotland
1845	Irish Potato Famine; Irish population falls by 50%
1850	Beaver extinct
1919	Woodland cover < 5%; coniferous afforestation starts
1950	Agricultural intensification starts, resulting in the destruction or neglect of much natural habitat
1958	The River Thames declared 'biologically dead' where it flows through London
2000	Habitat decline slowing after English lowland meadow declined by 97%, lowland heathland by 80%, Raised Bog by 94% and 45% of Scotland's Blanket Bog was afforested in 20th century; **British human population 58·6 million**
2010	125 fish species recorded in the River Thames

MAIN PICTURE: Lazy beds between Clare Island harbour and Portnakilly, Ireland. Lazy beds are a ridge and furrow farming system that can still be seen in parts of western Scotland and Ireland. In these areas seaweed is often applied as a fertilizer and the beds are used to grow potatoes. The field systems in much of Britain would have resembled lazy beds during the post-Roman period in the 5th and 6th centuries.

NATURAL CHANGE – SUCCESSION

Succession is the sequential change in the species present in a given place over time. The process of succession is referred to frequently in this book as it is the key natural mechanism through which changes occur, both within and between habitat types. Succession is a result of the adaptations of species to specific environments, and the way in which species change their environment.

Primary succession starts on bare ground that is colonised by pioneer species adapted to cope with exposed conditions and low levels of nutrients. Which species these are depends on the nature of the substrate – for example, lichens and mosses are primary colonisers of bare rock (*e.g.* Scree), and specialist flowering plants are colonisers of bare sand (*e.g.* pioneer Sand Dune). These species gradually change the environment, increasing the organic content of the substrate and its capacity to hold water, and in some cases stabilising the substrate and allowing it to 'build' (*e.g.* Saltmarsh and Sand Dune). These changes result in other, more vigorous species being able to colonise, which often outcompete the previous species and, in turn, change the environment. This may allow longer-lived species such as shrubs to become established and these eventually give way to trees. However, the succession need not stop here, as in particularly wet situations bog-mosses can start the process of peat formation. Where conditions become too wet for trees to become established, bog may develop.

The process of change continues until an equilibrium (often called a climax community) is reached where there is no further potential for new species to colonise, or until disturbance events or environmental change disrupt or reset the successional process. Most habitats in Britain and Ireland are maintained at a particular stage in their successional pathway by human activities (such as livestock grazing). This is called a 'plagioclimax'.

Secondary succession occurs when an existing community is disturbed (*e.g.* by natural tree fall or by tree-felling in woodland) and the process is set back to an earlier stage (*e.g.* grassland or heathland). The pathway that succession takes is not random, but is influenced by a variety of factors such as climate and seed source, and the degree of the disturbance involved – and it can happen at any scale. Disturbance events that cause a reversion to bare ground, and subsequent succession, are a key element in many habitats, and lead to the development of a diversity of vegetation types and structures that are suitable for a range of different species, for example in Lowland Dry Heath or Soft Cliff (see *pages 86* and *242*).

A range of successional stages can often be observed together in the landscape. This can be in situations where secondary succession is patchy or is at different stages with a given area, or where primary succession is resulting in an environmental gradient (e.g. in accreting Sand Dune or Saltmarsh).

Solway Firth, Dumfries and Galloway – successional stages from pioneer to upper Saltmarsh, Reedbed and woodland.

Reedbed

Woodland

Upper Saltmarsh

Pioneer Saltmarsh

Succession over time presents a major challenge when the conservation aim is to maintain a particular successional stage but the activities that traditionally achieved this are no longer carried out. The photographs shown here illustrate the colonisation of heathland by Scots Pine over a ten-year period.

Cerne Abbas, Dorset – a mosaic of successional stages is seen here with patches of Lowland Calcareous Grassland (LCG), Mixed Scrub and woodland intermingling on the hillslope.

HABITAT CLASSIFICATION

Several different systems are used to record or classify habitats in Britain and Ireland. These various systems have been devised for different purposes, for example to enable the legal protection of habitats or for survey purposes. The different systems can be initially confusing as they do not always correspond neatly. Some examples are illustrated here to show the complexity of the situation. The approach used in this book is straightforward, with habitat definitions largely similar to the UK Priority Habitats. To minimise potential confusion, the relationships between the most commonly used classification systems and the habitats described within this book are shown on *pages 256–265*, together with sources of further information.

Priority Habitats were identified in the UK as part of the UK Biodiversity Action Plan, the UK's response to the 1992 Convention on Biological Diversity. They are habitats considered to be under threat due to rarity or rate of decline, or for which the UK has particular international responsibility. They were placed within a framework of *Broad Habitat Types*. This Priority Habitat list is still used as the basis of much ongoing biodiversity work.

The Habitats Directive is European legislation that requires member states to designate, maintain, restore and protect sites to form a coherent network across Europe. Annex I of the Directive lists 189 habitat types (of which 79 occur in the UK and/or Ireland) considered to be rare or vulnerable in a European context. These are referred to as *Annex I habitats.* The habitat accounts in this book encompass all Annex I habitats types found in Britain and/or Ireland (with the exception of marine habitats).

Classification systems include the *Phase 1 Habitat Classification* and the *National Vegetation Classification* (NVC). Phase 1 provides a standardised system to record semi-natural vegetation and other wildlife habitats in the UK at a broad level through field surveys. The *National Vegetation Classification* is a far more detailed classification of the vegetation types (rather than habitat types) of Great Britain based on field surveys and covers 250 different plant communities. The Joint Nature Conservation Committee has published classification schemes for British rivers and lakes, both based on aquatic plant communities.

Limestone Pavement (seen here on The Burren) can be classified in a variety of ways. **CORINE Land Cover** has a category for *Bare rock* and the **Countryside Survey Land Cover** for *Inland rock*. Limestone Pavement is categorised by **Fossitt** as *ER2 Exposed calcareous rock*. There is one relevant **Annex I** habitat – *Limestone pavements*, and three main **NVC** communities may apply (and possible overlaps with eight others). In the UK, Limestone Pavement falls within the **UK Priority Habitat** *Inland rock outcrop and scree habitats*.

The *Integrated Habitat System* was developed to integrate some of the above systems within the UK and is focussed at helping users combine data from a range of different sources, for example NVC and Phase 1 maps.

In Ireland, there is a standard scheme for describing habitats, often referred to as the *Fossitt Habitat Categories* after its author, Julie Fossitt. The scheme includes 11 broad habitat categories, split into a 117 individual habitat types.

There are several national-level surveys of habitat extent. Within the UK, the *Countryside Survey* is a regularly repeated survey that has been running since 1978 and is designed to detect changes in the UK's countryside over time. There are two components to the survey: field surveys record data from a sample of 1 km squares, while the *Land Cover Map* uses satellite data to produce a digital map. These data cross-reference to Broad Habitat Types and Priority Habitats and provide estimates of the extent of a range of habitats. In Wales, this is supplemented by the *Habitat Survey of Wales* produced by the then Countryside Council for Wales (now Natural Resources Wales). The estimates of the extent of each habitat presented in this book draw on these published data.

CORINE Land Cover is a European-level database of land cover based on satellite imagery (the name is derived from its full name Coordination of Information on the Environment) and uses a broader classification system, with 44 different habitat types recognised. The maps are derived from satellite imagery and use a minimum parcel size of 25 ha. CORINE Land Cover data cover twelve European countries and are used to examine environmental change (such as the disappearance of wetlands, or agricultural intensification) across a wide area. The CORINE data cover the whole of the UK and Ireland, and are therefore used as the basis for many of the maps presented in this book. EUNIS (the European Nature Information System) is a successor to CORINE with classes that can be cross-matched to those used in the CORINE Land Cover Map.

A diversity of habitats seen in **Morecambe Bay**, **Whitbarrow** and the **Pennines** from **Yewbarrow, Cumbria**, including Upland Calcareous Grassland (A), Upland Birch Wood (B), Scree (C), Yew Wood (D), Coastal and Floodplain Grazing Marsh (E), Raised Bog (F) and Upland Acid Grassland (G).

Saltmarsh (seen here on the Solway Firth) is a **UK Priority Habitat** and mapped as a single habitat type on the **Countryside Survey Land Cover Map** and the **CORINE Land Cover Map**. However, **Fossitt** differentiates between two saltmarsh categories (*CM1 Lower Saltmarsh* and *CM2 Upper Saltmarsh*; the image includes both types), and there are four **Annex I** saltmarsh habitat types that occur in Britain and Ireland (the Solway is designated for *Atlantic salt meadows* (Glauco-Puccinellietalia maritimae). The **NVC** describes 25 different saltmarsh vegetation communities within Great Britain, of which *SM13* Puccinellia maritima *saltmarsh* and *SM16* Festuca rubra *saltmarsh* can be seen in this photograph.

Although **Coastal and Floodplain Grazing Marsh** (seen here in the Frome Valley in Dorset) is a **UK Priority Habitat**, there is no habitat type listed on **Annex I** to which it corresponds. **CORINE Land Cover** maps *Pastures*, and **Countryside Survey Land Cover** maps *Improved Grassland* and *Rough Grassland*, but both incorporate a much wider range of grassland habitats than just **Coastal and Floodplain Grazing Marsh**. Two **Fossitt** categories apply to the habitat: *GS4 Wet grassland* and *GA1 Improved agricultural grassland*. There are four main **NVC** communities that are relevant, and overlaps with a further 12 NVC types.

CONSERVATION OF HABITATS

Habitats have varying requirements and vulnerabilities. Today there is a multitude of different conservation organisations, including both statutory bodies and non-governmental organisations, working to protect habitats and species. They provide a considerable body of expertise about nature conservation combined with plenty of experience – species and habitat loss has been occurring for a long time! Once a case of protecting species, conservation now involves re-creating and restoring habitats, reintroducing species, lobbying and campaigning. However, despite the best efforts of the conservation sector, without which the habitats and species of Britain and Ireland would undoubtedly be much poorer today, 40% of Priority Habitats in the UK are still declining, and more than one in 10 of over 3,000 monitored species are at risk of extinction (and the status of only about 5% of terrestrial species is known, with much less known about marine species). On the flip side, 40% of species are increasing, including some seabirds and generalists such as Jackdaw and Woodpigeon. There have been some celebrated successes, such as the return of the Bittern, Red Kite and Large Blue butterfly, the expansion of Otter back into most of our major waterways, the return of wildlife to the Thames, and the re-creation of nearly 2,500 ha of lowland heathland. Nevertheless, our wildlife is in a state of flux and we are losing more than we are gaining.

Faced with the apparently inexorable decline of habitats and species, the conservation movement has tended to look back to a time when these particular habitats and species were more abundant. In the desperate struggle to save vanishing species and fragments of habitat, there has been limited opportunity in the past for looking forwards and searching for ways to create more space for nature. However, schemes for wildlife-friendly farming and a move towards landscape-scale conservation are now moving in this direction. There is also a growing interest in 're-wilding' that focuses on ecological processes and involves reducing deliberate human intervention and reintroducing missing species such as Beaver that play a key role in ecosystem dynamics. Discussion is growing about how the habitat of large areas of semi-natural countryside that are of relatively limited conservation interest (*e.g.* upland rough grasslands) could be enriched. In an environment that is increasingly urbanised and impoverished, an interest in more 'naturalistic' habitats is developing, and the need to find ways of helping people to reconnect with nature is becoming a priority within the conservation movement.

More than one designation can apply to sites. **Strumble Head, Pembrokeshire**, falls within the Strumble Head - Llechdafad cliffs SSSI, the St David's/Ty Ddewi SAC and forms part of the Pembrokeshire National Park. This headland supports Maritime Heath, Hard Cliff and Slope, and Rocky Shore, and is famous for passing seabirds and cetaceans.

How Habitats are Protected

Name	Aim	Legislation/convention	Number in the UK	Number in Ireland
International				
Special Areas of Conservation (SACs)	To maintain, restore and protect sites to form a coherent network across Europe of habitats that are rare or vulnerable in a European context (listed in Annex I)	The Habitats Directive (European)	652	423
Special Protection Areas (SPAs)	To protect sites classified as important for birds at a European level	Wild Birds Directive (European)	270	154
Ramsar Sites	To protect wetlands of international importance	Ramsar Convention (global)	148	45
UNESCO World Heritage Sites	To protect sites of outstanding cultural or natural importance to all humanity	Convention Concerning the Protection of the World Cultural and Natural Heritage (global)	3 (natural)	–
National				
Sites of Special Scientific Interest (SSSIs) and Areas of Special Scientific Interest (ASSSIs)	To protect sites noted for their biological or geological interest	Wildlife and Countryside Act 1981 in England and Wales; Nature Conservation and Amenity Lands (Northern Ireland) Order 1985; Nature Conservation (Scotland) Act 2004	approx. 6,800	n/a
Natural Heritage Areas (NHAs)	To protect areas considered important for the habitats present or which hold species of plants and animals whose habitat needs protection	Wildlife (Amendment) Act 2000	n/a	148

Special Areas of Conservation (SACs) (shown here) are the key sites for natural and semi-natural habitats in Britain and Ireland. Together with **Special Protection Areas (SPAs)** they are commonly referred to as **Natura 2000** sites and are afforded strict legal protection. The selection criteria for individual sites (available from the JNCC and NWPS websites) are a useful source of information, often containing detailed descriptions of the vegetation and species present.

THE HABITATS

In this book, habitats are grouped under 10 sections: **Woodlands, Scrub, Heathlands, Grasslands, Mountains, Rocky Habitats, Wetlands, Freshwaters, Coastal Habitats** and **Other Habitats** (marine habitats are not covered). Each section has an introduction providing background information on the range of habitats found and themes common to the habitats within it. Within each section, accounts are provided for individual habitat types. Each account follows the same format and includes information on how to recognise the habitat, its ecology, any overlaps with similar habitats, its origins, its conservation and particular features to look out for (this section is expanded for especially complex or diverse habitats). Range maps are provided for all habitats, where appropriate. Each habitat account can be read on its own – it is not necessary to read the preceding accounts, although these will provide additional context.

Maps

The range maps have been derived from a variety of sources depending upon the data available. For the overall maps given in the introduction to each section, and for some of the individual habitat maps, it was possible to map the actual occurrence of the habitat(s) in question. In other cases, it was only possible to map the general distribution of the habitat by indicating in which 10 km grid squares it has been recorded. The maps are intended as a guide only. CORINE Land Cover data (which includes habitat patches of 25 ha and above) have been used for all the main habitat sections and for some individual habitats such as Coniferous Plantation. Data from the Annex I Habitat Reports that are compiled periodically by the government agencies in Ireland and the United Kingdom have also been used. These data are plotted according to 10 km grid cells that contain the habitat (the grid cells are aligned to a grid based on a European map projection rather than the British or Irish National Grid). Another source of data is the national inventories that are available for some habitats, including the Priority Habitat layers derived by Natural England, the Habitat Survey of Wales, and various others including the Traditional Orchard inventory, the Scottish Native Woodland Inventory, the Irish Survey of Native Woodland and the Turlough Database. Data concerning canals and rivers are derived from OpenStreetMap (a crowd-sourced geographic dataset available online). For habitats that are specifically upland or lowland, the upland boundary shown earlier in the introduction has been used to separate the two. Sources for the map data and copyright information are given on *page 274*.

For each habitat, additional context on its distribution is given in a box below the map headed **Distribution and extent**. This also gives the area of each habitat type in England (Eng), Scotland (Sco), Wales (Wal), Northern Ireland (NI) and Ireland (Ire). Areas are indicative only and are not directly comparable where it has been necessary to use different sources (which include Countryside Survey Land Cover Map, Annex i reports, Priority Habitat descriptions, individual habitat inventories and Landmap, a GIS-based resource on landscape characteristics for Wales). Where

The habitats of Britain and Ireland contain a great diversity of plant and animal species, of which over a thousand are referred to in this book. For identification guides to different species groups, the Princeton **WILD**Guides Britain's Wildlife series is recommended http://press.princeton.edu/wildguides/.

appropriate an indication of the European distribution is given for habitats for which Britain and Ireland are of particular importance.

For some habitats, extent data have been derived from the 2013 Habitats Directive Reports submitted to the European Commission by the UK and Ireland. This is indicated by the annotation '(ANN I REP)' in the map caption. In cases where the Annex I habitat does not fully correspond with the habitat as described and only includes a proportion of it (see *page 256*), these figures are likely to be an underestimate of the total area. In instances where the extent of a habitat type is not known the annotation 'n/k' is used.

Key for maps

The following colour-coding system is used on the habitat maps:

- data for the area are unavailable
- habitat range based on mapped habitat patches.
- habitat range according to 10 km squares within which it is known to be present.

Species and habitat names

Common (English) species names have been used throughout this book. For consistency and accessibility, such names have been used for groups such as mosses, liverworts and some invertebrates for which scientific names are more often used. A list of the scientific names of all the species mentioned in the text is provided on *pages 266–272*. The nomenclature used for higher plants follows the *New Flora of the British Isles* by Clive Stace (Cambridge University Press, 2001). For birds the names follow *The British List: a checklist of birds of Britain*, 8th ed. (*Ibis* 155: 635–676). In most other cases, the names used are those adopted by the relevant society or recording group (Amphibian and Reptile Conservation Trust, Bees, Wasps and Ants Recording Society, British Bryological Society, British Dragonfly Society, British Lichen Society, British Phycological Society, Butterfly Conservation and The Mammal Society). The nomenclature used for the remaining groups follows the national checklists provided by the Natural History Museum. Species names are capitalized, unless more than one species of the same genus are referred to or the species is not identified to species level. For example, 'Sessile Oak' refers to that species, while 'oaks' refers to either (or both) Sessile and Pedunculate Oak.

Habitat names are capitalized where they refer to the habitats described individually in this book. Other broader habitats names are not. For example, 'Lowland Dry Heath' refers specifically to the habitat described on *page 86*, while 'heathland' refers to any heathland habitat.

WOODLANDS

ORIGINS

The development of woodland after the last glaciation has mostly been inferred from tree pollen preserved in wetland peat. Montane species of birch and willow and Common Juniper were the first tree species to colonise the tundra-like landscape left behind by the retreating ice around 12,000 years ago. They spread from small pockets of woodland that persisted in the unglaciated (although still very cold) southern extremity of England and from the European mainland (of which Britain and Ireland were still a part), and were then followed by other birches and Aspen and then by Scots Pine. As the climate became wetter and milder, the pinewoods retreated north and were followed by broadleaved species such as Hazel, Alder, oaks, elms and limes. Beech and Hornbeam were relative latecomers, arriving when climate became drier again about 6,000 years ago, and spreading as far as the Brecon Beacons in South Wales (their further spread may have been inhibited by the subsequent reduction in overall woodland cover rather than climatic factors). Beech, Hornbeam and Small-leaved Lime did not reach Ireland; presumably because they failed to cross the land bridge before it sank under the Irish Sea (several other characteristic woodland species did not make it either, including Hazel Dormouse, Roe Deer, Nightingale, Willow and Marsh Tit, woodpeckers, Pied Flycatcher and Purple Emperor and White Admiral butterflies, although Strawberry-tree, absent from the UK, did).

By the beginning of the Neolithic period (6,000 years ago), most of Britain was covered in woodland except for the arctic-alpine tundra of areas like the Cairngorm plateau and the boggy northernmost tip of Scotland. Pine forest covered much of Scotland (and also Connemara in western Ireland), with birch dominant towards the far north. Oak – Hazel woodland covered lowland Scotland, most of northern England and Wales, parts of the West Country and the western tips of Ireland. Lime woods covered the English Midlands, East Anglia and much of southern England, with Hazel and elm woods in Cornwall, south-west Wales and much of Ireland. Willow and Alder carr covered wetland areas that were not bog. These woodlands were home to animals such as Auroch (wild cattle) and Wild Boar, which would have maintained clearings opened by tree fall or along river banks.

Woodland had already been exploited by humans for wood and food, but human impacts increased markedly as settled agricultural lifestyles became prevalent in the Neolithic period and significant woodland clearance began on lighter, more fertile soils. Clearings were not permanent to begin with, and when cleared plots were abandoned they reverted to woodland. However, woodland clearance accelerated through the Bronze

Under the feudal system, land and trees were usually owned by Lord of the Manor, with villagers (commoners) having various rights to graze animals (including turning out pigs to eat acorns and beechmast in the autumn), and collect firewood.

Age (4500–2500 years ago) with the development of metal tools, and a wetter and cooler climate stimulated the development of bogs in oceanic areas, preventing tree regeneration. By the end of the Iron Age (2,000 years ago, when the human population in Britain was over one million), 50% of woodland cover had gone. Tree composition also changed: the amount of elm had already decreased (possibly due to a pandemic elm disease), Small-leaved Lime decreased (possibly due to climatic changes use as fodder for livestock) and there was a corresponding increase in Hazel. Secondary woodland spread after the end of the Roman period, but clearance began again in Saxon times, and by the Norman period (11th century, human population three million) only about 15% remained, by which time ownership of woodlands in much of Britain was defined under the feudal system and their use regulated. Norman management of Irish woods within their control was more exploitative, and some may have been completely felled and the timber exported. However in both countries coppice management was widespread. Deer parks and Royal Forests were also created at this time.

By the 14th century, woodland cover had declined to around 10% in Britain, and remained roughly at this level into the 19th century despite the vicissitudes of plague and famine – probably because the remaining woodland was by this time an integral part of local economies. The need for charcoal increased with the spread of the blast furnace in ironworks throughout the early 17th century, while the growth in merchant and naval shipbuilding in Britain around this time required timber and as a consequence the remaining woodlands were carefully managed. The replanting and selective weeding of less useful tree species then began to have a significant impact on the composition and structure of woods. The same demands for wood were felt in Ireland, which had a woodland cover of about 20% around this time. However, the English monarchy handed over large areas of land to non-Irish settlers, who cleared woodland to use as farmland. A large increase in the population

HABITAT	DESCRIPTION
Lowland Mixed Oak and Ash Wood *page 34*	Mixed broadleaved woodland on relatively rich soils, usually with a history of coppice management. Includes classic lowland Bluebell woods.
Lowland Dry Oak and Birch Wood *page 38*	Oak and birch-dominated woods on dry, acid soils in heathland areas, often managed as high forest.
Beech Wood *page 40*	Beech-dominated high forest with a limited shrub and field layer found on a range of soils, famous for rare orchids and helleborines.
Yew Wood *page 42*	Yew-dominated woodland on chalk and Yew groves within Upland Mixed Ash Wood on limestone.
Wet Woodland *page 44*	Varied woodland of Alder, willows or birches found on wetlands, in river floodplains and strongly flushed situations. Includes bog woodland.
Wood Pasture *page 48*	Includes sites with a long-standing history of grazing that support veteran or ancient trees (usually Beech or oaks). Usually found on relatively infertile land, often common land, royal forests or deer parks. Rich in invertebrates and lichens.
Atlantic Oak Wood *page 52*	Oceanic woodland in the uplands often supporting a diverse range of lower plants. Strong oak dominance is partly a consequence of management.
Upland Mixed Ash Wood *page 56*	Mixed woodland on calcareous outcrops in the uplands, often with a rich flora, naturally limited in extent.
Caledonian Forest *page 58*	Native pinewoods found only in the Highlands of Scotland.
Atlantic Hazel Wood *page 62*	Woodland with a natural Hazel canopy, rich in lower plants, confined to the Atlantic fringe.
Upland Birch Wood *page 64*	Widespread, dynamic woodland dominated by birches in the uplands. It is often transient.
Coniferous Plantation *page 66*	Plantations of pine, spruce and fir, usually found on nutrient-poor soils and particularly widespread in the uplands.

Looking east towards Farnham, Surrey from Farleigh Wallop, Hampshire – arable fields and settlements interrupt a mix of both managed and unmanaged Lowland Mixed Oak and Ash Wood, a scene that has remained relatively unchanged for centuries.

saw further clearance in the 17th and 18th centuries and the woodland cover in Ireland is thought to have dropped as low as 2%, although planting was also encouraged during this time.

The development of the rail network in the 19th century meant that coal could be widely used. As a consequence, coppicing for firewood declined but woodlands were still cleared for cultivation. At the beginning of the 20th century woodland cover reached an all-time low of 5% in Britain and < 2% in Ireland. However, demand for home-grown timber increased during the First World War, and new planting (mostly coniferous) was undertaken on an unprecedented scale, mostly on infertile land but also within existing woodlands. Agricultural intensification from the 1950s saw further clearance of broad-leaved woodland, but around this time the rate of woodland loss became a concern, and the conservation movement started protecting ancient woodland sites. Woodland now covers around 10% of Ireland and 12% of the UK. A large proportion of this is coniferous plantation (75% in Ireland, 52% in the UK), although the area of broad-leaved woodland has also increased through planting and the expansion of secondary woodland. The area of semi-natural ancient woodland is tiny at 1·2% in the UK, while in Ireland, mapped ancient or long-established woodlands cover about 0·1% of the land area.

TYPES OF WOODLAND

Eleven types of semi-natural woodland are described in this book, as well as Coniferous Plantation. Woodland classification can be complex but in the UK the systems most commonly referred to are Peterken's stand types (which includes 12 main and 39 subsidiary types based on the presence of species of long-established trees), the National Vegetation Classification (based on samples of all vegetation present, which has over 50 woodland communities grouped under 18 main types) and the UK Priority Habitat types (nine types based on threat and vulnerability). In Ireland, woodland has been classified into seven semi-natural types and five highly modified types mainly according to vegetation characteristics. In this book, a pragmatic approach has been adopted based on the tree species present (linked to geology and climate) and conservation interest. The table on *page 27* summarises the main features of each woodland habitat for which an account has been provided.

The woodland habitats described may be found on ancient woodland sites, and can be primary woodland, although all are likely to have been managed to a greater or lesser extent. Some occur as secondary woodland (*e.g.* birch wood that develops on heathland if grazing pressure is relaxed) or are naturally transient (*e.g.* willow carr, a type of Wet Woodland) and are likely to develop into other woodland types over time. Atlantic Hazel Wood, which is sometimes considered to be a coastal

Wildwood is used to refer to the natural woodland cover of Britain and Ireland before significant human impacts. If there are any remaining areas of wildwood that have never been significantly influenced by humans, they are likely to be small remnants in remote and inaccessible places such as ravines and perhaps small islands in lochs.

Semi-natural woodland has not been planted, but has experienced periods of more or less intense management that may have included coppicing, grazing, selective felling and planting.

Ancient woodland refers to sites where woodland is known to have been present since at least 1600 (1750 in Scotland), a date chosen because planting was not common before this. Some have been replanted but retain a ground flora typical of ancient woodland.

Primary Woodland is semi-natural ancient woodland that has never been cleared and replanted and so has physical continuity with the wildwood, even though it has been managed.

Secondary woodland develops by a natural process of succession on open habitats or arable land that is no longer managed. It takes woodland species a long time to colonise, and so many secondary woodlands lack specialist species. Secondary woodland can be ancient woodland if it colonised previously cleared land before 1600 (1750 in Scotland).

Plantation is artificially established woodland planted with the intention of obtaining a timber crop. Most plantations are coniferous and can be monocultures, although broadleaves are also planted. Many semi-natural woodlands include areas in which trees have been planted at some point.

form of Upland Mixed Ash Wood or Atlantic Oak Wood (depending on the substrate), is described separately here as it is unique to Britain and Ireland and is of particular value for the suite of lower plants it supports. Yew Wood, often considered together with Beech Wood on chalk, is also given a separate section due to its distinctive character. Although essentially a crop, Coniferous Plantation is included because it can support scarce or rare species or those associated with the habitat it replaced. Wood Pasture is anomalous as it is a product of a particular type of management used over a long time period. It is usually derived from Lowland Dry Oak and Birch Wood or Beech Wood but is very distinctive and of such conservation interest that it merits its own description. Traditional Orchards, which have some similarities to Wood Pasture, are covered in the Other Habitats section (*page 248*).

Climate and soil type are the key natural factors influencing the character and distribution of woodlands. Broadly speaking, oaks are the commonest dominant species in established woodland on more acid soils and on acid rocks. Ash is found on limestone and chalk and also on moist soils (and is the commonest woodland dominant in Ireland); Small-leaved Lime and Wych

COMMON TREE FORMS

Coppice – a multi-stemmed tree that has been cut at ground level and allowed to re-grow. Coppice stools can be hundreds of years old. Many woods, such as Garston Wood in Dorset, were traditionally managed as coppice with standards (*i.e.* coppice with well-spaced pollards or maiden trees). This periodically opened up the canopy and provided the edge habitat favoured by many woodland specialists. Coppicing was widespread, although the technique did not become widely practiced in Scotland until the 17th century.

A veteran lime **stub** in the Wye Valley, Gloucestershire. Stubs are short pollards or high coppice stools.

A **phoenix willow** at Salhouse, Norfolk. Phoenix regeneration happens when a tree falls over and new shoots develop perpendicularly from the main trunk or branches.

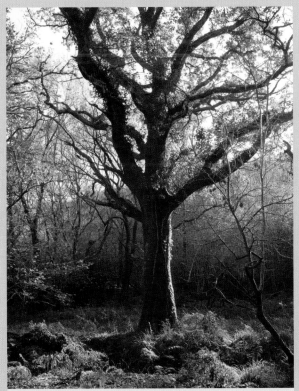

A **maiden** oak at Arne, Dorset. A **standard** or maiden tree is one that has never been cut, coppiced or pollarded.

Recently **pollarded** willows at Cricklade, Wiltshire. Pollards are cut above animal grazing height to allow the regrowth to be harvested for wood or timber. Pollards are still found as standards within woods, on boundary banks, in hedgerows and along rivers, although many are no longer cut regularly.

Elm also prefer more calcareous soils. Hazel is widely distributed and is found both as an understorey shrub and, on the Atlantic fringe, as a canopy species. Beech and Yew can tolerate thin, drought-prone soils and birches are pioneer woodland species found in a wide range of conditions. Alder grows on strongly flushed sites and in river floodplains and, like willows, grows readily in wetlands. Climatic factors are particularly evident in northern Scotland and Ireland, where high rainfall can inhibit tree growth (favouring bogs). Conditions in the Highlands are sufficiently harsh that species such as Scots Pine and birches, which would be out-competed in more favourable situations, can be dominant. In the west of Britain and Ireland, moist, oceanic conditions favour the growth of a rich suite of lower plants within woodlands. In southern England, species such as Field Maple, Beech and Hornbeam, which did not reach Scotland naturally, are found.

The character of most woodland is the product of thousands of years of often quite intense human management interacting with these natural factors. In many areas, woodland has been managed to favour particular species (*e.g.* oaks and Beech). Other species have been weeded out and key species planted. Elsewhere, planting has included non-native species *e.g.* Sweet Chestnut and ornamentals such as Rhododendron. Non-native shrub species have often been planted as cover in woodlands used for pheasant-rearing. Sycamore is a component of many sites, particularly (but by no means exclusively) secondary woodland. It is thought to have been introduced in the Roman or Medieval period, possibly to Scotland, although it did not become widespread until the 18th century. It is now considered an invasive species in some semi-natural woodland (although it has been argued that it may in fact be native as its pollen does not preserve well in peat and is not possible to separate from that of Field Maple).

This variety of human and natural influences contributes to the lack of conformity in woodland, much of which does not fit neatly into one category or another, particularly in the case of young secondary woodlands. The descriptions for the woodland types in this book should be treated as nodes on a continuum, rather than as self-contained woodland types.

THREATS AND ISSUES

Britain and Ireland are among the least wooded countries in Europe and the tiny amount of ancient woodland that remains is still under threat. Long-term monitoring of many woodland birds and a range of woodland butterflies has shown steep population declines, suggesting that all is not well within our woodlands.

Development pressure is particularly a problem in the south-east of England, and the irreplaceable nature of semi-natural woodland appears not to be

Despite a resurgence of interest in traditional woodland management techniques for cultural, historical and environmental reasons, the lack of such management still threatens the fauna and flora that developed under coppice regimes.

A sapling is used as the return spring for the treadle in a pole lathe, which is known to have been used to turn green wood since at least Viking times and is now used by those with an interested in green woodworking.

fully understood or appreciated by decision-makers. Woodland wildlife is also threatened by changes in management. Traditional coppice management is no longer economically viable, and many woods are either neglected or managed for timber, both of which lead to structural changes and the lack of appropriate niches for species that flourished under traditional management. Many woodland habitats are fragmented into isolated patches and, as woodland species are generally not very mobile, local extinctions easily become permanent. A widespread increase in the deer population and, in the uplands, the number of livestock grazing woodlands (a traditional practice), is threatening regeneration within woods and 'fixing' the naturally dynamic boundaries of upland woodlands. Although disease and pests are a part of natural ecosystems and have always affected trees, the arrival of new species (*e.g.* through international trade in plants) to which trees have not had the opportunity to develop resistance can be far-reaching. Currently, the likely impact of Ash dieback (caused by the fungus *Chalara fraxinea*) is unknown. Climate change may increase vulnerability to pathogens. Projected increases in temperature, changes in rainfall seasonality and an increase in storm events are also likely to change the composition, structure and distribution of woodlands.

Key Woodland Areas

1. New Forest
2. South Dartmoor
3. Wye Valley
4. Vale of Ffestiniog
5. Killarney Woods
6. Borrowdale
7. West coast Atlantic Oak and Hazel Woods
8. Speyside/Deeside
9. East Anglian mixed coppice
10. Weald

This map shows all woodland habitats and illustrates that they are widespread. South-east England has the highest concentration of broad-leaved ancient woodland, whereas Coniferous Plantation is more common in the north and west, including Scotland, Wales and Ireland. Woodland patches tend to be small and scattered in lowland arable areas, such as East Anglia, while former wetlands such as the Fens and Somerset Levels hold little woodland cover. Large, extensive patches often indicate old hunting forests or individual estates.

Some key locations are labelled on the map; this selection is not intended to be exhaustive but highlights a few of the most important areas.

CULTURAL IMPORTANCE

Woodland is a much-loved feature of the landscape. For many people it provides a place for spiritual renewal and contemplation as well as fresh air and exercise, and of course the chance to see wildlife that is not encountered in the wider countryside. Stepping inside an ancient wood can be a welcome escape from the monotony of modern agriculture or the abrasive urban environment. The woodland boundary is often out of sight and out of mind; it is possible to be fully immersed in the structural complexity of a habitat that is three-dimensional at the human scale and where natural processes at least appear to predominate. The enduring nature of woodland can also engender a feeling of continuity with the past. Many woods are historical features in their own right, and have been documented for hundreds of years. Wood banks, old boundary pollards and coppice stools, charcoal hearths and other archaeological features all have a tale to tell about past lives and add to the historical value of woodland sites.

Woodlands are also valued as a source of traditional products such as locally produced charcoal and firewood, and Hazel for wattle hurdles and thatching spars – and the skills required for woodland crafts are valued in their own right. There is also interest in reinstating traditional coppice management to provide woodchip as a source of fuel. The rise of the forest school movement, which offers children hands-on learning experiences in an outdoor environment, is also raising the profile of woodlands among young people. The role of woodland in carbon sequestration and flood control is becoming increasingly apparent, although the lack of market value for these services provides little incentive to landowners to maintain or expand woodland.

CONSERVATION IMPORTANCE AND PROTECTION

Woodland includes some or our richest habitats and supports a huge range of species, many of which are rare or scarce. The varied geology and climate of Britain and Ireland had led to the development of a diverse range of woodland types, including ten Annex I habitats, of which half are priority features (*i.e.* considered to be particularly vulnerable and/or mainly restricted to Europe). However, only a small proportion of ancient woodland is legally protected (*e.g.* around 15% is designated as SSSI (see *page 23*) in the UK), and in the UK the conservation status of the majority of designated sites is deemed unfavourable, largely due to inappropriate forestry management, overgrazing (in the uplands particularly) and the presence of invasive non-native species. Much woodland is in private ownership, and conservation efforts often revolve around promoting appropriate management for conservation.

The area of some woodland types has increased in recent years and there are several key projects working to expand woodland, often for community benefits in addition to those for nature conservation. For example, in the English Midlands the National Forest is creating a multi-purpose forest landscape within 200 square miles of an ex-mining area. There is also increasing interest in reconnecting or buffering remaining areas of woodland to increase their resilience.

The value of continuing or reinstating coppice management on sites that have a history of such management is widely promoted, but there is also value in allowing abandoned coppice to revert to more 'naturalistic high forest'. Although this will not favour rare specialist butterflies requiring open conditions or encourage a high diversity of flowering plants, it will benefit decomposer species that require dead plant material and flourish in moist, sheltered conditions. Many species also depend on mature trees. For example, the abundance of leaf miners and spiders has been

Stoborough, Dorset – secondary woodland is often afforded little if any protection, although some sites are recognised as being of importance at a county level. Secondary woodland is greatly valued as green space in both urban and rural settings and can provide a relatively robust location for recreation.

shown to increase with the age of coppice, and many moths are dependent upon mature canopies. However, most of these species are hard to see and even harder to identify, and therefore receive only limited recognition in the world of conservation. Coppicing is not appropriate in Atlantic woodlands with rich lower plant communities.

KEY ELEMENTS

Woodlands include our most structurally diverse habitats, and can comprise a canopy layer usually of taller tree species, a shrub layer of smaller trees and shrubs such as Rowan, Wild Cherry, Hazel, Wild Service-tree, willows and Guelder-rose, and a field layer of grasses, herbs, ferns, lichens, mosses and liverworts. The balance between these layers is determined by factors such as the amount of light penetrating the canopy and grazing pressure. Within this diverse structure a wide range of microhabitats can be found. Key microhabitats to look out for are deadwood, ancient trees and edges. Deadwood and leaf-litter are used by a huge diversity of organisms including fungi, bacteria and invertebrates. It is estimated that 13% of species in Britain are associated with deadwood. These saproxylic species play a vital role in the woodland food chain by recycling nutrients. Many are too small to see with the naked eye or are out of sight, but look out for fungal fruiting bodies in a great variety of forms and macro-invertebrates such as Stag Beetle. Ancient and veteran trees (see Wood Pasture, *page 48*) provide an important range of deadwood habitat within living trees that is used by fungi and invertebrates, and for nesting by birds such as woodpeckers. Ancient trees are also important for epiphytic lichens as their longevity provides the continuity of conditions needed for the development of a diverse flora. Glades, rides and woodland edges are important for species dependent on sunny, sheltered conditions, including rare fritillary butterflies. Many woodland plants favour these more open conditions, and will be found flowering in recently coppiced areas or along ride edges.

FURTHER INFORMATION

Woodland Conservation and Management by George Peterken (Springer, 1993)
Woodlands by Oliver Rackham (HarperCollins, 2010)
Atlantic Hazel Action Group – a group that aims to protect Scotland's unique Atlantic Hazel woodlands
– sites.google.com/site/atlantichazelgroup/
Trees for Life – aims to restore functioning Caledonian Forest (and its missing wildlife such as Beaver and Lynx) to a swathe of Scotland – www.treesforlife.org.uk/
Ancient Tree Forum – provides information on the ecology, management and conservation of veteran trees
– www.ancient-tree-forum.org.uk/ancient-tree-forum/

The presence of a range of particular species is considered to indicate the likely ancient origins of woodland, although this varies according to the type of woodland (and the individual species are not necessarily confined to ancient woodland). Species include vascular plants (*e.g.* Moschatel, Ramsons, **Wood Anemone** (ABOVE), Pignut, Opposite-leaved Golden-saxifrage and Bluebell), a suite of epiphytic lichens, and tree species such as Wild Service-tree and Small-leaved Lime.

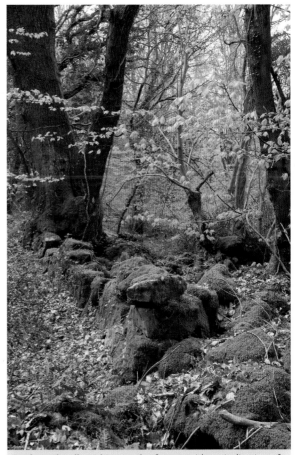

Banks and walls within woods often provide an indication of past use. **The Hudnalls,** in the **Wye Valley, Gloucestershire** was inhabited by squatters in the 18th century. Woodland recolonised cleared areas and old stone walls are all that now remains of the settlements. It has not been cut for 100 years and is now high forest (*i.e.* the trees are not pollarded or coppiced).

Lowland Mixed Oak and Ash Wood

Lowland Mixed Oak and Ash Wood encompasses a range of vegetation types resulting from long-term interactions between human activity, substrate and climate. While oaks and/or Ash are usually present, limes and Hornbeam can dominate the canopy (and are sometimes differentiated into separate woodland types). In many woods, Sycamore, suckering elms and Sweet Chestnut have colonised or been planted. Where the typical deep-brown earths are more acidic, Bluebell woods are found, with oaks and Hazel (also Holly, Rowan, Wild Cherry, Ash, and Yew) over Bracken, rambling Bramble and Honeysuckle and an eye-catching ground flora of Bluebell, often with Wood Anemone. In more calcareous situations, the woods become more species-rich. Ash joins or replaces oak in the canopy, and Field Maple is characteristic. Lime-loving shrubs such as Dogwood, Spindle and Wayfaring-tree may be common, while Dog's Mercury tends to dominate a ground flora that may contain woodland rarities. Ferns include shield-ferns and Hart's-tongue, but they are not as prominent a feature as in Upland Mixed Ash Wood. In Ireland, Ash and Hazel tend to dominate this type of woodland, but without Field Maple.

Similar habitats

Lowland Mixed Oak and Ash Wood is replaced by other woodland types where the soil is very dry and limey, strongly acid and leached, or wet, but overlaps with these types where soils are deeper. Gradations to upland woodland types are common in the upland fringes or where the topography changes abruptly.

Distribution and extent

Scattered across the lowlands, very limited in extent in Ireland. Eng: 69,500 ha; Sco: 28,000 ha; Wal: 26,600 ha; NI: n/k; Ire: 26,900 ha.

FAR LEFT: **High forest** developed when coppiced woodland was overplanted with dense oak in the 19th century and from the growth of suckering elms and un-cut coppice in the 20th century. LEFT: **A coppice coup** of recently cut Hazel with young oak standards. Rotational coppicing traditionally created a variety of open conditions that allowed a diversity of plants and invertebrates to persist.

BELOW LEFT: **Hornbeam-dominated woods** are mostly confined to Kent, Sussex and East Anglia. Generally coppiced (for firewood), Hornbeam is also found with lime. BELOW: Lime woods are prominent in the Midlands and East Anglia and often found where there has been a long continuity of woodland cover.

Origins and development

Enshrined in folklore as remnants of wildwood, these woods have in fact been shaped by human intervention over millennia. By the Middle Ages, coppicing (with or without standards) was almost universal. It finally ceased around the mid-20th century, although by then many coppices had been overplanted or were already neglected. Subsequent clearance and replanting with non-native trees led to a 30–40% reduction in area, and the loss of hedgerows reduced connectivity between sites. More recently, planting and small-scale natural regeneration have increased the area of this woodland type.

Conservation

Traditional management is usually no longer economically viable and management for timber or abandonment has simplified the structure of woodlands, resulting in a closed canopy with few open patches. In many instances overgrazing by deer is preventing regeneration. Many woods are surrounded by intensive agriculture, making them vulnerable to nitrogen pollution and reducing the amount of valuable edge habitat. Ash die-back caused by *Chalara fraxinea*, which was first found in the UK in 2012, could have a significant impact on nutrient cycling and species composition. Massive declines in some woodland birds, moths and butterflies in recent decades indicate that appropriate conservation measures are urgently needed. To be sustainable, these need to re-integrate woodland management within local economics (*e.g.* through sensitive management for woodfuel). While the continuation or reinstatement of coppicing is generally favoured to maximise diversity, there is also a case to be made for allowing natural processes to function in non-intervention high forest.

Garston Wood – a classic coppice-with-standards Bluebell wood in Dorset.

How to recognise

Small, contained by banks or ditches and often ancient, these woods are oases of wildlife amidst the sterile monotony of the lowland agricultural countryside. They are at their most vital in May when the canopy trees can still be easily differentiated by their colours. The air is pungent with Ramsons and alive with birdsong, and the intense hue of thousands of Bluebells can be captivating – for this woodland type includes the iconic Bluebell woods so central to our notion of British woodland.

In most woods traditional coppicing has been abandoned and high forest has grown up, which, although more naturalistic in appearance, is proving a challenge for many of the specialist inhabitants. However, open rides and glades can provide warm, well-lit and sheltered patches, while mature trees supply dead and rotting wood for beetles and fungi. Where coppicing is still practiced (usually on nature reserves), rare woodland butterflies and a spectacular spring flora can still be found. Many of these woods are quite close to urban centres, and can be much visited and loved for their beauty and the continuity they provide with the past.

When to visit

April–May for spring flora, late May–August for butterflies.

35

What to look for

Look for glades, rides and woodland edges, as this is where many of the most interesting species will be found. Sheltered and well-lit, open areas provide structural variety including mature trees, scrub, tall herbs, short vegetation and bare ground; east–west rides are best as they receive most sunlight. Look for Spotted Flycatchers hunting from trees on the edges of clearings in the summer, and listen out for other summer migrants such as Garden Warbler and perhaps Nightingale in the scrub. Purple Hairstreaks tumble over the canopy top, and Silver-washed Fritillaries fly strongly along rides. In shorter vegetation, Common Dog-violet and Wild Strawberry provide food for the caterpillars of fritillary butterflies and Grizzled Skipper respectively. The nocturnal Hazel Dormouse is found in Lowland Mixed Oak and Ash Woods with dense undergrowth. Mature trees host hole-nesting birds such as woodpeckers, whose excavations are also used by roosting Noctule bats, while cracks behind peeling bark are preferred by Barbastelle bats. Dead and rotting wood are vital, and provide deadwood for invertebrates (*e.g.* Stag Beetle) and fungi (*e.g.* Chicken of the Woods, a distinctive bright orange-yellow tiered bracket fungus). Lowland Mixed Oak and Ash Woodland is famed for its spring flora. Carpets of Bluebells can be breathtaking where the canopy is broken, accompanied by patches of Wood Anemone. The more calcareous sites are not so colourful but can be more species-rich, supporting plants such as Dog's Mercury, Pignut, Sanicle, Yellow Archangel, Bugle, Enchanter's-nightshade and Primrose (or Oxlip in East Anglia), with Moschatel (INSET BELOW) and Opposite-leaved Golden-saxifrage in flushes around springs and moist places. Keep an eye open for more unusual plants such as Solomon's-seal, Herb-Paris and Greater Butterfly-orchid.

Hazel Dormouse can be hard to see, but look out for empty nut shells with oblique tooth marks around the hole.

Did you know?
The average size of a Lowland Mixed Oak and Ash Wood is less than 20 ha. Lime woods are prominent in the Midlands and East Anglia and are often found where there has long been continuity of woodland cover.

The Hudnalls in the Wye Valley is dominated by oaks, limes and Beech and is managed on a 'minimum intervention' basis with dead wood left in situ.

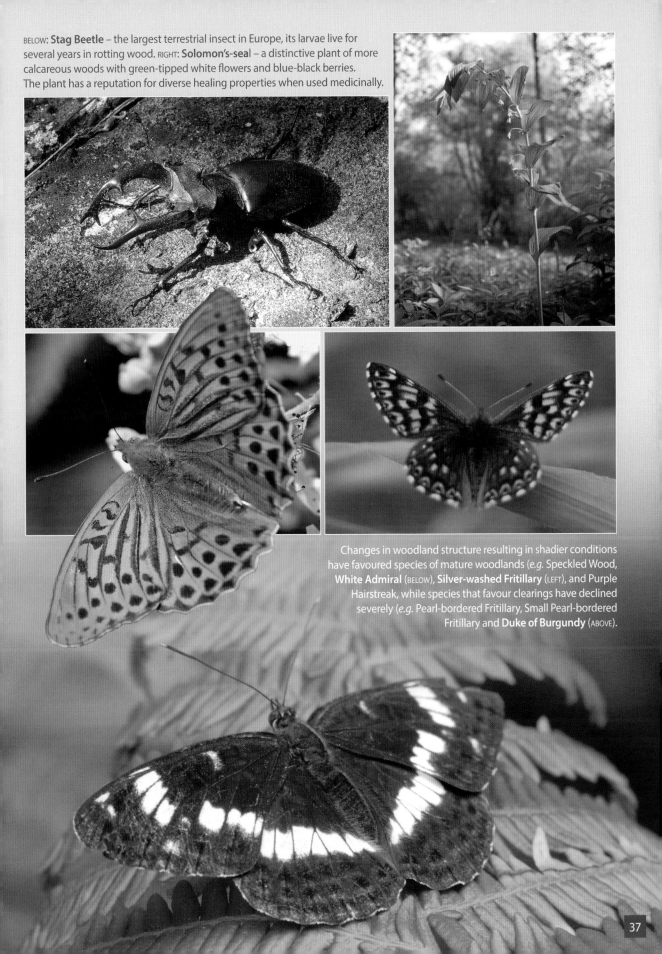

BELOW: **Stag Beetle** – the largest terrestrial insect in Europe, its larvae live for several years in rotting wood. RIGHT: **Solomon's-seal** – a distinctive plant of more calcareous woods with green-tipped white flowers and blue-black berries. The plant has a reputation for diverse healing properties when used medicinally.

Changes in woodland structure resulting in shadier conditions have favoured species of mature woodlands (*e.g.* Speckled Wood, **White Admiral** (BELOW), **Silver-washed Fritillary** (LEFT), and Purple Hairstreak, while species that favour clearings have declined severely (*e.g.* Pearl-bordered Fritillary, Small Pearl-bordered Fritillary and **Duke of Burgundy** (ABOVE).

Lowland Dry Oak and Birch Wood

Lowland Dry Oak and Birch Wood is found on gently undulating acid sands and gravels in the warm and dry south-east, and has a simple floristic composition. Pendunculate Oak is the most common oak, although pockets of Sessile Oak also occurs in places, becoming more common where the climate is wetter. Both Silver and Downy Birch are frequent, and although dense birch thickets suggests recent succession (*e.g.* from heathland), birches are also associated with canopy gaps and abandoned coppice. The shrub layer is mostly limited to Holly and Rowan that are able to persist in the shade of oaks and may in places reach the canopy. Wavy Hair-grass is characteristic of the field layer, and where Bracken is not too dominant species such as Heather, Broad Buckler-fern, Foxglove, Wood Sage and Heath Bedstraw are found. Bluebell is rare, and there is no showy display of spring flora. Bilberry and mosses are more frequent toward the northern limit of the habitat, and Bristle Bent replaces Wavy Hair-grass to the west. Taken in isolation, these woods are relatively species-poor, but many old stands include veteran trees important for their lichen, fungi and invertebrate assemblages, and other notable species are associated with patches of heathland or mire (peat-forming wetland).

Similar habitats

Lowland Dry Oak and Birch Wood intergrades with the more acid end of the spectrum of Beech Wood where both occur (*e.g.* the Chilterns and the New Forest) and often merges with open habitats and scrub. Many examples were historically managed as Wood Pasture. The lack of Hazel and the dominance of oaks differentiate it from Lowland Mixed Oak and Ash Wood, in which oaks tend to occur as sporadic pollards over Hazel.

Distribution and extent

South and east England only. Eng: 4,500 ha (ANN I REP). Lowland Dry Oak and Birch Wood occurs on suitable soils across Europe but is extremely local.

FAR LEFT: **Common Cow-wheat** – an ancient woodland indicator species found on well-drained nutrient-poor soils.
LEFT: **Dark Crimson Underwing** can sometimes be seen by day on oaks with sap runs.
BELOW LEFT: **Staverton Park, Suffolk** – a classic Lowland Dry Oak and Birch Wood site previously managed as Wood Pasture. Veteran oak pollards are surrounded by large Holly trees that have grown up in the absence of grazing.
BELOW RIGHT: In the **New Forest**, Lowland Dry Oak and Birch Wood often merges with Beech Wood and heathland.

Origins and development

Lowland Dry Oak and Birch Wood developed in areas once dominated by Small-leaved Lime after this species declined, perhaps as a consequence of increased livestock grazing during the Neolithic. By medieval times Lowland Dry Oak and Birch Wood was used as Wood Pasture, although coppice and high forest forms were also present. In the 18th century many coppices were planted with Sweet Chestnut.

Conservation

Lowland Dry Oak and Birch Wood suffers the threats common to most woodland habitats, particularly deer browsing (preventing regeneration), airborne pollution, and invasion by non-native species such as Rhododendron and Shallon. In heathland contexts, restoring heathland vegetation is often a priority over maintaining or enhancing Lowland Dry Oak and Birch Wood. However, where there is ancient woodland present, the woodland boundary may be allowed to expand.

What to look for

Older stands can support birds such as Lesser Spotted Woodpecker and Redstart. Look out for Common Cow-wheat, whose large seeds are distributed by ants.

BELOW: **Arne, Dorset** – secondary birch woodland is a very common sight on southern heathlands, but in some cases contains a core of Lowland Dry Oak and Birch Woodland. It also often includes pine from nearby plantations. Dense, even-aged Silver Birch can regenerate rapidly within woods following disturbances such as felling. RIGHT: **Lesser Spotted Woodpecker** is decreasing across most of its range, but can still be found in open Lowland Dry Oak and Birch Wood.

BEECH WOOD

Few woodland habitats are found on the same variety of substrates as Beech Wood. Calcareous Beech Wood (found on the Downs, Chilterns and Cotswolds) often includes some Ash or Sycamore in canopy gaps, while Yew and whitebeams may form a sub-canopy. Dog's Mercury is common, with Sanicle where steeper ground produces more open woodland. At the other end of the spectrum on acid sands and gravels (*e.g.* the High Weald, London Basin, New Forest), oaks join Beech in the canopy, and the heathy ground flora often merges into heathland. At intermediate sites on more neutral and waterlogged brown earths, Beech gains the greatest stature and is overwhelmingly dominant, with only Bramble and Holly frequently persisting in the understorey. These three types of Beech Wood often intergrade.

Beech is native to southern England and Wales. Its slow spread after the last glaciation meant that it had probably not reached its climatic limit before habitat fragmentation impeded its expansion northwards. However, Beech is now stretching existing notions of vegetation types by recolonising sites where it was removed to favour Hazel coppice, by naturally colonising sites outside of its historic range, and by invading vigorously from places where it has been introduced.

Similar habitats

Beech Wood is often found in intricate mosaics with other lowland woodland, grassland and heathland communities. Acidic stands that are managed as Wood Pasture are described more fully under that habitat.

BOTTOM LEFT: **Yellow Bird's-nest** – like the incredibly elusive Ghost Orchid also found in Beech Wood, this species lacks chlorophyll and gains its energy from a network of underground fungi. BOTTOM CENTRE: **Beech mixed coppice and Wood Pasture** were once more common, but the removal of less favoured species and management for timber has resulted in Beech-dominated high-forest, which is now just old enough to be considered traditional. RIGHT: The **Yellow-ringed Comb-horn** breeds in rot holes in Beech trees. FAR RIGHT: The lack of undergrowth makes **Beech Woods** easy to places to explore, although the speciality helleborines, such as **Broad-leaved Helleborine** (CUTOUT), can be hard to find (except where caged against the depredations of herbivores).

Origins and development

Beech was slow to return after the last ice age, but gradually replaced limes in woodlands disturbed by cutting and pasturage. Existing stands have been strongly influenced by sylvicultural practices. While its low commercial value has meant that Beech Wood has suffered less from clearance than other woodland types, replanting with conifers and non-native species has nevertheless reduced its area.

Conservation

Deer and Grey Squirrel damage is currently impacting on the age structure and natural regeneration of Beech Wood, while pollution may be resulting in vegetation change. Beech is particularly susceptible to drought and storm damage, so the impacts of climate change are likely to be significant. Urban growth threatens sites where increased human activity results in trampling, disturbance and pollution. Conservation effort has focussed on restoring areas replanted with conifers, and promoting expansion on suitable sites. Within existing stands, allowing natural processes of recruitment and decay will maximise the structural diversity needed by invertebrates. Long-term planning is important to ensure continuity of veteran trees.

What to look for

Beech Wood on chalk may support uncommon and rare species such as White, Narrow-lipped, Violet, Green-flowered, Red and Narrow-leaved Helleborines, Bird's-nest Orchid and Yellow Bird's-nest. Specialist invertebrates can be hard to find and identify, but look out for the Yellow-ringed Comb-horn, a striking black-and-yellow striped cranefly (see picture opposite).

New Forest, Hampshire. On some sites the Beech canopy can reach 30 metres: the soaring trunks and spaciousness are often likened to a cathedral.

YEW WOOD

Yew Wood develops where exposure and the dry, shallow soils of steep slopes discourage other woody species. In Yew Wood on south- and west-facing chalk slopes in southern England, Yew is overwhelmingly dominant, its dense evergreen shade excluding all but a scatter of whitebeams, Ash and Elder and sparse, patchy Dog's Mercury. These woods generally develop when a relaxation of grazing pressure on chalk grassland allows Common Juniper or Hawthorn scrub to grow. The scrub protects the more palatable but shade-tolerant Yew seedlings, which gradually shade out the scrub and out-live any faster growing species (*e.g.* Ash) that may colonise canopy gaps. Yew Wood is dynamic, and can spread, senesce and reinvade in a slow progression around coombes.

On the Carboniferous and Magnesium limestone of northern England, Yew forms more diverse groves on steep rocky slopes, cliffs and in ravines. Ash and elms join Yew in the canopy, and the ground flora is an impoverished version of that of the surrounding Upland Mixed Ash Wood. The Yew Wood of the Killarney limestone pavements in Ireland includes Holly and Hazel with Ash where soils are deeper, and the rocks are thickly covered with bryophytes.

Similar habitats

Yew Wood forms transitions and mosaics with Lowland Calcareous Grassland and Mixed Scrub on chalk. In northern Britain it occurs in mosaics with Upland Mixed Ash Wood and Atlantic Oak Wood, whilst in the south it is also associated with Beech Wood.

Origins and development

On inaccessible limestone sites, Yew Wood may be primary woodland that has never wholly been cleared. On the southern chalklands it is mostly secondary, having colonised when grazing pressure on grassland has relaxed. Historically, Yew wood has been used for wood-turning and, more famously, for long bows, but rarely for timber production.

Distribution and extent

Scattered throughout England and Ireland. Eng: 1,250 ha; Wal: 50 ha; Ire: 80 ha (ANN I REP). Pure Yew Wood is rare in Europe.

How to recognise

Yew Woods are only found on chalk escarpments, chalk coombes and steep limestone slopes and cliffs. They are easy to spot in the landscape as from a distance the dark, evergreen foliage of Yew stands out against surrounding vegetation (often calcareous grassland).

Inside Yew woods, the contorted yet fluid forms of individual Yew trees are the prominent feature. Little else distracts the attention in these stark, species-poor woods; there is no real understorey, although the deadwood remains of Juniper Scrub that once protected the Yew seedlings may still scent the air. The ground is a soft carpet of slowly decomposing needles over bare rock and soil, with only a very patchy ground flora surviving in the dense shade.

When to visit

Year-round.

Individual **Yew** trees may reach several hundred or even thousand years in age. Yew has an important role in ancient mythology and religion due to its longevity and powers of regeneration.

Conservation

Current threats are linked to limited ecological functionality. Browsing by deer limits natural regeneration, while afforestation of surrounding slopes prevents the small-scale migration once typical on chalk. This has resulted in relatively uniform stands. Air pollution may be a significant pressure on the structure and functioning of Yew Wood, and it may become geographically restricted due to the impact of climate change. Yew in tree nurseries has been affected by imported pathogens, but there is no evidence that these have spread to Yew Wood. Reducing deer pressure and releasing surrounding land from static management may allow natural processes to reassert themselves and reinvigorate many woods that are slowly deteriorating.

What to look for

The inconspicuous Triangle Spider, found on Yew and Box, spins a very characteristic triangular web from four radial threads, making up three sections of the normal orb. Locally, Box can be a significant part of the understorey, and has a distinctive smell.

BELOW LEFT: **Yewbarrow, Cumbria**. The Yew groves found on the Carboniferous limestone of northern England are sometimes considered to be part of the surrounding Upland Mixed Ash Wood, although they have a distinct character of their own. BELOW RIGHT: In the nearly continuous semi-natural woodland of the Wye Valley, where Yew either forms a dense canopy on rocky slopes or is scattered amongst other species. In spring, the dark needles contrast vividly with the luminous spring colours of deciduous trees. BOTTOM, INSET: **Yew bark**, needles and seeds are toxic, but birds can ingest the berry (the fleshy 'aril' is edible), helping to disperse the seeds.

Kingley Vale, West Sussex is the largest area of Yew woodland in Britain and is unusual in showing a full range of habitat structure and function.

WET WOODLAND

Wet Woodland includes willow and Alder carr, floodplain, hill and plateau Alder woods, and bog woodland. Carr is essentially a transient feature of peaty landscapes that develops as accumulating organic matter raises the soil surface above the water level, allowing scrub and trees to colonise. These dry the habitat out further and eventually more terrestrial woodland types become established. In some cases the trees are inhibited by the development of bog-mosses (fed by rainwater) so that a cyclical relationship between mire and carr develops. Willow carr is also very widespread in damp places on mineral soils, where it may gradually dry out and develop into other woodland types, although on exposed western coasts it can form a climax community.

Flood events and the slow meandering of rivers once made many floodplain woodlands dynamic. However, natural processes have largely been curtailed by drainage and intensive land-use, with only a few significant areas remaining in un-drained floodplains in northern Scotland. In hilly country, Alder woods are also found on mineral soils along spring lines and in wet gullies, and can be quite species-rich, while plateau Alder woods develop where water seeps between boulder clay and capping sands or wind-blown sediment.

On some mires, a scattering of stunted Scots Pine or Downy Birch with the rich epiphytic flora of ancient woodlands is found; these are bog woodlands. Largely confined to Scotland, small patches are also found in the New Forest, on the Dorset heaths and in Ireland. A balance between the very slow tree growth and the development of the bog creates a stable habitat where the drainage patterns of the bog are unaltered by the trees. Little is known about this woodland type in Britain, although it is common in Scandinavia.

Similar habitats

Wet Woodland frequently occurs in mosaics with other woodland types and open habitats. In Alder woods, transitions to the wetter Ash-dominated end of Lowland Mixed Oak and Ash Wood are found, while Downy Birch carr is often transitional to Upland Birch Wood.

Distribution and extent

Scattered throughout Britain and Ireland where conditions are suitable. Map and extents do not include carr. Eng: 2,600 ha; Sco: 3,100 ha; Wal: 2,700 ha; NI: 300 ha; Ire: 1,900 ha (ANN I REP).

ABOVE: **River Tay** – the largest areas of remaining floodplain Alder woodland are found along active river channels in Scotland, such as the Spey and the Tay. LEFT: Carr woodland may form part of a successional series of habitats from open water to dry woodland. Here in **The Broads**, open water is fringed with swamp and Wet Woodland, but the succession stops abruptly at the boundary with agriculturally improved drier land.

Origins and development

Wet Woodland first developed on open, wet habitats after the last glaciation, and has continued to colonise open habitats ever since. Where periodically disturbed (*e.g.* by flooding or coppicing), or where it forms stable transitions to dry woodland, Wet Woodland can persist, but it often succeeds to drier woodland types. Much carr is of recent origin, having developed on semi-natural open habitats. Although willow has been cropped for craft uses (such as basket making) and Alder coppices easily, Wet Woodland is hard to access and has little economic value compared to other woodland types. It has, therefore, suffered extensively from clearance and drainage for agriculture.

Insh Marshes, Speyside – in some cases carr vegetation forms in the middle of mire such as this floodplain Transition Mire.

Did you know?
Submerged Alder does not rot, and was used to build crannogs (loch-dwellings) in the Iron Age.

Studland, Dorset – In many cases carr is secondary, having colonised open vegetation in the last 100 years or so since traditional management such as grazing or cutting has ceased.

Conservation

Conserving a dynamic habitat in isolation within a static framework of intensive land-use presents challenges. Current threats include the lowering of the water-table through water abstraction, eutrophication, the clearance of newly established sites and invasion by vigorous non-native plants such as Himalayan Balsam. Much Wet Woodland is successional, and will therefore particularly benefit from large landscape-scale conservation projects that provide the space for habitats to change and develop. At the site scale, re-establishment of natural hydrological systems will allow dynamism within the habitat, creating microhabitats of different structure suitable for different species.

What to look for

The most extensive stands of carr are found in The Norfolk and Suffolk Broads and the Shropshire and Cheshire Meres and Mosses. These calcareous carrs can be quite species-rich, with scrub such as Buckthorn, Alder Buckthorn, Guelder-rose, Dogwood and Red Currant, and a ground flora of Meadowsweet, Greater Tussock-sedge, Royal Fern and Yellow Iris. A distinctive northern form with a low canopy of Bay Willow includes herbs such as Wood Stitchwort, Marsh Hawk's-beard and Angelica, and can support the rare Coralroot Orchid. Widespread, but also more common in the north, is a calcifuge community of Downy Birch growing over bog-mosses or Purple Moor-grass on the drier edges of mires.

Floodplain Alder woodlands of any size are harder to find. Isolated strips and patches can still be found in the loops and backwaters of meandering rivers and streams, and larger areas occur in remnant floodplains and shingle islands along active, braided river channels in Scotland. Look out for the scarce Black-poplar on river banks. The ground is usually

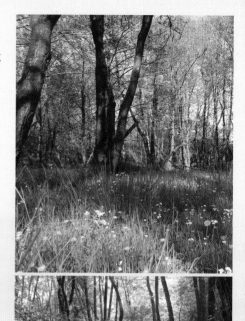

BELOW: **River Bure, Norfolk** – where Wet Woodland develops at the water's edge, it provides shade and detritus for aquatic invertebrates and fish.
INSET: **Hoveton Great Broad, Norfolk** – accessible only by boat, this swamp Alder carr is floating on unstable mud and peat over medieval peat workings.

TOP: **Kingcombe, Dorset** – drier Alder woods can have a relatively species-rich ground flora.
ABOVE: **New Forest, Hampshire** – strips of floodplain Alder woodland can be found along winding streams where they are grazed by free-ranging livestock.

ABOVE LEFT: **Morden Bog, Dorset** – this old-growth bog woodland of Downy Birch is located in the centre of a valley mire. **Greater Tussock-sedge** tussocks at least one metre in height are surrounded by peaty water. ABOVE RIGHT: **Upton Fen, Norfolk** – carr ground flora often reflects the flora of the preceding fen, and can include shade-tolerant species such as **Marsh Fern**. RIGHT: **Siskin** is often seen feeding on Alder catkins.

dominated by ruderal species such as Common Nettle and Great Willowherb, fed with nutrients from river-borne silt. Drier Alder woods with Ash on slopes and plateaux tend to be more species-rich, with a flora including Wood Anemone and Creeping Buttercup.

Wet Woodland has few specialised animals but its humidity and the abundance of dead, rotten wood make it attractive to many species. Willow Tit prefers wet, scrubby woodland and excavates its nest holes in rotten wood. Siskin and Lesser Redpoll feed on Alder catkins and birch seed. Wetland trees, wet seepages and semi-submerged deadwood are home to a suit of invertebrates, some of them rare. Willows in particular support a rich assemblages of moths and other insects. Otter can use Wet Woodland for cover and breeding sites.

WOOD PASTURE

Wood Pasture is an ecological structure rather than a specific vegetation type. Trees of different ages grow at varying densities in more or less open conditions, a function of light grazing. Grazing suppresses vigorous tree regeneration and the resulting semi-shade, together with the long-term presence of ancient trees, promotes a particularly rich epiphytic flora of lichens, mosses, liverworts and ferns, and an invertebrate fauna of deadwood specialists. Over the centuries, fluctuations in grazing pressure would have allowed the periodic recruitment of younger trees. However, both overgrazing and the cessation of grazing eventually result in the loss of Wood Pasture, either to closed-canopy woodland or to open heathland or grassland. The long life-span of veteran trees means that they can persist for many years amongst younger trees or conifers, but in such shaded conditions the diversity of species hosted by the veterans is greatly diminished and their vigour much reduced.

Wood Pasture is found from sea level right up to the tree line, often on nutrient-poor acidic soils that are unsuitable for cultivation, although it is by no means confined to these. Many well-known sites are in southern England but a few parklands are scattered throughout Wales and Northern Ireland. In Scotland, a continuum from closed-canopy woodland through grazed woodland to Wood Pasture is often seen.

Similar habitats

Wood Pasture is a particular expression of Lowland Dry Oak and Birch Wood and acid Beech Wood (parkland is also sometimes derived from Lowland Mixed Oak and Ash Wood).

Distribution and extent

Map shows English distribution only. Scattered across Britain, scarce in Ireland. Eng: 57,800 ha; Sco: 10,500 ha; Wal: n/k; NI: 1,100 ha; Ire: n/k. Britain holds a significant proportion of north-west European Wood Pasture.

RIGHT: The **New Forest, Hampshire** contains the largest area of Wood Pasture in NW Europe. It is one of very few sites that are known to have a continuous history of grazing since the medieval period. Light grazing helps to maintain the diversity of grassland species and creates a varied vegetation structure, including regenerating scrub and trees.

BELOW LEFT: **Borrowdale, Lake District** – pollards were still cropped for livestock fodder within living memory. These Ash trees have been re-pollarded by the National Trust.

BELOW RIGHT: **Burnham Beeches, Buckinghamshire** – an old wooded common where the classic squat forms and retracted crowns of veteran pollards can be seen.

Origins and development

Wood Pasture may be derived from the post-glacial wildwoods, where fluctuations in the woodland canopy and the actions of wild herbivores created open areas. It developed through the complex interactions between human use (livestock grazing; collecting of leaf fodder, leaf-hay, firewood, timber and bark; and hunting) and natural processes. By medieval times such uses had become formalised under the system of common rights. Royal Forests and hunting parks were established, and included large areas of Wood Pasture. The subsequent decline of Royal Forests saw the loss of much Wood Pasture, although medieval parks were revived during the Tudor period in the 16th century, and again in the 18th century (when many were formally landscaped). The loss of Wood Pasture was exacerbated when communal grazing land was enclosed from the 17th Century onwards and by conversion to plantation during the Napoleonic Wars at the beginning of the 19th century and again after the Second World War. In the uplands, a balance between grazing and regeneration was maintained until the agricultural revolution of the late 18th/early 19th centuries, when woods were enclosed or were grazed more heavily as year-round sheep pasture.

How to recognise

Veteran trees (see *page 50*) are the defining feature of this habitat. Often knarled, contorted into fabulous shapes and encrusted in lichens and fungi, they are scattered with other trees and scrub in a serene, savannah-like landscape.

Wood Pasture on former Royal Forests and wooded common is often extensive. Ancient, open-grown trees are interspersed with thickets of scrub and younger trees and they often merge into a mosaic of woodland and heathland or grassland.

Upland Wood Pasture may be associated with remnant ravine or cliff woodland, and often contains ruined sheilings (a hut, or collection of huts) or drove roads.

Wood Pasture found in old deer parks is usually more confined, with fences or banks demarcating an abrupt transition to farmland. In wooded commons it often has a more irregular boundary. All types are deeply cultural landscapes of historical interest, legacies of a multi-purpose tradition of land-use long since abandoned.

When to visit

Year-round for veteran trees and lichens.

LEFT: The classical Wood Pasture landscape holds wide appeal, and many people are drawn to veteran trees because of their character and links with the past.

Staverton, Suffolk

49

Conservation

A surge of interest in veteran trees in the late 20th century has resulted in efforts to manage and reinvigorate lapsed Wood Pasture. These efforts have focussed on how to renew and extend existing areas through appropriate grazing and the sensitive management of veteran trees. The full biodiversity benefits of extending Wood Pasture will be a long time coming, but such areas make good stepping stones between fragmented patches of woodland and open habitat. A long-term view is required, such as the 500-year management plan the Corporation of London has developed for Burnham Beeches in Buckinghamshire.

What to look for

The ground flora of Wood Pasture tends to be quite species-poor, although it can include grassland, heathland and woodland species, including fungi such as waxcaps (see *page 103*). Of the trees, oaks and Beech are the most frequent, but Ash, Hornbeam, Holly, elms, Alder, birches and, in Scotland, Scots Pine are all common. Parkland can also include planted non-natives such as Turkey Oak and Cedar-of-Lebanon. However, the overriding wildlife interest of Wood Pasture lies in the myriad species associated with veteran trees. Many of these trees have been pollarded in the past, extending their lifespans. However, such management is not a prerequisite since open-grown trees, with large, spreading canopies and horizontal branches, are also of great value.

As trees gradually age, their limbs die back, fungi hollow out the dead heartwood, and bark becomes craggy and loose. Nevertheless, they can still last for centuries, and this continuity is important for the sedentary species that colonise them. Fungi decompose standing and fallen deadwood, releasing nutrients for other fungi and feeding invertebrates. Mosses, liverworts and ferns colonise damp hollows, and lichens, fungi and algae grow on the bark, providing habitats for invertebrates in their turn. Beetles and flies use deadwood, sap runs, lightning strikes and old wounds, and are themselves prey for other invertebrates, birds and bats. Some birds excavate nest holes in softened wood, and others use crevices for breeding, as do bats. The open canopy of trees also favours foliage-living invertebrates, while others depend on the micorrhizal fungi associated with tree roots, or with dung. Groups of veteran trees provide a greater range of microhabitats and support a more diverse fauna and flora than single trees.

The diverse nature of a veteran tree

A veteran tree (FACING PAGE) can be defined as one that is of interest biologically, culturally or aesthetically because of its age, size or condition. Age depends upon the species – oaks might reach a millennium and Yews pre-date Christianity, but a veteran birch may be just a few decades old. Individual veterans are often named, well-loved, and enshrined in legends and stories. For example, the Fortingall Yew is said to have shaded the play of Pontius Pilate as a child. These trees speak to our souls, and their tenacity, the complexity of their ecology and the richness of the species they support is truly awesome. However, our veteran trees are a legacy from the past that we are failing to renew.

ABOVE: **Bracket fungus.** BELOW: **Staverton, Suffolk** was once a medieval deer park. The thick Bracken growing under these venerable pollards shows that this area is no longer grazed.

Rot hole

Snag where limb
has broken

'Bird' or 'air' tree, in
this case a Holly,
rooted in a fork

Damp holes
colonised
by bryophytes

Bracket fungus

Swollen base

Deadwood

ATLANTIC OAK WOOD

Atlantic Oak Wood is often dominated by oaks (mostly Sessile, but sometimes Pedunculate). In some sheltered situations species such as birches, Rowan, Holly, willows and some Ash and Alder are also present, but in many cases these were weeded out in the 19th century. Some Atlantic Oak Wood is in fact oak plantation, dating from the same time. Most woods are grazed, and heavy grazing (and browsing) prevents woody regeneration and promotes a grassy field layer with bulky mosses. On un-grazed loch islands or in enclosures the lack of grazing is immediately apparent in the more complex understorey and a lush field layer dominated by Great Wood-rush.

The field layer is also influenced by the underlying soil. Heather and Bilberry can be found on more acid substrates, with grass and Bracken (often sheltering Common Dog-violet and Wood-sorrel) on more neutral soils. The least acidic sites support a more herb-rich community and may have elms and Ash in the canopy; Ash also occurs in flushed areas along streams, and wet bog-moss hollows or springs covering wet mineral soils can support Alder. A dense growth of pioneer birch or Rowan in canopy gaps is often indicative of an earlier period when grazing was relaxed.

Similar habitats

Oak tends to give way to birch upslope in northern Scotland until Upland Birch Wood becomes dominant. Downslope it often grades into Upland Mixed Ash Wood or Alder or birch-dominated Wet Woodland. In coastal locations (particularly Argyll), Atlantic Hazel Wood is found over a similar field layer. Where a long history of grazing has resulted in very open, grassy woodland and associated veteran trees, Atlantic Oak Wood is considered as Wood Pasture.

Distribution and extent

Locally extensive on the western and northern upland fringes and coast. Once more widespread around the oceanic western rim of Europe, Britain and Ireland now hold most of the Atlantic Oak Wood in Europe.
Eng: 2,000 ha; Sco: 31,900 ha; Wal: 48,000 ha; NI: 1,000 ha; Ire: 5,900 ha (ANN I REP).

LEFT: **Erraid, Ross of Mull** – exposed coastal oak woodland is often stunted. BELOW LEFT: **Borrowdale, Cumbria** – the age and canopy species of some woods are quite uniform in structure either because species other than oaks were weeded out, or because they were in fact planted. These woods are likely to become more diverse over time. BELOW RIGHT: **Wistman's Wood, Dartmoor** is famed for its knarled, twisted trees and epiphytic flora. Photo evidence shows that the wood has spread and the trees gained in height since the late 19th century.

Origins and development

Most of the original Atlantic Oak Wood was destroyed in prehistory, and the fragmented remaining patches were exploited for timber and managed as coppice to provide tanning bark and charcoal used in iron smelting (mid-18th–mid-19th centuries). They were also used for sheltered grazing. Sheep pasturage increased markedly from the mid-18th century, and in recent decades deer browsing has added significantly to the grazing pressure. During the second half of the 20th century, clearance and thinning for conifer plantation, combined with conversion to rough grazing, reduced the area of Atlantic Oak Wood by nearly 40%. However, more recently, designation and initiatives to protect this habitat mean that it is likely to be increasing through both planting and natural regeneration.

Conservation

Encouraging the remaining islands of Atlantic Oak Wood to expand is a priority. Promoting natural recolonisation and planting seeds of local provenance will buffer and link existing sites, allowing marooned specialist species to expand their range. Within existing Atlantic Oak Wood, non-intervention is generally the best approach, except where threatening exotics or conifers need to be removed and where, in the absence of natural predators, deer management is needed to ensure natural regeneration is not suppressed. Seasonal low-intensity grazing is often advocated in order to prevent a thick ground flora developing and shading out lower plants where these have become limited in extent. Coppicing, although favourable for spring flowers and some warmth-seeking insects, does not allow the development of rich epiphytic communities.

How to recognise

This is the cool, moist oakwood of the western upland fringes. It is often found in places where the characteristic hard rock has eroded into crags, ravines or tumbles of boulders. Both Sessile and Pedunculate Oaks occur, and may grow as standards, with multiple stems, or as crooked gnarly hulks. On the coast, where stunted by Atlantic gales, they may even be prostrate.

The mild, wet climate and clean air of the west coast promote the lush growth of myriad lower plants, many growing in the fissures and crevices of old bark. Trunks and branches are clothed in bryophytes, which form a background for large leafy-lobed lichens, ferns and dripping beard lichens, while mosses carpet rock under open Holly, Rowan and Hazel.

Archaeological remains (such as levelled charcoal hearths), boundary walls, pollards and evidence of previous management as coppice or Wood Pasture often add a historic element to the atmosphere of these woods.

When to visit

From mid-April for birds (easiest to see when the leaves are not quite out!), May–early June for butterflies, and year-round for lichens, mosses and scenery.

Did you know?
The epiphytic lichen assemblages of Atlantic Oak Wood are among the richest in Europe.

What to look for

Four characteristic summer migrant birds to listen for and look out for in the spring are Redstart, Pied Flycatcher, Tree Pipit and Wood Warbler. Mammals are less likely to be seen but Pine Marten (Scotland only), Red Squirrel (in the north), Badger and Polecat are all found in Atlantic Oak Wood. In sheltered woodlands in north-west Scotland look for Chequered Skipper in sunny clearings and rides. Pearl-bordered Fritillary is another scarce butterfly that may be present, and more common butterflies may include Speckled Wood, Silver-washed Fritillary and White Admiral.

A wide range of lower plants are favoured by the moist, clean air. Lichens include dangling beard lichens, leafy protruding lungworts and creeping and crustose species of the Parmelion community. Look out for the distinctive lichen Common Tree Lungwort (see Atlantic Hazel Wood, *page 62*), which is an indicator of ancient woodland, and other rarer species. Some of the more conspicuous mosses include the golden-green fingers of Neat Feather-moss; dark green, thyme-like Swan-necked Thyme-moss; and the bright, fern-like Common Tamarisk-moss; and inside the moist woodland interior rare woodland species can be found.

ABOVE, LEFT TO RIGHT: **Redstart** typically nest around the edges of woods or near clearings. Listen for the distinctive accelerating song of the **Wood Warbler**, which is sometimes likened to the sound of a spinning coin. **Pied Flycatcher** is associated with open Atlantic Oak Wood where the understorey is sparse.

ABOVE: **Snowdonia** – although often remote and wild in feel, almost all Atlantic Oak Wood has been used by humans for generations. Look for areas on cliffs or ravines to find possible unfelled remnants of wildwood. ABOVE RIGHT: **Chequered Skipper** occurs in damp grassland (the larval food plant is Purple Moor-grass) on the edge of woodland. The best time to see adults is at the end of May/early June. RIGHT: **Loch a' Mhuilinn, Sutherland** – oceanic Atlantic Oak Woods with particularly rich lower plant floras, including many of our rarest bryophytes, are temperate rainforests.

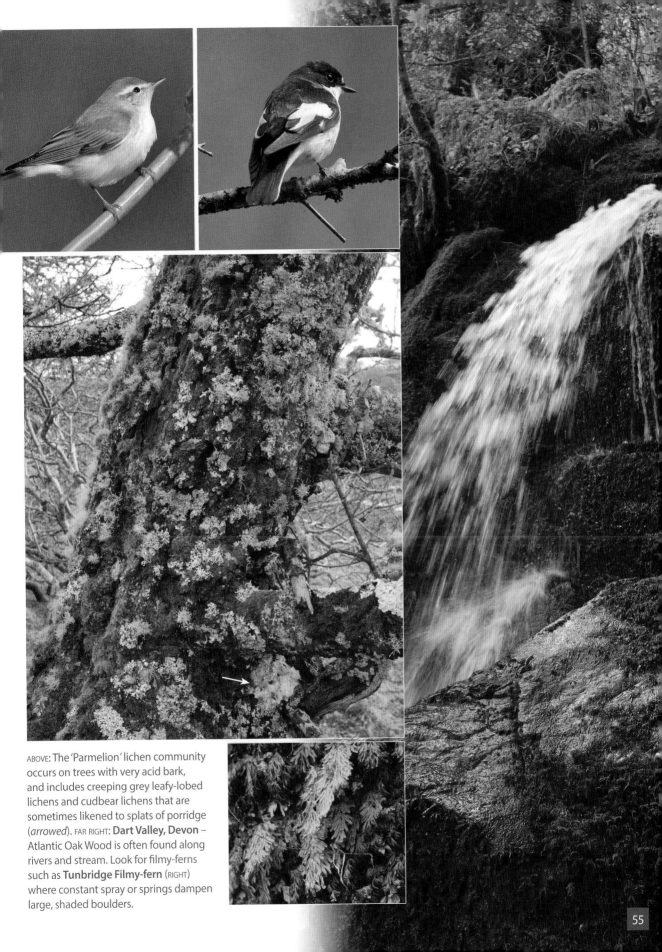

ABOVE: The 'Parmelion' lichen community occurs on trees with very acid bark, and includes creeping grey leafy-lobed lichens and cudbear lichens that are sometimes likened to splats of porridge (*arrowed*). FAR RIGHT: **Dart Valley, Devon** – Atlantic Oak Wood is often found along rivers and stream. Look for filmy-ferns such as **Tunbridge Filmy-fern** (RIGHT) where constant spray or springs dampen large, shaded boulders.

UPLAND MIXED ASH WOOD

The species composition of Upland Mixed Ash Wood varies from north to south, and also locally according to slope, aspect and the degree of moisture. In the north, characteristic species include Rowan, Hazel, Downy Birch, oaks and Bird Cherry, while in the south, Small-leaved Lime, Field Maple, Wych Elm and Beech (which is probably native in South Wales and the Lower Wye Valley) are common. Sycamore is frequent and although native to this woodland type on the continent, is an introduced species.

The light shade and calcareous substrate of Upland Mixed Ash Wood mean that it is typically species-rich. Un-grazed woods can be carpeted with Ramsons or Dog's Mercury, together with less common species such as Lily-of-the-valley, Solomon's-seal and Herb-Paris and, in the north, Wood Crane's-bill, Globeflower, Marsh Hawk's-beard and Lady's-mantle. Where grazed, the ground flora tends to be grassy with Bracken and thick mosses covering the rocks. In the oceanic climate of north-west Scotland and southern Ireland, epiphytic bryophytes and ferns are particularly abundant, creating a characteristic winter greenness, while lichens can include the distinctive Lobarion communities found in other Atlantic woodland types. Upland Mixed Ash Wood has a rich invertebrate fauna, and is particularly important for specialists of flushes and for molluscs (which require calcium for their shells). Dead elms are a frequent sight and are good for insects that require decaying wood.

Similar habitats

Upland Mixed Ash Wood can merge with other woodland types due to irregular topography and soil conditions. Where grazed, it can form mosaics with limestone grassland or pavement communities.

Distribution and extent

Found mainly on limestone in the north and west. Eng: 7,500 ha; Sco: 2,000 ha; Wal: 3,000 ha; NI: 300 ha; Ire: n/k (ANN I REP).

LEFT: **Colt Park Wood, North Yorkshire** – wooded Limestone Pavement is uncommon, but provides an intriguing insight into how unmodified open limestone landscapes may have looked in the past. BELOW LEFT: **Scar Close, North Yorkshire** – open patches are important in Upland Mixed Ash Wood, supporting grassland species not found under the canopy. BELOW RIGHT: **Rassal Ashwood, Wester Ross** – in the cool oceanic climate of northern Scotland, Upland Mixed Ash Wood can be found almost at sea level, and often supports rich epiphytic communities. Rassal is the most northerly sizeable Ash wood in Britain, probably at its climatic limit.

Origins and development

Ash spread rapidly after the last glaciation, reaching its current range around 6,500 years ago and Upland Mixed Ash Wood probably represents the last vestiges of a more widespread climax vegetation type on calcareous soils in cool, sub-montane areas. Clearance, and more latterly overgrazing, quarrying and replanting with non-native trees have greatly reduced its extent, although the required substrate has always been more fragmented than for other upland woodland types. Many woods were coppiced for timber and firewood and often had oak standards. Young groves of single-stemmed Ash are now found in some woods where preferential management for oaks reduced the amount of Ash in the past.

Conservation

Upland Mixed Ash Wood often forms part of pastoral farming systems and grazing by deer and livestock continues to constrain regeneration, reduce structural diversity within woods and limit the field layer. Light grazing regimes can maintain some open patches. Coppicing is not recommended where there are rich lichen and bryophyte floras. Ash die-back, first seen in the UK in 2012 could significantly impact on this habitat in the future.

What to look for

Rarities include Dark-red Helleborine, Jacob's-ladder, Large-leaved Lime and rare whitebeams. Oceanic epiphytic lichen and bryophyte communities can be particularly rich.

How to recognise

Although often small or fragmented, Upland Mixed Ash Wood can be particularly beautiful places with a colourful ground flora and rich diversity of plant and invertebrate species. Found in the upland fringes of pastoral landscapes, they are now confined to rocky limestone outcrops, crags, ravines and river gorges, where the elegant form of Ash can be picked out from a medley of other species.

Upland Mixed Ash Wood can also be found hidden away in valley heads and on hillsides forming smaller zones and patches within other woodland types, with which it intergrades.

Ash regenerates readily in the absence of grazing and woods often include old boundaries, pollards, limekilns and quarries that have been subsumed by younger trees.

When to visit

Late spring–summer for flora.

LEFT: Ravine woodland near **Cowgill, Yorkshire Dales** – such woods can provide oases of wildlife in barren upland landscapes. BELOW RIGHT: **Lily-of-the-valley** is frequently found in Upland Mixed Ash Wood, but also on Limestone Pavement, in some lowland woods and as a garden escape.

Did you know?

A related woodland type (missing in Britain but still found in Scandinavia) of Ash, birches, willows and Bird Cherry over a tall-herb field layer is probably the origin of the distinctive Northern Hay Meadow flora.

CALEDONIAN FOREST

Caledonian Forest is the only indigenous pine forest in Britain and Ireland, and is restricted to Scotland. It is found on infertile, acid soils from valley bottoms up to about 650 m; in most places the natural tree line is depressed by the effects of grazing rather than climate. Regeneration – or rather the lack of it – is a key factor in shaping the forest. Where browsing pressure is not too high, the forest regenerates readily, with young trees blurring the interface with heathland. Sparser forest with older, larger trees may be a product of selective thinning as well as grazing. Charismatic older trees with deep crowns growing in more open conditions ('Granny Pines') can also be relics of previous forest where regeneration was suppressed by browsing deer. Areas of dense young pines with high crowns result from planting, natural regeneration following felling, fire or changes in management. Species composition varies between regions, with Scots Pine dominating in the cold, dry east, while more humid, milder conditions in the west are more favourable for birches, Rowan, Holly and Hazel. Sessile Oak is found in the north-east.

Similar habitats

This distinctive habitat merges with other upland woodland habitats and with wetlands and heathlands. It can be hard to distinguish relatively natural Caledonian Forest, which has regenerated following felling or fire or in old stands, from planted areas.

Distribution and extent

Confined to around 85 sites in the Scottish Highlands. Sco: 17,900 ha. Caledonian Forest is an oceanic form of the boreal forests that encircle the globe at relatively high latitudes.

LEFT: **Rothiemurchus, Inverness-shire** – a typical transition between forest and heathland.
BELOW: **Abernethy, Inverness-shire** – old-growth forest is characterised by a range of tree ages and shapes and standing deadwood (*left*), plantation and regeneration in felled areas is more uniform (*right*).

Origins and development

Following the last glaciation, Common Juniper, willows and, later, Scots Pine colonised the Highlands of Scotland, and by 4,000 years ago some 1·5 million hectares of pine-dominated mixed woodland had developed. Felling and climate cooling during the Neolithic period started an ongoing decline. This increased from the 17th century onwards until only isolated remnants were left, largely in the more inaccessible upper glens. The removal of crofters and subsequent management of Red Deer for sport shooting led to a spurt of regeneration, although this was then contained by increased sheep-grazing. In the 20th century, reforestation programmes were initiated.

Conservation

The area of Caledonian Forest is limited by grazing animals, while the quality of existing forest is influenced by past and present sylvicultural practices. In the north-central Highlands, the Trees for Life project (see *page 33*) aims to restore significant areas to natural forest and eventually reintroduce its missing species: Beaver, Eurasian Lynx, Wolf and Wild Boar. Restoration involves planting as well as facilitating natural regeneration by fencing out Red Deer and livestock. At Abernethy, the RSPB plan to increase the forest by 2,000–3,000 ha through natural regeneration, using light grazing to optimise conditions for key species. Some areas, such as Abernethy, are managed primarily for their wildlife interest, but in others, such as Glenmore, commercial timber management is more of a priority. Recreational access is often an important factor influencing management.

(see *page 33*)

How to recognise

Caledonian Forest has a feeling of wildness and expanse that is rare in Britain and Ireland. It is easily identified by its geographic location (the central and north-east Grampian Mountains and northern and western Highlands) and characteristic species.

Scots Pine forms an open canopy with birches and Rowan above a richer layering of shrubby Common Juniper, Heather, Bell Heather and Bilberry. In places it grows more densely over a diminished shrub and field layer.

Many of the remnant areas are vast (*e.g.* Abernethy Forest is 28 km^2) and show natural functions such as intact transitions to other habitat types and natural regeneration. This, together with the apparent lack of human intervention, contributes to a pervading sense of naturalness in the landscape.

When to visit

Year-round for characteristic birds, July–August for rare plants and Heather in bloom.

Did you know?

Caledonia, the Roman name for Scotland, is derived from the early celtic word "caleto" meaning hard or strong. Caledonian Forest is often considered one of the last real wildernesses in Britain.

Beinn Eighe, looking across Loch Maree – above the altitude that this photograph was taken, the pines largely give way to Upland Birch Wood.

What to look for

Caledonian Forest supports relatively few species (and often at low density) compared with more fertile lowland woodlands, but many of those that do occur are absent or very rare elsewhere in Britain and Ireland. Red Squirrel, Wild Cat and Pine Marten are closely associated with Caledonian Forest, but were more widespread in the past. Pine Marten and Wild Cat were heavily persecuted and Red Squirrel has disappeared from much of England due to disease and competition from Grey Squirrel – Caledonian Forest has provided sanctuary for these species. While a chance encounter with either predator is unlikely, the knowledge that they are still present adds to the wild feel of the habitat. Red squirrels are still relatively common and can be easily seen at sites such as Abernethy or Rothiemurchus.

Key bird species include Crested Tit, Capercaillie and crossbills. Crested Tit nests in holes in dead standing trees and can occur in pine plantations, but is found at higher density within Caledonian Forest. It is found in forests in Easter Ross, Glen Affric, Strathspey and the Moray Firth coast. Capercaillie occurs mostly south of the Great Glen and prefers old forest with a dense understorey. Crossbills prefer large, broad-crowned and isolated trees and three species breed in Caledonian forest (Common, Scottish and Parrot Crossbills). Notoriously hard to separate, the species differ in their calls and morphology (particularly beak shape). The Scottish Crossbill is Britain's only endemic bird species.

*View across Caledonian Forest in **Rothiemurchus** with the Cairngorm massif in the background.*

ABOVE LEFT: **Capercaillie** – the world's largest grouse became extinct in Britain over 200 years ago, but was reintroduced in 1837. Bilberry is an important food source.
ABOVE RIGHT: **Pine Marten** – an omnivorous species that eats a range of fruit and caterpillars, as well as small mammals, Capercaillie chicks and Red Squirrels. It is most easily seen at dedicated feeding stations and bird feeders.
BELOW: **Crested Tit** – endemic to Europe with an endemic subspecies in Scotland, this bird is strongly associated with Caledonian Forest and is often seen in or around old trees.

With a bit of luck (and persistence) some unusual flowering plants can be found among the Heather and Bilberry. Creeping Lady's-tresses, Twinflower and One-flowered Wintergreen all have white or very pale flowers. Mosses are abundant and Glittering Wood-moss is particularly characteristic and very common. Tooth fungi are mainly associated with Caledonian Forest, Orange Tooth and Blue Tooth fungi being restricted to native pinewoods.

Caledonian Forest is also important for hoverflies, flies and beetles, including a number of species with very restricted distributions. Many of the important species, such as the Bumblebee Robberfly, are saproxylic, relying on dead pine wood. There are also up to seven species of wood ant that occur in Caledonian Forest, including the Narrow-headed Ant which has its stronghold around Loch Morlich in the Cairngorms. This rare ant can only persist in areas with an open understorey.

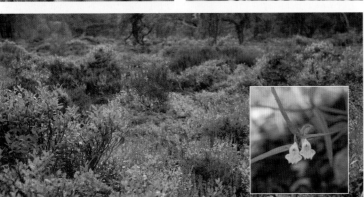

TOP: The **Bumblebee Robberfly** is a large and dramatic fly – look for it on fallen pine trees and stumps, where it sits ready to ambush other insects.
ABOVE, LEFT: **One-flowered Wintergreen** occurs in both old-growth forest and pine plantations.
ABOVE, CENTRE: **Twinflower** is a boreal species predominantly associated with old Caledonian Forest and is confined to approximately 50 sites in Scotland, mainly in drier woods in the east. ABOVE, RIGHT: **Green Shield-moss** is an endangered species known from just 13 sites (most of which are in Caledonian Forest). It is a deadwood specialist that mostly grows on boughs bigger than 20 cm diameter. Unlike most other mosses its leaves are invisible.
LEFT: **Forest Lodge, Abernethy** – thick field layer vegetation of Bilberry, Heather and abundant mosses can include species such as Cowberry, Wavy Hair-grass, and **Small Cow-wheat** (INSET).

ATLANTIC HAZEL WOOD

Hazel's natural growth form is that of a multi-stemmed shrub and the longevity of an individual 'tree' is not therefore limited by the lifespan of a single trunk. As a consequence, in places where exposure and thin soils prevent other woody species from establishing themselves, Atlantic Hazel Wood can persist indefinitely. Single-stemmed 'trees', the product of extensive grazing, are found in heavily grazed woodlands and Wood Pasture. In some places Hazel rings are evident. These are created when satellite stools grow up around a 'mother' plant that is eventually shaded out and leaves a circle of clones behind. It is conjectured that some of these trees may be many hundreds of years old, providing stable conditions for epiphytes to flourish.

Variations in the underlying substrate are reflected in the ground flora, which typically includes woodland spring flowers such as Primrose, Wood Anemone, Bluebell, Common Dog-violet and Wood-sorrel, together with ferns and bryophytes. The flora is richest on limestone substrates, where it is comparable to that of Upland Mixed Ash Wood. Leafy lichens are also present, and include the 'Lobarion' community of large, lobed species, smaller, more adpressed species, and those with a jelly-like consistency.

Similar habitats

The ground flora tends to be the same as either Atlantic Oak Wood or Upland Mixed Ash Wood, depending on the substrate. Canopy transitions are found where deeper soils or less exposed situations allow other species to overtop Hazel, which can remain a part of the understorey.

Origins and development

Older by far than Atlantic Oak Wood, and even some Caledonian Forest, these woods are thought to be a survivor of the pioneer Hazel woods that colonised Britain and Ireland after the last glaciation. Protected from livestock grazing and felling because they occur on rough ground and because Hazel can regenerate, they have had a continuous presence for over 10,000 years. During this time it is likely that some woods have been selectively cut (although entire stools were not generally cut-over) and used for pasturage, particularly to shelter livestock. Where the Hazel growth is impenetrably low and dense, it is hard to imagine these woods have ever been used. Current threats include coppicing and overgrazing, which reduce suitability for lower plants, destroy the internal structure and in the case of grazing, prevent regeneration.

Distribution and extent

Found on the western seaboard of Scotland between Knapdale and Sutherland, also some sites in western Ireland. Extent unknown. Considered unique to Britain and Ireland.

ABOVE, TOP: The rubbery orange fingers of the fungus **Hazel Gloves** only occurs in ancient Atlantic Hazel Wood.
ABOVE, BOTTOM: **Assynt, Sutherland** – light grazing has created a grassy field layer, but has not prevented regeneration of Hazel shoots.
LEFT: **Cathir Chomáin, Co. Clare** – large areas of pioneer Atlantic Hazel Wood have developed on the limestones of Co. Clare and Co. Fermanagh as a result of farming changes. They included more ancient core areas, but mostly lack the species-richness of old-growth areas.

Conservation

Atlantic Hazel Woods do not fit into the National Vegetation Classification of British plant communities, nor are they currently recognised by the European Habitats Directive. Few sites fall within protected areas, and the habitat does not easily fit the criteria of current management grants. To ensure its conservation, greater recognition is needed of the ancient origins of this habitat and its unique lower plants. Light seasonal grazing is recommended to help create and maintain small glades. Areas of Hazel without the distinctive lower plant communities of the ancient sites are widespread and have value as potential future habitat, allowing linkage and expansion of current sites.

Also known as Celtic rainforest, these ancient woods are strange and magical places.

Always close to the sea and on steep or rocky ground, Atlantic Hazel Wood can form self-contained stands, or may be part of other woodland. The low canopy of Hazel filters out the light, making them shady and cool even in summer. The regular, abundant rainfall and moist sea-mists, together with an equable, mild climate allow incredibly rich assemblages of oceanic mosses, liverworts and lichens to flourish, including species that occur nowhere else in the world. Mosses carpet the ground and creep up trunks. In exposed places, the smooth bark of young stems appears pale, mottled with patches of crustose lichens.

Deeper in, large leafy-lobed lichens emerge from thick moss on older branches whose fissured bark traps moisture. Sometimes these heavy stems lean out or are wrenched over in storms, creating a canopy gap that is rapidly filled with young whips sprouting from the base of the stool, and allowing the wood to perpetuate.

When to visit

Year-round for lichen interest.

LEFT, TOP TO BOTTOM: the moss **Dwarf Neckera**; the lichens *Pyrenula occidentalis;* and **Golden Specklebelly**. RIGHT, TOP TO BOTTOM: the lichens **Common Tree Lungwort**; *Arthonia cinnarbarina*; and **Octopus Suckers** – a jelly lichen.

Isle of Eigg, Hebrides. The impenetrably dense canopy of exposed Atlantic Hazel Wood.

63

UPLAND BIRCH WOOD

Upland Birch Wood varies according to altitude and climate. At lower elevations, Silver Birch is most common, while the tougher Downy Birch survives in wetter and colder places, growing with Rowan, willows and Hazel. In the cool and windy north-west Highlands, a shrubby form of Downy Birch reaches no more than 10 m in height. In the north and east Highlands, both species form almost pure stands, with the presence of a little Common Juniper and Scots Pine hinting at a past continuum with Caledonian Forest. In other places, birch dominance can be a result of selective felling for timber. In northern England and Wales, where there is little remaining woodland at high altitudes, birch woods are scarce, tending only to occur in patches within other woodland types or, more rarely, as wet, valley bottom woodlands with an understorey of bog-mosses and Purple Moor-grass (see Wet Woodland *page 44*). Downy Birch stands are considered a part of upland oak woodland in Ireland.

Birches are pioneers, their small, wind-blown seeds allowing them to colonise open areas quickly. As birches are short-lived and easily shaded out by other species, Upland Birch Wood tends gradually to move across the landscape as older stands either senesce and revert to moorland or succeed to other woodland types, and new stands develop on open ground. Newer woods tend to be relatively species-poor and even-aged, occurring where a temporary relaxation of grazing pressure results in a pulse of regeneration, leading to even-aged stands of trees.

Similar habitats

Upland Birch Wood is closely related to other upland woodlands types, and can often be seen as a cyclical stage within these.

ABOVE LEFT: **Assynt, Sutherland** – Birch Wood often forms mosaics with other habitats, including Upland Dry Heath as seen in this stream gorge. ABOVE: **Borrowdale, Cumbria** – oak woodland gives way to birch on the upper slopes. LEFT: **Yewbarrow, Cumbria** – Upland Birch Wood is intrinsically transient, although individual woods are known to have persisted for hundreds of years.

Distribution and extent

Widely distributed in the uplands, especially in Scotland. Around 15,000–25,000 ha is probably ancient, but much is more recent secondary woodland. Eng: n/k; Sco: 45,000 ha; Wal: 4,400 ha; NI: n/k; Ire: n/k.

How to recognise

Upland Birch Wood cloaks large swathes of the uplands (particularly in Scotland) where infertile, poorly drained soils are challenging for other species.

Birch woods often have a transient feel. They are generally open and grassy, quite even-aged, and dotted with glades, rocky outcrops and damp hollows. They can range from a scattering of individual trees over heathy vegetation to more established woods with dense thickets, mature trees and veterans that have changed the flora beneath them to grass and just a few herbs such as Sheep's Sorrel and Tormentil.

Although the flora is generally quite limited, inaccessible ledges in damp, base-rich ravines can support tall herbs. Upland Birch Wood provides habitat for typical upland woodland birds, and as birch wood rots rapidly, it provides excellent habitat for a great diversity of invertebrates and for fungi.

When to visit

Late spring/early summer for butterflies and flowers.

Origins and development

Birch colonised rapidly following the last glaciation and persisted where harsh conditions prevented other tree species from flourishing (*e.g.* in the north of Scotland and possibly on McGillycuddy's Reeks and the Wicklow Mountains in Ireland). The extent of Upland Birch Wood often fluctuated in a slowly changing mosaic of other woodland types, heathland and wetland, and they were generally not as intensively managed as other woodland types. However, their dynamic nature is now often constrained by land management practices (overgrazing and burning) that prevent regeneration and result in isolated and sometimes moribund stands. In the second half of the 20th century, overgrazing and replanting with non-native species led to significant losses, but planting under grant schemes and restructuring of conifer plantations may be reversing this trend.

Conservation

Upland Birch Wood is currently used for shelter and grazing for livestock, with some wood extraction for firewood. Overgrazing of woodland and adjacent habitats needs to be reduced to allow Upland Birch Wood move, change and regenerate. A strategic approach is needed to join new areas to existing stands, to allow cohesive forest ecosystems to develop, and to conserve genetic diversity across its range. Climate change may reduce longevity and affect regeneration.

What to look for

Boreal plants including Chickweed-wintergreen and Globeflower; stands of Aspen (which can support rare and scarce insects) in Upland Birch Wood in the Highlands; Pearl-bordered Fritillary.

TOP: **Chickweed-wintergreen** – although not species-rich, Upland Birch Wood provides habitats for flowering plants typical of northern Britain. BOTTOM: **Pearl-bordered Fritillary** can be seen in clearings where there are abundant violets (the larval food plant) and nectar sources, but populations can die out when clearings become overgrown.

Like Atlantic Oak Wood and Atlantic Hazel Wood, the Upland Birch Wood of the Atlantic fringe can support rich lichen and bryophyte communities, including many rarities.

Did you know?
In the past, birch was used for firewood and for making small tools, herbal remedies and a fermented drink.

CONIFEROUS PLANTATION

The wildlife of Coniferous Plantation reflects the type of semi-natural habitat that was afforested or replanted (usually heathland, bog and less profitable woodland types), and the age and structure of the plantation. In dense plantations, deep shade and needle-litter can inhibit plant growth, but where light can penetrate along rides or in thinned areas, Bracken or heathland species can develop. In plantations within broad-leaved woodland, an impoverished woodland flora can persist.

Large sites that are a complex matrix of different plantation stages and open habitats may support more species than the open habitat would alone, as they can include woodland species that do not inhabit the open habitat (*e.g.* bats such as Brown Long-eared Bat or Noctule that roost in mature trees). Within woodland sites, conifer-loving species benefit, and plantations have extended the range of some species (*e.g.* Firecrest and Common Crossbill in England). Early growth stages may support high densities of birds that favour scrub, such as warblers, and young pine is particularly important for Black Grouse, but the lack of structure inhibits many woodland birds.

Similar habitats

Larger sites usually contain patches of semi-natural habitat including mires, heathland, secondary woodland and ancient woodland. Coastal sites can include Sand Dune.

TOP LEFT: **Bentley Wood, Wiltshire** – clearings within plantations on woodland sites can support rare butterflies such as Pearl-bordered Fritillary and Duke of Burgundy. TOP RIGHT: **Holkham, Norfolk** – Scots Pine was planted in the late 19th century to stabilise the sand dunes. Rare fungi have been recorded here, together with uncommon plants such as Yellow Bird's-nest and Creeping Lady's-tresses. ABOVE: **Dentdale, Cumbria** – uniform blocks of dense conifers jar the eye in upland landscapes but can (when young) support species such as Small Pearl-bordered Fritillary and Black Grouse.

Distribution and extent

Found throughout Britain and Ireland, particularly in the uplands. Eng: 303,300 ha; Sco: 993,800 ha; Wal: 143,100 ha; NI: 65,400 ha; Ire: 500,000 ha.

How to recognise

Plantations are easily identified. Our only indigenous coniferous tree – Scots Pine – is now only native to Scotland and dark, geometric blocks of uniformly aged trees planted in straight lines with little by way of shrub or field layer do not look any more natural than a field of wheat. However, many plantations (which can include pine, spruce and fir) are now managed more sympathetically than in the past.

Open ride-edges, firebreaks and clearfells can support natural vegetation, and animals including reptiles and Woodlark, while clearings in replanted woods may still support rare butterflies. Raptors including Goshawk and Osprey nest in tall pines, Common Crossbill and Red Squirrel forage for pinenuts and Red or Roe Deer may seek cover.

After dusk, plantations can be great places to see Nightjar, Long-eared Owl and bats, and big sites in particular offer superbly dark skies for star-gazing.

When to visit

Warm, still evenings May–August for Nightjar; year-round for Red Squirrel.

Origins and development

Large-scale coniferous afforestation started after the First World War, when woodland cover in Britain had reduced to 5% and in Ireland to less than 2%. In 1919, the Forestry Commission (FC) was formed to set up strategic reserves of timber, and extensive areas where poor soil fertility had precluded agriculture (mainly heaths and mires) were afforested. State afforestation commenced in Ireland in the 1920s. By the 1920s, large areas such as the New Forest, Thetford Forest and Kielder Forest were afforested, and planting moved into the uplands. Scotland now contains the largest sites and greatest area of Coniferous Plantation. In the 1980s, vast areas of natural peatlands in the Flow Country in northern Scotland were afforested due to tax breaks and forestry grants. Nature conservation now forms part of FC's remit, and some areas are being restored to their former important habitats.

Conservation

While Coniferous Plantations can support a diversity of wildlife, their overall conservation value is generally less than that of the semi-natural habitat they replaced, and restoration projects are now underway to restore areas of heathland, mire and broadleaved woodland (*e.g.* through the Forestry Commission's Open Habitats Policy and the efforts of conservation organisations). The size of many plantations offers scope for creating habitat networks in the landscape.

Where coniferous cover is retained, focus should be on providing rich edge habitats and a shifting mosaic of clearfell and young plantation, retaining old stands and managing watercourses sensitively. Recreation is increasingly part of the remit for state-owned sites, and a balance between such activities and maintaining and enhancing the wildlife interest can be difficult to achieve.

What to look for

Nightjar, Sand Lizard and Smooth Snake in southern heathland areas; Red Squirrel and Common Crossbill.

ABOVE: **Godlingston, Dorset** – the interface between pine plantation and heathland can support higher densities of Nightjar than heathland alone.
RIGHT, TOP: **Red Squirrel** – Coniferous Plantation in the north of England and Scotland remains a stronghold for Red Squirrel after the decline caused by the introduction of Grey Squirrel. Dense stands with continuous cover and a diversity of conifers to provide an ongoing food supply are important.
RIGHT, BOTTOM: **Creeping Lady's-tresses** – a rare orchid found in pine woods in Scotland, Cumbria and East Anglia, which may have colonised naturally or been introduced with tree seedlings.

SCRUB

Scrub can be hard to define precisely, as it is usually a changing successional phase found in a mosaic with other vegetation types. Typically, scrub is thought of as vegetation dominated by shrubs or bushes (*i.e.* woody plants with many stems) reaching no more than about five metres in height and forming a canopy over at least 50% of the habitat patch. It can range from scattered bushes on open habitats to dense, impenetrable patches. The term is also often used loosely to include young trees often associated with these shrubs.

ORIGINS

There has been much debate amongst ecologists as to how much scrub and open habitats existed in the 'natural' (pre-Neolithic) vegetation of Britain and Ireland. Scrub developed rapidly in some places after the last glaciation and was largely replaced by woodland, but the extent of the woodland canopy is questioned. Some argue that a shifting mosaic of scrub, woodland and open habitats was always present; there is certainly evidence that scrub has a long history in Britain and Ireland (*e.g.* Blackthorn has been found in pollen cores dating back at least 5,000 years ago and evidence of Blackthorn and Hawthorn has been found in Mesolithic deposits).

Scrub plants are pioneer woody species. They grow fast once established and do best where there is ample light, and as a consequence can colonise open habitat quite quickly. Scrub species also have a range of adaptions that enable them to respond rapidly to changing environments and colonise new areas (see below for some examples).

Scrub is spreading onto grassland from the woodland edge after a reduction in grazing pressure.

Many shrubs have fleshy berries that are distributed in the droppings of a range of species, including birds such as thrushes. Seed fall is much heavier under trees and bushes where birds perch than in open grassland, but few seeds will germinate in dense shade. The highest density of new seedlings is therefore usually around the edges of scrub or under lone trees, so patches of scrub tend to spread outwards. Since huge numbers of berries are produced, some seeds are deposited in open grassland where they germinate readily and can form new scrub patches. Experiments involving planting Hawthorn seedlings in grassland have shown that those close to scrubby edges are less likely to be grazed down and have the highest probability of survival.

Scrub can expand rapidly in open habitats such as farmland, grassland or heathland as soon as they are less intensively grazed, cut or otherwise managed. Once established, scrub patches are rarely static, and scrub edges may fluctuate depending on grazing levels and conditions. Over time the canopy may close between

Adaptations of scrub species

Scrubby plants produce **high volumes of seeds**. Many, such as Bramble, produce berries which are dispersed by birds; Traveller's Joy (ABOVE) is wind-dispersed.

Woody stems and spines (seen here on Hawthorn) are effective in deterring browsing animals.

Backwards-pointing thorns help the quick-growing stems of species such as Dog-rose to scramble over other plants.

Once arching **stems** of Bramble **touch the ground** they **root and produce new shoots** and new plants develop. Some species, such as Blackthorn, spread through underground suckers.

Scrub species that form an integral part of other habitats:

TOP LEFT: **Bog-myrtle** suckers and forms dense patches in wet heathland and mires where there is some movement of groundwater. Several moth larvae feed on Bog-myrtle including the day-flying Argent and Sable. TOP CENTRE: **Gorse** and Western Gorse are very common on light well-drained soils and can provide breeding habitat for Dartford Warbler, Stonechat, Linnet and Yellowhammer. A number of scarce invertebrates are also reliant on gorse. TOP RIGHT: **Sea-buckthorn** spreads by rhizomes and layering, and can form dense thickets. Widespread in the late-glacial period, it is now only native on fixed dunes along the east coast of Britain. However, it is often used as an amenity shrub and become widely distributed, and can be problematic. RIGHT: **Shrubby Sea-blite** grows on upper Saltmarsh, on shingle drift lines (seen here) and more rarely behind sea walls in Coastal Grazing Marsh in East Anglia, south-east England and Dorset.

bushes, and the vegetation of the surrounding habitat is shaded out and replaced by species such as Common Nettle and Cleavers. Tree species may become established as the scrub canopy becomes taller and thins a little and, after about 50 years or so, woodland will develop. The complete succession through to woodland does not always occur, and may be halted if disturbance, levels of exposure or lack of seeds limits tree regeneration.

TYPES OF SCRUB

Some scrub is dominated by a single species such as Bog-myrtle, Gorse, Sea-buckthorn or Shrubby Sea-blite, and is best considered as a component of the habitat within which it is found. Common Juniper can also form single-species stands of scrub, but is of particular conservation interest (see box on *page 70*). In other cases, scrub is more varied, and can be treated as a habitat in its own right. **Mixed Scrub** (*page 72*) is the common scrub of waste ground, abandoned farmland and grassland, and is typically found in the south and in the upland fringes. It is closely linked to grassland and woodland habitats but supports a distinctive suite of species. Mixed Scrub on calcareous grassland can be quite species-rich. **Hedgerow** (*page 74*) is essentially linear scrub and forms a distinctive habitat of cultural importance. It can support unusual woodland-edge species. **Montane Scrub** is very rare and is unusual among scrub types in being a natural climax community; it is described further in the Mountain Habitats section (*page 132*). **Bracken** (*page 78*) is included here because, although not a shrub, it is forms a component of other habitats, can be transitional, and has some similar conservation issues.

THREATS AND ISSUES

Scrub has had a bad press – seen as something undesirable that needs to be tidied away. It is controlled on both farmland and on nature reserves, where it generally spreads at the expense of other, preferred (and often much rarer) habitats, which may not regenerate readily even if the scrub is removed. Similarly, farmland and roadside hedges are kept tightly trimmed to stop them from encroaching on fields and to minimise labour. In many upland areas, scrub has been lost through heavy grazing and that which remains is even-aged, tall and mature. However, scrub can be excellent for wildlife, and naturalists often gravitate towards the interface between scrub and open habitats. Fortunately, the value of scrub has become better appreciated in recent decades, and it is now established as an important component of semi-natural sites. This does not make it any easier to manage, as it is a dynamic habitat that needs space to move and deteriorates if fossilized in one place. The small size of many sites in the lowlands makes this a challenge, while difficulties in finding graziers for semi-natural sites means that scrub can overwhelm open habitats. In any case, grazing alone is unlikely to control scrub (unless it is at levels that are also likely to damage the open habitat), and in the past scrub was often cut for fuel and small timber. Cutting scrub is labour-intensive if carried out manually; done with machinery, it requires an all-or-nothing approach that can make it difficult to achieve a range of scrub types and ages.

JUNIPER SCRUB

Juniper is generally encountered as a component of the vegetation within other habitats. However, in some cases it forms a distinct association with other shrubs, shade-tolerant herbs, grazing-sensitive tall herbs, bryophytes and ferns (*e.g.* on chalk and Carboniferous limestone) and can also form a type of woodland (*e.g.* in the eastern Highlands). In these situations it is considered to be a habitat in its own right and one of European importance. Juniper can occur both as scattered individuals in other habitats and as a distinct association of its own. It was one of the first woody species to colonise Britain and Ireland after the last glaciation around 12,400 years ago and has a huge global distribution encompassing America, Europe and Asia. It occurs in a wide range of habitats, from sea level to 900 m, including Mixed Scrub, Calcareous Grassland, Lowland Dry Heath, Coastal Vegetated Shingle and Sand Dune (in north-east Scotland only), Limestone Pavement, Upland Dry Heath, Caledonian Forest, Montane Dwarf-shrub Heath and Montane Scrub.

Juniper occurs in a range of shapes and growth forms. There are two main subspecies: Common Juniper (the most frequent, found across Britain) and Dwarf Juniper (found on the Atlantic fringe of Ireland, in Scotland, Cumbria and North Wales). A third very rare subspecies is found in coastal heath in Pembrokeshire and on The Lizard in Cornwall. Many Common Juniper populations are isolated and genetic studies show a high degree of variability. Clusters of 50 or more plants are thought to be capable of recruitment and long-term survival without inbreeding, yet in many locations numbers are much lower than 50 and regeneration is very limited. After the bushes reach about 50 years of age the fruits they produce become increasingly sterile, so Common Juniper depends on regular recruitment of new seedlings. The seedlings require bare ground to germinate, but are very vulnerable to grazing. The outbreak of myxomatosis was the last time there was significant recruitment of seedlings in southern populations, many of which are no longer fertile.

Particularly large numbers of invertebrates are specific to Common Juniper and a high proportion of them are Red Data Book species. These include a range of moths (including the Juniper Carpet), gall midges and mites. Common Juniper also provides winter cover for Black Grouse in the uplands.

RIGHT, TOP: Well-developed Common Juniper 'woodland' is associated with Bilberry, Heather, Wood-sorrel, Heath Bedstraw, the distinctive branched mosses Common Tamarisk-moss and Glittering Wood-moss, and sometimes Chickweed-wintergreen (**Rothiemurchus, Speyside**). In Scotland, Common Juniper can occur where the canopy of Caledonian Forest is missing. RIGHT, MIDDLE: Juniper Scrub at **Burnham Beeches, Buckinghamshire**, on acid soil. RIGHT, BOTTOM: Juniper Scrub at **Noar Hill, Hampshire**, on chalk grassland. BELOW: Prostrate Common Juniper on rocky outcrops in Blanket Bog in **Roundstone Bog, Connemara**.

Key locations for Juniper Scrub

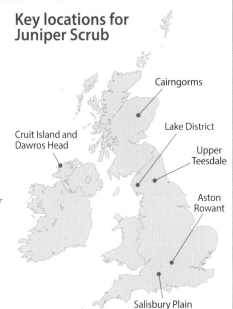

Cairngorms

Lake District

Cruit Island and Dawros Head

Upper Teesdale

Aston Rowant

Salisbury Plain

Near **Llanfachreth, Gwynedd** – in Welsh, *ffridd* (seen in this valley) refers to a complex mosaic of scrub, heath, Bracken and other habitats of uncultivated valley sides in the transition between upland and lowland. Often continuous, it can provide important habitat and corridors for fritillary butterflies and birds such as Whinchat.

Mature, established scrub has a limited ground flora.

Removal of mature scrub does not always mean a return to species-rich swards. Grassland seed banks are short-lived and impoverished swards can result from scrub clearance.

CULTURAL IMPORTANCE

Scrub has always been an important part of the rural economy, providing fuel and wild foods. Even today many people still mark the seasons by making elderflower cordial, blackberry jam and sloe gin. Some scrub species have also played an important role in cultural traditions. Hawthorn (also called Whitethorn or May) is a symbol of May Day, and has a strong role in pagan beliefs. Hedgerows are particularly valued for what they tell us about the development of the landscape. Many are ancient, and follow boundaries established in the medieval period or even earlier. They are quick to grow and suitably impenetrable. The Old English name for Hawthorn is *haegporn* from *haga*, which means haw. The abundance of Hawthorn in hedges (it is the most frequently mentioned tree in Anglo-Saxon boundary charters) led to the name *haeg* or hedge for a boundary of Hawthorn.

CONSERVATION IMPORTANCE AND PROTECTION

Scrub occurs widely in SSSIs (although it is rarely a reason for their designation), around one quarter of the Special Areas of Conservation (SACs) in the UK are estimated to contain scrub habitats of nature conservation importance, and scrubby vegetation is a component of eleven different Priority Habitats in the UK. However, with the exception of Montane Scrub and Juniper Scrub, for which the UK has an international responsibility under the European Habitats Directive, scrub is rarely recognised in its own right. Its nature conservation interest generally lies in the species associated with it. These depend on particular characteristics, including patchiness and structural diversity, which are best achieved at large spatial scales.

FURTHER INFORMATION

Hedgelink – www.hedgelink.org.uk/
National Hedgelaying Society – www.hedgelaying.org.uk/

KEY ELEMENTS

Scrub is important for a range of individual species that often require quite specific conditions. For example, Nightingale prefers dense scrub patches that include open ground; Dingy Mocha (a moth) seeks out isolated young willows on the edge of heathland, and Barberry Carpet (another moth) requires Barberry bushes with young, vigorous growth. Structural diversity within a wider mosaic of other habitats is often key in ensuring suitable niches are available for a variety of species, and the interface between scrub and open habitats is of particular importance.

There are not many words in English to describe different types of scrub, so ecologists have borrowed terms from elsewhere. *Saum* refers to the fringe of taller herbs and grasses around the edge of scrub patches, and can support rare plants and invertebrates. *Mantel* is the woodland edge zone supporting woody plants such as wild roses, Brambles and thorns. In North Wales the term *ffridd* refers to unenclosed land in the transition between upland and lowland, while in South Wales it refers to enclosed land, with the term *coedcae* being used to describe similar unenclosed areas.

MIXED SCRUB

Mixed Scrub is variable and depends on the soil characteristics and location. Hawthorn and Bramble scrub is the commonest type, typically occurring with Ivy on well-drained soils that are mildly acidic to calcareous. Blackthorn is also common and on the coast can persist in a natural climax community. Elder is often found where disturbance has created local nutrient enrichment. On acidic soils gorse is frequent, while a suite of lime-loving species, including Dogwood, Wild Privet, Wayfaring-tree, Guelder-rose, Spindle and Buckthorn and (rarely) Box, is found on calcareous soils, often with climbers such as Traveller's-joy and Black Bryony sprawling over the canopy.

Mixed scrub is a successional habitat that develops between open herbaceous vegetation and woodland, and each stage is accompanied by changes in light and nutrient levels, and soil moisture. Initially the field layer is that of the preceding habitat, but as the canopy closes the ground flora changes and is eventually lost. Later, as the canopy becomes taller but thins, woodland species such as Ash and Sycamore can colonise and eventually woodland becomes established.

The dynamic boundary between scrub and open vegetation is the most important component for wildlife. The scrub edge provides structure, shelter, fruits and seeds, and may protect grassland plants from grazing and trampling, while the herbaceous vegetation allows light to penetrate and supplies nectar for invertebrates. This interface may support a range of plants and invertebrates not found in either habitat on its own. Scrub within ancient woodland, Wood Pasture and Calcareous Grassland can be particularly rich.

Similar habitats

Hedgerow supports similar vegetation but is linear and subject to a very specific management regime. Mixed Scrub can occur with and alongside many other habitats and may conceal features such as ponds.

Origins and development

In a few circumstances (*e.g.* eroding and slumping cliffs, screes or quarries) Mixed Scrub can be entirely natural, forming part of a primary succession. However, it is generally part of secondary succession, occurring after grazing has been relaxed on grassland or heathland or on abandoned arable land. Unless the succession is arrested by some form of disturbance or particularly harsh conditions (or seed sources are sparse), the scrub will succeed to woodland within 50 years or so.

The decline in Rabbit numbers due to myxomatosis in the 1950s, combined with a general reduction in grazing, resulted in an increase in scrub on semi-natural open habitats in lowland areas. By contrast, in upland hill farming areas, decades of intensive grazing has resulted in scrub habitats becoming scarcer.

Conservation

The most valuable areas of scrub are dynamic and shift and change over time; the largest number of species will occur where there is a range of successional stages. Rotational scrub cutting is generally required to maintain structural diversity, while grazing is often used on the surrounding habitat to help prevent excessive scrub encroachment.

Distribution and extent

Widespread, particularly in southern England, on south-western coasts and on marginal land in the uplands. Extent unknown. Map shows patches of 25 ha or more, including gorse, so may not reflect true distribution.

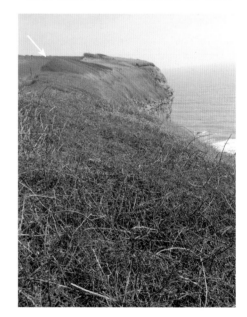

ABOVE: **Dancing Ledge, Dorset** – Blackthorn can withstand wind-exposure better than Hawthorn and on cliff tops can form natural climax vegetation. Such areas provide important shelter for migrant birds in the spring and autumn. The abrupt edge (*arrowed*) is created by grazing. Farther west along the Dorset coast, high densities of Hazel Dormouse have been found in coastal scrub.

ABOVE LEFT: **Noar Hill, Hampshire** – some scrub control and rotational management is required if a species-rich mosaic of grassland and scrub is to be maintained.
ABOVE RIGHT: **Port Eynon, Gower** – dense Mixed Scrub on limestone outcrops including Ivy, whitebeams, gorse, Blackthorn and Elder.

What to look for

Endemic whitebeams on shrubby limestone outcrops in the west of Britain; rare plants such as Bastard Balm, Purple Gromwell, also rare orchids (*e.g.* Fly, Man, Military, Monkey and Lady Orchid) on base-rich *saum* (see *page 71*); Black Hairstreak (Blackthorn in the Midlands). Listen for Nightingale, Whitethroat, Lesser Whitethroat, Willow Warbler, Garden Warbler and, in the uplands, Whinchat and Redstart.

(see *page 71*)

How to recognise

Typical Mixed Scrub of thorny shrubs such as Hawthorn, Blackthorn and Bramble and other species occurring along woodland edges, roadsides and railway embankments, on abandoned agricultural land, commons, grasslands and heaths, in quarries, and on the coast.

Particularly eye-catching in the spring, when Blackthorn is one of the first plants to flower, and provides an early nectar source for invertebrates. At this time of year it can be alive with bird song, while later in the summer bush-crickets creak and rasp from tall herbage.

The best scrub for wildlife has a diverse range of species with a complex canopy structure and plenty of gaps and edges and transitions to short vegetation.

When to visit

Spring for Nightingale and other breeding birds; summer for plants and invertebrates at the scrub/grassland interface; spring and autumn for migrant birds near the coast.

Bentley Wood, Wiltshire – this woodland clearing with Hawthorn and Bramble scrub supports a range of butterflies including Duke of Burgundy and Pearl-bordered Fritillary.

HEDGEROW

Hedgerow is essentially woodland edge habitat, without the wood. The combination of woody structure and more open conditions provides many nesting, roosting and feeding opportunities for wildlife. Hedges can also act as wildlife corridors between isolated patches of woodland and scrub. However, their linear nature means they have a lot of edge, and land management practices adjacent to hedgerows have a disproportionately strong influence. Many hedges are affected by agricultural spray-drift (leading to loss of species through nutrient enrichment and damage from pesticides) in addition to unsympathetic management.

Traditional management involves hedge-laying (bending partially cut stems over at an angle and weaving them between stakes to provide a stock-proof barrier), which is repeated every 20 years or so. This rejuvenates the hedge, retains deadwood (often kept to provide initial protection from livestock) and subsequently allows it to grow tall over a broad, thick base. Hedge-laying is labour-intensive and has generally been abandoned in favour of annual mechanised trimming, which creates more homogenous hedges with limited structural variation. Repeated severe cutting can also cause hedges to die back.

Ancient hedgerows are often the most species-rich, and the presence of certain plant species can be used to identify older hedges, particularly Field Maple (in the UK), Dogwood, Hazel and Spindle, which are relatively poor colonisers and are rarely planted. Ancient hedges also often include giant coppice stools or old pollarded trees.

Distribution and extent

Map shows pasture and arable land where Hedgerow may be present. Species-rich hedges are found particularly in south-west England and South Wales. Eng: 558,100 km; Sco: 48,700 km; Wal: 88,700 km; NI: 118,600 km; Ire: 300,000 km.

LEFT: **Sedbergh, Cumbria** – a recently laid Ash hedge. There are over 30 different styles of hedge-laying around the UK. Studies have shown that laid hedges support the largest numbers of invertebrates. BELOW LEFT: **Rackenford, Devon** – a relic hedge-bank that has developed into a line of Beech trees. Beech hedge-banks are a particular feature of north Devon. BELOW: A thick hedge with standard trees adjacent to an arable field margin.

Near **Port Isaac, north Cornwall** – Cornish hedges comprise an earthen bank and stone-faced sides with or without shrubby vegetation.

Similar habitats

Hedgerows include similar species to woodland edges and scrub, but are linear features subject to regular cutting or laying. Unmanaged hedgerows can develop into shaws (thin strips of woodland found on field boundaries, often adjacent to a road), although shaws may also be woodland remnants.

Origins and development

Many hedgerows were planted but some have more natural origins as relics of woodland that has long since disappeared. Some West Country hedge-banks date from the Bronze Age and many hedges are medieval, planted to mark ownership boundaries, retain livestock and provide shelter. Some of these hedges have a distinctive 'S'-shape, a result of the need for space where a plough could be turned. During the enclosure of common land in the 18th and 19th centuries, an estimated 200,000 miles of hedge were planted in England, particularly in the Midlands. These are often dominated by Hawthorn and tend to be straight, sometimes cutting through other landscape features. After the 1950s, the fortunes of hedgerows declined as agricultural intensification resulted in tens of thousands of miles of hedgerows being removed, damaged by brutal trimming and spray-drift or simply neglected.

*An irregular patchwork of small fields bounded by hedgerows (near **Cahersiveen, Co. Kerry**). The commonest field enclosures in Ireland are earth banks topped with scrub.*

Did you know?

Hooper's rule of thumb that the number of tree and shrub species in a 30-yard length of hedge equates to the age of the hedge in centuries is generally true in many areas.

Conservation

Much attention has been focussed on how best to manage hedgerows for wildlife. Left unmanaged, they turn into lines of trees and lose the structure and variety that is so important. However, tight annual trimming is damaging, and can result in patchy hedges with little body. Periodic hedge-laying or coppicing is considered best, followed by some trimming to encourage a dense structure to develop before the hedge is allowed to grow up ready for laying or coppicing again. Late winter is the best time to manage hedges, so that berries are retained for as long as possible throughout the winter but the bird nesting season is avoided. Encouraging sensitive harvesting for woodfuel, and increasing the awareness of the role that hedges play in reducing soil erosion and water run-off, could help protect the habitat.

What to look for

Hedges that are good for wildlife provide nesting sites, song posts, roosting sites, foraging habitat and corridors for movement. Some 600 plant, 1,500 insect, 65 bird and 20 mammal species have been recorded in hedgerows. In addition to the suite of ancient hedgerow shrubs, keep a look out for veteran trees (including Black-poplar), Plymouth Pear (restricted to a few hedgerows in the south-west) and the endemic Devon Whitebeam (which is found in south-east Ireland as well as in Devon). An endemic herb, Purple Ramping-fumitory, is particularly associated with hedge-banks.

Hedgerows are good places to look for invertebrates. Bramble, Honeysuckle and thorn blossom provide nectar and pollen for a range of insects, some of which depend on Ivy flowers in autumn. Many beetle species can occur in the litter and tussocky vegetation at the base of hedges, including Stag Beetle, while hedgerow ditches adjacent to hedgerows are good for caddisflies. Bumblebees nest in hedgerows and use hedges as guides to their foraging sites. White-letter Hairstreak breeds on elm suckers, and also feeds on aphid honeydew on Field Maple. Look for Small Tortoiseshell and Red Admiral butterflies around hedgerow nettles, and Orange-tip on Garlic Mustard. The Barberry Carpet moth is occasionally disturbed from its foodplant (Barberry) during the day.

Most bird species prefer tall hedges with many trees, although Whitethroat, Linnet and Yellowhammer are found in shorter hedges. Uncommon species associated with hedges include Cirl Bunting, Turtle Dove and Tree Sparrow. Hazel Dormouse is famously found in hedges but Bank Vole is more common, and Harvest Mouse may also be seen. At dusk look out for bats – Serotine follows hedges to foraging areas, and species such as Greater Horseshoe Bat and Natterer's Bat glean insects from hedgerows.

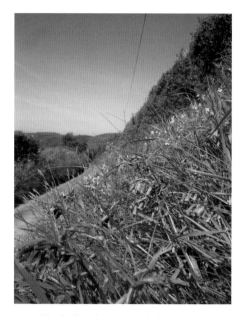

ABOVE: **Bluebell** and **Greater Stitchwort** growing in a hedge margin in Purbeck, Dorset. Herbaceous vegetation growing alongside and within hedges provides a rich nectar source for invertebrates and a welcome splash of colour along roadsides. BELOW LEFT: **Grey Partridge** – widespread but now uncommon, this species prefers open fields with uncultivated margins bordered by hedgerows, particularly those with grass litter at the base, where they nest. Declines since the 1950s have been attributed to increased pesticide and herbicide use, predation and removal of hedgerows. BELOW: The **Hazel Dormouse** weaves summer nests of stripped bark (often Honeysuckle) about the size of a grapefruit for breeding. Hedgerows can be an important habitat for this species and also provide links between woodland and scrub patches along which it can disperse.

TOP LEFT: Hedgerows provide nest sites for a range of species including **Yellowhammer** which often nest in the base of shrubby hedges with vegetated ditches and uncultivated margins.

TOP CENTRE: The dense wood of **Spindle** was, as its name suggests, traditionally used for spindles. The berries are poisonous to humans but are eaten by a range of birds.

TOP RIGHT: **Guelder-rose** is a widespread and attractive shrub found in hedges on neutral and calcareous soils. Look for the distinctive white flowers in May–June.

ABOVE: **Brown Hairstreak** – rare and relatively secretive, this butterfly breeds mainly on Blackthorn in hedgerows. Annual cutting is disastrous as the eggs overwinter on young twigs.

RIGHT: **Greater Stitchwort** – a typical hedgerow plant that is often seen along roadside hedges.

BRACKEN

Bracken is the most common (and largest) fern in Britain and Ireland. It occurs within 36 different National Vegetation Classification communities, a reflection of the range of habitats in which it can be found. It favours dry, acid soils (up to around 450 m), and can spread at a rate of one metre per year by underground rhizomes. It regenerates from spores only on relatively bare ground, such as after burning. Livestock grazing increases the dominance of Bracken by reducing competitors, although cattle in particular can reduce its vigour through trampling.

Bracken produces plant toxins that, together with its shady canopy and deep litter, inhibit the growth of other plant species. Dense stands of Bracken often hold little wildlife interest, although a woodland flora is sometimes found (particularly on the coast) and Wild Gladiolus (restricted to the New Forest) only occurs under Bracken. A range of invertebrates feed on Bracken, including some rare sawflies, flies and moths, and it is linked to some of our most threatened and rapidly declining butterflies: High Brown Fritillary and Pearl-bordered Fritillary are virtually restricted to Bracken and Dark-green Fritillary and Small Pearl-bordered Fritillary may also be associated with it. Bracken is also a favoured habitat of the Sheep Tick.

Similar habitats

Bracken is considered as a habitat type in its own right where it occurs in continuous swathes. Patchy or scattered Bracken is common in a range of other habitat types of which it is considered part.

Origins and development

Bracken is often perceived to be spreading and its dominance is a management challenge at some sites. However, Bracken spores found in cores taken for pollen analysis show that the species has a long history in the landscape. In many cores Bracken peaks are associated with the loss of woodland cover at least 2,000 years ago. The amount of Bracken declined at some locations during the 14th century, coinciding with agricultural abandonment linked to the Black Death and a period with a colder climate. Current levels are perhaps, therefore, not exceptional, but historically Bracken was a valued resource (used for bedding, thatch and potash for soap and glass) and widely harvested, which would have helped contain its spread.

BELOW: **Common Dog-violet** can grow under Bracken and is the main food plant for caterpillars of several fritillary butterflies. RIGHT, TOP: **Dark-green Fritillary** is found in a range of grassy habitats including acid grassland with Bracken. RIGHT, MIDDLE: **Small Pearl-bordered Fritillary** is widespread and locally common in woodland clearings and moorland. RIGHT, BOTTOM: **High Brown Fritillary**, together with Pearl-bordered Fritillary, favours warm, dry slopes. To raise their body temperature, the caterpillars bask on dead Bracken stems.

Distribution and extent

Widespread across Britain and Ireland.
Eng: 91,100 ha; Sco: 131,500 ha;
Wal: 62,700 ha; NI: 2,600 ha; Ire: n/k.

RIGHT: **Rhossili Downs, Gower** – in August, Bracken forms conspicuous bright green patches in the landscape.

INSET: **Bracken** sometimes allows plants to grow that otherwise require a woodland canopy – in this case **Bluebell**.

Conservation

Bracken is not considered as a Priority Habitat for conservation and in many situations conservationists seek to control its spread or reduce the area present. It spreads at the expense of other habitats and can be problematic in other ways – its spores have been implicated as a carcinogen, it harbours sheep ticks and it can damage archaeological features. Bracken can be managed by spraying, cutting or bruising, but such treatments have to be maintained to be successful. On hill slopes, areas where Bracken has been eradicated can be vulnerable to erosion, or may be colonised by species such as Common Nettle. Woodland reversion may, in the long term, be a better solution for such locations.

Although ineffective in controlling large patches of established Bracken, grazing is ideal on butterfly sites, where the paths and trampled areas created by livestock provide sunny patches that are ideal for violets – the foodplant for many fritillaries. Mosaics of Bracken and grassland with abundant violets and open areas are optimal for butterflies but can be difficult to maintain.

What to look for

Basking Adder; Whinchat and other breeding birds (uplands); Wild Gladiolus (New Forest); several species of fritillary butterfly.

How to recognise

Bracken can cloak hillsides, form dense stands within woodland, and cover large patches of lowland grassland and heathland. Although it generally occurs within other habitats, extensive patches can be considered a habitat in their own right.

The bright green, tight-curled fronds emerge in late spring once the frosts have passed and grow quickly; by midsummer Bracken can form a closed canopy, often over head-height and impenetrable. It also has a distinctive smell at this time of year that is intensified by sunshine and is sometimes likened to almonds. In the autumn it dies right back, leaving rusty-brown fronds that litter the ground in winter.

When to visit

Look for fritillaries in the spring and summer: Pearl-bordered from late April–end of June, Small Pearl-bordered in June–July, High Brown and Dark-green mid-June–mid-August. Bracken can form a colourful part of the landscape in the autumn.

Did you know?
Bracken is one of the most widely distributed plants in the world, occurring in every continent apart from Antarctica.

Glasdrum, Highland – an extensive area of Bracken within a large woodland clearing.

HEATHLANDS

ORIGINS

Heathlands are semi-natural habitats that developed on relatively nutrient-poor and acidic soils as a result of forest clearance that in some cases may have started at least 5,000 years ago. Combined with subsequent use of the land for livestock grazing, the removal of trees contributed to a reduction in soil fertility and increase in acidity. This enabled heathland vegetation, which perhaps previously existed in clearings and under sparse canopies, to expand. Many current heathlands date from the Bronze Age, some 3,000 years ago, although in the uplands of Ireland and the Scottish Highlands transitions occurred much later. Heathland and woodland existed in a dynamic state, fluctuating according to the scale of human activity. In southern England, its coverage was probably greatest in the medieval period.

Unsuitable for cultivation, heathland became part of a farming system that integrated the use of infertile parts of the landscape with that of tilled areas. However, from the mid-19th century, changes in land management led to the breakdown of the more traditional, extensive systems that had evolved over centuries. In the lowlands, about 85% of the heathland in existence in 1800 was lost. Developments in farming techniques meant that heathlands were fertilized and cultivated. Many of those that survived were afforested, set aside for military training or built on (even into the 1980s). Small fragments that remained fell out of use, and natural succession (aided by the proximity of coniferous plantations) led to the development of secondary pine and birch wood. In the uplands, the change from mixed farming to sheep rearing from the mid-18th century saw a change in the way heathland was grazed and, in the Highlands, led to the brutal restructuring of local communities which had played a fundamental role in maintaining the cultural landscape. The rise of shooting estates in the 19th century meant that management priorities shifted; burning became widespread and increasing grazing pressure converted heathland to grassland. In the 20th century, huge areas were engulfed by forestry plantations.

TYPES OF HEATHLAND

Heathland is found from sea level up to about 1,000 m in both dry and periodically waterlogged situations, giving way to bog (see Wetlands, *page 160*) where waterlogging increases. Essentially, it occurs where nutrient-poor, acidic conditions favour the growth of dwarf-shrubs, particularly Heather, Bell Heather, Cross-leaved Heath, Dwarf Gorse and Bilberry, and where grazing or burning prevents the development of scrub and woodland. At high altitudes where conditions are too exposed for woodland (around 600–700 m, but variable), heathland

Cannock Chase is the most extensive area of lowland heathland in the Midlands. The site is unusual in that the vegetation is intermediate between lowland sites in southern England and more northern/upland sites, supporting Bilberry, Cowberry and Crowberry.

communities are natural, and these are considered in the Mountain Habitats section (see *page 132*). The low-nutrient status and early-successional stage of heathland vegetation is reflected in the relatively low number of plant species it supports – but despite this, wide variation is seen throughout Britain and Ireland. Four heathland habitats are described within this section, but transitions and variations occur. **Lowland Dry Heath** (*page 86*) encompasses the dry heaths of southern England and Wales (including humid-heath). Some other types of Lowland Dry Heath are described in this section, including Maritime Heath, which is also found in Scotland and Ireland, and the peculiar heathland mosaics of Breckland. **Upland Dry Heath** (*page 94*), which is widespread throughout the uplands, supports different vegetation communities from Lowland Dry Heath and, like Lowland Wet Heath, faces quite different pressures and issues, particularly those concerning grouse moors. **Lowland Wet Heath** (*page 92*) is differentiated from **Upland Wet Heath** (*page 98*) as although it supports similar vegetation, it faces different management and conservation issues and the two types can support different specialist species. Heathland rarely occurs in isolation and, particularly in the uplands where it is far more extensive, it usually occurs within a mosaic of other habitat types, including Blanket Bog, Upland Acid Grassland and upland woodland habitats. In the lowlands, heathland often occurs with Valley Mire, Lowland Dry Acid Grassland and secondary woodland. Fifteen heathland vegetation communities and their sub-communities are described in the UK National Vegetation Classification.

The origins of the word **heath** lie in the old English word for untilled land, and heathland has long been regarded as wasteland, much to its detriment. Today the word heath usually refers to land dominated by dwarf shrubs such as Heather, but also encompasses similar low-growing and nutrient-poor vegetation that may be dominated by lichens and grasses.

Moorland is generally used to refer to open upland landscapes beyond the limit of agricultural improvement and enclosures but below the climatic tree line. Moorland can include Upland Dry Heath, Upland Wet Heath, Upland Acid Grassland, Upland Calcareous Grassland and Blanket Bog. The derivation of the word is unclear, although it may stem from an Old English word meaning morass or swamp, and perhaps its use in the uplands is related to the low fertility of the habitats. Locally, moorland is also referred to as fell, wold, or simply 'the hill'. There is more moorland in Britain and Ireland than anywhere else in the world.

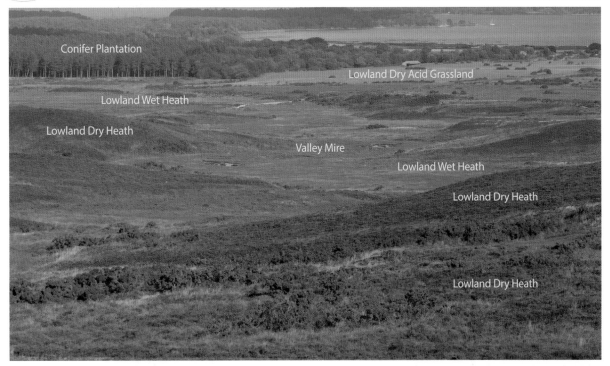

ABOVE: Lowland heathland at **Godlingston, Dorset**.
BELOW: Steep, glaciated slopes of the **Lake District**, showing upland heathland alongside other upland communities.

81

THREATS AND ISSUES

Surviving lowland heathland is, in most cases, divorced from the agricultural practices and economics of the surrounding countryside, and this presents a challenge for conservation management. The functionality of the cultural landscape has essentially been lost, and modern conservation organisations are left trying to replicate historical grazing, cutting and burning regimes, often on relatively small areas of land, in an attempt to safeguard the remaining populations of heathland species. In other cases, heathland is surrounded by, or close to, urban conurbations, and provides much-needed green space. However, proximity to urban centres can pose problems, including increased risk of fire, eutrophication from dog waste, dumping, disturbance to birds and predation by cats. Often local residents have strong feelings about their local heathland, and wish to see it managed in a particular way or left to its own devices.

The situation in the uplands is different, as extensive tracts of open heathland have been maintained, and are still grazed as part of agricultural systems, even where the primary use is game shooting and deer hunting. Past subsidies, based on the number of livestock, encouraged high stocking rates, and many areas are heavily grazed and in some cases this grazing has converted heathland to grassland. Changes in the way subsidies are allocated has reduced this stress, but many areas remain very heavily grazed. There is increasing interest in expanding the area of semi-natural woodland in the uplands, as it is recognised that to restore functionality and safeguard species, bigger, connected areas of wood are needed. In many cases this will be at the expense of heathland.

Several hardy pony breeds are native to the mountains and moorlands of Britain and Ireland (in the sense that they were bred here – wild horses became extinct after the last glaciation). They are often seen leading a semi-feral existence in unenclosed heathland in places such as Dartmoor, Exmoor, the New Forest and parts of Wales, although all are owned. These animals are well adapted to surviving in heathland habitats, and are often now used for conservation grazing.

CULTURAL IMPORTANCE

Heathland is particularly valued as a cultural landscape, one that has evolved through the long-term interactions between people and nature. Some of the evidence of human presence can still be seen today, including prehistoric worked flints and Bronze Age burial mounts. More recent boundary banks, enclosures and other features all indicate a time when heathland was used more intensively than it is today and played an intrinsic role in agricultural livelihoods. Farming encompassed both arable land close to dwellings and more extensive areas of heathland farther afield, which were often

Exmoor Pony – one of the hardy native breeds that is able to withstand the challenges of grazing on heathland.

Modern cultural links between heathlands and local communities are more likely to be through daily dog walks than people's livelihoods.

common land. Heaths were used by local people for grazing livestock (including animals used for farm work), turf was cut for fuel, gorse for livestock fodder and to use in bread ovens, Bracken for livestock bedding and Heather for thatch. In some areas, such as East Anglia, the management of arable land and heathland was further integrated through manuring. Animals that grazed on the heaths during the day were folded on arable land during the night so that their dung could fertilize the fields. Research into similar practices in Denmark suggests that around ten hectares of heathland was needed to provide manure for one hectare of arable land. Heathland burning was also practiced to provide a flush of new young growth for the livestock.

Today, lowland heathland provides extensive tracts of open countryside that are not intensively farmed. Both upland and lowland heathland are valued for the recreational opportunities and sense of wilderness they provide.

CONSERVATION IMPORTANCE AND PROTECTION

Heathlands are not intrinsically species-rich habitats, but are greatly valued for the specialist species they support, many of which are rare and largely confined to heathland. In the lowlands these can include reptiles (such as Sand Lizard and Smooth Snake), birds (such as Nightjar and Dartford Warbler) and many invertebrates at the northern edge of their range. Particular suites of plant species are also associated with heathland microhabitats in the lowlands. Upland heathland

Key Heathland Areas

1 New Forest
2 Dorset Heaths
3 Pebblebeds
4 Dartmoor
5 The Lizard
6 Exmoor
7 Pembrokeshire Coast
8 Brecon Beacons
9 Snowdonia
10 Berwyn
11 The Lake District
12 Mourne Mountains
13 SW Ireland Uplands
14 NW Ireland Uplands
15 Antrim Mountains
16 The Highlands
17 The Southern Uplands
18 The Pennines
19 North York Moors
20 Breckland
21 Suffolk Sandlings
22 Ashdown Forest
23 Thames Basin Heaths
22 Wealden Heaths

The map shows all heathlands. In the lowlands, heathland occurs in fragmented patches across southern England and Wales. Extensive tracts of heathland habitats are found across the uplands, particularly the Scottish Highlands.

Some key locations are labelled on the map; this selection is not intended to be exhaustive but highlights a few of the most important areas.

HEATHER

The life-cycle of Heather involves four stages. Individual plants can take 13–50 years to go through the cycle, depending on the characteristics of the location, including soil, climate and management.

Pioneer – up to about 6 years from seedling to bush, vertical growth

Building – up to about 15 years old, dense lateral growth

Mature – up to about 25 years old, growth slowing, centre opening

Degenerate – central branches collapse, allowing seedlings and other species to grow

There are nine native heather species found in Britain and Ireland, three of which are widespread.

Species	Distribution	Habitat types	Flowers
Heather	Widespread	Dry and wet heaths (also bogs)	Jul–Sep
Cross-leaved Heath	Widespread	Wet heath (also bogs)	Jun–Sep
Bell Heather	Widespread	Dry heaths	Jul–Sep
Dorset Heath	Dorset, S. Devon, Cornwall and Connemara	Wet heath	Jun–Sep
Blue Heath	Central Scotland, rare	Rocky upland heath with prolonged snow-lie	Jun–Jul
St Dabeoc's Heath	Connemara and Galway	Dry heaths	Jul–Sep
Mackay's Heath	Connemara and Donegal	Wet heath (also bogs)	Aug–Sep
Cornish Heath	Cornwall, Fermanagh	Dry and wet heaths	Jul–Aug
Irish Heath	Galway and Mayo, rare	Wet heath (also bogs)	Mar–May

Heather

Cross-leaved Heath

Dorset Heath

St Dabeoc's Heath

Cornish Heath

Bell Heather

Blue Heath

Mackay's Heath

Irish Heath

Furze cutters *ca.*1890, **Dorset Heaths**.

Intensive management is required to maintain heathlands today, here conducted by the RSPB.

can support Red Grouse, Black Grouse, Hen Harrier, Merlin, Mountain Hare and some globally rare plant communities, including one rich in rare liverworts and mosses. Oceanic heathland is confined to north-west Europe, and over 20% is found in Britain and Ireland.

A substantial majority of heathland sites are protected through designation as SSSI (or equivalent) or SAC (four Annex I habitats cover most of the heathland types found in Britain and Ireland). However, in the UK heathland is considered to be in a worse condition than any other habitat category. In the lowlands this is largely due to lack of appropriate management, leading to scrub and Bracken encroachment; in the uplands it is due to overgrazing and burning leading to a loss of species and structural diversity. Fortunately, a considerable proportion is believed to be improving. Substantial funding has been put into conserving lowland heathland in the 21st century, but ongoing effort is required to ensure that heathland communities are sustained following restoration efforts. Conservation of upland heathland is mainly being addressed through agri-environment schemes, but it is not known how long it may take before a significant improvement in its condition can be detected.

KEY ELEMENTS

A key element determining the conservation interest of heathlands is structural variety. The structure of heather depends on its age (see opposite) and different stages are suitable for different species. For example, caterpillars of the Silver-studded Blue butterfly require the soft shoots of pioneer or building heather; so does Red Grouse, which also requires taller heather nearby for shelter. Mature heather supports the largest number of invertebrate species, and reptiles bask amongst degenerate heather that provides shelter and warmth. Nightjar nests are also often in degenerate heather.

A variety of other vegetation structures adds to the overall diversity of heathlands. For example, gorse bushes provide habitat for web-spinning spiders.

The Lizard, Cornwall. In the past trackway species were found in areas with heavy poaching by livestock or cart ruts; now conservationists deliberately create localised rutted/poached areas with machinery in the winter.

Dartford Warbler nests in gorse, which is also a source of invertebrate prey, even in the winter, and young, dense gorse bushes provide it with protection from heavy snow. Woodland fringes also support a diversity of invertebrates, and flowering verges are an important source of nectar when heathers are not in flower.

Bare ground is an important microhabitat within heathland. Bare sand is used by insects for basking, hunting and nesting, and south-facing slopes are particularly good for solitary bees and wasps. Sand Lizards lay their eggs in warm bare sand. A suite of plant species is associated with very open, damp, compacted ground, and can be found in puddles and wheel ruts in heathland tracks. These include Allseed, Yellow Centaury, Chaffweed and, on The Lizard, Three-lobed Crowfoot and Pygmy Rush. Marsh Clubmoss is another species that can be found on bare, damp ground.

FURTHER INFORMATION

Heaths and Moorlands. Cultural Landscapes. Thompson, D.B.A., Hester, A.J. & Usher, M.B. eds. (HMSO, 1995)
Heathlands. A Natural History. Webb, N. (Collins New Naturalist, 1986)

Lowland Dry Heath

Lowland Dry Heath varies according to climate, soil, drainage, altitude and historical management (grazing and burning). It typically occurs on infertile and free-draining acid sands, gravels and other superficial deposits from sea level up to about 300 m. The dry, eastern heaths of Breckland and the Suffolk Sandlings tend to be species-poor, and are dominated by grasses and Heather, with Gorse along roads and tracks joined by Bracken in disturbed places. Bell Heather and Dwarf Gorse are common in the slightly wetter climate of the Wealden heaths, Ashdown Forest, the Thames Basin and the New Forest heaths. In the more oceanic west, Dwarf Gorse is replaced by Western Gorse, and Bristle Bent and Purple Moor-grass become common, the latter increasing where drainage is impeded. Some distinctive variants are described in the section *Some Different Types of Lowland Dry Heath* (pages 90–91).

Lowland Dry Heath is a dynamic habitat and is reliant upon some form of disturbance – usually grazing or burning – to remain open. Natural succession would otherwise lead to the development of scrub and pine and birch woodland. However, much of the diversity of heathland is determined by its structural variation, and the extent and nature of associated scrub. The presence of open areas and patches of tall herbs and grasses are also important. Bracken, gorse or other scrub are frequent on heaths, but extensive patches can indicate where natural succession is leading to the development of scrub and woodland communities, which conservation management aims to prevent. Brambles, nettles and lush green grass are signs of nutrient enrichment.

Similar habitats

On wetter ground, Lowland Dry Heath can grade into Lowland Wet Heath and Valley Mire (which are distinguished by the presence of Cross-leaved Heath, Deergrass and wetland species including bog-mosses). It also grades into Lowland Dry Birch and Oak Wood or birch-dominated secondary woodland. Some areas show characteristics intermediate between lowland and upland heaths, often with Bilberry (*e.g.* Cannock Chase and moorland fringes in the south-west peninsula).

Distribution and extent

Scattered across the lowlands. Extent figures overestimate as include Lowland Wet Heath. Eng: 58,000 ha; Sco: 18,900 ha; Wal: 8,800 ha; NI: 5,800 ha; Ire: n/k. Globally limited to the Atlantic fringe of Europe (from Norway to Portugal).

BELOW LEFT: Near **Kynance, Cornwall** – gorse intermingled with Cornish Heath forms a characteristic heathland community limited to The Lizard in Cornwall. BELOW: **Sutton Heath, Suffolk** – the dry Sandlings heaths of the Suffolk coast are by tradition sheep-grazed. Some sites are a mosaic of heathland and Lowland Dry Acid Grassland similar to those in nearby Breckland.

Did you know?

More than 80% of the lowland heathland that once covered much of southern England has been lost since the 1800s, and the remainder is fragmented.

Canford Heath, Dorset – one of the few remaining fragments of the extensive Poole Basin heaths that once covered what is now Bournemouth and Poole. The last major losses to development occurred just before SSSI designation. It now suffers from urban pressures.

Origins and development

The origins of Lowland Dry Heath lie in forest clearance and management extending back to the Bronze Age or even the Mesolithic period. Heaths were maintained as open habitat through a diverse range of activities, which included livestock grazing accompanied by burning and the use of cut Bracken for livestock bedding, heather turves for fuel and gorse for bread ovens. Perceived as wasteland, huge areas of heathland were agriculturally improved, afforested or subject to urban development. Declines started before 1800, but escalated in the second half of the 20th century. During this time many patches developed into secondary woodland as the realities of agricultural economics resulted in the removal of grazing animals.

How to recognise

Lowland Dry Heath is an open habitat, characterised by low, shrubby vegetation of heather with scattered pine or birch trees and areas of gorse scrub. The prickly and scratchy vegetation can be impenetrably thick, or quite open and springy, but in either case there are usually plenty of tracks or livestock paths to follow.

In spring the vegetation is slow to come alive although Gorse flowers early and adds a splash of colour (and a faint scent of coconut). By summer, heaths come into their own; Bell Heather colours slopes a rosy purple, turning towards lilac as it starts flowering in August. Summer sunshine brings the sound of popping gorse seed pods, the smell of warm pines and the buzz of insects, and on warm evenings Nightjar can be heard churring. The heathland colours last well into autumn, but by winter become muted; sites often have names that reflect their dour winter appearance such as Blackhill, Blackheath and Blackdown.

Many heaths occur in areas of high human population density and the wide open spaces are a marked contrast to the urban conurbations surrounding them.

When to visit

Reptiles are easiest to see in spring (adders emerge in February) when the air is still cool and they need to bask in the sun to warm up; summer is best for Nightjar and invertebrates; heathers flower from July.

Coombe Heath, Arne, Dorset. Young pine trees are cleared regularly from this heath. Some mature trees are retained and provide suitable perches for Nightjar.

Conservation

Extensive livestock grazing is usually the preferred management, together with some burning and cutting and rotational scrub management. Removal of top soil (scraping) to remove nutrients is also an option but care needs to be taken to preserve archaeological features that have often been preserved on undisturbed heaths. On restoration sites, there can be public opposition to tree-felling and scrub-clearance, which are initially unattractive and can seem counter-intuitive to visitors. The challenge is to reintegrate heathland management into local economies (*e.g.* through extensive grazing and technological advances in biofuel production) and to help people move away from a perception of heathland as empty wasteland.

What to look for

The density of wildlife may be quite low, but Lowland Dry Heath supports a host of rare and specialist species, particularly invertebrates and reptiles. Continuous, even-aged Heather is poor in species, so look for variation, including edges, damp hollows, banks, old diggings, patches of scrub and bare sand. Bare ground is especially important for many insects and for reptiles – look for sandy patches that catch the sun and are not too churned up by feet or wheels. Rare invertebrates that are hard to see include the Purbeck Mason-wasp and Ladybird Spider; like many species they are on the edge of their range in the UK and are limited to a small number of sites. Green Tiger Beetle and day-flying moths such as Emperor Moth and Fox Moth are easier to see, and flowery verges and scrub edges are good places to look for nectar feeders.

Heathlands are a good place for look for reptiles (all six British species can be present) including Sand Lizard, which requires bare, sandy patches to lay eggs and mature vegetation for cover, and Smooth Snake, which needs sunny, mature heath. Heathlands also support internationally important populations of Nightjar, Woodlark and Dartford Warbler. Nightjar uses surrounding habitat, including gardens, for foraging, and will travel as far as 7 km to find good feeding sites. Nightjar density tends to be greatest where there is some tree cover, such as along the interface between open heath and forestry.

Heathlands support very distinctive vegetation but this includes few rare species. On the humid heaths of the south-west look out for Dorset Heath, which hybridizes readily with Cross-leaved Heath. On The Lizard in Cornwall, Cornish Heath grows over base-rich Serpentine rock with Common and Western Gorse and Bell Heather. St. Dabeoc's Heath can also be found on dry heath, mainly in Connemara in Ireland.

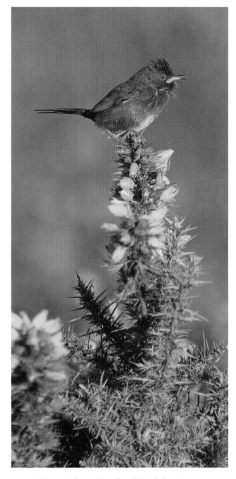

ABOVE: The resident **Dartford Warbler** is particularly susceptible to harsh winters and needs mature gorse for shelter. BELOW LEFT: **Sand Lizard** – look along path edges and on stumps that catch the sun in spring when the green colouration is brightest. Sand Lizards also occur in some sand dune systems. BELOW RIGHT: **Smooth Snake** – found almost exclusively on lowland heath, it is largely restricted to Dorset and Hampshire, with small populations in other southern counties, and is hard to see.

TOP: **Nightjar** – listen at dusk between May and August for churring, "*quip*"s and the distinctive wing clap. It is present on all major southern England heaths, in southern Ireland and north into Scotland.

MIDDLE, LEFT: **Beewolf** – the adults feed on nectar and pollen, but catch and paralyse honey bees to feed their larvae. MIDDLE, RIGHT: **Heath Tiger Beetle** – a specialist of open bare ground, their larvae live in funnel-like pits that help them to catch ants and other prey. Adults chase prey over the surface. BOTTOM, LEFT: **Mottled Bee-fly** – this rare and declining species is thought to parasitize the **Heath Sand Wasp** (BOTTOM, CENTRE), which in turn relies upon moth caterpillars that are captured and placed in burrows to provide a larder for the offspring. BOTTOM, RIGHT: **Great Ovens, Dorset** – a range in structure from bare ground to scrub is important to accommodate the needs of a diversity of species.

Hartland Moor, Dorset.
Bell Heather and Heather
mingle with Dwarf Gorse
and Bristle Bent.

SOME DIFFERENT TYPES OF LOWLAND DRY HEATH

MARITIME HEATH

On sea cliffs on the west coast of Britain and Ireland, and also the north and east coast of Scotland, Maritime Heath can be found on gently sloping land above maritime cliffs on suitable soils. The short vegetation is often wind-clipped and scorched by salt on the windward side of tussocks. It is quite species-rich, including plants such as Spring Squill, Sea Plantain and Buck's-horn Plantain, sometimes with Thrift and Sea Campion. Heather is the most common dwarf-shrub, but in places Crowberry or Bell Heather are co-dominant and, in Cornwall, Cornish Heath can extend some way into the vegetation. Some of the Cornish rarities also find their way into the Maritime Heath, including Chives, Fringed Rupturewort, Spring Sandwort and Twin-headed Clover, as wall as prostrate forms of Broom, greenweeds and Common Juniper. Autumn Ladies-tresses, Autumn Squill and Portland Spurge extend farther north, and Scottish Primrose is found in northern Scotland and on the Orkney Islands. Maritime Heath is generally maintained by a combination of grazing and exposure, but a climax community with maritime forms of Cock's-foot, Hairy Greenweed, and Kidney Vetch identified in Cornwall and Wales is thought to be rare.

DUNE HEATH

Heath can develop on old, stabilised sand dunes including those where sand mixed with calcium from marine organisms (including shells) has become leached over hundreds of years. Leaching is particularly widespread in the north and west where conditions are wetter. Provided grazing pressure from Rabbits or livestock is not too heavy, Heather can become established on fixed acid dunes (with Bell Heather in more western situations) and may be quite dense, although the sward can still contain some dune plants such as Sand Sedge or even Marram. Crowberry also occurs, but is restricted to Scotland and the north-west coast of Ireland. Dune Heath is most common in Scotland, although Winterton in Norfolk and Studland in Dorset both support Dune Heath.

TOP TO BOTTOM: MARITIME HEATH: Near **Claddaghduff, Connemara** – Crowberry, Bell Heather and Heather in a wind-clipped sward on an exposed headland; **The Lizard, Cornwall** – tussocks of Western Gorse growing with Cornish Heath are scorched on their seaward side. DUNE HEATH: **Studland, Dorset** – an acidic dune system with stable dunes supporting Heather, in places mingled with Marram. FACING PAGE, TOP TO BOTTOM: BRECKLAND HEATH: **Wangford Warren, Suffolk** – the short sward contains Sand Sedge and the rare Grey Hair-grass, and several lichen species including reindeer lichens (*e.g. Cladonia arbuscula*), and a distinctive branched, shiny brown lichen *Cetraria aculeata*. SHINGLE HEATH: **Dungeness, Kent** – scattered Heather plants growing in a short, lichen-rich sward on stabilised coastal shingle. LIMESTONE HEATH: **Lullington Heath, East Sussex** – in the 1950s, myxomatosis decimated the Rabbit population that had previously maintained a short sward. Dartford Warbler and Stonechat and more recently Nightingale and Whitethroat, have colonised as the amount of scrub has increased.

BRECKLAND HEATH

A unique mix of Lowland Dry Acid Grassland and Lowland Calcareous Grassland with dwarf-shrub heath has developed on the patchy, wind-blown sands over chalk of the East Anglian Breckland. These heaths experience a more continental climate, with hotter summers and colder winters and lower rainfall than the western heaths. As a result they are more lichen-rich and include some continental species such as Grey Hair-grass. The heathland and grassland communities occur in close proximity due to stone-striping (soil patterning caused by freeze-thaw conditions at the end of the last glaciation) and variations in the depth of the sand. In the past, heavy Rabbit- and sheep-grazing meant that in places the sand was mobile, and in the 17th century created inland dunes (reportedly up to 20 yards in height) which practically engulfed the village of Santon Downham and blocked the river for several miles. A remnant of inland dune can be seen at Wangford Warren.

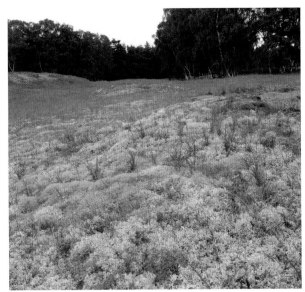

SHINGLE HEATH

Found on stabilised shingle either on the coast (see Coastal Vegetated Shingle, *page 234*) or in rivers, Shingle Heath usually supports a sparse community of grasses, lichens, small herbs and Heather. The term 'Shingle Heath' is often used rather loosely to describe a range of vegetation communities that can include lichen-rich acid grasslands (sometimes with Bell Heather) and more conventional heathland dominated by Heather or Crowberry, often with gorse. It is also used to describe some transitional lichen-rich grassland communities that occur on shingle but do not fall readily within the National Vegetation Classification, such as those with False Oat-grass, Sea Campion, Biting Stonecrop and a variety of *Cladonia* lichens. Coastal Shingle Heath tends to be limited to the largest shingle sites such as on the Solent (Browndown), Dungeness and Spey Bay, and is particularly well developed in the north where unique communities occur. Riverine Shingle Heath is even rarer, but examples are found in actively braiding river systems in Ceredigion and in central and northern Scotland. It can support unique lichen assemblages, including montane species.

LIMESTONE HEATH

Limestone Heath occurs where thin superficial deposits of sand overlay limestone (including chalk), often on plateaux or the top of slopes. This sand, blown from the front of glaciers farther north and deposited on downland, allows species such as Heather to grow alongside lime-loving plants such as Common Milkwort, Dropwort and Salad Burnet. Once more widespread, many sites were lost under the plough, but natural leaching plus the accumulation of acidic humus (aided by a decrease in Rabbit grazing) has also led to increased acidification.

LOWLAND WET HEATH

Lowland Wet Heath occurs on seasonally waterlogged shallow peat and mineral soils where the degree of moisture favours the more shallow-rooted Cross-leaved Heath over Heather, which, although present, is generally sparser. Lowland Wet Heath shares many plant species with bogs, including some with an oceanic distribution such as Brown Beak-sedge and Marsh Clubmoss. More common species include Compact Bog-moss, Deergrass, Tormentil, Heath Spotted-orchid and Lousewort, while Round-leaved Sundew and White Beak-sedge are limited to wetter hollows. However, frequent uncontrolled burning, heavy grazing or drainage can impoverish the sward, leaving only Purple Moor-grass, Heather and Cross-leaved Heath. Conversely, a lack of burning or grazing can allow Downy Birch, Grey Willow and pine to colonise, often with a field layer of dense, tussocky Purple Moor-grass. Climate and substrate also influence the vegetation. In the Poole Basin and Cornwall, Dorset Heath can be locally abundant and on The Lizard, Cornish Heath contributes to a very localised plant community with Black Bog-rush, Purple Moor-grass, Western Gorse and Petty Whin.

The mosaics formed by Lowland Wet Heath with Valley Mire and Lowland Dry Heath are important for invertebrates and several rare and scarce species can be seen. For example, the Southern Damselfly, which needs base-rich runnels or streams that can be found in Lowland Wet Heath over clay substrates. The Purbeck Mason-wasp may visit damp heathland in search of moist clay with which to seal the entrance of its nest, and the Large Marsh Grasshopper may occur where Lowland Wet Heath and Valley Mire form a mosaic.

Similar habitats

Lowland Wet Heath grades into Valley Mire, but typical peat-forming mosses such as Papillose and Magellanic Bog-mosses are largely absent. Bell Heather and Western Gorse indicate transitions to Lowland Dry Heath, and Bristle Bent is characteristic of a humid variant found in the south and south-west.

Origins and development

Lowland Wet Heath develops where soils conditions are suitable within heathland landscapes. It has suffered similar losses to Lowland Dry Heath, but the habitat has also been degraded through changes in hydrology including groundwater extraction, pollution and drainage associated with agricultural improvement, forestry and housing developments.

Distribution and extent

Found throughout lowland Britain and Ireland within heathland areas. Extent unknown. In Europe it is restricted to the Atlantic fringe (from Scandinavia to Normandy), with 85% of the resource in Britain and Ireland.

ABOVE: **Goonhilly Downs, Cornwall** – The Lizard holds a unique kind of Lowland Wet Heath dominated by Black Bog-rush with Cornish Heath. FAR LEFT: **Stoborough Heath, Dorset** – Purple Moor-grass can dominate Lowland Wet Heath, usually where the soil is derived from a slightly more base-rich substrate, or is influenced by the flow of enriched groundwater. LEFT: Red Devon cattle on **Hartland Moor, Dorset**. The loss or decline of several characteristic Lowland Wet Heath and Valley Mire plants was attributed to the cessation of traditional grazing in Dorset; grazing has, however, been reinstated on many sites for conservation purposes.

Conservation

Lowland Wet Heath is usually managed as an integral part of a heathland complex. Free-ranging livestock are often used with other heathland management techniques such as rotational scrub cutting to maintain open, diverse swards.

What to look for

Silver-studded Blue in open, heathery swards; Southern Damselfly where there are runnels; a suite of scarce plants including Marsh Gentian, Brown Beak-sedge, Marsh Clubmoss and Petty Whin.

RIGHT: **Marsh Gentian** is typically found where there is some seasonal movement of surface water, it can flower (August–September) profusely following burning. BELOW: **Silver-studded Blue** – look during June and July in areas with a short sward, such as along firebreaks. BELOW RIGHT: **Petty Whin** is hard to see except when it flowers in April, this woody species may persist for some time un-observed in un-grazed Purple Moor-grass dominated Lowland Wet Heath, flowering again when grazing resumes.

How to recognise

Look for Lowland Wet Heath in depressions, around pools and anywhere that drainage is a little impeded on heathlands. It often forms a narrow band between Lowland Dry Heath and Valley Mire, although in some places it can cover significant areas. Lowland Wet Heath is characterised by Cross-leaved Heath, which comes into flower earlier than other heathers, and its clustered rose-pink heads speckle the ground from June, enlivening the sward of Purple Moor-grass, Heather, Deergrass and cushion-like Compact Bog-moss.

The ground may squelch underfoot, but it is generally possible to walk through the short vegetation with relative ease, except in situations where Purple Moor-grass has become dominant and formed large tussocks, in places interspersed with Bog-myrtle.

When to visit

April–August depending on species for scarce plants, June–July for Silver-studded Blue and Southern Damselfly.

Did you know?

Female Silver-studded Blues only lay eggs where they detect suitable ant pheromones (the caterpillars are taken by ants into their nests and tended there).

Hartland Moor, Dorset. The pale litter of Purple Moor-grass can give Lowland Wet Heath a distinctive pale hue, seen here around the pool and in the shallow valley bottom surrounded by the darker brown of Heather-dominated Lowland Dry Heath.

UPLAND DRY HEATH

Upland Dry Heath is usually found between enclosed agricultural land and the montane zone (about 300–700 m), although in the harsh climate of northern Scotland it can occur right down to sea level. It grows on thin peat and mineral soils that are usually fairly well-drained but kept moist by rain, mist and snow. The vegetation is largely influenced by climate, altitude and management. Much of this habitat type is characterised by a deep canopy of young Heather and Bilberry, sometimes with Crowberry and Cowberry, overtopped by Wavy Hair-grass and growing out of thick mats of large leafy mosses and reindeer lichens. Bell Heather is found in more oceanic areas, and Bearberry in the boreal heaths of north-east Scotland. In south-west England, Western Gorse and Heather grow together and create a distinctive yellow and purple sward when in flower.

Upland Dry Heath is found within the woodland zone and falls midway on the successional spectrum between grassland and woodland. Succession to woodland is generally prevented by grazing and burning. Heavy grazing can eliminate Heather and Bilberry (resulting in acid grassland), while burning encourages the regeneration of Heather but eliminates other species.

Similar habitats

An increase in Purple Moor-grass, Deergrass, Cross-leaved Heath, bog-mosses and Hare's-tail Cottongrass indicates transitions to Upland Wet Heath and, in wetter areas, Blanket Bog. Gradations to Montane Heath with prostrate and small dwarf-shrubs occurs at higher altitudes in mountainous areas.

Distribution and extent

Widespread in the uplands. Extent figures overestimate as include Lowland Dry Heath: Eng: 320,000 ha; Sco: 479,000 ha; Wal: 69,600 ha; NI: 16,800 ha; Ire: 109,422 ha (ANN I REP). Britain holds a significant proportion of the global resource, which is restricted to north-west Europe.

FACING PAGE, TOP: **Creag Meagaidh, Central Highlands** – with reduced grazing, and provided there is a nearby seed source, Upland Dry Heath gradually reverts to woodland. Here deer control and the deliberate removal of sheep is resulting in the development of Upland Birch Wood.

LEFT: **Derwent Valley, Lake District** – The darker vegetation on the steeper crags is Heather and Bilberry (BELOW), while the paler green on less steep terrain indicates where intense grazing has converted heathland to acid grassland. Ring Ouzel can be found on the heathery crags.

Origins and development

Most Upland Dry Heath is a modified form of the understorey of woodland or scrub communities that were extensively cleared by people from the Neolithic period onwards. At high altitudes, some communities may be near-natural, but most are prevented from succeeding to woodland through livestock grazing and burning. The last 200 years have seen many changes. In the 19th century, heathland was lost through agricultural improvement and deteriorated with the rise of sheep ranching, shooting estates and associated heather burning. In the 20th century, huge areas were afforested, and loss and deterioration through agricultural improvement, heavy sheep and deer grazing and burning continued – 27% was lost in England and Wales during this period and about 80% of designated heath is currently in poor condition.

Strath Nethy, Cairngorms. Upland Dry Heath on the slopes grades into Upland Wet Heath and Blanket Bog on flatter ground beside the burn.

How to recognise

Upland Dry Heath covers slopes and crags in the wild, open moorland and mountain landscapes of the British and Irish uplands.

From a distance, the low canopy of dark Heather and lush green Bilberry contrasts with the paler vegetation of upland grasslands and Blanket Bog. Vertebrates are few and far between in this bleak and windswept landscape, although the haunting calls of breeding Golden Plover can be heard and the songs of Meadow Pipit and Skylark over the associated grasslands are a constant presence in spring.

The rolling moors of the Southern Uplands, Pennines and North York Moors are managed heavily for grouse shooting and are often little more than monocultures of Heather, coloured a pretty purple in late summer, and striped and patched where they have been recently burnt to promote young growth for Red Grouse.

When to visit

Late summer for scenic beauty.

Conservation

In many cases, Upland Dry Heath is impoverished and modifications to grazing and burning practices are widely needed. Atmospheric pollution is an issue in the South Pennines, and may be contributing to the poverty of lower plant communities. Upland Dry Heath has high recreational value and activities such as mountain biking, off-road driving, skiing, fell walking and running can be damaging where they are not carefully managed.

Upland Dry Heath is valued as a cultural landscape, and unlike lowland heathland remains integrated into the economics of local communities through (subsidised) farming practices and management for game. An increasing awareness of water catchment and carbon storage issues, and a growing interest in re-wilding, are all factors that will contribute to the much-needed debate over the future of the British uplands.

What to look for

Upland Dry Heath vegetation is typically quite species-poor, but there are interesting variations to be seen. Look out for more oceanic heathland plant communities in the north-west (or on warm south-facing slopes in the north) with Bell Heather, moorland grasses, Wild Thyme and small herbs such as Fairy Flax and Selfheal, and, higher up, the distinctive Woolly Fringe-moss. In the cold climate of the east Highlands, stony soils support a more boreal heathland type, and Bilberry gives way to the bright green, net-veined leaves of Bearberry. Wherever there are richer brown earths or the underlying rock is more base-rich, more species-rich heath can be found with Intermediate Wintergreen, Common Bird's-foot-trefoil, Wood Anemone, Bitter-vetch and northern species such as Lesser Twayblade,

Damp, oceanic heath in the west of Scotland and Ireland can support large, leafy liverworts such **Wood's Whipwort** (TOP RIGHT) and **Bird's-foot Earwort** (RIGHT) in a community that is globally restricted to these areas and Norway. Known as the northern hepatic mat, this community extends into snow-beds in the montane zone and is suceptible to burning, particularly when followed by heavy grazing.

*Foel Cynwch, near **Llanfachreth, Gwynedd** – Heather, Bell Heather and Western Gorse*

Chickweed-wintergreen and Mountain Everlasting. Shady, steep north- or east-facing slopes often support damper heath with richly coloured carpets of bog-mosses. In places this damp heath includes rare oceanic liverworts and the tiny Wilson's Filmy-fern, which looks more like a moss than a fern.

Notable groups of species include upland birds and moorland invertebrates. Look out for Red Grouse (in open heather), Black Grouse (in habitat mosaics and moorland fringes) and Twite (moorland edges), as well as Merlin, Hen Harrier and Short-eared Owl (all of which nest in open heather but are often scarce or absent around grouse shooting estates due to illegal persecution). The invertebrate fauna is diverse, with up to 15% of British ground beetles, and 20% of British spiders found in areas with a range of moorland vegetation types and structures.

TOP LEFT: The endemic **Red Grouse** – listen for the distinctive "*go-back, go-back*" call, or the whirring of wings when a bird is disturbed from the ground.
TOP RIGHT: **Mountain Hares** are native to the Highlands of Scotland, and were introduced to the Peak District in the 19th century. The Irish Hare is smaller and does not grow a white coat in winter. RIGHT: Near **Balnakeil, Durness** – here, Upland Dry Heath defies stereotypes by growing over limestone almost at sea level. The patterning is a result of severe wind-pruning. BELOW LEFT: **An Creagan**, near **Balmoral** – Heather burning (also referred to as muirburn) is a widespread practice, particularly on grouse moors, and results in a distinctive patchwork of different aged Heather. Its impact on the structural and species diversity of heathland is dependent on rotation length, the amount of old degenerate heather retained, and the interaction with grazing. Larger areas are also burnt by sheep farmers to give an early bite. BELOW RIGHT: Near **Carn Lochan na Beinne, Cairngorms** – rocky ground at about 700 m supporting Crowberry and Bearberry among low Heather.

UPLAND WET HEATH

Upland Wet Heath is found at moderate altitudes on shallow peats and acid mineral soils that are waterlogged for at least part of the year, but are too dry or too shallow for active peat formation. It generally occupies gently sloping hillsides where there is some movement of water, often above Blanket Bog but below the better drained steeper slopes where drier heath is found. These habitats often intermingle. Drier areas on mineral soils often support grasses, particularly Mat-grass and Wavy Hair-grass, while Heath Rush is common on shallow peats. Where the heath is slightly flushed with moving water, Carnation Sedge grows with other sedges and Round-leaved Sundew. Reindeer lichens are common on steeper, higher slopes in the Northern Highlands, but are replaced in the wetter and milder conditions farther west by Woolly Fringe-moss and Bell heather in a more open sward. In areas where it is heavily grazed, Upland Wet Heath can be characterised by Deergrass, Mat-grass and Heath Rush. There is a degree of overlap between the wetter moorland habitats.

Similar habitats

It can be difficult to distinguish Upland Wet Heath from Upland Dry Heath and Blanket Bog, particularly as drained Blanket Bog can support Purple Moor-grass and Heather. However, Upland Wet Heath lacks the typical peat-forming species characteristic of Blanket Bog such as the pale greenish-ochre Papillose Bog-moss and Hare's-tail Cottongrass. Upland Dry Heath tends to have a thicker Heather canopy and usually lacks Cross-leaved Heath, although damper versions with bog-mosses are similar to Upland Wet Heath.

Origins and development

Upland Wet Heath may have occurred in boggy glades when the upland landscape was still primarily forested, but most probably developed on shallow slopes on the waterlogged ground that resulted from tree clearance that began about 4,000 years ago. Much habitat has deteriorated through overgrazing, burning and drainage, while losses have been caused by afforestation and, more recently, the development of tracks and renewable energy infrastructure.

Distribution and extent

Found in the western uplands. Extent figures overestimate as include lowland wet heath: Eng: 25,000 ha; Sco: 37,000 ha; Wal: 9,400 ha; NI: 58,300 ha; Ire: 143,000 ha (ANN I REP). Britain and Ireland form the global stronghold of Upland Wet Heath.

LEFT: **Rothiemurchus, Speyside** – hollows within Caledonian Forest support Upland Wet Heath in a range of transitions with Upland Dry Heath. The rare montane ground-beetle *Amara alpina* is associated with Upland Wet Heath in the Cairngorms, and feeds on the seed-heads of Deergrass. RIGHT, BOTTOM: **Beinn Eighe, Wester Ross** – Upland Wet Heath covers extensive tracts of land on the relatively shallow lower slopes. In Scotland look around bog margins in sheltered Upland Wet Heath for **Scotch Argus** (RIGHT, TOP).

ABOVE: **Twelve Pins (Na Beanna Beola), Connemara**. Much of the landscape is clothed with Upland Wet Heath, with Blanket Bog on flatter areas.

Conservation

Although some grazing is beneficial in promoting floristic diversity by preventing Heather or Purple Moor-grass from smothering smaller species and lower plants, a reduction in grazing levels would benefit many upland sites. Burning, which is often carried out in large patches to stimulate fresh growth for livestock, can damage lichens and bryophytes. Many upland woodlands are adjacent to Upland Wet Heath, and so woodland expansion is often likely to be to the detriment of Upland Wet Heath.

What to look for

Flushes with butterworts, sundews, White Beak-sedge and Many-stalked Spike-rush. Bog Asphodel adds colour from July. Rare mosses and western liverworts can be found in the northern hepatic mat community (see Upland Dry Heath, *page 94*). Look for Mackay's Heath in western Ireland.

(see Upland Dry Heath, *page 94*)

How to recognise

Upland Wet Heath only occurs to any great extent in Britain and Ireland, where it dominates much of the moorland landscape of the wet western uplands, particularly in Scotland and Ireland. It is a little less heathy in appearance than Upland Dry Heath, although the warm green-ochre tones of Deergrass are broken by pinky-purple patches of Cross-leaved Heath and Heather in summer. The knee-high vegetation is spiked with Bog Asphodel and Common Cottongrass and the distinctive pale straw of Purple Moor-grass (Britain's only deciduous grass) litters the underlying mosses. Upland Wet Heath is often found within tracts of Blanket Bog but although wet underfoot, it is generally firm enough to walk over.

When to visit

Late summer for flowering heather and drier conditions.

*Below **Carn Lochan na Beinne, Cairngorms**– the warm glow of Deergrass and pale pink flowers of Cross-leaved Heath contrast with the darker Heather-dominated Upland Dry Heath on the steeper slopes behind.*

GRASSLANDS

ORIGINS

Almost all grasslands in Britain and Ireland are semi-natural, a result of millennia of human activity that has favoured grassland over woodland and wetland, generally to provide animal fodder. However, this does not mean that grassland did not exist before the Neolithic period, when the clearance of woodland began. Pollen records suggest that tundra and tall-herb communities predominated over Britain and Ireland for a period at the end of the last glaciation. As woody species colonised, these communities were able to persist at high altitudes beyond the natural limit of tree growth, on exposed cliff slopes and shorelines, in dynamic river floodplains, and in glades within woodland maintained by large wild herbivores such as Auroch. Tree clearance, drainage and grazing with domestic livestock allowed these communities to expand and adapt on suitable soils, and grassland became a key feature in the landscape from about 6,000 years ago. On more acid soils where these activities resulted in heathland, grassland sometimes developed subsequently as a result of heavy grazing and burning. Grassland has ebbed and flowed with changing human population pressure but remains a defining feature of the British and Irish countryside today.

The extent of almost all semi-natural habitats in Britain and Ireland has declined significantly, but the loss of lowland grassland has been particularly severe, with a 90% decline in the 20th century. Cultivation and re-seeding became widespread by the 18th century amongst wealthy landowners, but it was in the 1940s and 1950s that destruction escalated. Technological advances and the drive for increased national self-sufficiency in food led to the extensive use of new chemicals and grass varieties, increased intensity of cutting and grazing, and the use of incentives to encourage farmers to plough up meadows, pastures and downland. Conversely, in the uplands, subsidies encouraged high stocking rates, which adversely affected grasslands, but also increased the areas of Upland Acid Grassland at the expense of heather-dominated habitats.

Some **semi-natural grassland** has become established relatively recently as a consequence of development, such as on railway cuttings and road embankments where the substrate has been exposed. It is sometimes reseeded with wildflowers, in this case Oxeye Daisy.

Corfe Common, Dorset. In the lowlands, grasslands often only survived because multiple ownership or common rights made gaining consensus for 'improvement' difficult.

HABITAT	DESCRIPTION
Lowland Calcareous Grassland *page 108*	Species-rich, on limestone and chalk mainly in the southern lowlands, of particular interest for invertebrates.
Lowland Dry Acid Grassland *page 112*	Species-poor, but supports specialist species, part of heathland landscapes on dry acid soils.
Lowland Meadow and Pasture *page 114*	Rich in generalist species, highly fragmented and limited in extent on neutral soils. Meadow is cut for hay or silage, pasture is generally grazed throughout the year.
Purple Moor-grass and Rush Pasture *page 116*	Marshy grassland with specialist species found in the lowlands.
Coastal and Floodplain Grazing Marsh *page 118*	Seasonally flooded, mostly semi-improved, of interest for breeding and wintering waterfowl.
Upland Calcareous Grassland *page 122*	Species-rich, of naturally limited extent on limestone and other basic rocks in the uplands.
Northern Hay Meadow *page 124*	Species-rich, of very limited extent mainly in and near the Pennines.
Upland Rush Pasture *page 126*	Species-poor rough grazing, of interest for its bird fauna, widespread in the uplands margins.
Upland Acid Grassland *page 128*	Species-poor rough grazing, widespread and extensive in the uplands on siliceous rocks, of interest for breeding waders.
Calaminarian Grassland *page 130*	Supports specialist metalliferous species, widespread but very limited in extent.

TYPES OF GRASSLAND

Estimates vary depending on definitions and survey techniques, but grassland probably covers around 40% of the land surface of the UK and over 60% of that of Ireland. In the UK, over half of this is permanent pasture, about 40% is rough grazing (*i.e.* semi-natural permanent pasture in the uplands). The remaining 10% is grass ley. Of the permanent pasture, the majority is improved or semi-improved (see box), with only a fraction remaining unimproved. Estimates for unimproved grassland are around 100,000 ha for England. To put this into

Magdalen Hill Down, Hampshire – an area of species-rich chalk downland of particular note for its butterflies.

Improved grasslands

Improved grassland includes swards that have been drained, fertilized and re-seeded, usually with Perennial Rye-grass and White Clover. Grass Ley is the term used for grassland that is sown in rotation with other crops and ploughed every few years.

'Semi-improved' is used to refer to swards that are not particularly species-rich, having been drained and fertilized, but are nonetheless of greater interest than re-seeded pasture and leys. Such swards may include rushes, a range of other grass species and herbs such as buttercups. Some semi-improved swards are of great wildlife value as they still provide habitat for breeding and wintering waterfowl (*e.g.* Coastal and Floodplain Grazing Marsh, *page 118*).

perspective, the total area of grassland in England is over 4·5 million hectares.

There is a tiny amount of near-natural grassland in Britain and Ireland. It is found where climate, exposure, or changing environmental conditions naturally prevent woody species from becoming established (*e.g.* in montane situations, in exposed places, and where the substrate shifts such as in sand dune and shingle systems). The remainder of unimproved grassland is generally referred to as semi-natural because, without human intervention, successional processes would otherwise result in scrub and woodland developing (some types could revert to wetland habitats). Semi-natural grassland is generally found within agricultural systems, and much is either in protected areas or managed through agri-environment schemes.

Grassland is, by convention, divided into upland and lowland, with the 300 m contour taken as an approximate delimiter. This is because cooler, wetter and more exposed conditions in the uplands favour different species from those adapted to the generally warmer and drier conditions in the lowlands. However, as in all habitat types, transitions occur, and some 'upland' communities are found at sea level where conditions are harsh. The division also has practical relevance as the fate of lowland grassland has been different from that of the uplands, and a different approach to the conservation of each is needed.

Hay meadow management

With the widespread development of efficient metal tools in the Iron Age, hay-making became a possibility. Dried herbage, rather than tree-forage, became the winter mainstay for livestock in Britain (although tree-lopping persisted into the 19th century) and meadows evolved. In Ireland, the milder climate meant that stock could be out-wintered more readily, and hay-making was not so ubiquitous.

In meadows, the livestock are excluded from around the beginning of May and moved to alternative pasture, often common land, downland or hill grazings. The mixed sward of grass and herbs is cut from about midsummer onwards, ideally after it sets seed. It is then left to dry in the field for three days or so. Historically, it was cut by a team of people with scythes and turned by hand. Nowadays the process is mechanised but is still time-consuming; the hay generally needs to be turned several times and 'rowed up' overnight. Hay-making is entirely dependent upon fair weather, and in a poor season can be delayed until September, although by this time the rank herbage can be difficult to dry properly. Traditionally, hay used to be stacked on tripods or built into haycocks to minimise the impact of dew or rainfall overnight. Now, it is more likely to be big-baled and wrapped for silage in inclement weather. After the crop has been removed, livestock are let back in to graze the regrowth (known as 'aftermath') and any uncut corners and margins. Grazing usually continues throughout the winter and, in the spring, farmyard manure and sometimes lime are applied to help maintain fertility.

Mechanisation (and the widespread availability of plastic) has made silage-making comparatively easy, and it has now largely replaced hay-making. Silage is more nutritious than hay (although not suitable for horses). The grass is cut green, then fermented in anaerobic conditions, causing carbohydrates to be converted to acids that preserve the silage and improve digestibility. The grass can be cut earlier, does not need drying, and more than one cut can be taken in a year. Expensive equipment also requires greater returns, and artificial fertilizers are used to maximise the crop. Early and repeated cutting and fertilization greatly reduce the plant species diversity of the sward and can be devastating for birds and invertebrates.

Inishbofin, Connemara – traditional hay-making still takes place in western Ireland and occasionally in the Hebrides, generally in small, rocky fields. Hay-making was a major event in rural life and was celebrated accordingly.

Grassland can also be defined according to the pH of the substrate, and is often described as acid (*e.g.* on sands, gravels and siliceous rocks) or calcareous (on rocks rich in magnesium as well as different limestones). Both acid and calcareous grassland support specialist species, although calcareous swards tend to be significantly more species-rich. Some species are found in both. Grassland that supports species that are able to tolerate intermediate pH is called 'neutral' and is generally found on clays and loams. This type of grassland is also referred to as 'mesotrophic', as it is inherently more productive than acid or calcareous grassland.

Management is another key factor. Pastures are often grazed year-round, and are not cut. Meadows are shut off from livestock in the spring to allow vegetation to be harvested and stored for the winter – traditionally as hay but now more often as silage. Wet grasslands generally experience regular flooding, mostly in the winter, and in some cases this is actively managed. However, there is variation in how particular habitats are managed; for example, pastures can be cut for hay in some years and wet grasslands may be meadow or pasture. In some cases grassland has survived by accident, for example in churchyards and on road verges where it is also cut sporadically.

Semi-natural grassland in Britain and Ireland is very varied, a product of the diverse substrate, soil, topography, climate and land-use history of these islands. Ten types are described this chapter but these are, as always, nodes on a continuum, and transitional types are of no less interest.

CONSERVATION IMPORTANCE AND PROTECTION

Semi-natural grassland supports distinctive communities of plants, fungi and invertebrates in particular, including species that are greatly valued for their attractiveness and rarity. For example, 206 of the UK BAP priority species are found in lowland semi-natural grasslands, and 41 in Upland Calcareous Grassland and Northern Hay Meadow. Although often celebrated as being species-rich (and it is wonderfully species-rich in comparison to the improved grassland that has so often replaced it), grassland is not intrinsically species-rich compared to woodland it generally replaced if all life-forms are taken into account. It is an early-successional habitat that lacks the complexity of later stages. However, it supports species for which those later stages are too enclosed, and which presumably would once have occurred in natural openings. Most woodland remnants are now too small, fragmented and constrained for such natural openings to occur, and species dependent upon open conditions are limited to semi-natural grassland and Wood Pasture. In Europe as a whole, around 50% of the endemic plant species are dependent on grassland.

FUTURE THREATS
Nitrogen deposition has affected the species diversity and composition of acid and calcareous grassland respectively. While major changes have probably already occurred, ongoing deposition may see further change.
Neglect of semi-natural lowland grassland has resulted in a decline in condition, and is a reflection of the poor economic returns from low-productivity grassland. Funding for conservation grazing is needed if this decline is to be reversed.
Climate change is likely to directly impact on semi-natural grasslands, although exactly how is still unclear. Changes in hydrology may result in wet grasslands becoming drier, and areas where the climate is suitable may be reduced for northern species such as Globeflower and Wood Crane's-bill.

Waxcap grasslands are particularly rich in fungi, although not necessarily in plant species, and are found in short, nutrient-poor swards across the spectrum from acidic to calcareous. The most striking species are the waxcaps, which can be white, pink, purple, yellow, orange or red, and colours in between. They generally have smooth glossy or sticky caps and thick, waxy gills. Fairy clubs, pinkgills and earthtongues are also characteristic of waxcap grasslands. The presence of particular species can be used as 'indicators' of the quality of a site. Waxcap grasslands occur principally in Europe, and are most extensive in Britain.

Conservation branding is seen as a way to add value to produce from semi-natural grasslands. There is also some evidence to suggest that the quality of meat from semi-natural grassland is better than that from improved grassland. The importance of the botanical diversity of forage for cattle in terms of cheese favour has already been established.

European designation helps to protect six types of grassland in Britain and Ireland. This excludes Coastal and Floodplain Grazing Marsh, most Lowland Dry Acid Grassland, Upland Acid Grassland and Upland Rush Pasture, although the former is recognised as a Priority Habitat for conservation within the UK and all four can be found within Special Protection Areas (SPAs) notified for their internationally important breeding or wintering birds. Unusual or species-rich variants of Upland Acid Grassland are sometimes notified as SSSIs, but in general, together with Upland Rush Pasture, the impoverished sward is of less interest than that of the other moorland habitats such as Upland Dry Heath, Upland Wet Heath and Blanket Bog from which they are derived. There is growing interest in exploring how some of these impoverished habitats could be reinvigorated. The removal of heavy grazing pressure would result in an increase in dwarf-shrubs and eventually woodland (although given the distance to seed sources in many cases, this could take many years). In wetter situations some habitat would revert to Blanket Bog. Changes in the Common Agricultural Policy, which used to link subsidies directly to numbers of livestock, has seen a decline in grazing pressure, but about 75% of protected Upland Calcareous Grassland remains in poor condition largely due to overgrazing by sheep.

Information on how much grassland is designated is most readily available in England, where around 68% of semi-natural grassland is thought to be protected by SSSI notification. However, this proportion varies widely between grassland types, with, for example, a much great proportion of calcareous grassland protected than Purple Moor-grass and Rush Pasture. Designated sites are, on the whole, in better condition than undesignated sites, but their condition is deteriorating. In contrast, the condition of some non-SSSI semi-natural grassland has improved slightly, a consequence of agri-environment schemes and increasing expertise in grassland restoration. Species-rich grassland is still being lost (although the rate has slowed), and the ongoing declines in associated species are alarming: 22 butterfly species found on farmland saw a 37% decline between 1990 and 2009; declines in breeding Yellow Wagtails in Northern Hay Meadows accelerated through the 1990s; and populations of breeding waders continue to dwindle. A major change in policy is needed, so that the multi-faceted value of species-rich grassland is better appreciated and low-intensity management is better supported. The advent of ecosystem services valuation, does raise the profile of the environmental benefits provided by grassland in terms of flood prevention, carbon storage and water purification, as well as the benefits to heath and well-being and contributions to tourism. It is, however, important not to lose sight of the intrinsic value of habitats.

CULTURAL IMPORTANCE

Wildlife-rich grassland is valued as a cultural landscape, a serendipitous product of thousands of years of human impacts on ecological processes. Once an intrinsic part

Uffington White Horse, Oxfordshire – many archaeological features have been preserved in semi-natural grassland including Bronze Age figures such as this and the Cerne Abbas Giant in Dorset, whose origins are obscure.

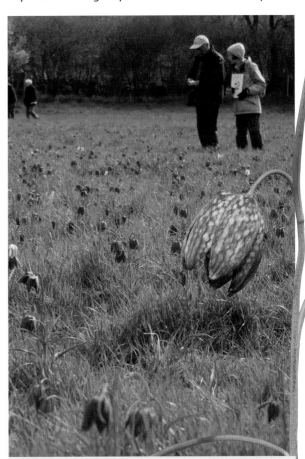

Fox Fritillary Meadow, Suffolk – open days on privately owned flower-rich grasslands are popular – an indication of the affection with which meadows are regarded, and of how difficult it can otherwise be to see them.

Key Grassland Areas

1. South Downs
2. Salisbury Plain
3. Somerset Levels and Moors
4. Culm Grasslands
5. Mendips
6. Rhôs Pasture
7. Cotswolds
8. Great Orme
9. The Burren
10. Aran Islands
11. River Shannon Callows
12. Durness
13. Ben Lawers
14. The Pennines
15. Breckland
16. The Fens
17. Thames Valley

KEY

Semi-natural grassland
Improved grassland

The map shows all grasslands. Lowland grassland sites are often very small and scattered. In many parts of the uplands, grassland habitats are extensive, including large parts of Wales, the Pennines, the Southern Uplands and the Scottish Highlands.

Some key locations are labelled on the map; this selection is not intended to be exhaustive but highlights a few of the most important areas.

of every farm, flower-rich grassland is deeply embedded within our culture and has recurred as a theme for artists and writers for centuries. Much loved for its sheer beauty in an increasingly monotonous countryside, such grassland is becoming increasingly scarce – it is unusual to come across any by chance and, for younger generations, uniform green fields are the norm in pastoral landscapes. There is the danger that some types will soon be limited to folk memory and literature unless declines in extent and quality are halted.

Semi-natural grasslands also have a range of historical management practices and traditions associated with them that are valued for their cultural significance. For example, in Wessex, flocks were shepherded on the chalk downland, then enclosed on arable land to fertilize it. From the 17th century, water meadows were an important part of the system, and had their own customs and skills linked with them. 'Drowned' or 'floated' using a system of channels, drains and sluices, usually in early spring, they were managed to provide an 'early bite' in the spring, and hay for the winter. The famous Lammas meadows of the Thames Valley were common land. Commoners drew lots for 'doles' marked with boundary stones from which hay had to be cut and carted away by Lammas Day in August.

KEY ELEMENTS

Grazing plays a crucial part in the ecology of almost all semi-natural grasslands. Grazing or mowing is essential to maintain floral species diversity and abundance by preventing bulky, competitive species and scrub from engulfing finer grasses and herbs. Grazing (at appropriate stocking densities) creates a more diverse sward structure than mowing and can result in a mosaic of patches with short, tall and tussocky vegetation and bare ground. The dung produced by livestock is also important, as it attracts coprophagous beetles and flies. For example, the larvae of the rare Hornet Robberfly feed on dung beetle larvae that are reliant on cattle dung. Grazing is also less of a catastrophic event than mowing for invertebrates and breeding birds.

Anthills (typically formed by Yellow Meadow-ant) indicate long-established semi-natural grassland. The ants (which farm underground aphids) create the mounds while excavating underground galleries where they care for their young. The mounds, which are warmed by the sun and act as storage heaters, support individual colonies that may be over 100 years old. They can be found on dry acid or calcareous grassland, and the fine material often supports different species of plants from the surrounding sward, including scarce species such as Nit-grass. Green Woodpeckers feed from anthills using their particularly long tongues. Anthills are also used by basking Common Lizard and by Common Field Grasshopper for egg-laying.

The structural diversity created by grazing is particularly important for invertebrates, whose requirements can be complex. For example, blue butterflies have a fascinating relationship with ants, secreting a sweet liquid that the ants feeds on before taking the caterpillars into their nest under the misapprehension that they are ant grubs. The caterpillars eat the real grubs, and hibernate in the nest until the following summer, safe from predators. The butterfly is therefore reliant on the specific conditions required by the relevant ant species (usually very warm, short swards).

In general, any kind of variation in the sward composition, structure or wetness of grassland is a good indication of the likely presence of different species. For example, flushes in Northern Hay Meadow can support localised plant species such as Bird's-eye Primrose and Grass-of-Parnassus. Moist areas (and animal dung) on Lowland Calcareous Grassland can sometimes attract clouds of butterflies (*e.g.* Small and Chalkhill Blue) in search of mineral salts. Bare patches can be particularly valuable – a biodiversity audit in Breckland found that the presence of bare, disturbed ground was more important than habitat type in determining how many species were present on a site. Margins, ditches, and transitions to other habitat types also add to the diversity of species that may be found. The transition to scrub is particularly important, as it provides a sheltered microclimate but without too much loss of light, and is considered an integral part of most grassland habitats. A balance between ensuring that adequate scrub is present and maintaining the area of open grassland can be difficult to achieve. The small size of most sites makes managing this interface labour-intensive.

FURTHER INFORMATION

Meadows by George Peterken (Brit. Wildlife Publishing, 2013)
Jewels beyond the plough, a celebration of Britain's Grassland by Richard Jefferson (Langford Press, 2012)
Nature's Tapestry. The story of England's grasslands and why not all grass is green by Miles King (Grassland Trust, 2011 www.grasslands-trust.org)
Flora Locale promotes the restoration of wild plants and habitats (www.floralocale.org)

Pasqueflower – an iconic species of calcareous grasslands in Britain, flowering during late April and early May. Its decline (due to agricultural improvement) has been long-term, and it is now restricted to a handful of sites.

Common Rock-rose is a small evergreen shrub typical of calcareous grassland that is widely distributed throughout Britain and Ireland. Flowering from June to September it is a food plant for several butterflies and moths, including Brown Argus, Green Hairstreak, Silver-studded Blue and the iridescent green day-flying moth Cistus Forester.

Yellow-rattle is widespread in dry neutral grassland and flowers from June to September. It is a hemi-parasite, tapping into the roots of grasses to obtain nutrients; this reduces their vigour and dominance in the sward, providing opportunities for other less robust species to become established. It can play a key role in grassland restoration.

LOWLAND CALCAREOUS GRASSLAND

Classic chalk grassland is mostly found in the warm and dry southern chalk country (Dorset, Wiltshire, the twin ridgeways of the North and South Downs and the Chilterns), where its character is determined by the climate, rather than the particularly type of limestone on which it occurs. Towards the cooler and wetter north it becomes increasingly limited to south-facing slopes. Famous for its incredible floristic richness (up to 40 or more species per square metre), it usually contains a mixture of fine-bladed grasses and small herbs such as Meadow Oat-grass, Quaking-grass, Wild Thyme, Small Scabious, Dropwort, Common Bird's-foot-trefoil, Salad Burnet and Yellow Feather-moss. Hawthorn and Blackthorn scrub is common, and Common Juniper thrives locally. The diversity of plants is mirrored by that of invertebrates, which favour the open, well-drained conditions of calcareous sites, particularly where there is a good diversity of structure within the vegetation.

In Breckland, the dry climate and lack of fertility of the wind-blown sands have shaped a chalk grassland that is more akin to the continental steppes. Frost-sorting (repeated freeze-thaw cycles that sort small stones according to size, resulting in patterned ground) following the last glaciation has formed a patchwork of grassland and heath. Distinctive smooth, grey-green patches indicate plentiful reindeer lichens, while close inspection of the broken turf of Sheep's-fescue, Wild Thyme and Mouse-ear-hawkweed reveals tiny spring-flowering annuals such as Parsley-piert, Thyme-leaved Sandwort, Early Forget-me-not and Little Mouse-ear.

BELOW: **The Manger,** near **Uffington, Wiltshire** – a dry chalk valley whose rippled sides were created by retreating permafrost during the last glaciation.
BOTTOM LEFT: Near **Port Eynon, Gower** – on exposed limestone headlands and rocky places, the inhospitable, sparse soils and degree of exposure prevent inundation by thick grass, scrub and trees, and may have provided a refuge for rare species like Hoary Rock-rose and Yellow Whitlowgrass ever since the last glaciation.
BOTTOM RIGHT: **Ballard Down, Dorset** – un-grazed chalk grassland on cliff slopes, kept short on the cliff top by exposure and the thin, friable soil, develops into a taller sward farther back and includes Nottingham Catchfly.

Distribution and extent

Largely confined to southern England, the north and south coast of Wales and central Ireland. Eng: 38,700 ha; Sco: 700 ha; Wal: 1,100 ha; NI: 0 ha; Ire: 1,400 ha (ANN I REP).

Chalk grassland only occurs in north-west Europe, and the UK holds a significant proportion; it is found from Dorset, through Wiltshire and Hampshire into the South Downs of Sussex and Kent and the North Downs of the Chilterns, up into East Anglia and as far north as the Yorkshire Wolds.

Limestone grassland is found on the western and southern coastal strips, notably in Dorset, around Torbay in Devon, on The Burren, on the Isle of Wight, and on the Gower Peninsular and Gt. Orme's Head, as well as in the Mendips, the Cotswolds and the central plain of Ireland.

LEFT: The flora of **Breckland** chalk grassland contains a high proportion of rarities, including Spanish Catchfly (seen here), Purple-stem Cat's-tail, Spiked Speedwell, and Maiden Pink. RIGHT: **Cressbrook Dale, Peak District** – Scrub is an integral part of most Lowland Calcareous Grassland, and is of particular importance to breeding birds and invertebrates, some of which are dependent upon scrub-edge microhabitats. Transitional scrubby vegetation can host uncommon and rare plants such as Bloody Crane's-bill or Lizard Orchid.

In contrast, the oceanic climate of southern and western coastal fringes, where most hard limestone is found, favours species such as Carline Thistle, Yellow-wort, Black Medick, rock-roses and squills. On shattered, rocky outcrops conditions are often quite disturbed, and annuals such as Fern-grass and Early Gentian (which is endemic to the UK) are found. The Irish limestone grasslands of The Burren have more affinity with Upland Calcareous Grassland.

Similar habitats

Transitions occur with Mixed Scrub and Beech and Yew Woods in particular. In Breckland, chalk grassland is found with Lowland Dry Heath. Limestone Heath (see Lowland Dry Heath, *page 91*) includes plants characteristic of Lowland Calcareous Grassland.

How to recognise

Typically found in open, rolling landscapes strongly influenced by the underlying limestone or chalk, Lowland Calcareous Grassland is easily identified from a distance by its soft, moss-green colour, which contrasts with the more strident, uniform green of nearby improved grassland. The sward appears more textured and has scrubby patches, and is typically found on steep slopes. In summer, the short, springy turf is alive with butterflies and the air is scented with aromatic herbs and alive with sound of grasshoppers and crickets. This rich diversity is on a small scale, and often merits getting down on hands and knees so that the more diminutive species are not missed.

Chalk grassland has an ancient feel, and is often found on prehistoric burial mounds, hill forts and trackways. Today, the notion of settled pastoralism evoked by chalk landscapes is often tempered by the close proximity of urban centres and the effects of cultural eutrophication. By comparison, the limestone sites of exposed coasts feel wilder, while the desolate flat grass-heaths of Breckland have their own special quality.

When to visit

April–August for flowering plants and invertebrates, depending on species (the extremely rare Fringed Gentian has been overlooked in the past becuase it flowers in the autumn).

Noar Hill, Hampshire – chalk grassland is characterised by species such as Stemless Thistle, Horseshoe Vetch and Squinancywort, and can support rarities such as Chalk Milkwort, Bastard Toadflax, Chalk Eyebright and Common Juniper.

Origins and development

Chalk and limestone grassland is the product of millennia of livestock grazing following woodland clearance that started in the Mesolithic, and may have focussed on the relatively sparse, well-drained woodland of limestone. Changing agricultural pressures meant that grassland was increasingly ploughed up from about 1700 onwards, although much remained until the mid-20th century, after which destruction accelerated. Now, of a habitat type that used to dominate whole landscapes, only scattered pockets are left on slopes too steep to plough or in areas whose military use precluded modern agricultural practices. Grassland on remaining sites has often succeeded to Mixed Scrub, partly due to the impact of myxomatosis on Rabbit populations. Outright habitat loss has mostly been stemmed, but there has been a notable decline in characteristic species in recent years.

Conservation

Conservation management generally aims to create a structurally diverse sward that includes short areas on south- and west-facing slopes. Low intensity sheep or cattle (also Rabbit) grazing is mostly preferred but, unfortunately, agricultural policies do not necessarily favour appropriate stocking rates. Fragmentation is a real concern and in some areas is being addressed through projects to re-create and reconnect sites – Lowland Calcareous Grassland may otherwise be facing extinction debt (the likely future loss of species as a consequence of past habitat loss). It is not yet clear how the impacts of climate change will manifest, but connecting more areas of habitat will increased the ability of species to respond.

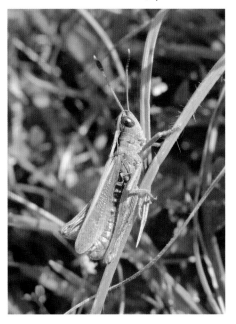

Although grasshoppers and crickets are common in this habitat, only the **Rufous Grasshopper** (BELOW) and Stripe-winged Grasshopper are considered to be characteristic of old, species-rich turf.

Over 30 of Britain's butterfly species occur on chalk grassland, and at some sites still occur in great numbers. The blues are particularly associated with this habitat, with five species and many thousands of individuals flying at exceptional sites. Each of the key chalk grassland butterfly species has different habitat requirements, as summarised in the following table:

Species	Main Food Plant	Calcareous Grassland Preferences
Silver-spotted Skipper	Sheep's Fecue	Hot, sun-baked chalk grassland, short turf, often steep south-facing scarp
Lulworth Skipper	Tor Grass	Dense mature clumps of Tor-grass at least 20 cm tall
Small Blue	Kidney Vetch	Sheltered grassland with a mix of short turf and taller plants
Brown Argus	Common Rock-rose	Short vegetation on steep south-facing downs, banks or earthworks
Chalkhill Blue	Horseshoe Vetch	Short, open grassland
Adonis Blue	Horseshoe Vetch	Short, sun-baked turf
Large Blue	Thyme	Closely grazed grassland, warm (often south-facing)
Duke of Burgundy	Cowslips or Primroses	Warm pockets of grassland among scrub, medium sward height
Marsh Fritillary	Devil's-bit Scabious	Chalk grassland with a short-medium sward, often on south-facing slopes
Marbled White	Red Fescue	Tall, unimproved grassland

Lowland Calcareous Grassland sites can be important for a wide diversity of orchids.

CLOCKWISE FROM TOP LEFT: **Early Spider-orchid, Bee Orchid, Frog Orchid, Pyramidal Orchid, Fragrant Orchid.**

Did you know?

Salisbury Plain is the largest area of chalk grassland in Europe. Extending to more than 21,000 ha, it contains over half the Lowland Calcareous Grassland in the UK.

Eggardon Hill Fort, Dorset *– the best habitat is often found where the ground is steep, well-drained and thin-soiled, such as on scarps and ancient earthworks. It can also develop in disused limestone quarries and chalk pits, on spoil heaps, road verges and railway cuttings.*

What to look for

The tremendous abundance of plant species in Lowland Calcareous Grassland is possibly due in part to the sparseness of the woodland that colonised the thin soils after the last glaciation, which perhaps allowed species requiring open conditions to persist. A long list of scarce and rare species may be found, many of which are particularly attractive or intriguing, such as Pasqueflower, Round-headed Rampion, Monkey Orchid and the spider orchids.

Bare areas and short swards on south-facing slopes are often excellent places to look for insects. Sites with good structural and botanical diversity are best for insects. Over-wintering species use taller tussocks for shelter, while butterflies, bees and hoverflies need flowering plants for nectar and pollen, and some craneflies rely on the leaf-litter underneath scrub. Still, sunny days are best for seeing invertebrates, but around July, a night-time visit might reveal Glow-worms; the flightless females of this beetle give off a soft yellowish-green light at night to attract a mate. Birds are more limited, but look out for Skylark, Corn Bunting, and in Breckland and at some Wiltshire sites, Stone-curlew.

Fertilized downland swards are of limited wildlife interest but easily identified as they contain far fewer species and include generalists such as Crested Dog's-tail, Yorkshire-fog and White Clover.

CHALK GRASSLAND BLUE BUTTERFLIES
FACNG PAGE, LEFT TO RIGHT: **Small Blue**, female; **Large Blue**, female; **Chalkhill Blue**, male. THIS PAGE, RIGHT: **Adonis Blue**, male.

LOWLAND DRY ACID GRASSLAND

Lowland Dry Acid Grassland is found on acid soils derived from sandstone and igneous rocks, and on sands and gravels, and varies across the country according to climate and soil characteristics.

Sometimes called lichen-heath or grass-heath, parched acid grassland is found in Breckland, the Suffolk Sandlings, the New Forest, the Dorset heaths and the Wealden heaths. It is the most species-rich acid grassland type, containing up to 25 species per square metre, many of which are uncommon, including Mossy Stonecrop, Annual Knawel, Bur Medick, Clustered Clover and Smooth Cat's-ear. In the more humid south-west, parched acid grassland gives way to species-poor swards dominated by Bristle Bent, particularly where humid heathland has been burnt. In the moister north and west, the sward tends to be tighter and quite species-poor, although the border hills of Powys and Shropshire contain some species-rich examples. In Scotland, Lowland Dry Acid Grassland can occur on rock outcrops in the hills and on shingle river banks.

Lowland Dry Acid Grassland is important for specialist invertebrates. Dry sandy patches in particular support ground-dwelling and burrowing invertebrates such as solitary bees and wasps, and very rare species such as Field Cricket. Good habitat includes taller swards where flowering plants provide nectar and pollen and south-facing banks that provide warm nesting and basking areas. A little scrub adds to the range of niches; however, where grazing has ceased, encroaching Bracken and scrub can smother the distinctive grassland species.

Similar habitats

Often found in a mosaic with Lowland Dry Heath, transitional vegetation between the two is common. It can grade into wetter grassland types (look for Purple Moor-grass and Sharp-flowered Rush) and coastal grass (with Red Fescue, Buck's-horn Plantain and maritime species such as Thrift). In Breckland, abrupt transitions to chalk grassland create 'stone stripes' (see *page 108*).

BELOW LEFT: **Brockenhurst, Hampshire** – in the New Forest, look out for dry 'lawns' kept tightly grazed by ponies. Such areas are worth searching for uncommon plants such as Hairy Bird's-foot-trefoil and Smooth Cat's-ear, and in the autumn and winter you might see the distinctive and rare Nail Fungus on pony dung.
BELOW RIGHT: **East Wretham Heath, Norfolk** – The characteristic red sheen of **Sheep's Sorrel** in flower. Other species in the sward (ABOVE RIGHT) include **Early Hair-grass**, **Biting Stonecrop**, **Smooth Hawk's-beard**, **Common Whitlowgrass**, **Little Mouse-ear**, the reindeer lichens *Cladonia ciliata* and *C. portentosa*, and **Broom Fork-moss**.

Distribution and extent

Scattered, mainly in England. Eng: 20,100 ha; Sco: 4,300 ha; Wal: 36,000 ha; NI: 700 ha; Ire: n/k. Occurs widely throughout north-west Europe; Britain may hold a significant proportion of European parched acid grassland.

Origins and development

Lowland Dry Acid Grassland is an intrinsic part of heathland landscapes. From the Mesolithic onwards it developed where Lowland Dry Oak and Birch Wood was felled and heathers were excluded through heavy grazing, spasmodic cultivation or other disturbance. The relative proportions of heathland and grassland in extensive heathland landscapes have probably always fluctuated according to changes in agricultural economic and social pressures. However, the second half of the 20th century saw significant losses in both habitats through agricultural intensification and extensive use of what was considered to be unproductive land for afforestation and urban development.

Conservation

The area of Lowland Dry Acid Grassland is still reducing, and declines in butterflies and specialist plant species within extant grassland are ongoing (despite much of it being designated or managed as nature reserves). The decline in plant species-richness has been linked to increased acidification through atmospheric pollution. Efforts have been made to restore and expand the habitat, although it is unlikely to be prioritised over heathland. Generally used as pasture (but also found on golf courses and air fields), almost all Lowland Dry Acid Grassland needs grazing (or cutting) to maintain its distinctive flora and invertebrate fauna. Changing agricultural policies and economics have seen a decline in traditional grazing, resulting in scrub and Bracken encroachment. Conservation of this habitat depends on the restoration of functioning pastoral landscapes.

What to look for

In very early spring listen out for one of the loveliest sounds of the lowlands: the spiralling, liquid song of the Woodlark. The eerie whistling of the Stone-curlew is a sound peculiar to dawn and dusk on Breckland grass heaths. Characteristic butterflies include Small Copper, Grayling and Green Hairstreak. In Breckland look out for a classic suite of rare species including Spiked Speedwell, Sand Catchfly and Perennial Knawel.

RIGHT: **East Wretham Heath, Norfolk** – many areas of Breckland were managed as Rabbit warrens from the 12th until the early 20th centuries. Rabbit grazing is encouraged as it can maintain the short, disturbed sward required by many Breckland specialities.

How to recognise

Short, dry grassland found within heathland landscapes is likely to be Lowland Dry Acid Grassland. It can be found along tracks and around outcrops on sites otherwise dominated by Heather, but also forms extensive areas in its own right. Also look out for it on commons, in ancient parkland, on coastal grasslands and stable shingle.

Lowland Dry Acid Grassland is characterised by a short, open sward of fine grasses, mosses and reindeer lichens scattered with tiny ephemeral annual plants such as Early Hair-grass, Shepherd's Cress, and Common Stork's-bill, and often forms transitions with heathland vegetation. In the spring it can take on a distinctive red sheen created by thousands of flowering stems of Sheep's Sorrel. In summer it burns off and by August the turf becomes brown and scrunches underfoot.

When to visit

March–April is best for Woodlark and Stone-curlew, April–July for a characteristic suite of plants (flowering times vary within this period).

Middebere and Stoborough Heath, Dorset – a patchwork of Heather and Lowland Dry Acid Grassland in an area that was cultivated briefly in the mid-20th century, and is now reverting to heathland (INSET). Cat's-ear, Sweet Vernal-grass and bent grasses characterise a lightly grazed sward in July. Earlier in the season, Suffocated Clover, Clustered Clover and Subterranean Clover can be seen on the track.

Lowland Meadow and Pasture

Lowland Meadow and Pasture is generally found in moist conditions on deep neutral clay and loam soils. This habitat type includes flood meadows and water meadows that are found on the floodplains of large rivers (including the Shannon, Thames, Yorkshire Ouse, Trent and Severn), as well as on stream floodplains, and are periodically subject to inundation during the winter. On moist but not waterlogged soils, characteristic grasses include Red Fescue and Crested Dog's-tail, which are dependent upon adequate surface drainage during the growing season. Where the water-table remains high throughout the summer and around springs and seepages, Marsh-marigold and small sedges are typical. On more freely draining soils, clovers, buttercups, Yellow-rattle, Rough Hawkbit and Common Knapweed can form very herb-rich vegetation. Churchyards, road verges and railway embankments can also support this type of vegetation.

Lowland Meadow and Pasture provides habitat for a wide range of invertebrates, including butterflies, grasshoppers and Yellow Meadow Ant, and many support strong populations of common species. The abundance of nectar sources means that meadows can be important for threatened bumblebees, and associated features such as paths, banks, livestock dung and flushes add to the diversity of species present. However, only a handful of specialists are found. Corncrake, once a common denizen of hay meadows, has been banished by modern farming practices to the Hebrides (although reintroductions have now taken place).

Similar habitats

Lowland Meadow and Pasture can grade into Purple Moor-grass and Rush Pasture in wetter areas or into Lowland Acid or Calcareous Grassland (depending on the substrate) in drier areas.

Origins and development

The pre-Neolithic landscape probably contained clearing, glades and floodplains which supported the species that are now associated with Lowland Meadow and Pasture. These areas were expanded through forest clearance and drained where necessary. From the Iron Age onwards, grasslands were used for making hay (see *page 102*) and by the 13th century most floodplains were probably managed as meadows. However, since 1935, 97% of Lowland Meadow and Pasture has been lost, largely through agricultural improvement or gravel extraction, but also through neglect and unsuitable mowing regimes. A tiny fraction has survived, generally where older farmers resisted modern intensification, or where common rights or multiple ownerships thwarted change. The remaining habitat is now highly fragmented; most sites are under 10 ha and occur in isolation. Put together,

Distribution and extent

Widely but very sparsely distributed. Eng: 36,100 ha; Sco: 1,000 ha (includes traditional crofting areas in the west of Scotland, which are not mapped); Wal: 1,300 ha; NI: 900 ha; Ire: 100 ha (ANN I REP).

BELOW LEFT: **Martin's Meadow, Suffolk**. One of three ancient meadows known in Suffolk. A succession of species is seen, from Cowslip and Early-purple Orchid in spring to Meadow Saffron in late August. BELOW RIGHT: **Itchen Stoke, Hampshire**, on the occasion of its first 're-floating'. Water meadows were irrigated from adjacent rivers and streams to encourage early grass growth in the spring. The practice peaked by 1800 but has now largely ceased, although a few sites have been restored and are 'drowned' annually.

ABOVE LEFT: **Clattinger Farm, Wiltshire** – flood meadows are found in river valleys. Often flooded in winter, they are used for grazing and hay cropping and include the iconic Lammas Fritillary meadows of the upper Thames. ABOVE RIGHT: **Adder's-tongue** – a small fern considered to be an indicator species for ancient meadows and pastures. BELOW RIGHT: **Meadow Crane's-bill** – a hay meadow species that has become increasingly restricted to roadsides because of changes in agricultural practices.

the remaining lowland meadows would occupy an area 1/10th the size of Greater London. However, a slight increase was recorded in the first decade of the 21st century, thought to be due to re-creation projects.

Conservation

Early conservation legislation did little to protect Lowland Meadow and Pasture, perhaps because it was so enmeshed in the farmed landscape, and only about half of the remaining area is designated. A large proportion of sites is in private ownership, and conservation initiatives are focussing on disseminating information and advice to landowners.

What to look for

Rare plants such as Fritillary, Meadow Saffron, Pepper-saxifrage, Dyer's Greenweed and Adder's-tongue can still be found on some sites. Large meadows can support breeding waders.

Lowland Meadow and Pasture is now mostly found tucked away in corners of farms that have for one reason or another escaped agricultural improvement. Meadows are allowed to grow tall and are then cut for hay, whereas pastures are grazed through the summer, but both support a similar assemblage of quite widely distributed species.

Situated on low-lying ground enclosed by hedges, Lowland Meadow and Pasture are bright with Dandelions and Cowslips in spring. By summer, these are over-topped with a medley of other flowers such as Oxeye Daisy, Great Burnet and Meadowsweet, and are busy with invertebrates. Pasture is not as showy as meadow in the summer, but can support large anthills or ancient features such as ridge and furrow or the remains of old settlements.

When to visit

April for Cowslip and Marsh Fritillary, June–July for hay meadows in flower.

Did you know?

'Ridge and furrow' topography created by traditional ploughing techniques is often considered to indicate grassland that may be of medieval origin, although in some cases it can date from as recently as the early 19th century.

Corfe Meadows, Dorset – old, undisturbed hay meadows can be very rich in herbs (up to 90% cover).

PURPLE MOOR-GRASS AND RUSH PASTURE

Purple Moor-grass and Rush Pasture is found on moist peaty-mineral soils poor in nutrients on the better-drained margins of wetlands where it is not regularly flooded. In the south-west of England and Wales, north-west Ireland and locally in south-west Scotland, it is often found with heathy vegetation on more acid soils. In these areas, Compact Rush grows with Meadow Thistle, Tormentil and Cross-leaved Heath in a tussocky sward of Purple Moor-grass. A distinctive and particularly short form is found in the heavily pony-grazed lawns of the New Forest. In the north of England and Scotland, cold-sensitive species such as Meadow Thistle are replaced with Globeflower and Marsh Hawk's-beard. Where Purple Moor-grass and Rush Pasture is derived from Lowland Fen on more base-rich soils (*e.g.* in East Anglia, central Ireland), Purple Moor-grass is joined by rhizomatous rushes and sedges such as Blunt-flowered Rush and Lesser Pond-sedge; often mown, it is known as Fen Meadow. A rich sward with Devil's-bit Scabious, Ragged-Robin, Marsh-marigold and other herbs flourishes where the rush and sedge cover allows, sometimes over-topped by tall-herb fen species such as Wild Angelica and Meadowsweet.

Throughout the cool and wet west, acidic peats support a much more widespread type of rush pasture typified by abundant Soft Rush and/or Sharp-flowered Rush with species such as Greater Bird's-foot-trefoil and Marsh Bedstraw. This community is often found in patches where drainage is impeded within improved pasture, and is of limited interest for wildlife.

Similar habitats

This habitat can show similarities to wetlands, heathlands and drier grasslands. Fen Meadow is related to Lowland Fen but occurs on drained or drier soils where traditional management has created a species-rich sward.

Origins and development

Purple Moor-grass and Rush Pasture supports a distinctive vegetation type that was originally derived from wetland vegetation through grazing and/ or annual mowing for livestock fodder and bedding, and can be ancient. Much Purple Moor-grass and Rush Pasture of conservation interest has been lost through agricultural improvement. Some of this loss is recent – almost 50% of Culm Grassland was destroyed in the last two decades of the 20th century.

Conservation

Britain and Ireland hold a significant proportion of the European resource of relatively species-rich Purple Moor-grass and Rush Pasture. Conservation effort it focussed on linking fragmented sites and reinstating appropriate grazing regimes, particularly where populations of Marsh Fritillary butterfly are present or nearby.

What to look for

Look out for butterflies (particularly Marsh Fritillary) and Narrow-bordered Bee-hawkmoth. Orchids can include Heath Spotted-orchid and Lesser Butterfly-orchid, and Whorled Caraway may be present. Other species to look for are breeding Curlew and Snipe, Common Frog and Grass Snake.

RIGHT, TOP: Purple Moor-grass and Rush Pasture scattered with Heath Spotted-orchid. RIGHT, BOTTOM: **Marsh Fritillary** – the gregarious larvae, which feed on Devil's-bit Scabious, spin protective webs that are easily seen in late summer. Threatened across Europe, this species is restricted to Purple Moor-grass and Rush Pasture and Lowland Calcareous Grassland on chalk sites.

Distribution and extent

Widespread in the lowlands, particularly in the west, extending east in England where soils are wetter. Eng: 21,500 ha; Sco: 6,800 ha; Wal: 32,000 ha; NI: 18,500 ha; Ire: 600 ha (ANN I REP).

Did you know?

Culm Grassland is the term given to Purple Moor-grass and Rush Pasture overlying the Culm Measures of north Devon and north-east Cornwall. Rhôs Pasture refers to similar vegetation in Wales, while the East Anglian fen meadows are sometimes known as Litter.

ABOVE: **Cefn Bryn, Gower** – Purple Moor-grass and Rush Pasture forms transitions with Lowland Wet and Dry Heath on the Gower commons, where management includes grazing, Bracken control and mowing firebreaks. BELOW, LEFT AND CENTRE: **Heath Spotted-orchid** and **Lesser Butterfly-orchid** – In the more oceanic south-west, Atlantic species such as this, Lesser Skullcap, Ivy-leaved Bellflower and Wavy St. John's-wort (absent from Ireland) can be found. BELOW, RIGHT; **Meadow thistle** – a classic species of Purple Moor-grass and Rush Pasture.

How to recognise

Purple Moor-grass and Rush Pasture is a damp type of grassland found within the enclosed agricultural landscape, on unenclosed common land or as part of Lowland Fen. It is generally grazed and sometimes mown for hay.

Though not as colourful as Lowland Meadow and Pasture, it can be species-rich and has its own distinctive character. The thick, tussocky sward of rushes and coarse grasses can be specked yellow with Meadow Buttercup in the spring and purple a little later with Devil's-bit Scabious, Meadow Thistle, Water Mint, Selfheal and vetches – and may include scarce species such as Whorled Caraway. Some areas of Fen Meadow (*e.g.* in the East Anglian fens) support tall herbs such as Meadowsweet. In the west it is a key habitat for the threatened Marsh Fritillary butterfly.

When to visit

Late May–early July for Marsh Fritillary; summer for a suite of interesting plants.

Rackenford and Knowstone Moor, Devon – Purple Moor-grass can form distinctive tussocks where grazing levels are low. A patchwork of short swards and taller tussocks is ideal for Marsh Fritillary.

COASTAL AND FLOODPLAIN GRAZING MARSH

Coastal and Floodplain Grazing Marsh is grassland that is seasonally flooded or has a high water-table. It is dependent on hydrology, topography and management rather than vegetation or substrate type (which can be alluvial or peat soil). Grazing Marsh that is extensively flooded with shallow water (< 50 cm) throughout the winter can support huge numbers of wintering wildfowl. The most diverse assemblages are found where there are a range of conditions suitable for dabbling, diving and grazing species. Marshes with a mixture of tussocky vegetation, short turf and long grass also provide good nesting habitat for a variety of waterfowl. Where the water-table remains within about 20 cm of the surface, it pushes invertebrates to the surface and the ground remains soft, ideal for probing waders (although areas under water for prolonged periods become deplete of invertebrate prey).

Almost all Grazing Marsh has experienced some degree of agricultural improvement and less than 5% of marshes in the UK are semi-natural. The sward is often species-poor, dominated by Perennial Rye-grass, Yorkshire-fog and rushes, although inundated areas can support characteristic communities with Creeping Bent, Marsh Foxtail, Floating Sweet-grass and Silverweed. The few remaining unimproved sites are often too small to support significant bird populations.

Distribution and extent

Found along the lower reaches of lowland rivers and on low-lying coasts.
Eng: 218,100 ha; Sco: n/k; Wal: 80,200 ha; NI: 20,000 ha; Ire: n/k.

TOP LEFT: **River Ant and Ant Marshes, Norfolk** – a wetland landscape including embanked Floodplain Grazing Marsh, Reedbed and Lowland Fen. BOTTOM LEFT: **Wareham Marshes, Dorset** – floodplain grazing marsh in the valley of the River Frome. RIGHT: **Tinker's Marsh, Walberswick, Suffolk** – light cattle-grazing has created a diverse sward structure and range of microhabitats.

Cliffe Marshes, Kent – a typically flat and expansive Coastal Grazing Marsh adjacent to the Thames.

Similar habitats

Grazing Marsh often adjoins Lowland Fen and Reedbed but does not support extensive patches of tall-herbs and reeds. Saltmarsh, present just over the seawall on most coastal grazing marsh sites, supports very different vegetation. Purple Moor-grass and Rush Pasture tends to be on more sloping ground that does not experience regular flooding.

Origins and development

Most Grazing Marsh was created through the embankment and drainage of floodplain and coastal marshes from medieval times onwards. Embanked washlands were created for the purpose of floodwater storage, notably in the East Anglian Fens in the 17th century. Some floodplain marshes owe their existence to the ongoing management of water flow and ditch levels in otherwise well-drained floodplains, which allows water to be retained in the summer to provide drinking water, lush grazing swards and wet fences for livestock. Most grazing marshes are grazed, usually by cattle, and some are cut for hay or silage.

Aldeburgh, Suffolk – shallow winter flooding provides ideal habitat for wintering waterfowl in the RSPB's North Warren reserve.

How to recognise

Coastal and Floodplain Grazing Marsh is found on low-lying, wet ground in the valleys of slow-flowing rivers and along estuaries and on low-lying coasts. It is often behind sea walls where saltmarsh has been 'reclaimed' from the sea and converted into pasture, or behind natural barriers such as sand dunes and in places, the sinuous curves of old saltmarsh creeks can still be visible. Earlier sea walls are found inland where coastal marshes have been progressively enlarged.

Ditches, seasonally wet hollows and pools can be teeming with invertebrates and rich in plants, far more so than the grassland, which has generally been agriculturally 'improved' and is, in itself, of little interest.

It is the birds that really define Grazing Marsh. In winter huge flocks of ducks, geese, and swans congregate on the wide, open expanses of flooded grazing marshes, while in the spring waders nest and probe in the damp grassland.

When to visit

October–March For wintering waterfowl, mid-March–June for breeding waders.

Did you know?
Of an estimated 1,200,000 ha of wet grassland (all types) found historically in England and Wales, only 300,000 survived until the 1930s, and only 100,000 ha now hold significant bird populations.

TOP LEFT: Icelandic **Black-tailed Godwits** spend the winter in the UK and feed on mudflats. They switch to wet grassland as their food is depleted on the estuaries before returning to Iceland to breed. TOP RIGHT: **White-fronted Goose** – most grazing wildfowl prefer short grass (< 15 cm) and grazing can be managed to achieve this. BOTTOM: **Lapwing is** the breeding wader most commonly found on Coastal and Floodplain Grazing Marsh. It requires a short sward, and is less dependent on wet conditions than other species.

Summer flooding can disrupt traditional management such as grazing and cutting for hay.

Conservation

Much of Britain and Ireland's grazing marsh has been lost in the past century, generally through drainage and conversion to cereal production. Remaining marshes are often too dry, too heavily grazed or cut too early/ frequently to support significant populations of breeding waders; most species have declined severely in the last few decades. Conservation management focuses on providing a range of conditions and is dependent on the ability to regulate water levels and stocking densities. A more strategic approach to restoration is beginning to see wetland recreation in whole river catchments. In some places on the sinking east coast of England, marshland will be lost as sea defences are realigned, and some of its value is seen in its potential for the re-creation of other wetland types.

What to look for

During the winter months Grazing Marshes can draw spectacularly large flocks of waterfowl, many migrating from northern Europe, including Bewick's Swan, Whooper Swan, Teal, Bean Goose, Brent Goose, Wigeon, and Golden Plover. In the spring, several species of breeding wader can be seen: look for Lapwing tumbling overhead, listen out for the eerie drumming of snipe, and search for the scarce Black-tailed Godwit. Other scarce breeding species include the secretive Garganey (look in vegetation around pool edges), Spotted Crake and Yellow Wagtail (which favours cattle-grazed areas). Cranes occur in some east-coast sites, and their astonishing trumpeting calls can also be heard in the Somerset Levels and Moors, where they have been reintroduced. Floodwater provides protection from terrestrial predators, but not from birds of prey such as Marsh Harrier and Peregrine, which are drawn by the large numbers of waterfowl, while Barn Owl and Kestrel hunt for small mammals.

Although hundreds of plant and invertebrate species have been recorded from Grazing Marsh, the invertebrate and plant interest is mostly associated with ditches (see Ditch) rather than the grassland itself. However, Grazing Marsh supports a range of invertebrates including ground beetles, snails and the adult forms of many species (such as dragonflies) whose larval forms are aquatic. Dragonflies strongly associated with drainage ditches in Grazing Marsh are Scarce Emerald, Variable Damselfly, Norfolk Hawker, and Hairy Dragonfly (which can tolerate brackish conditions). Scarce plants such as Sea Clover, Slender Hare's-ear and Divided Sedge can be found on coastal sites where there is a brackish influence.

ABOVE: **Scarce Chaser** – found from May until early August) in lowland floodplains and water meadows in southern England. Its habitat requirements include ditches with thick emergent vegetation and nearby scrub. BELOW: **Mousetail** – a distinctive and scarce annual (flowering May–July) of seasonally flooded, poached gateways and ruts that persist on Grazing Marsh. BOTTOM LEFT: **Black-poplar** – Pollarded willows and Black-poplar, whose branches have a distinctive droopy shape, are characteristic features of floodplains. BOTTOM RIGHT: **Cuckooflower** – a distinctive spring flower often found in less improved Grazing Marsh.

UPLAND CALCAREOUS GRASSLAND

Upland Calcareous Grassland occurs mainly on limestones and basic metamorphic schists, generally above about 300 m. High rainfall means that the soils are more leached than those of Lowland Calcareous Grassland and, as a consequence, some of the more exacting calcicoles of southern grasslands are absent, while those that favour more acidic conditions, such as Mat-grass, Tormentil and even a little Heather, are found. The total area of the habitat is less than the distribution of calcareous bed-rock would indicate, as its influence is often limited by deposits of boulder clay or thick glacial drift.

The vegetation varies according to soil characteristics, climate and altitude. On Carboniferous limestone (*e.g.* the Morecambe Bay area, the Craven Dales, Upper Teesdale, The Burren and the Dartry Mountains in Co. Sligo/Leitrim), Blue Moor-grass dominates in a short, species-rich sward that includes Limestone Bedstraw and Common Rock-rose. It is typically found on skeletal soils where there is no glacial drift obscuring the underlying limestone, and can include a number of rarities. On more mature, but still fairly base-rich soils covering large areas of hillsides, less calcicolous species (*e.g.* Common Bent, Selfheal, Harebell and Glittering Wood-moss) join Sheep's-fescue and Wild Thyme. Over about 600 m in the cool, wet climate of the Lake District and the Highlands (but lower in north-west Scotland), Alpine Lady's-mantle becomes abundant, often joined by Viviparous Fescue, Pill Sedge and arctic-alpines. Species-rich swards found on more siliceous rocks, particularly in the western Highlands, are often considered with this habitat, and include tall mesotrophic herbs such as Wild Angelica, Wood Crane's-bill and Wood Avens.

Under the particular climatic conditions of the north of Scotland and The Burren, a procumbent dwarf shrub, Mountain Avens, dominates in a characteristic community with Glaucous Sedge, Sheep's-fescue, Fairy Flax, Ribwort Plantain, Sea Plantain and tufts of mosses. In places it is joined by other dwarf-shrubs such as Bearberry, Crowberry, Creeping Willow and Bell Heather. This community is found on strongly calcareous, skeletal soils and wind-blown shell sand from just above sea level to about 450 m; although found a low altitudes, it is sub-montane in character.

Similar habitats

Upland Calcareous Grassland often grades into more species-poor Upland Acid Grassland. At high altitudes the addition of Moss Campion and an array of rare arctic-alpines indicate a montane dwarf-shrub community (see High Montane Heath and Snow-bed, *page 140*), and un-grazed swards can support typical Mountain Ledge species such as Wild Angelica.

Origins and development

Most Upland Calcareous Grassland types were derived through prehistoric clearance of woodland and subsequent livestock grazing. Mountain Avens heath is a surviving example of the type of vegetation that developed across Britain on base-rich, gravelly soils left behind as the ice retreated after the last glaciation, and was subsequently out-competed by more robust herbs, and then scrub and trees. It could probably persist naturally due to exposure and the harsh climate on the north coast of Scotland, but is dependent upon grazing in more sheltered areas.

RIGT, TOP: **Yewbarrow, Cumbria** – swards of **Blue Moor-grass**, the shiny purple-blue panicles of which (BOTTOM) are conspicuous in April and May, are often on steep slopes under limestone crags, or among rocky outcrops.

Distribution and extent

Scattered across the uplands. Eng: 10,300 ha; Sco: 7,000 ha; Wal: 800 ha; NI: 1,100 ha; Ire: n/k.

Did you know?

Genetic analysis of Fringed Sandwort from Ben Bulben in Co. Sligo has shown that the species survived the last glaciation in situ.

Conservation

In common with most of the uplands, Upland Calcareous Grassland is usually heavily sheep-grazed, and many sites would benefit from a relaxation in grazing pressure. However, without grazing, most Upland Calcareous Grasslands would succeed to herb-rich Upland Mixed Ash Wood, with the loss of characteristic species. Conservation grazing with hardy cattle is used in some key areas to achieve a balance. As Mountain Avens heath is more accessible than other types of Upland Calcareous Grassland, it has suffered more from conversion to improved pasture.

What to look for

Arctic-alpines and other plants to look out for include Spring Sandwort, Hoary Whitlowgrass, Alpine Forget-me-not, Alpine Pearlwort, Shrubby Cinquefoil, Spring Gentian, and Limestone Bedstraw. Look out for Bird's-eye Primrose, Scottish Asphodel and False Sedge in flushed areas. The invertebrate fauna is not as rich as that associated with Lowland Calcareous Grassland, but in June, keep an eye out for Northern Brown Argus (the larvae feed on Common Rock-rose). Skylark, Wheatear and Lapwing nest in Upland Calcareous Grassland.

This habitat type includes the famous Teesdale assemblage of plants that is found on metamorphosed 'sugar' limestone and comprises both arctic-alpines (at only 350–353 m) and lowland species. It includes Teesdale Sandwort and Teesdale Violet (both unique to Teesdale), Spring Gentian (also found in The Burren), Hair Sedge, False Sedge, Scottish Asphodel, Alpine Bartsia (also found in the Highlands) and Dwarf Milkwort and Hoary Rock-rose (also found farther south).

*Near **Slieve Carron, Co. Clare**. The dry calcareous grasslands of The Burren support arctic-alpine species such as Spring Gentian and Mountain Avens, together with Mediterranean species like Hoary Rock-rose and Dense-flowered Orchid.*

How to recognise

Moist, dense and springy, or sparse and summer-parched over crumbly rock, Upland Calcareous Grassland comprises a sward of fine grasses such as Sheep's-fescue starred with Wild Thyme and other small herbs. In upland limestone country it is a key component of the landscape, but also occurs in patches around outcrops of basic rocks or flushed areas in siliceous landscapes. Since it is favoured by livestock, it is generally hard-grazed; so much so that in many places plants rarely flower and the short, green swards free of plant litter often stand out against the surrounding vegetation. Where grazing is less intense, its intrinsic species-richness becomes more apparent.

When to visit

May to July for flowering plants (a little earlier for Spring Gentian) before more parched swards burn off.

BELOW, TOP: **Ben Lawers, Perthshire**. In the cool, wet Highlands **Alpine Lady's-mantle** can become so abundant that the community is referred to as grass-heath rather than grassland.
BOTTOM: **Balnakiel, Sutherland** – Mountain Avens heath is now one of the rarest vegetation types in Britain and Ireland. It can contain many rarities including Scottish Primrose, Arctic Sandwort, and Dark-red Helleborine. **Mountain Avens** *Dryas octopetala* was so widespread towards the end of last glaciation, that three time periods were named Dryas after it.

Northern Hay Meadow

Northern Hay Meadow is found on brown earth soils in a cool, submontane climate on level or gently sloping sites between about 200 and 400 m where non-intensive hay meadow management has been carried out. Hay meadow vegetation can also be found along river banks and on road verges. A variety of grasses is found throughout, but none is dominant overall, and it is the abundance and diversity of herbs that is distinctive. Typical species include Sweet Vernal-grass, various lady's-mantles, Yellow-rattle, Water Avens and less common plants such as Melancholy Thistle and Globeflower. The mix of northern species (*e.g.* Wood Crane's-bill) and southern species (*e.g.* Great Burnet) is also distinctive. The best meadows support up to 120 species and around 30 species per square metre.

The flora has been shaped by the practice of hay-making and the associated grazing, liming and manuring of the sward. The regular removal of vegetation excludes more robust, coarse species that would out-compete the finer grasses and herbs. Applications of farmyard manure and lime offset the loss of nutrients and gradual leaching of the soils and maintain relatively fertile conditions. Variation between fields is common and is often due to differences in farming practices, particularly the timing of the hay cut. Although hay meadows provide abundant nectar for invertebrates, the radical change brought about by cutting is inimical to many species, and there is only a limited fauna adapted to the conditions. They can, however, provide nesting sites for birds such as Yellow Wagtail and Lapwing, and Snipe and Redshank can breed in damp flushes.

Similar habitats

The flora is similar to that found on calcareous mountain ledges, although these also contain arctic-alpines, and some characteristic species are also found in the ground flora of Upland Mixed Ash Wood.

Origins and development

Northern Hay Meadow vegetation is probably derived from the post-glacial tall-herb flora that survived in open woodland glades and which is still found on some mountain ledges. Following large-scale woodland clearance, grazing-tolerant versions of this vegetation type were able to expand, and by the Iron Age hay-making was underway. The importance of meadows in providing winter feed for livestock meant that many persisted in the landscape into the second half of the 20th century. Since then, severe losses and degradation have been as a consequence of increased use of artificial fertilizers, a switch to sheep-grazing in the winter, and conversion to silage-based systems in addition to ploughing and reseeding.

Distribution and extent

Found in upland valleys in northern England, with outliers in Scotland. Eng: 900 ha; Sco: 30 ha. The floristic composition differs from that of equivalent mountain hay meadows in Europe.

BELOW LEFT: **Dentdale, Cumbria** – a hay meadow prior to cutting. Hay is cut in the summer, often in July, and a run of dry days is required so that it can be dried on the fields.
BELOW RIGHT: The pale sward of recently cut meadows can be picked out along the valley bottom in late July (ARROWED).

Conservation

Agri-environment schemes have targeted species-rich grassland, and have perhaps helped maintain existing meadows, but have had mixed success. Expertise in improving and re-creating flower-rich meadows (*e.g.* using seed collected and spread as 'green hay') is now well-developed and current initiatives are involving the wider community in hay meadow conservation through diverse projects, events and festivals.

What to look for

Look for Bird's-eye Primrose and Grass-of-Parnassus in wet flushes. Orchids can include Early-purple Orchid, Common Spotted-orchid, Frog Orchid, Fragrant Orchid, Twayblade and Small-white Orchid. Twite can sometimes be seen feeding on seed heads.

How to recognise

Northern Hay Meadow is found within a distinctive upland landscape of small fields enclosed by stone walls, each often with its own small stone barn. Typically found in the Yorkshire Dales and parts of Durham, Cumbria and Lancashire, it occurs in valley bottoms and on shallow valley slopes, giving way to permanent pasture then open fell above. It is at its best at midsummer, when the yellow sheen of buttercups gradually sweeps along the valley bottoms, reaching the upper meadows by late June. Close-up, the knee-high sward is made up of many different textures and colours, with deep red Common Sorrel, frothy white Pignut, and vivid blue splashes of Wood Crane's-bill. After hay-making, the muted green fields are geometrically patterned with lines left by mowers and balers, and it is no longer easy to distinguish flower-rich meadows from those that are species-poor due to agricultural intensification.

When to visit

June–July for flora.

LEFT: Uncut corners are important for invertebrates and species intolerant of cutting such as the **Giant Bellflower**.
ABOVE: **Wood Crane's-bill** – an iconic species of the Yorkshire Dales hay meadows. Its cup-shaped flowers are more up-turned than those of the similar Meadow Crane's-bill.

Did you know?

The characteristic sweet scent of new hay comes from the coumarin found in Sweet Vernal-grass, which is widely used in perfumes, nowadays in synthesised form.

UPLAND RUSH PASTURE

Upland Rush Pasture is found on soils kept permanently moist by ground or surface water in the upland fringes up to about 400 m. Farther north it is found at lower altitudes, and is common in the Inner Hebrides, but scarce in the Highlands. It usually comprises a grassy sward dotted with varying amounts of Soft Rush and (particularly in the west) Sharp-flowered Rush. Hard Rush is also found where the habitat occurs on limestone (*e.g.* the north Pennines and Craven Dales). Rushes can form separate tussocks or thick swards. The underlying grasses, which can be heavily grazed, include Yorkshire-fog, Creeping Bent, Red Fescue and Sweet Vernal-grass, and there is often a little Creeping Buttercup and other mesophytic herbs such as Common Sorrel and White Clover. On more acidic, peaty soils, Marsh Bedstraw may twine through the rushes. On drier soils, the grassy understorey can resemble Upland Acid Grassland or improved grassland.

Upland Rush Pasture is most notable for the distinctive suite of breeding waders it can support. Curlew, Redshank, Snipe, Lapwing and Oystercatcher all breed where there is a suitable mosaic of rushy tussocks and shorter grassier patches, but each species requires slightly different conditions: for esample, Snipe needs tall, rushy tussocks and damp ground; Lapwing is found in shorter swards and slightly drier conditions; while Redshank prefers short swards with tussocky areas for nesting.

Similar habitats

Upland Rush Pasture is often found on the edge of the fells between improved pasture (or Northern Hay Meadow) on flatter ground in valley bottoms and Upland Acid Grassland above the limit of improved grazing. It supports some of the same vegetation types as its lowland counterpart, Purple Moor-grass and Rush Pasture.

Origins and development

Ultimately derived from woodland through clearance and then heavy grazing of the ensuing heathland, Upland Rush Pasture is dependent upon grazing. In many cases, Upland Rush Pasture has been converted through drainage to Upland Acid Grassland, and through subsequent liming and fertilizing to Perennial Rye-grass–Crested Dog's-tail swards. Agricultural intensification after the 1950s, and particularly increases in stocking densities, resulted in a significant decline in the populations of Lapwing, Curlew and Redshank, and the local loss of Snipe.

Conservation

Conservation management of Upland Rush Pastures revolves around ensuring appropriate cover of rushes for breeding waders, usually using light cattle-grazing. Where rushes become too widespread, open areas needed for feeding are lost (and suitability for grazing animals, which maintain the sward, decreases) but where tussocks are very sparse, not enough cover is available for nesting. Swards are often topped in late July, after chicks have fledged, to help prevent the spread of rushes.

What to look for

In addition to breeding waders, look out for Little Owl, which sometimes breeds in stone barns. Merlin, associated with nearby heathland, can occasionally be seen hunting for pipits.

Distribution and extent

Ubiquitous through the uplands. Extents are for Upland Acid Grassland and Rush Pasture combined. Eng: 376,000 ha; Sco: 903,000 ha; Wal: 137,300 ha; NI: 9,700 ha; Ire: n/k.

Dentdale, Cumbria – tightly sheep-grazed Upland Rush Pasture in early spring.

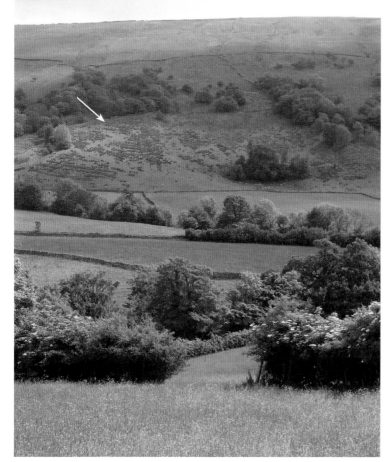

The stippled brown of rush clumps marks out Upland Rush Pasture mid-slope (ARROWED), with Northern Hay Meadow below and Upland Acid Grassland above.

How to recognise

Upland Rush Pasture is the rather degraded, tussocky grassland found on poorly drained hillsides in the upland fringes where it forms a key part of upland agricultural systems, providing relatively accessible year-round pasture. It may be cattle-grazed, although sheep are now more common.

Within (and sometimes beyond) enclosure walls, clumps or patches of rushes stand proud of the often quite closely cropped grassy sward, and this coarse texture makes it easy to differentiate from the more 'improved' pasture or meadow found lower down the valley sides. The vegetation is a brighter green than the Upland Acid Grassland often found just beyond the walls, and lacks mosses and plant litter. Upland Rush Pasture is of limited wildlife interest, but the best swards can support breeding waders and in spring the calls of Redshank, Lapwing and Curlew are a characteristic feature.

When to visit

March–June for breeding waders.

BELOW, TOP: **Redshank** probes damp ground for insects and earthworms. Its distinctive piping call can be heard in the upland fringes, although it is more commonly seen in its wintering grounds on estuaries and coastal lagoons.

BOTTOM: **Curlew** – easily recognised by its long, down-curved bill, evocative call, and distinctive display flight over breeding grounds in spring.

Gruinart, Islay – sheep grazing rush pasture at sea level.

Upland Acid Grassland

Upland Acid Grassland includes short, smooth swards of fine grasses, rich in mosses, and thick tussocky vegetation with rushes or Purple Moor-grass. It is generally found over sandstones, acid igneous rocks or superficial sands and gravels. The specific vegetation type is generally determined by the soil characteristics and grazing pressure. On mildly acidic brown earths on the steep lower slopes of hillsides, Sheep's-fescue and Common Bent grasses (or Bristle Bent in the south-west) are usually shorn by sheep, speckled in summer with the tiny flowers of Tormentil and Heath Bedstraw, and springy with branched mosses such as Cypress-leaved Plait-moss, Red-stemmed Feather-moss and Springy Turf-moss. On the moist, peaty mineral soils of shallower slopes or on degraded bog, short, dense swards of bristly and unpalatable Mat-grass are widespread. Where the climate is cooler and the peat deeper, Mat-grass is replaced by a distinctive longer and looser sward of Heath Rush and Common Hair-cap moss with bog-mosses in the wettest places. Patches of taller rushes are common where moderate slopes are wet throughout the year. On the peaty hillsides of the western upland fringes, tussocky Purple Moor-grass covers huge areas; this vegetation can be quite acid and boggy, and include Upland Wet Heath species.

Similar habitats

This habitat is linked to the heathland and wetland communities from which it is derived, and may often show transitional characteristics where grazing pressure is reduced. Where soils become base-rich it can merge with forms of Upland Calcareous Grassland, distinguished by the presence of calcicoles such as Wild Thyme, Harebell, Fairy Flax and Quaking-grass.

Origins and development

Upland Acid Grassland is generally derived from heathland and mire through livestock grazing and often also burning and draining. The increasing predominance of sheep from the 18th century onwards resulted in an increase in the habitat, which continued with the promotion of high stocking rates through agricultural subsidies in the late 20th century. The loss of mixed grazing regimes saw further changes, with an increase in Mat-grass (unpalatable to sheep but eaten by cattle). More recently a change in incentives has seen some decreases in stocking levels, and localised return of heathland species.

Distribution and extent

Ubiquitous throughout the uplands. Map shows all upland grassland (of which acid grassland is by far the most abundant). Extents are for Upland Acid Grassland and Rush Pasture combined. Eng: 376,000 ha; Sco: 903,000 ha; Wal: 137,300 ha; NI: 9,700 ha; Ire: n/k. There is similar vegetation in Europe, although particular communities are unique to Britain and Ireland.

ABOVE: Looking south-west from **Catbells, Cumbria** – Upland Acid Grassland forms vast areas of rough grazing in the Lake District, where it is much appreciated both as a key part of the landscape and for its amenity value.
LEFT: **Northern Glyders, Snowdonia** – Upland Acid Grassland covers huge areas of upland Wales, where grass-heath mosaics are thought to indicate the impact on Upland Dry Heath of recent increases in sheep numbers.

ABOVE LEFT: **Rise Hill, Yorkshire Dales** – the pale sheen of Mat-grass contrasts with the brown Heather that is recolonising the less-grazed steep slope following a reduction in overall grazing pressure. ABOVE RIGHT: **Whernside, Yorkshire Dales** – Heath Rush and Common Hair-cap moss with patches of Hare's-tail Cottongrass in a sward that is transitional to Blanket Bog.

Conservation

This habitat is valued as part of a cultural landscape resulting from centuries of upland farming. However, with the exception of species-rich variants in flushed conditions, it is usually of less wildlife interest than the habitats it replaces, and is only protected where it falls within sites supporting other vegetation types of conservation interest. Given its ubiquity and impoverished nature, and the reliance on agricultural subsidies to support the upland farming practices that maintain it, there is increasing interest in modifying grazing and burning regimes to restore heathland or even woodland.

What to look for

Species-rich flushes with Globeflower (INSET BELOW) and Grass-of-Parnassus; waxcap fungi on short swards; Mountain Ringlet in the Lake District and Highlands; sparse populations of breeding Curlew and Snipe in tussocky areas; Black Grouse (Wales, Pennines, Scotland) in mosaics with heathland and Mixed Scrub or Coniferous Plantation.

How to recognise

Great swathes of the hill-country of Britain and Ireland are dominated by rather dull Acid Grassland that nonetheless contributes to the overall diversity of the upland landscape.

Beyond the limit of inbye walls, the mossy tones of these unimproved swards contrast with the more luminous green of improved pasture below and (where these are still present) the browner tones of Blanket Bog or the more intense purple-brown of Heather above.

This is an impoverished habitat, but the wide open spaces are heart-lifting, and in summer there is the distinctive mossy, peaty tang of the uplands in the air, while the sound of Skylark and Meadow Pipit is never far away. In spring, the bubbling song of Curlew is still common.

When to visit

Early summer for waders, midsummer for Mountain Ringlet, autumn for waxcaps.

Did you know?

The Heath Rush community has developed through a long history of grazing and burning in an oceanic climate and is thought unique to Britain and Ireland.

*View from **Knoutberry Hill, Yorkshire Dales** – Cloudberries (known locally as Knoutberries) have long since been grazed away, and the landscape is patterned with Upland Acid Grassland, Upland Rush Pasture, Blanket Bog and Coniferous Plantation. A little Upland Dry Heath persists on the railway cutting.*

CALAMINARIAN GRASSLAND

The ecology of Calaminarian Grassland is driven by soil chemistry. High concentrations of toxic heavy metals (commonly lead, copper and zinc), usually as a consequence of mining, result in a sward that is often very sparse and quite species-poor. Discarded minerals such as fluorspar, calcite, and barites present in spoil heaps also influence the vegetation, and overall it can be quite varied within (and between) sites, occurring in a mosaic with other vegetation types associated with the parent rock. Zinc is the most challenging metal for plants, and is often present as a waste product at lead mines (*e.g.* in North Wales and the Pennines). Tin and copper mines also support Calaminarian Grassland (*e.g.* in Cornwall) and near-natural examples of this habitat type are found on skeletal soils rich in nickel, chromium and cobalt

A distinctive suite of metal-tolerant vascular plants is found in Calaminarian Grassland and can include Moonwort, Pyrenean Scurvygrass, Spring Sandwort and Alpine Pennycress. Some species, such as Thrift and Bladder Campion, have particular genetically adapted forms that occur in Calaminarian Grassland. Areas of bare ground offer suitable habitat for stress-tolerant lichens and liverworts, including Greater Copperwort and other rare threadworts. Widespread plants such as Sheep's-fescue, Harebell and Wild Thyme are common, while other less common species like Fragrant and Frog Orchid can benefit from the general paucity of plant minerals that prevents other more robust species from become established.

Similar habitats

Transitions tend to be fairly clearly demarcated, but occur with upland grasslands (particularly calcareous), heathland and some montane habitats.

Origins and development

Mines at Calaminarian Grassland sites often date back to Roman times, and many were subsequently more extensively exploited in the 19th century, meaning that much of the habitat is of recent origin. Natural sites may be far older, as the toxicity of the heavy metals tends to hold back succession, allowing a grassland sward to persist, and many are in any case grazed. In some places Calaminarian Grassland communities may have occurred naturally on rock that has since been quarried away, and now only persist on spoil heaps. In a handful of rivers, such as the Tyne and Allen in northern England, heavy metals from mine-washes have accumulated in exposed river shingle that supports Calaminarian Grassland species.

Distribution and extent

Widely distributed in diverse locations.
Eng: 200 ha; Sco: 80 ha; Wal: 50 ha; Ire: 10 ha (ANN I REP). Approximately 29% of Europe's designated Calaminarian grasslands are in the UK.

LEFT: **Greenhurth Mine, Upper Teesdale** – bare ground often indicates areas where metal levels are high and it is difficult for plants to grow, but species such as **Alpine Pennycress** (CENTRE) can survive here. RIGHT: **Cwmystwyth, Ceredigion** – spoil heaps, screes and rocky outcrops have been colonised by heavy-metal tolerant plants including the rare Lead Moss. Mining waste has helped shape Shingle Heath on river gravel downstream.

LEFT: **Glen Isla, Caenlochan** – open serpentine debris on the plateau supports species such as **Alpine Catchfly** (TOP RIGHT). BOTTOM RIGHT: **Spring Sandwort** is a good indicator of Calaminarian Grassland (although it also occurs in parched calcareous grassland); its local name in Derbyshire is 'leadwort'.

How to recognise

Calaminarian Grassland is a strange habitat, where rare and specialised plants grow among spoil heaps and the derelict paraphernalia of mine-workings. It can be found in obviously post-industrial landscapes, but also where old diggings have softened with time into gently undulating grassland.

It is always limited in extent, but sometimes sites follow distinct lines in the landscape (called rakes in the Peak District), reflecting the mineral veins where mining activity was focussed. In a few places, serpentine rock and mineral veins support near-natural Calaminarian Grassland, but this is very restricted in distribution, found mainly in the Scottish Highlands and Islands. Stable, exposed riverine sediments also support Calaminarian plant communities, although in some cases this is a result of mining activity within the catchment.

Conservation

Many Calaminarian Grassland sites have strong historical and cultural links that make each site unique, and management needs to be sensitive to the particular conditions and history at each location. Sites tend to be very small, often in a mosaic with other habitats, and this can lead to problems protecting them and ensuring appropriate management. Scrub control and grazing is used in some cases to prevent succession that would result in the loss of characteristic plant species. Threats include agricultural improvement and reworking for minerals.

What to look for

Scarce species to look out for include Northern Rock-cress, Forked Spleenwort and Young's Helleborine. Northern sites support boreal species such as Arctic Sandwort and the endemic Shetland Mouse-ear. Lower plant enthusiasts will find a suite of rare and specialist species.

When to visit

Most of the speciality plants can be seen flowering between June and July.

Did you know?

Calaminarian Grassland is named after Zinc Violet Viola calaminaria, which is characteristic of metalliferous soils in continental Europe.

Gang Mine, Derbyshire – the undulating topography of spoil heaps and old mine shafts is clearly visible.

MOUNTAINS

Mountains are forced into being as the earth's surface shifts, and in Britain and Ireland are ancient stumps of a range once as huge as the Himalaya. Sculpted by numerous ice ages and constantly eroded and weathered, they are now patchily covered with a thin layer of hardy vegetation and sparsely inhabited by some of our rarest wildlife. Mountains are generally defined as peaks that extend at least 600 m above their surroundings, although some lower peaks are montane in character. They can occur as single, isolated peaks (such as Suilven in Assynt), but are more often found as part of a range (such as the Cairngorms). Above the natural limit of tree growth is the montane (or alpine) zone. This usually starts at around 600–700 m above sea level, although montane vegetation is found at lower altitudes in more exposed situations (*e.g.* from around 300 m in northern Scotland). Above 900 m, mountains support particularly specialised communities of plants and animals. There are around 300 such peaks in Britain and Ireland, the majority of which are in Scotland, with a handful in each of Ireland, North Wales and the English Lake District.

ORIGINS

Our mountains have been shaped by immense geological forces over huge time periods. The oldest rocks are Lewisian Gneiss and Torridian Sandstone (around 3,000 million and 1,500 million years old respectively). These are found in Wester Ross and Sutherland in Scotland, which were once part of the ancient continent of Laurentia that included much of North America. When Laurentia collided with the European continental plate 300–400 million years ago, the Caledonide mountains were thrust up. The north and central Highlands are the worn down stumps of these mountains that stretched into North Wales and parts of northern and western Ireland. Volcanic activity resulted in vast areas of granite, which formed mountains such as the Cairngorms and those of Donegal. During the same period, the sediments of the ocean floor were uplifted and now form the Southern Uplands of Scotland and parts of Northern Ireland. In south-west Ireland, material eroded from the Caledonides built up into layers of sandstone, which were forced up into mountains some 250 million years ago when another collision of continents occurred. This collision also caused folding and faulting in the Pennines and created the granitic uplands of southern England. During the ice ages that followed, glaciers sculpted the landscape, carving out corries and scoring deep 'U'-shaped valleys.

The current interglacial started about 11,500 years ago. Open tundra-like vegetation spread from the unglaciated south and included arctic plants such as Mountain Avens, Crowberry and Dwarf Willow, with scattered

The distinctive peaks of **Inverpolly, Assynt**, are formed of Torridian Sandstone. A capping of hard Cambrian Quartzite prevented them from being eroded down to the underlying Lewisian Gneiss, one of the oldest rocks in the world that forms the cnoc and lochan landscape surrounding them.

Common Juniper and Dwarf Birch. A rich tall-herb community followed on the raw, lime-rich soils but gave way to woodland as tree species colonised. However, woodland was prevented by climatic conditions from ascending beyond about 800 m, a limit known as the tree-line. This limit has fluctuated with climatic variation, and is now considered to be at around 700 m. It is also dependent upon geography, occurring much lower in exposed northern or western situations (*e.g.* about 500 m in Ireland). Above the tree line tundra-like habitats were able to persist, but progressive leaching of the soils created more acidic conditions than were initially found, and the tall herb and scrub communities became restricted to calcareous rocks, whilst acid-loving dwarf-shrubs became widespread.

TYPES OF MOUNTAIN HABITAT

Montane habitats are generally found on peaks, ridges, high plateaux, boulder fields and steep-sided corrie walls. They are characterised by low-growing perennial

Ingleborough, North Yorkshire (723 m). The high hills of the northern Pennines are formed of Carboniferous Limestone often capped with Millstone Grit, sedimentary rocks tough enough to stand proud of the surrounding landscape but also sculpted by glaciers. Although not usually considered to be mountains, the highest peaks of these hills support montane vegetation including rare arctic-alpine species.

HABITAT	DESCRIPTION
Montane Dwarf-shrub Heath *page 136*	Low growing heath of montane dwarf-shrubs such as Mountain Crowberry and Arctic Bearberry.
High Montane Heath and Snow-bed *page 140*	Moss, sedge and rush heath found on very exposed shoulders, plateaux and summits; mossy communities found under melting snow-beds.
Mountain Ledge *page 144*	Lush herb-rich vegetation protected from grazing on moist mountain ledges.
Montane Scrub *page 146*	Low-growing scrub of montane willows or Common Juniper found in un-grazed locations, often on mountain ledges. Also includes Dwarf Birch scrub that is found on blanket mire at lower altitudes.

woody dwarf-shrubs and dwarf-herbs with mosses and bryophytes, grasses, sedges and rushes, and can cover extensive areas. Shrubs and tall herbs are found on mountain ledges and moist, sheltered un-grazed areas, and are far more limited in extent and distribution. Rocky habitats that are too unstable or steep for a continuous cover of vegetation to become established and for soil to develop, are also very widespread and common on mountains – these are considered in detail in a separate section (see Rocky Habitats *page 148*). Montane forms of wetland habitats, particularly Upland Spring and Flush and Blanket Bog, and grassland habitats are also found on mountains (see Grasslands *page 100* and Wetlands *page 160*).

THREATS AND ISSUES

Montane habitats are vulnerable to climate change. They can only become more limited in extent as conditions warm, and it seems likely that some iconic mountain species, together with their lesser known associates, will be lost to Britain and Ireland. Montane vegetation has also been affected by atmospheric pollution, which has particularly impacted on high-altitude moss-heath (mosses gain most of their nutrients from rain and the air, and deteriorate rapidly if nitrogen levels are too high). Overgrazing is having a significant impact on much mountain habitat, reducing the ability of more palatable plants to reproduce and maintain themselves, and impacting on vegetation structure. Recreational pressure can be an issue along popular paths and climbing routes.

CULTURAL IMPORTANCE

Mountains were considered as bleak, forbidding places by early travellers. However, they became more appreciated during the Romantic era in the first half of the 19th century and mountaineering took off at about the same time. Mountains are now greatly valued for a variety of reasons including the beauty of the landscape, the wildlife they support and the recreational opportunities they offer – evoking as they do a unique sense of wilderness.

CONSERVATION IMPORTANCE AND PROTECTION

The oceanic climate of Britain and Ireland, with its cool summers, mild winters and abundant rain and wind, makes our mountain habitats distinctive. They also occur at lower altitudes than elsewhere in Europe. Nationally, they are greatly valued as examples of climax or near-natural communities that are otherwise rare in Britain and Ireland, where almost all habitats have a long history of modification by humans. Botanical excursions to explore the mountain flora started in the 19th century, but mountain habitats were not among those first protected by the fledgling conservation movement, and some were initially protected by virtue of their association with other habitats, such as Caledonian Forest, rather than in their own right. However, many mountains are now protected as SSSIs or equivalent,

The rolling, granite plateau of the **Cairngorms** (LEFT) contrasts with the steep-sided valleys, narrow ridges and shattered peaks of Moine schists in the **western Highlands** (RIGHT). Glacial action was more severe in the west where greater snowfall meant that glaciers were deeper and flowed faster.

and are designated as SACs for their alpine, boreal, and sub-arctic communities. Unfortunately, the majority of these sites are not currently considered to be in favourable condition for nature conservation, largely due to overgrazing. Projects to exclude sheep and deer from remnant patches of Montane Scrub and Mountain Ledge habitat have proved successful in reducing grazing damage, although regeneration remains an issue for scrub. The challenge facing conservationists is how to reduce grazing pressure over large areas to make montane habitats more robust in the face of climate change.

KEY ELEMENTS

The primary factors influencing montane habitats are climatic and relate to altitude and topography. Temperature drops by 0·6°C with every 100 m increase in altitude, so the growing season is shorter and snow lies longer higher up. Humidity increases too, as relatively warm, moist air rises up the windward side of a mountain and cools until the moisture condenses and falls as rain or snow. Conditions on mountains are also windier because wind speed increases as air density decreases with height and away from obstacles causing friction. These environmental gradients result in a marked vegetational zonation from upland heathland to Montane Dwarf-shrub Heath then High Montane Heath. While it is usually necessary to climb above about 700 m to find montane heath, it occurs much lower in exposed locations (which can make it easier to reach). Look for High Montane Heath on very exposed, high shoulders, ridges, peaks and plateaux. Look out for north- or east-facing corries and hollows that may shelter snow-beds and the local zonation of vegetation found around them. Grazing is another factor, as both Mountain Ledge vegetation and Montane Scrub are highly sensitive to grazing, and were probably more widespread on suitable substrates before the rise of sheep farming and deer estates. Anywhere out of reach of grazing animals, including steep slopes, is always worth investigating. However, the classic, calcareous tall-herb ledge community is only found on basic rock in moist conditions, and is unlikely to be encountered by chance. Similarly, Montane Scrub is, on the whole, so restricted in distribution that it is necessary to visit a known site.

FURTHER INFORMATION

Scrubbers Bulletin, an occasional publication produced by the Montane Scrub Action Group and hosted on the Highland Birchwoods website

The Nature of The Cairngorms: Diversity in a Changing Environment. The Natural Heritage of Scotland Series. Shaw, P., Thompson, D. (TSO, 2006)

Hostile Habitats – Scotland's Mountain Environment: A Hillwalkers' Guide to Wildlife and the Landscape. Wrightam, M. & Kempe, N. (Scottish Mountaineering Trust, 2006)

A rare example of a natural tree-line at **Creag Fhiaclach in the Cairngorms**. In Britain and Ireland, natural transitions from woodland to montane vegetation are incredibly rare, as prehistoric tree clearance followed by a deterioration in the climate and a long history of grazing and burning has eliminated trees and scrub at altitudes where the transition might be expected to occur. Instead, a more subtle transition between upland heathland or grassland and montane communities is generally found.

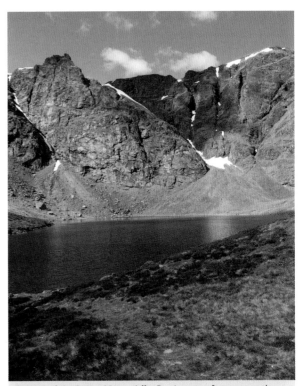

Coire Ardair, Creag Meagaidh. Corries are often on north- or east-facing slopes. The shadier conditions of hollows on these slopes meant that snow accumulated and, over thousands of years, formed glacier ice. This scraped out the rock and deposited debris on the lip, enlarging the corrie (called cwm in Wales). When the ice melted, a tarn often formed in the bottom of the hollow. The moist, sheltered conditions and protection from grazing animals means that corrie walls can be hot-spots for arctic-alpine plants. They are also used for winter ice-climbing.

Key Mountain Areas

1 Macgillycuddy's Reeks

2 Snowdonia

3 Lake District

4 Cuillin Hills

5 Foinaven & Ben Hope

6 Hoy

7 Shetland

8 Monadhliath

9 Central Highlands

10 Cairngorms

KEY

▲ Peak over 900 m

The map shows mountain habitats and peaks of 900 m or more. Mountain habitats are most extensive in Scotland, but also occur in the Lake District, the northern Pennines and south-west Ireland.

Some key mountain blocks are labelled on the map; this selection is not intended to be exhaustive but highlights a few of the most important areas.

MONTANE DWARF-SHRUB HEATH

Montane Dwarf-shrub Heath is one of very few natural climax communities in Britain and Ireland, its structure and flora being determined almost entirely by climate and topography. It is generally found on stony, acidic and well-drained soils above the potential altitudinal limit of woodland at around 600 m (500 m in Ireland), but descends almost to sea level in the extreme north-west of Scotland. It is also found where glacial moraine breaks through Blanket Bog in exposed locations. Some plant communities that occur on only a few high peaks in the Highlands form the southernmost outposts of tundra vegetation. Others are more widespread across the Scottish uplands, with outliers in the Lake District, northern Pennines and North Wales. The transition from woodland to Montane Dwarf-shrub Heath has largely been eliminated by woodland clearance and subsequent grazing, but the transition from Montane to High Montane Heaths is generally intact.

Montane Heath vegetation is quite diverse, showing clear altitudinal gradients and variation between oceanic and continental conditions. For example, Heather gives way to Bilberry with increasing snow-lie and abundant lichens are characteristic of the drier eastern heaths, while Woolly Fringe-moss and a suite of rare Atlantic liverworts are found in the more oceanic west.

Similar habitats

Moorland habitats also hold similar species but Montane Dwarf-shrub Heath can be distinguished from these by the prostrate growth form of dwarf shrubs and the presence of arctic-alpine species. High Montane Heath lacks abundant dwarf-shrubs.

Origins and development

Montane Heath is a natural (or near-natural) community maintained by harsh climatic conditions. Unlike most heaths it is not dependent upon some form of anthropogenic disturbance to prevent succession to other vegetation types, and is easily damaged by grazing and burning. In North Wales and northern England, a loss of lichen and bryophytes and corresponding increase in grasses has been attributed to nitrogen deposition and overgrazing.

Distribution and extent

Found mainly in the Scottish Highlands, with examples in other northern and western uplands. Eng: 1,200 ha; Sco: 41,000 ha; Wal: 30 ha; NI: 80 ha; Ire: 17,000 ha (ANN I REP). Similar habitat is found in Scandinavia, but oceanic bryophyte-rich versions are unique to Britain and Ireland.

ABOVE: In the north-west Highlands, **Dwarf Juniper** (a subspecies of Common Juniper) can form a continuous mat ('Juniper heath') that provides shelter for oceanic liverworts. It is very sensitive to fire, and may have once been more widespread, forming a continuum with more upright forms of Common Juniper in the east. LEFT: **Cul Mor, Assynt** – here, prostrate Heather forms a low sward with Bilberry, Fir Clubmoss and Woolly Fringe-moss on a stony plateau at about 600 m.

High Spy, Lake District – transitional Heather-Bilberry heath at around 600 m showing prostrate growth forms but no arctic-alpine species.

Creag Meagaidh, central Highlands – wind-shorn Mountain Crowberry with patches of pale Woolly Fringe-moss and spikes of Fir Clubmoss between boulders on the mountain plateau at around 850 m.

How to recognise

This is a distinctive habitat of high, exposed mountain spurs and ridges where fierce winds sweep away winter snow and expose vegetation to bitter, prolonged frosts. Prostrate forms of Heather and Bilberry only a hand span high hug the ground, which can be thick with spongy reindeer lichens and mosses. In very exposed places wind erosion creates patches of bare ground and the vegetation forms in parallel strips aligned with the prevailing wind. Although the vegetation may change gradually and subtly as it reaches the montane zone, at this altitude the magnitude of the landscape, its vastness and silence, and the overriding power of nature, are awe-inspiring and unmistakable.

When to visit

Summer months for arctic-alpine flora and breeding Dotterel, winter for Ptarmigan in its white plumage.

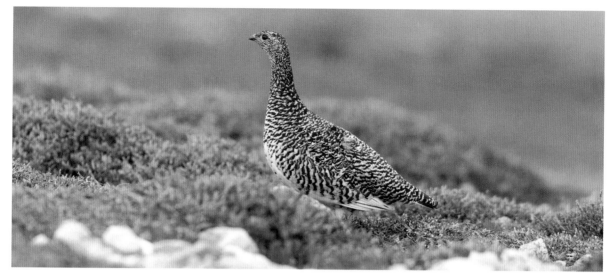

Conservation

Montane Heath is greatly valued as one of a series of montane habitats that together form the most extensive areas of natural vegetation in Britain and Ireland. The factors that need addressing are mainly the systemic issues of pollution and climate change rather than local management issues, although a reduction in grazing and the prevention of burning would be beneficial. Montane Heath can also be affected by trampling, as walkers often favour the ridges and spurs that support this habitat.

What to look for

In the eastern Highlands, look out for small arctic-alpines such as Mountain Crowberry, Bog Bilberry and Alpine and Fir Clubmosses in lichen-rich heath of prostrate Heather spiked with Stiff Sedge. Farther west, Dwarf Juniper, Alpine Bearberry and Trailing Azalea may be seen. On cold and wet rocky slopes, boulder fields and exposed ridges in the west of Scotland and North Wales, where the weather systems create an extreme oceanic climate (mild and wet), a community found nowhere else in the world supports rare Atlantic bryophytes. In steep, shaded places on moist peaty soils, look for Cloudberry and Dwarf Cornel growing with large, branched mosses. This community is more widespread, and can be found as far south as the Cheviots and North Wales.

Montane Heath in Scotland provides habitat for Ptarmigan and Dotterel (which also nests on High Montane Heath). Ptarmigan breeds in montane habitats and is a year-round resident, moving down to the forest edge in particularly harsh weather. A distinctive croak is often heard long before the bird is seen exploding up from behind nearby rocks. A small population of Snow Bunting breeds in Britain, joined by Arctic breeders over the winter. Look for these tough songbirds searching for insects among mountain-top lichens. Dotterel is harder to see, but a few hundred still breed on high plateaux among montane mosses, feeding on craneflies and spiders. After the first snow-melt in spring, look out for Mountain Hare, whose white winter coat stands out against the dark background.

Montane invertebrates are restricted by the extremes of microclimate and the limited number of plant species. Characteristic species are highly adapted, and populations may be long-standing. Several are very rare, and there are probably undiscovered species. In the Cairngorms, look out for the striking red-and-black Scotch Burnet (June–July). This moth hides amongst vegetation in poor weather, but in sunshine it can be seen flying close to the ground among flowers such as Mountain Everlasting.

TOP: **Ptarmigan** is seasonally camouflaged, moulting its snowy white feathers at the end of winter. It is thought that crows, attracted to the high tops by rubbish left behind by mountain walkers, are predating Ptarmigan chicks. MIDDLE: **Trailing Azalea** (Scotland only) can colour well-drained, exposed slopes a gentle pink when in flower, and individual plants may live for 50 years or more. Such long-lived woody plants can be irreparably damaged by a clumsily placed boot. BOTTOM: The distinctive leaf and five-petalled flower of **Cloudberry** is often found on upper slopes that face north-west or east and where snow lies relatively late into year.

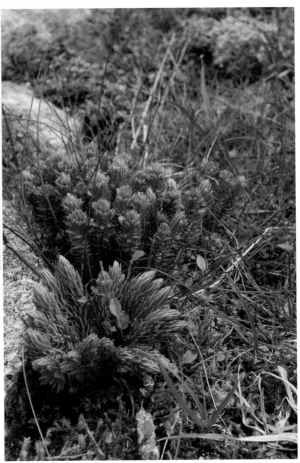

ABOVE: Male **Dotterel** are less brightly coloured than females, and have the job of incubation and chick rearing. Females sometimes leave the area and breed with a different male before returning to north Africa for the winter. RIGHT: **Fir Clubmoss** growing in a short sward of Stiff Sedge, Bilberry and Viviparous Fescue. Clubmosses belong to the most ancient group of land plants.

Did you know?
The impacts of climate change combined with atmospheric nitrogen deposition are likely to lead to a reduction in the range of arctic-alpine species.

Beinn Eighe, Wester Ross, supports the largest area of Juniper heath in Britain. This type of montane heath is unique to Britain and Ireland.

HIGH MONTANE HEATH AND SNOW-BED

High montane communities are determined by altitude and topography and further shaped by climate. With increasing altitude the snow lies for longer and the growing season is shorter, dwarf-shrubs give way to grass-heath, moss-heath, sedge-heath and rush-heath, and ultimately to snow-bed communities reminiscent of arctic tundra.

On the high summits, blasted free of snow by freezing, desiccating winds in winter and scorched by sun in the summer, only a handful of well-adapted species can survive. In the oceanic west, moss-heath dominated by Woolly Fringe-moss covers large areas. In the colder, drier east and central Highlands, where most precipitation falls as snow, this moss-heath is replaced by sedge-heath. As the environment becomes more extreme over about 1,000 m, sparse rush-heath grows on loose gravel around rocks.

Where snow is caught in hollows and against the headwalls of north- and east-facing corries, snow-bed communities are found. The snow insulates the vegetation from the worst of the weather, but deeper snow cuts off light for all but a few weeks of the year. Flowering plants need about three months to grow, flower and set seed, so only mosses and liverworts can survive where the snow lasts longest. An extensive snow-bed will have several communities, from grass-heath under the early melting snow around the outside, to colourful patches of mosses and liverworts under late-melting snow in the centre.

Similar habitats

Transitions to Montane Dwarf-shrub Heath and upland grasslands occur at lower altitudes. Snow-beds can include Upland Spring and Flush and northern hepatic mat (see Upland Dry Heath, *page 94*) communities.

Origins and development

In most cases high montane vegetation types are natural climax communities maintained through harsh conditions. Those communities dependent upon snow-lie are particularly vulnerable to climate change, and snow patch longevity is already declining. Rush-heath is not dependent on snow-lie and may be more resilient. Snow-beds in particular are damaged by atmospheric depositions. The impacts of grazing can interact with pollution in damaging vulnerable species such as Woolly Fringe-moss and result in the impoverished montane vegetation typical of the Lake District and Snowdonia.

Distribution and extent

Largely confined to the Scottish Highlands, with outliers in the Lake District, north-west Wales and the north Pennines. Eng: 1,100 ha; Sco: 70,700 ha; Wal: 90 ha; NI: 60 ha (ANN I REP).

BELOW LEFT: **Beinn Eighe, Wester Ross** – a thick mat of Woolly Fringe-moss and other bryophytes spiked with Stiff Sedge and Viviparous Fescue carpets broad ridges. Britain probably holds more moss-heath than anywhere else in the world.

BELOW RIGHT: **Beinn Eighe, Wester Ross** – the location of snow-beds in winter can often be identified by the vegetation in summer. In this case, grass-heath and sedge-heath indicate an early melting snow-bed, with the pale Mat-grass sward giving way to Stiff Sedge and bryophytes where drainage is more impeded.

Bright apple-green patches of **Mountain Thread-moss** are visible from a distance, and indicate the presence of springs.

Conservation

Huge challenges are presented by the threat of climate change in particular, and iconic montane species are likely to become extinct in Britain and Ireland. A reduction in sheep and deer grazing and trampling would increase the resilience of High Montane Heath to atmospheric pollution and climate change.

Cairngorm plateau – where water flow is impeded by frozen ground, saturated soil creeps gradually down the slope (solifluction), resulting in distinctive patterned mosaics of Three-cornered Rush (note the rills in the central hollow – see Upland Spring and Flush, page 174)

see Upland Spring and Flush, page 174

How to recognise

On the highest cols, shoulders and plateaux of mountains, the fierce winter wind scours away the snow, exposing the thin skin of vegetation to bitter and prolonged frosts. Only a sparse layer of brownish sedge and rush or silver-grey moss persists, patterned by frost-heave or solifluction and sometimes stretching for miles. In gullies, hollows and corries the wind carries the snow into deep drifts that remain well into the summer months, gradually melting to reveal a miniature community of mosses and liverworts where the snow was deepest. Incredibly rare and specialist species inhabit this stark landscape, and while challenging terrain and weather mean it is hard to reach, the remote beauty of one of Britain's wildest and most natural habitats makes the effort well worthwhile.

When to visit

The summer months once most of the snow has melted.

Did you know?
Some snow-bed communities are the last relics of genuine late-glacial vegetation.

LEFT: **Cairngorm plateau** – extending for miles, tufty orange-brown tussocks of Three-leaved Rush are interspersed with stony ground and large crustose lichens and mosses or a little Bilberry and Dwarf Willow.

FACING PAGE, TOP RIGHT: **Snow Bunting** feed on craneflies that emerge after the spring snow-melt. They also forage for insects blown up by the breeze from lower down the hillside and caught on the surface of the snow. These insects also provide prey for spiders that migrate to snow-beds to feed on them. INSET BELOW: **Mountain Ringlet** can be found on grassland from about 300 m up to the montane zone. It has a low, fluttering flight and is only active in sunny conditions, although it can be disturbed from the ground. Mountain Ringlets form discrete colonies, and can be seen in their hundreds at the best sites.

What to look for

A suite of small and rare arctic-alpine vascular plants, mosses and liverworts is found in High Montane Heathsand Snow-bed. On grass-heath look out for Alpine Clubmoss, Iceland Moss (a foliose lichen) and conspicuous cushions of the distinctive pale blue-grey liverwort Alpine Silverwort that

Creag Meagaidh, Central Highlands – a bryophyte community revealed in early June as the snow melts.

indicate places where icy water trickles slowly from springs. In snow-bed vegetation, look for rare rock-mosses, Dwarf Willow, Alpine Hair-grass, Starry Saxifrage and Dwarf Cudweed. Mosses such as Northern Haircap, Starke's Forkmoss and Bristly Fringe-moss can support a crust of tiny specialist liverworts.

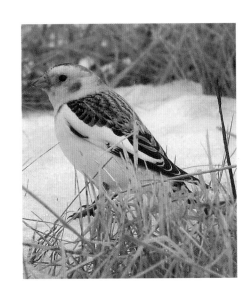

Most soils in the high montane zone are nutrient poor (being either based on acid rocks or strongly leached), but where soils are more base-rich or where frost heave has redistributed nutrients within the soil, more species can be found. In such situations, look for Alpine Lady's-mantle and rarities such as Alpine Mouse-ear and Alpine Cinquefoil on grass-heath and dwarf-herbs such as Moss Campion, Cyphel, Alpine Bistort, Alpine Meadow-rue, Purple Saxifrage, Sibbaldia, and a suite of rare species on moss-heath. Unsurprisingly, many montane species are rare and some (*e.g.* Diapensia, Norwegian Mugwort, Curved Wood-rush, Drooping Saxifrage and Highland Saxifrage) are restricted to a few or single locations.

Invertebrates can sometimes be found in the low sward – look out for Mountain Ringlet basking on grass tussocks in sunny conditions and a strikingly marked wolf spider *Tricca alpigena* in Mat-grass and Woolly Fringe-moss. It is worth looking up from the vegetation underfoot too: montane habitats provide a great vantage point for spotting Golden Eagle and there is always the chance of seeing Dotterel.

Mountain Ledge

Mountain Ledge vegetation varies according to both substrate and altitude. On base-rich rocks, classic tall-herb vegetation of Angelica, Meadowsweet, Roseroot, Water Avens, Wood Crane's-bill, Lady's Mantle and Marsh Hawk's-beard forms thick swards with Bilberry, Tufted Hair-grass and mountain sedges, and rushes over lush mosses. The tall vegetation precludes small arctic-alpines, but larger species include Alpine Meadow-rue, Alpine Bistort, Mountain Sorrel, Alpine Saw-wort and Holly-fern.

Acid ledges with deep soils are dominated by Great Wood-rush and Bilberry. Ferns are abundant, typically Broad Buckler-fern with Hard Fern, Lemon-scented Fern, and the soft green fronds of Beech and Oak Ferns. Starry Saxifrage may be present in wetter situations. Rowan and Aspen are sometime frequent in stands at lower altitudes. Rare species are found at higher altitudes, including montane willows such as Downy Willow, Dark-leaved Willow, Woolly Willow, Net-leaved Willow, and the very rare Alpine Blue-sow-thistle.

On skeletal soils where the base content is constantly replenished by the weathering of calcareous rocks, Mountain Avens can form extensive dark mats with cushion herbs such as Moss Campion and Cyphel; taller herbs such as Globeflower, Roseroot and Water Avens; and montane willows and saxifrages. This community supports lime-loving arctic-alpines such as Alpine Milk-vetch, Alpine Saxifrage and Alpine Bartsia, together with Round-leaved Wintergreen, Grass-of-Parnassus and Mountain Everlasting.

Similar habitats

There is strong floristic continuity with Downy Willow Montane Scrub and, at lower altitudes, with the ground floras of some types of upland woodland and with Northern Hay Meadow. Transitions to grazed Upland Calcareous Grassland also occur.

Origins and development

Mountain Ledge vegetation is entirely natural. Although to some extent limited by geological and hydrological requirements, it was probably once more widespread at suitable altitudes, but has been reduced and fragmented by grazing, to which it is highly vulnerable. Evidence for this is seen in its presence on un-grazed loch islands, the tops of large boulders out of the reach of grazing animals, and lightly grazed slopes.

LEFT: **Yellow Saxifrage** is often found sprawling over wet rock. RIGHT: **Alpine Saxifrage** is a small species found on ledges where taller vegetation is absent.

Distribution and extent

Found mainly in the Scottish Highlands. Eng: 7 ha; Sco: 200 ha; Wal: 65 ha; NI: 15 ha; Ire: < 80 ha (ANN I REP).

How to recognise

The 'hanging gardens' of inaccessible mountain ledges are astonishing oases of luxuriant vegetation within the barren upland landscape. Festoons of Yellow Saxifrage cascade down cliff faces, ledges lush with Great Wood-rush support leafy ferns and tall meadow herbs, cushion herbs intermingle with dwarf herbs, and a scattering of rare and beautiful arctic-alpine plants can be found.

Tall-herb mountain ledges are constantly wet, sometimes dripping with water, and mostly found on north- or east-facing cliffs that are shaded and sheltered from the prevailing wind. They are almost always out of the reach of grazing animals (and, by and large, people) but occasionally the vegetation spills over onto lightly grazed slopes and tumbled block Scree, offering a glimpse of how many such mountainsides could have looked in the past when grazing was less intensive. More accessible ledges have been impoverished through heavy grazing and tend to be dominated by Tufted Hair-grass with few herbs.

When to visit

Summer.

Conservation

Stands of Mountain Ledge vegetation in more accessible locations are usually overgrazed, and in some cases threatened by burning. The impact of grazing by feral goats is a particular issue in Snowdonia. Access to cliffs for recreation (climbing and ice-climbing) can damage vegetation. Fencing has been undertaken at some sites to relieve grazing pressure (*e.g.* at Cym Idwal in Wales and Ben Lawers and Caenlochan in the Highlands) and has resulted in the expansion of Mountain Ledge vegetation. Targeted reductions in grazing pressure elsewhere could result in further increases, and the aim should ultimately be the restoration of an intact transition from woodland through Montane Scrub to Mountain Ledge communities.

What to look for

An outstanding array of northern meadow and arctic-alpine plant species; Golden Eagle, White-tailed Eagle and Peregrine nesting on ledges.

BELOW, LEFT: **Yellow Oxytropis** is a very rare glacial relict found only on cliffs. BELOW, CENTRE: **Roseroot** is a classic Mountain Ledge species; seen here in bud, its flowers are yellow when open. BELOW, RIGHT: **Combe Scar, Dentdale** – Great Wood-rush, Rosebay Willowherb, Foxglove, Broad Buckler-fern, Oak Fern, Wood Sage, Goldenrod and Orpine under a patchy canopy of Aspen and Rowan hint at the kind of woodland that might have once been more prevalent.

Ben Lawers, Perthshire is celebrated for its Mountain Ledge flora and arctic-alpine rarities.

Did you know?

Some of Britain's rarest plants survive on base-rich ledges at high altitude and include Alpine Woodsia, Yellow Oxytropis, Alpine Bartsia and Alpine Gentian.

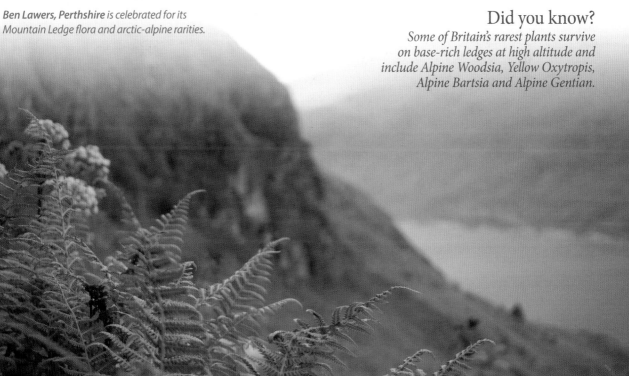

Montane Scrub

Tiny fragments of arctic-alpine willow scrub are found on moist, north- or east-facing base-rich mountain ledges or un-grazed gravelly slopes next to streams where the winter snow lies for long periods. It is dependent upon snow cover for insulation against air frosts, and on inaccessible locations for protection from grazing animals. It currently occurs between about 650–900 m above sea level in the Highlands. The largest patch (at Caenlochan) is only half a hectare in extent. The most common species is Downy Willow followed by Myrtle-leaved Willow. Mountain Willow is restricted to higher altitudes (concentrated in Breadalbane) and Woolly Willow is the rarest, found only on cliff ledges (notably at Caenlochan). Other more widespread species are also found (*e.g.* Eared Willow, Dark-leaved Willow, Tea-leaved Willow and Goat Willow), and Net-leaved Willow is sometimes found on ledges with Mountain Avens. Downy Willow also occurs in very small numbers on Helvellyn in the Lake District.

Alpine Juniper Scrub comprises short, upright Common Juniper scattered over Heather and dwarf shrubs without forming a continuous canopy. Its central location is the eastern Highlands, where it is locally frequent in the Cairngorms and can also form part of tree-line woods. Elsewhere it is found on cliff ledges.

Dwarf Birch is found scattered or in clumps on Blanket Bog and Upland Wet Heathland at moderate altitudes, although it can reach 850 m in the western Highlands, particularly Ben Wyvis and Beinn Dearg. In grazing exclosures it can reach almost a metre in height, but is usually shorter, at the same height as the surrounding vegetation. It is nationally scarce and populations are supressed by overgrazing and heather burning.

Similar habitats

Juniper Scrub (see *page 70*) is found in Caledonian Forest where the canopy has been removed, and more widely through the uplands where it colonises heathland and calcareous grasslands. Dwarf Juniper, which can be hard to differentiate from prostrate Common Juniper, forms a Montane Heath community with Heather. The flora associated with willow scrub is often that of Mountain Ledge.

Origins and development

Scrub dominated Britain and Ireland for a brief period as the climate ameliorated immediately after the last glaciation. As tree species colonised up to their altitudinal limit (at around 800 m above sea level when tree cover was at its greatest extent, lower in Ireland and west Britain), Montane Scrub became restricted to a narrow altitudinal band just above the tree-line, where it probably formed an ecotone (transitional habitat) between forest and montane heath. Rather than a continuous band, it is likely to have formed patches in more sheltered hollows (Common Juniper) or on wetter, flushed ground and base-rich rock (willows). There is evidence that the area of scrub began to decrease in prehistory, and this decline has intensified over the last 200 years as deer and sheep have increased in numbers.

Conservation

Much Montane Scrub is in poor condition and shows limited functionality due to the small population sizes of its characteristic species and its isolation; tiny populations are also particularly threatened by stochastic events (*e.g.* rock falls and landslips). The habitat is susceptible to grazing and burning and to climate change. Restoration projects are underway to conserve vulnerable populations and to allow complete natural

Distribution and extent

Highly fragmented and limited in extent, almost entirely restricted to the Scottish Highlands. Eng: 1 ha; Sco: 23 ha (ANN I REP).

TOP: **Dundreggan, Highland** – an unusually large Dwarf Birch with two **Downy Birch** behind. Dwarf Birch is found on gently sloping peatlands up to 800 m. BOTTOM: **Borrowdale, Lake District** – **Common Juniper** limited to a rock crevice on a heavily grazed hillside.

Ben Lawers, Perthshire – Woolly Willow flourishing in an exclosure erected in 1980. Arctic-alpine willow scrub has probably always been limited by its exacting requirements, but is likely to have been more widespread in places where it is currently limited by grazing pressure. RIGHT: **Creag Fhiaclach, Cairngorms** (600 m) – Common Juniper occurs with knarled Scots Pine in an almost unique expression of natural tree-line vegetation virtually lost from Scotland today.

successions from valley woodlands to open mountain tops (*e.g.* at Ben Lawers, Abernethy, Creag Meagaidh and Glen Affric). Efforts are concentrated on protection from heavy grazing and expansion of the habitat through planting where populations are too small or isolated for natural regeneration.

What to look for

Rare and scarce willows and their associated invertebrates, which include rare sawflies.

Montane Scrub of **Common Juniper** *in the Cairngorms.*
INSET: **Mountain** *Willow may be more tolerant of grazing than other montane willows.*

How to recognise

In a very few places in the Scottish Highlands upland woodland reaches the natural altitudinal tree line. Here, small, gnarled and twisted Scots Pines give way to a fringe of Common Juniper and then Heather and Bilberry heath. Where the trees do not grow up to their altitudinal limit, Common Juniper sometimes grows scattered over the heathland. Elsewhere, willows, sometimes only knee-high, form a silvery canopy on inaccessible crags and un-grazed burnsides. At lower altitudes on damp, peaty slopes, Dwarf Birch peeps out from the surrounding vegetation. These are all Montane Scrub communities, tiny relics of a natural transition between forest and montane heath that is now largely absent. Remote and fragmented, the habitat is scattered across the Highlands, but it is hard to find and often inaccessible.

When to visit

Summer when willows and Dwarf Birch are in leaf, year-round for Common Juniper (conditions permitting).

Did you know?

One of the best sites for willow scrub is in the Grampian mountains at Corrie Seileach (which means corrie of the willows); it has been known to botanists for centuries.

ROCKY HABITATS

ORIGINS

Inland rocky habitats are generally widespread in the uplands where the bedrock has been exposed through glacial action and the erosion of weathered material. Limestone pavement is also found at sea level, and in north-west Scotland, montane communities are found on rocky exposures near sea level. Caves, quarries and disused mine workings are also found in the lowlands.

The rock exposures of Britain and Ireland include rocks from almost all geological eras dating back early 3,000 million years. They can be divided into two main types, siliceous (acidic) and basic (alkaline), and this may be reflected in the plant communities they support. Siliceous rocks, those with a high silica content, include granite, gneiss, sandstone and quartzite and predominate in the upland landscape. Basic rocks are rich in calcium or magnesium and include limestone, calcareous-schists and some igneous rocks such as serpentine and basalt. They are more restricted in their extent, but tend to support a greater range of plant species.

TYPES OF ROCKY HABITATS

Rocky habitats include inland cliffs, crags, rocky outcrops, screes, boulder-fields, fell-fields, limestone pavements, caves and quarries, most of which typically support a sparse scattering of vegetation. Of these, habitat sections have been provided for three categories: **Rocky Slopes** (*page 152*) (including cliffs, crags, rocky outcrops and some boulder-fields where these support crevice vegetation), **Scree** (*page 154*) and **Limestone Pavement** (*page 156*). On cliffs and crags, vegetation is limited to crevices and narrow ledges (wider ledges supporting tall herbs or scrub are considered in the Mountain section under Mountain Ledge and Montane Scrub). Rocky outcrops on shallower slopes can also support grassland or heathland species, depending on the steepness and size of the outcrop. The term boulder-field is often used rather loosely to refer to both screes of larger boulders (also called block talus) and areas of boulders left behind by retreating glaciers. Fell-field is another term that is used variably. It is generally applied to gravelly or rocky areas on the most exposed mountain summits and high ridges that support very sparse vegetation. Fell-field vegetation is particularly well-developed in the western Highlands, Skye, Mull and Shetland. The sparse, scattered vegetation typical of fell-fields, bryophyte-dominated Scree and some crevice communities is not fully covered by the National Vegetation Classification.

Limestone Pavement is somewhat different from the other habitats, occurring at lower altitudes in karst landscapes (*i.e.* open limestone landscapes where water

Buckland Beacon, Dartmoor. The unglaciated tors of Dartmoor are of great interest geologically. Tors also support up to 60 lichen species, as well as a number of ferns that are otherwise uncommon in southern England.

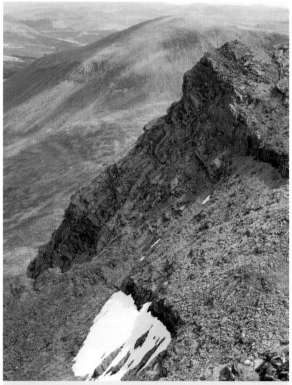

Creag Meagaidh, Central Highlands. Exposed rock predominates in mountain landscapes.

Balnakeil, Sutherland. Rocky outcrops, cliff and pavement are found almost at sea level on Durness limestone where they support montane plants.

Whernside, Yorkshire Dales. A barren fell-field of shattered rock lies above the tarns on an exposed shoulder of Whernside at about 650 m.

movement is mostly under rather than on the surface). Caves are also formed by the dissolution of soluble rock, usually limestone. Caves in Britain and Ireland, which have been relatively recently glaciated, are much less species-rich than their continental counterparts, but support bacteria, algae, fungi, and invertebrates adapted to low light levels (including a blind spider). They also provide roost sites for four protected bat species. Quarries are an artificial rocky habitat that can support a rich flora, particularly on limestone sites, and some species, such as the Bee Orchid, appear to favour such areas. Quarries also provide nesting habitat for Peregrine and Raven, and, in North Wales, Chough. Some bat species, such as the Greater Horseshoe Bat, are very dependent on quarry workings for roosting sites.

THREATS AND ISSUES

Rocky habitats are some of the most natural found in Britain and Ireland. Often remote, difficult to access and of little agricultural value, they have not been shaped by human activities in the same way as most other habitats. However, the uplands are generally grazed, and only sheer cliffs and the rockiest screes and boulder-

Coire an-t Sneachda, Cairngorms – a glaciated corrie with areas of active, largely un-vegetated Scree below the headwall, rocky outcrops on shallower slopes and boulder moraine in the valley floor.

Cliffed headwall

Active Scree

Rocky outcrop

Boulder field

fields are out of the reach of grazing livestock and feral goats. Limestone Pavement, particularly in Britain, is heavily influenced by grazing, which limits plants to crevices and prevents succession to woodland. It has also suffered from quarrying. At higher altitudes montane communities will be affected by climate change, and nitrogen deposition and associated acidification related to the high precipitation rates in upland areas may be an issue. Recreational pressure is an issue at some more accessible sites where activities such as climbing, bouldering and hill-walking can threaten vulnerable plant populations and disturb breeding or roosting birds, or, in the case of caves, bats.

CULTURAL IMPORTANCE

The diversity of British and Irish geology has inspired generations of pioneering geologists, and features of particular significance are often revealed by rocky habitats. Caves also have a special role to play in our understanding and appreciation of the prehistoric fauna and Paleolithic people. The 33,000-year-old skeleton known as the Red Lady of Paviland found in a cave on the Gower coast is the oldest ceremonial burial discovered in west Europe, and a nearby cave holds a 14,000-year-old carved reindeer. Unsurprisingly many caves also have prominent roles in legends. High, rocky place that feel close to the sky may also have had spiritual importance to our ancestors. For example, it is speculated that the Iron Age ramparts and hut circles at 723 m above the sheer Ingleborough scarp in North Yorkshire had ritual significance. Rocky places are undeniably awe-inspiring and often capture people's imagination. A wealth of paintings and literature have been inspired by craggy mountains, waterfalls and caves, such as Turner's paintings of Ingleborough. The Limestone Pavement of The Burren has a particularly rich archaeological heritage with megalithic tombs, burial cairns, prehistoric farmsteads, and more recent historic structures recording 6,000 years of human occupation. Until recently, there was also an unusual tradition of winter-only cattle-grazing on The Burren.

CONSERVATION IMPORTANCE AND PROTECTION

Rocky habitats contribute to the overall biological diversity of the uplands and are natural habitats in what is generally a semi-natural landscape. Montane cliffs can support a suite of rare arctic-alpine plants, and provide nesting places for Golden Eagle, Peregrine and Raven. Limestone pavements support a unique mix of rocky, woodland and calcareous grassland species, and are particularly well represented in Britain and Ireland. Caves and disused mine workings can support large populations of bats, including one of the biggest roosts in Europe.

King Arthur's Cave in the Wye Valley, Herefordshire. Excavations in the 19th century revealed the remains of Woolly Mammoth, Spotted Hyena and other extinct Pleistocene mammals. Current inhabitants include horseshoe bats.

The famous **Poulnabrone** portal tomb on Limestone Pavement in The Burren, Co. Clare, is one of nearly 2,000 monuments recorded there to date.

Knockan Crag, Assynt – famously the inspiration for the geological debate that revealed how tectonic forces can move rocks sideways. Here the Moine Thrust fault is revealed, showing older Moine rocks (some of the oldest in the world) forced up on top of much younger Cambrian and Ordovician rocks.

Some upland and montane Rocky Slope and Scree, caves (without public access) and Limestone Pavement are included within Annex I of the Habitats Directive. Limestone Pavement can also be protected under the Wildlife and Countryside Act (1984).

KEY AREAS

Rocky Slope and Scree are widespread in the uplands, particularly in the Lake District, the Scottish Highlands, and the north-west and west coast of Ireland. The best areas for Limestone Pavement are The Burren in Ireland, the Morecambe Bay area, the Craven Dales and Ingleborough in northern England and Durness in north-west Scotland.

KEY ELEMENTS

The key elements that influence the nature of rocky habitats are the underlying rock, stability of the substrate, altitude and aspect, all of which affect the availability of water, nutrients and shelter (including the shelter provided by snow). The harsh conditions suit species with specific adaptations that would be out-competed in other environments. Look for bryophytes and lichens on bare rock, and cushion-herbs with small, in-rolled leaves and strong root systems on exposed ledges. The lack of water-retaining soil means that crevice plants are found in gullies, under overhangs or near seepages that remain moist on north-facing cliffs. Scree retains moisture and also provides protection from frost, but plants must cope with the instability of the substrate. Some are able to regenerate from rhizomes if covered by rocks. At lower altitudes, a community rich in ferns and mosses is found in hedge banks and lanes, particularly in south-west Britain, with Polypody and Navelwort.

Grazing is a key factor, particularly at lower altitudes where the climate will allow tree growth. Below the tree line, trees can grow on exposed rock, and often the only trees in the upland landscape are those that have become established on rock faces out of the reach of grazing animals. Unstable rocky habitats such as active Scree are less likely to become wooded, although trees such as Ash, Rowan, Hazel and Yew can grow on stabilised Scree, and the high oakwoods of Dartmoor grow on slopes covered in granite blocks known as 'clitter'.

FURTHER INFORMATION

www.limestone-pavements.org.uk/ – general information about limestone pavements and their conservation
www.landforms.eu/ – about the geology and landscapes of Scotland
www.burrenbeo.com – about The Burren
Ingleborough: Landscape and History, by David Johnson (Carnegie, 2008)

Cyphel (ABOVE) and **Purple Saxifrage** (BELOW) – species of rocky places are often cushion-forming and deep-rooted, and have small and rolled or hairy leaves to reduce the impacts of exposure and maximise water absorption and retention.

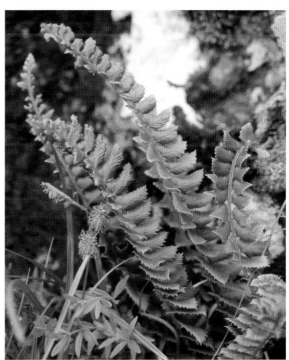

Holly-fern favours cool, moist positions on rocky ledges, in stabilised boulder scree and in deep grykes in Limestone Pavement.

Rocky Slopes

The plants of rock crevices and fissures ('chasmophytic vegetation') are unable to compete with more vigorous species in less challenging environments but, adapted to the stresses of drought, low nutrients, and poor shelter, they can persist in rocky habitats where there is little other competition. The vegetation tends to be sparse and scattered and is usually limited to more sheltered and humid situations. The suite of species present reflects the nature of the underlying rock. On acidic rocks, bryophytes include fringe-mosses and the vivid green rounded hummocks of Mougeot's Yoke-moss. Mountain crags shelter arctic-alpines such as Alpine Speedwell, Highland Cudweed and Mountain Sorrel and, where snow lies late in high, sheltered corries, a fern snow-bed community characterised by Alpine Lady-fern occurs among boulders and on ledges.

Calcareous cliff communities are less widespread. Found at some celebrated sites such as Ben Lawers in the Scottish Highlands and Moor House in Upper Teesdale, they can support a rich flora when out of reach of grazing animals, particularly at higher altitudes. Frizzled Crisp-moss (which shrivels into contorted spirals when dry) and cushions of Moss Campion, Cyphel and Snow Pearlwort grow on narrow ledges, as do rarities such as Alpine Woodsia, Alpine Gentian and rare saxifrages. At lower altitudes, crevice species include Green Spleenwort and Brittle Bladder-fern, and Maidenhair Spleenwort and Wall-rue are typical of sunny crevices and are often found growing from mortar in stone walls in the more humid west of Britain and Ireland.

Similar habitats

At lower altitudes more continuous woodland may develop in gorges and on Limestone Pavement (*e.g.* in the Avon Gorge and on the Morecambe Bay pavements) and crags can support rare whitebeams (*e.g.* in the Brecon Beacons).

Origins and development

Cliff vegetation grows on rock features that were exposed or formed during and at the end of the last glacial period and is not dependent upon any form of human management. However, grazing by sheep and feral goats limits the distribution of plants to the most inaccessible sites and is endangering some species.

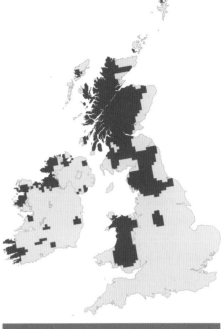

Distribution and extent

Widespread in the uplands. Eng: 1,500 ha; Sco: 37,600 ha; Wal: 1,200 ha; NI: 100 ha; Ire: 1,900 ha (ANN I REP).

ABOVE: **Oblong Woodsia** – this rare species of Rocky Slopes suffered serious declines due to 19th century plant collectors. Reintroduction projects have been more successful on Scree, from which it may have been eliminated through grazing and collecting.

FAR LEFT: **Northern Corries, Cairngorms** – mosses grow where water seeps continuously over the rock, and here provide niches for saxifrages to become established.

LEFT: Near **Seathwaite, Lake District** – at lower altitudes cracks in sheer cliffs can support Heather, and trees that are otherwise scarce in the grazed upland landscape, such as Rowan and Aspen, can also gain a foothold.

FACING PAGE: **Northern Corries, Cairngorms** – this corrie headwall provides habitat for plants such as **Arctic Mouse-ear** (INSET LEFT) and **Mountain Sorrel** (INSET RIGHT).

Conservation

Rocky slopes often support low numbers of individual species, making populations vulnerable. Climbing is of concern at some sites, particularly ice-climbing on north-facing, wet, vegetated slopes that are avoided in the summer. A reduction in grazing pressure would allow some species to spread from their current refugia, and increase their resilience to other stresses. Climate change is likely to alter the arctic-alpine component of the flora.

What to look for

Golden Eagle favours inaccessible cliff ledges for its eyries, and Peregrine and Raven also nest on cliffs. Look out for scarce and rare arctic-alpine flowering plants and ferns at high altitudes. The granite tors of Dartmoor in Devon are particularly good for lichens.

Did you know?

The iconic Snowdon Lily, known from just six rocky sites in North Wales, has been identified as the first arctic-alpine likely to go extinct in Britain as a consequence of climate change.

How to recognise

On cliffs, crags and rocky outcrops an attractive suite of mosses, liverworts, ferns and small herbs cling in crevices and spill down bare rock faces. Scattered plants find a home in fissures and on tiny ledges in the shelter of damp gullies and under overhangs dripping with water. Many of the more formidable cliffs are inaccessible (except to climbers) but some crags and smaller outcrops are quite easily explored on foot. A careful search (binoculars help) can reveal cushions of bryophytes, ferns sprouting from narrow cracks and, at higher altitudes, the intensely coloured flowers of small arctic-alpines.

When to visit

Summer for flora.

Scree

Instability, lack of soil and significant temperature differences between day and night make Scree (also called talus) a challenging environment. However, the stones give some protection from frost and also retain moisture. Epiphytic lichens are the first species to colonise, followed by bryophytes that can help to consolidate the loose rock. Parsley Fern is next to colonise, flourishing in more stable areas along the flanks and bottom edges of screes and behind boulders. Subsequent colonisation by other species depends on the build-up of decomposing fern fronds, which are slowly incorporated with decaying mineral material into a raw soil.

Species composition is variable, and is initially probably a result of chance colonisation, but fine grasses such as Wavy Hair-grass and Sheep's-fescue are frequent, together with Heath Bedstraw and Fir Clubmoss, and rhizomatous plants such as Bilberry and Bracken can gain a foothold around the peripheries. Calcareous Scree can support a wider range of species, including Limestone Fern and many other rarities. In the north-west Highlands, Woolly Fringe-moss forms extensive carpets over block Scree.

Scree is intrinsically unstable, and the successional process of vegetation development can be re-set at any time as the mobile surface layer shears away, leaving discrete patches of vegetation scattered across slopes. Patterns in the vegetation are formed where plants persists in the shelter of boulders but are prevented from spreading laterally by moving rocks, which tend to build up on either side, leaving it in a slight depression. Scree vegetation usually only covers a few square metres, but in some situations can extend over hectares.

Similar habitats

Similar vegetation can be found on shattered rocks on mountain summits and in the crevices of boulders left by retreating glaciers (boulder fields).

Distribution and extent

Widespread in the uplands. Eng: 3,200 ha; Sco: 60,100 ha; Wal: 300 ha; NI: 100 ha; Ire: 2,100 ha (ANN I REP).

ABOVE: A sparse woodland cover of **Hazel** and **Yew** over limestone Scree in Cumbria. RIGHT, TOP: Crustose lichens are the first species to colonise. RIGHT, MIDDLE: In the north-west Highlands screes provide an important habitat for Atlantic bryophytes, such as the dark and glossy **Donn's Notchwort**, Juniper Prongwort and Bird's-foot Earwort, all species of the northern hepatic mat community. RIGHT, BOTTOM: The fresh, green fronds of **Scaly Male-fern**, another species found on Scree, stand out in the summer, and turn rusty-red as they die back in the winter.

Origins and development

Rock gradually disintegrates as a consequence of physical and chemical weathering. Rock falls, frost heave, avalanches and summer storm water all result in rocky material building up at the base of cliffs. Continued weathering and the addition of new material causes the rock to move downslope. The material varies in size from fine gravel brought by water to jumbles of bigger rocks from falls, and becomes sorted according to size as it flows down the slope, creating patches of evenly sized material. Larger rocks, which travel the furthest, tend to accumulate at the base of the scree. Over long time periods, Scree can consolidate and within the woodland zone would eventually support woodland, but this is generally prevented by livestock grazing and heather burning, and stable Scree tends to support heathland or grassland. Climatic conditions prevent succession at higher altitudes.

Conservation

Recreational activities (such as scree-running and hill-walking) impact on fragile vegetation and alter the structure of Scree, resulting in finer material sliding to the bottom of the slope. Atmospheric pollution may be preventing the establishment of fern communities in the southern Pennines. Screes are generally subject to the management practices of the surrounding land and a relaxation of livestock grazing and heather-burning would, in many cases, be beneficial in promoting the development of plant communities and allowing some natural succession to open woodland.

What to look for

Scree can support a rich fern flora, including Parsley Fern, Holly-fern, Limestone Fern, Oak Fern and Mountain Male-fern. The rare arctic-alpine Alpine Lady-fern is characteristic of a snow-bed community occurring at high altitudes on block talus. Ring Ouzel and Wheatear nest in crevices. Look under stones for scarce invertebrates, including ground beetles, money and jumping spiders, and whorl snails.

Knotts, Stonethwaite, Lake District – a typically fan-shaped scree spilling out from the bottom of a gully.

How to recognise

Scree is formed of drifts of broken rock that fan out on slopes beneath crags and the headwalls of corries in the uplands. From a distance, these smooth skirts of stone look completely bereft of life. At closer quarters, a scattering of vegetation becomes apparent, but the grey expanses of shifting rock still seem inhospitable. In late spring, as the ice melts, the clatter of falling rocks from the cliff above reminds the unwary that the process of scree formation is ongoing, while underfoot the rocks are unstable and easily dislodged. Around the margins and on more stable areas the fresh green of fern fronds catch the eye in summer. A closer look reveals crustose lichens and bryophytes, and screes in the montane zone can host a suite of small, rare arctic-alpines.

When to visit

Late spring to summer for ferns and arctic-alpine rarities.

Did you know?

The term scree comes from the Old Norse term for landslide, skriða

INSET: **Parsley Fern**, an early coloniser, growing on stabilised Scree.

LIMESTONE PAVEMENT

Limestone Pavement is formed of exposures of Carboniferous limestone (*e.g.* The Burren, the Pennines and around Morecambe Bay) and Durness and Dalradian limestones (*e.g.* north-west Scotland). The exposed rock is scored by repeated fissures (known as grykes) that are usually 1–2 m deep, (although they have been recorded up to 6 m deep) and about 10 cm wide. The intervening blocks (clints) are washed clean of soil by rain. Their variable size and shape is a reflection of the composition and structure of the bedrock and the direction of the ice movements that exposed it. In some places the limestone is shattered, and chunks and chips lie scattered across the ground.

Limestone Pavement can have a very diverse flora, the result of the wide variety of microhabitats it creates. Thin, well-drained turf develops around clints on shattered Limestone Pavement and between terraces of pavement on hillsides, and supports species typical of Upland Calcareous Grassland (which sometimes shows a regular pattern of hummocks and dips where pavement is hidden under the turf). Shady, humid grykes, shallow pans and other solution features formed by the action of rainwater hold water and can be rich in ferns. Small rock fissures and cracks allow species typical of Rocky Slopes to take root. Overall, the vegetation of Limestone Pavement is strongly influenced by livestock grazing. Heavy grazing confines plants to grykes, but without grazing, scrub and trees can develop and shade out the specialist flora. Climate also plays a role in the variability of pavement flora, with montane species occurring at higher altitudes and in the north of Scotland.

Similar habitats

Limestone Pavement supporting long-established woodland is considered under Upland Mixed Ash Wood. Extensive areas of The Burren now support secondary Hazel scrub.

Origins and development

Limestone Pavement occurs where hard, horizontally bedded limestone was scoured or plucked (in the case of shattered pavement) by glacial action. Subsequent weathering by meltwater and rainwater along lines

Distribution and extent

Widely distributed but limited in area. Eng: 2,900 ha; Sco: 300 ha; Wal: 100 ha; NI: 200 ha; Ire: 32,000 ha (ANN I REP). Britain and Ireland holds a globally significant amount of Limestone Pavement.

BELOW LEFT: **Yewbarrow, Cumbria** – grazing promotes the growth of grasses (*e.g.* Blue Moor-grass and Sheep's-fescue) and, in this case, has created odd-shaped Yew. BELOW RIGHT: **Scar Close** on the flanks of **Ingleborough, North Yorkshire** has been protected from grazing since the mid-1970s and supports a rich and relatively tall flora of ferns and herbs together with Ash, Hazel and other tree species.

Cattle-grazing with a hardy breed such as these **Blue-Greys** on Whitbarrow in Cumbria is more suitable than sheep-grazing in areas with Limestone Pavement.

of weakness in the rock created grykes, although some larger grykes in smooth pavement are considered to have been formed during the Carboniferous, some 300 million years earlier. Rainwater percolating through woodland and soil became more acidic, furthering the development of solution features. Soils may then have washed into the grykes, sometimes vanishing into the subterranean drainage systems characteristic of limestone country. Human clearance of the woodland and subsequent grazing speeded up the process of exposure.

Conservation

Limestone Pavement generally forms part of agricultural systems and subsidies have promoted overgrazing. However, on The Burren, the traditional practice of winter grazing with hardy breeds of cattle has declined markedly, resulting in a recent increase in Hazel scrub. Light grazing is ideal, as it can prevent succession to closed woodland and maintain open areas without eliminating tall herbs.

*Wild Boar Fell, Mallerstang, Cumbria –
Limestone Pavement can occur in small
patches within moorland where there
are outcrops of limestone.*

How to recognise

Limestone Pavements are unique and unmistakable; strange, stony deserts where bare grey rock cut by deep fissures into striking geometric patterns can stretch to the horizon. Worn smooth and sculpted into swirled hollows and runnels, they are a testament to the power of millions of years of rainwater. On many pavements, any vegetation is closely cropped by livestock, but the deep, moist grykes can harbour a luxurious flora of ferns and there is sometimes a scattering of dwarfed and knarled trees and bushes. The richest sites support a beautiful flora of woodland species together with those of open, calcareous conditions. The smooth, stepping-stone like rocks combined with the possibility of rare species in the next gryke, make pavements inviting places to explore. Hollowed-out rock can ring underfoot, and the stone becomes warm to the touch in the slightest sunshine, although it can be slick with water in rainy weather.

When to visit

Late April (Spring Gentian) through to July/ August (Bloody Crane's-bill) for flowering plants; ferns can still be seen into autumn.

What to look for

It is the combination of different floristic elements that makes the flora of Limestone Pavement so interesting. The humid microclimate and protection from grazing livestock provided by grykes is ideal for ferns, notably Limestone Fern, Rigid Buckler-fern, Green Spleenwort and (in Ireland) Maidenhair Fern, but also more widespread species such as Hard Shield-fern, Rustyback, Hart's-tongue and Male-fern. The shady conditions also suit woodland species (possibly relics of earlier woodland cover), and wherever a little soil has built up plants such as Wood Anemone, Primrose, Dog's Mercury and Lily-of-the-valley can be found. Look out also for plants associated with more open, calcareous conditions such as Burnet Rose, Bloody Crane's-bill, Limestone Bedstraw and Greater Knapweed. The thin turf between terraces, amongst shattered pavement and around pavements can be particularly rich in calcareous grassland species. Leached soils can support acidic heathland species, and the bizarre juxtaposition of Heather and Tormentil with calcareous species is a regular sight.

The botanical richness of Limestone Pavement is its most obvious feature, but it also provides a variety of niches for invertebrates. A specialist aquatic fauna capable of withstanding desiccation is found in solution hollows. Mossy and shaded clint tops support scarce snails, rove beetles and woodlice. The Wall Mason Bee (black, with metallic blue glints) needs full sunlight, an\d collects pollen from Common Bird's-foot-trefoil. On warm days butterflies can be abundant – look out for the threatened High Brown and Pearl-bordered Fritillaries as well as more common species. Limestone Pavement is not particularly attractive to birds, but Wheatear and Wren may nest in crevices and holes, and Meadow Pipits are rarely far away. In Ireland, The Burren is a stronghold for Pine Marten, which is associated with Hazel scrub. Look for Common Lizard basking on top of clints.

RIGHT, TOP: a wealth of orchids, including **Dark-red Helleborine** and other rare and scarce plants occur on Limestone Pavement; other specialities to look out for include Baneberry, Angular Solomon's-seal, Alpine Cinquefoil, Downy Currant, Bird's-foot Sedge and, in Ireland, Spring Gentian and Hoary Rock-rose.
RIGHT, MIDDLE: **Spring Gentian** – an iconic plant of The Burren. The Burren supports 75% of the plant species found in Ireland and includes Mediterranean species as well as arctic-alpines such as this gentian. RIGHT, BOTTOM: **Bloody Crane's-bill** is named after the deep red of its leaves in autumn. BELOW: **Limestone Fern** is particularly abundant on the Morecambe Bay pavements

LEFT: **Hard Shield-fern** (on the *right*) and **Hart's-tongue** (*in gryke*), two typical gryke species.
BELOW: **Southerscales, Ingleborough, North Yorkshire** – exposed conditions give little space for root growth and the lack of nutrients and water can result in dwarfed or even prostrate tree growth.

Did you know?

Hollows in the surface of clints collect rainwater, which gradually eats away at the limestone aided by acidic enzymes secreted by a blue-green algae. On The Burren, these solution hollows provide habitat for Mudwort, a rare annual.

The Burren, Co. Clare – most pavements are flat or gently sloping but in karst landscapes such as The Burren they can be terraced.

WETLANDS

ORIGINS

Wetlands occur in a diversity of situations as a consequence of several different hydrological mechanisms, and most are peat-forming. Peat accumulates where conditions are too waterlogged for vegetation to decompose fully, which instead builds up into a layer of organic matter. This helps to retain moisture, raising the local water-table. Peat can reach several metres in depth, and in bogs isolates the vegetation from the more mineral-nutrient-rich groundwater. In contrast, fens still receive groundwater, for example in floodplains or open water transitions. Bog peat is of entirely vegetative origin, whereas fen peat tends to include a greater proportion of inorganic matter that has accumulated as silt in open water situations. Although it is often straightforward to identify the habitats present in a particular wetland (see *page 163* for a summary of habitat types described in this section), it is not always clear-cut where transitions occur. For example, areas that are predominantly Blanket Bog may also include wetland features associated with moving water; both Lowland Fen and Blanket Bog can include areas of Raised Bog; and Lowland Fen, Valley Mire and Raised Bog can all have patches of Quaking Bog.

Some wetlands are entirely natural while others have developed as a consequence of environmental changes created by humans. Some wetlands, such as Raised Bog and some Blanket Bog, are apparently relatively stable end-points in a successional trajectory that started with open water or bare rock after the last glaciation (or more recently, as in the case of the wetlands of the Norfolk and Suffolk Broads). Others, such as Reedbed and Lowland Fen, are inherently transitional and would generally

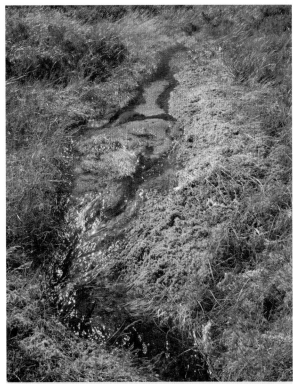

ABOVE: Wetlands can be very small in size, such as this spring in the **Cairngorms**, or cover whole landscapes (see main image on *page 163*)

develop into a different wetland type or woodland if left undisturbed.

Because of the constrained nature of lowland wetland habitats in particular, and perhaps also because of the overridingly dominant influence of anthropogenic factors, it is all too easy to lose sight of the natural dynamism of many wetlands in an attempt to safeguard the species typical of particular successional stages.

Wetland terminology	
Wetland terminology is notoriously confusing, largely because of the variability of wetlands and the lack of vernacular words to describe different conditions. Some frequently used key terms are defined here.	
Ombrogenous	Wetlands formed on soil or rock through *paludification*, whereby water derived from precipitation is prevented from evaporating by a humid climate. They form peat and are hydrologically isolated from the landscape. Most are found in the wetter north and west.
Topogenous	Wetlands formed where the water-table reaches the surface in low-lying hollows or other places where landforms impede drainage. Waterlogging promotes the development of wetlands through the *terrestrialisation* of shallow open waterbodies. They form peat.
Soligenous	Wetlands formed where the water-table reaches the surface in springs or seepages. They are found on slopes, and the ground surface is usually wet. They may or may not form peat, are most frequent in the north and west, and can also be found in association with the above wetland types.
Ombrotrophic	Wetlands fed only by rainfall, snowfall and mist ('cloud fed') and isolated from relatively mineral rich groundwater, resulting in acid and nutrient poor conditions *e.g.* Blanket Bog and Raised Bog.
Geotrophic or minerotrophic/rheotrophic	Wetlands fed by the earth or mineral groundwater / flowing water, which can be acidic or base-rich *e.g.* Lowland Fen, Valley Mire, Upland Spring and Flush.

Key Wetland Areas

1. New Forest
2. Dorset Heaths
3. Dartmoor
4. Somerset Levels & Moors
5. Lleyn Fens
6. Anglesey fens
7. Raised bogs of Midlands of Ireland
8. Iveragh Peninsula
9. Blanket bogs of Galway
10. Blanket bogs of Mayo
11. Blanket bogs of Donegal
12. Garron Plateau
13. Lewis Peatlands
14. Flow Country
15. The Highlands
16. Raised bogs of Central Scotland belt
17. The Pennines
18. West Midlands/Mid Wales Meres & Mosses
19. Fens
20. Norfolk & Suffolk Broads
21. Suffolk Coast

The map shows all wetland habitats. Wetland sites are relatively scarce in the lowlands but there are extensive tracts (mostly Blanket Bog) in the uplands and in western Ireland.

Some key wetland locations are labelled on the map; this selection is not intended to be exhaustive but highlights a few of the most important areas.

Fens (LEFT) receive their nutrients from rocks and soils via groundwater and are relatively high in mineral nutrients, allowing lush, diverse vegetation to develop. Most bogs (RIGHT) receive their nutrients via precipitation that is acid and low in mineral nutrients and therefore support less diverse vegetation.

TYPES OF WETLAND HABITAT

Wetland habitats can be categorised in terms of their hydrology (including the source, base-status, and nutrient status of the water), their topography, the vegetation they support, and how they have been used. Hydrology can be complex and difficult to establish simply from observation and vegetation can be similar in wetlands formed by quite different processes.

In this book, wetlands are categorised according to their physical attributes and their vegetation using names that are, on the whole, commonly used and understood, although there is some variation in how they are applied. Six types of wetland are described in the following sections: three types of bog (Blanket Bog, Raised Bog and Valley Mire) as well as Lowland Fen, Reedbed and Upland Spring and Flush (which includes upland small-sedge fens). Transitional types can also be found (see *page 164*). Although marshy grasslands such as Coastal Floodplain and Grazing Marsh and Purple Moor-grass and Rush Pasture are covered within the Grassland section, they can also be considered as wetlands.

CONSERVATION INTEREST AND PROTECTION

Wetlands are greatly valued for the richness and diversity of the vegetation and wildlife they support, and for the

ecological processes that functioning examples still demonstrate. They also play a key role in maintaining water quality and in flood alleviation. Intact peatlands sequester carbon – some of the carbon captured by plants is locked into peat rather than released back into the atmosphere during decomposition, and a significant amount is stored within the surface vegetation. However, this means they can also be a carbon source, and millions of tonnes of carbon dioxide are released into the atmosphere through peatland exploitation globally.

All wetland habitats, or components of them, are recognised as being of European importance (see *page 23*), with the exception of Reedbed. Blanket Bog and Raised Bog are locally rare peatland types for which Britain and Ireland are of particular importance. Some wetland habitats are naturally limited in their extent (*e.g.* Upland Spring and Flush), while others are very extensive (*e.g.* Blanket Bog, which covers huge areas in the uplands). In the lowlands in particular, many wetlands have been destroyed or greatly reduced in area through drainage. The remaining area of Lowland Fen and Reedbed is a tiny fragment of that in existence before drainage intensified in the 17th century. Much has also developed naturally into Wet Woodland as traditional management practices have died out over the last 100 years.

'Bog bursts' occur when the surface of a bog ruptures and releases a torrent of liquid peat. Such bursts, which can be hazardous, tend to occur after intense rainfall. In the similar (if less eloquently named) case of 'peat failure', rafts of peat break away and are transported down-slope. Bog bursts are largely confined to Ireland and Northern Ireland; peat failure is also observed in Britain. Both can be triggered by anthropogenic factors, and may be affected by climate change.

HABITAT	DESCRIPTION	NOTES
Blanket Bog *page 168*	Bog that has developed on dry land in wet climates and is rain-fed. Vegetation is relatively short and dominated by dwarf-shrubs, sedges and bog-mosses due to the low availability of minerals. Widespread and extensive in the uplands.	'Blanket mire' refers to landscapes mantled in peat that include Blanket Bog with areas of Raised Bog and transitional communities which can be hard to distinguish at first glance.
Raised Bog *page 172*	Bog that has developed from open water and is now rain-fed. Vegetation is relatively short and dominated by dwarf-shrubs, sedges and bog-mosses due to the low availability of minerals. More common in the wetter north and west, but can form in drier areas.	Can include Quaking Bog (see *page 164*) where rafts of vegetation develop over a lens of water.
Upland Spring and Flush *page 174*	Springs and associated flushes of water seeping over vegetation in upland settings. Acid or base-rich vegetation, usually characterised by bryophytes and small sedges.	Includes small-sedge fens.
Lowland Fen *page 176*	Calcareous fen in floodplains, open water transitions and basins fed by base-rich ground and surface water (as well as rainwater), supporting diverse and lush vegetation including swamp vegetation and calcareous fen meadows.	Sometimes used to encompass 'poor fen' or valley Transition Mire (see *page 164*).
Valley Mire *page 180*	Valleyhead mire that develops where water flows through a shallow valley in a heathland system, fed by groundwater and surface water (as well as rainwater).	Can technically be Transition Mire (see *page 164*) where more base-rich water enters from seepages.
Reedbed *page 184*	Swamp vegetation dominated by Common Reed, fed by ground and standing water of variable base and nutrient status.	

NOTE: **Mire** is a term used for any ecosystem that accumulates peat; the name comes from the Scandinavian *myr*.

*The oceanic climate of western Britain and Ireland allows blanket mire to develop over huge areas of the uplands, such as here in **Connemara**.*

TRANSITION MIRE AND QUAKING BOG

Transition Mire and Quaking Bog (called after the Annex I habitat of that name) is transitional between acid bog and alkaline fen habitats. It occurs where there is lateral movement of water or groundwater influence that can ameliorate the acidic and nutrient-poor influence of the peaty substrate. This is a very wet, quaggy habitat of floating rafts of bog vegetation that tremble underfoot, of swampy open-water fringes of Bottle Sedge, or of seepages delineated with green sedges in mires. Quaking Bog of floating vegetation is also known as hover, scraw or schwingmoor, and is referred to independently in the text where it is useful to differentiate it from Transition Mire. It develops in a wide range of situations varying from the huge floodplain mire of the Insh Marshes in Speyside to the blanket mire of Rannoch Moor and quaking bogs in the valley mires of the New Forest and Dorset. It is also indicative of successional transitions (*e.g.* between Lowland Fen and Raised Bog). A characteristic feature is the presence of Bottle Sedge, a tall sedge with bottle-brush shaped heads that catch the wind, and the grey-green sward may be enriched with the white flowers of Bog Bean and the strikingly geometric, silvery leaves of Marsh Cinquefoil. Where conditions are less acidic, the sward can be more species-rich, and 'brown mosses' (a group of yellow, brown and red coloured mosses typical of mineral-rich fens) replace bog-mosses. On the margins of lakes and pools it forms a buoyant swamp community, often with Common Sedge, Common Reed or Common Cottongrass and tall herbs including Ragged-Robin, Meadowsweet and Angelica. It is found in ladder fens and water tracks (see *page 167*) in Blanket Bog, on the marginal lagg (see *page 172*) of Raised Bog and on lochsides where water seeps down slopes. In basin mires, mobile rafts of transition vegetation can float over more base-rich water. It can also develop on the surface of cut-over mires or on partially drained bogs that have re-flooded. Transition Mire can reach into the montane zone, where small stands in hollows in calcareous montane grasslands can include arctic-alpine species.

Transition Mire and Quaking Bog is usually a component of larger wetlands, and management therefore needs to take into account the hydrological integrity of whole sites. The tendency for rafts to consolidate and succeed to woodland contributes to habitat loss if not balanced by the development of new habitat, and sometimes artificial rejuvenation of the hydrosere may be needed.

ABOVE RIGHT: **Bottle Sedge** – a typical species of very wet mires. Its seed cases are filled with air, allowing them to float in the surrounding water.
BELOW: **Insh Marshes, Speyside**, is the largest Transition Mire in Britain, occupying a five-mile stretch of the River Spey floodplain.

In Ireland, Raised Bog has been especially devastated by peat extraction in addition to drainage for agriculture and forestry, and only around 8% now remains.

Many wetlands are currently in poor condition, although a relatively high proportion are protected through designation (*e.g.* in England about 75% are within SSSIs). Current threats to wetland habitats revolve around water availability and quality and land management practices. Many raised bogs are still threatened by commercial peat cutting, and overgrazing is an issue on many upland blanket bogs. In contrast, lack of management is impacting on raised bogs, lowland fens and reedbeds. The degree of fragmentation of lowland wetland habitats means that many are surrounded by arable land, with the consequent problems of nutrient run-off and nitrate contamination of groundwater, drainage and water extraction, and lack of grazing animals. Water availability is likely to be an ongoing issue given the increases in water consumption and the existing and predicted impacts of climate change. Peatbogs have adapted to climate change in the past, but future resilience will depend upon their condition, and specifically how active they are in terms of bog-moss growth and peat formation. Restoration projects have been carried out on many bogs of European importance, and there have been significant improvements in water quality in areas such as The Norfolk and Suffolk Broads. The Great Fen project in East Anglia is an ambitious long-term project to re-create a whole wetland landscape.

CULTURAL IMPORTANCE

It is hard to imagine the extensive wetland wildernesses that existed in the lowlands until some 400 years ago. However, although wild in aspect, many were used extensively: reed and sedge were cut for thatch, peat was cut for fuel, and they were used for grazing livestock and for wildfowling. The cultural significance of some of these practices is still appreciated today. In contrast, wetlands still remain a key feature in upland landscapes in the form of blanket mires, and their presence is taken for granted. In Ireland, bog (both upland and lowland) still holds a unique place in the national culture, perhaps because of its prevalence. Bogs abound in Irish mythology, folklore, music and poetry, and bog is even explored as a symbol of the Irish psyche by Irish poet Seamus Heaney.

Peatlands are unique among habitats in their capacity to record the story of the landscape, and sometimes of the people who lived there. They are museums of the past, preserving in layers of peat evidence of environmental and cultural change. The Sweet Track in the Somerset Levels is one of a number of prehistoric marsh tracks that have been found within peat, and demonstrates highly developed woodworking and woodland management

Reed was traditionally cut to provide thatching material, but the practice declined rapidly in the 20th century. Commercial reed-cutting has recently experienced a small resurgence (particularly in Norfolk) and is also carried out for conservation purposes.

Peat cutting for fuel has been practiced for millennia. Traditional, small-scale peat cutting is limited in extent and is rotational, allowing vegetation to recolonise. The cultural value of traditional peat cutting is strongly upheld where it still takes place such as here in Connemara.

skills on the part of the Neolithic people who built it nearly 6,000 years ago. Artefacts and even human bodies uncovered in peatlands (such as the 2,000-year-old Lindow Man found in a Cheshire bog) suggest that some bogs were sacred places where people went to offer sacrifices to placate their gods. Paleontological records are also particularly well-preserved in wetlands. Analysis of pollen preserved in peat, and also invertebrate and wood remains, have provided invaluable insights into the development of peatlands and their responses to environmental and anthropogenic factors both spatially and through time.

KEY ELEMENTS

The hydrosere

Wetlands can show a variety of transitional stages represented by different vegetation types and structures. The classic development from open water through swamp and fen to carr woodland or ombrotrophic bog is referred to as a hydrosere, and reaches is full expression in the lowlands. The process of succession can take anything from 1,000 to about 4,000 years, which means that most shallow, post-glacial waterbodies have long since completed their hydrosere development. However, secondary succession can occur, as is the case in the Norfolk and Suffolk Broads, and succession is often seen in ponds and other artificial waterbodies. Succession from open water to swamp, via submerged and emergent aquatic plants, depends on the water depth being less than about one metre. Once this has occurred through siltation and the deposition of organic matter, swamp vegetation can swiftly take hold, provided there is no erosion. Fen vegetation follows and, as the sward becomes drier, the surface rises above the surrounding water-table. In some cases woody species may colonise but, where surface conditions become acidic, the growth of bog-mosses can trigger the development of Raised Bog. In some cases, paleo-ecological evidence suggests that bog-mosses have replaced woody species. Most of these stages in the hydrosere can be reversed, and are likely to be quite variable depending on local conditions. Succession plays out differently on Blanket Bog, where a wet climate creates waterlogged conditions

The Norfolk and Suffolk Broads are of particular interest in terms of hydrosere development as they demonstrate how it can be re-set by human activities. Peat originally developed in shallow valleys during the Atlantic Period, and eventually came to be dominated by carr (see Wet Woodland *page 44*). However, sea-level rise caused a return to open fen conditions and between the 12th and 14th centuries the area was extensively dug for peat. The dug areas subsequently re-flooded, creating the broads. Gradually, the open water silted up and swamp vegetation developed. Until the mid-20th century, many reed and sedge beds were cut, preventing succession to tall-herb fen and carr woodland, but recent decades have seen a rapid increase in the amount of carr.

on previously dry land, leading directly to the formation of ombrotrophic bog, although in some cases bog may have replaced woodland as the climate became wetter during the Atlantic Period 5,000–8,000 years ago.

Hummocks and Hollows

In bogs, hummocks and hollows formed of bog-mosses result from the vertical zonation of species in response to hydrological conditions. Hummocks and ridges are formed of Red and Imbricate Bog-mosses and support Round-leaved Sundew. Hollows are formed of Papillose and Soft Bog-mosses and pools tend to support Feathery and Cow-horn Bog-mosses, with Oblong-leaved Sundew, Common Cottongrass, White Beak-sedge, or bare peat. Distinctive bog pool patterning can occur and larger bog pools may persist for thousands of years.

Hydrological features

There are a number of hydrological features which are not directly related to successional processes that are found in wetlands and add diversity to the structure and vegetation. The terms used to describe these can be applied variably, so their usage in this book is defined here. **Seepages** occur where groundwater flows out from a mineral aquifer to the surface of a wetland. **Runnels** or **rills** are small lines of quite rapidly flowing water on slopes. **Soakways** are linear zones of flowing water and are distinguished by differing vegetation from the surrounding wetland (*e.g.* Marsh St. John's-wort and Bog Pondweed). **Water tracks** are similar but wetter, with flowing water visible on the surface running between tussocks or patches of mire vegetation. **Ladder fens** comprise a series of narrow pools separated by ridges aligned with the contour, which tend to support Transition Mire vegetation.

TOP TO BOTTOM:

Red Bog-moss grows in loose carpets or soft hummocks; its red colouration is eye-catching.

Papillose Bog-moss is a distinctively chunky moss.

Feathery Bog-moss is the most aquatic bog-moss and is found in pools, runnels and ditches; it forms structure-less mats if removed from the water.

Golden Bog-moss is locally common in pools and hollows on the Dorset Heaths; its colour and the neat arrangement of its leaves are distinctive.

FURTHER INFORMATION

Raised Bog Conservation – a website providing information on bog conservation in Ireland – rbc.cfram.com/

Great Fen – a long-term project to restore an extensive area of wetland in the east of England www.greatfen.org.uk/

Bogs. The Ecology, classification and conservation of ombrotrophic mires by R. Lindsay (SNH, 1995; available online).

Conserving bogs. The management handbook by Brooks and Stoneman (The Stationery Office, 1997)

BLANKET BOG

Blanket Bog can be found from Dartmoor to Shetland and from Co. Cork to Co. Donegal between sea level and 1,000 m. It forms over mainly acidic soils and rock in wet, cloudy climates where rainfall outstrips evapotranspiration and causes the formation of iron pans in the soils, creating waterlogged conditions. Bog-mosses flourish on wet, acidic ground and are resistant to decomposer microbes. Dead plant material slowly accumulates as peat, which increases waterlogging and isolates the vegetation from the groundwater and underlying soils and bedrock, further reducing nutrient availability. The resulting wet, very acidic and nutrient-poor conditions suit only a limited number of key species, particularly bog-mosses (*e.g.* Papillose, Red and Soft Bog-mosses). Cross-leaved Heath and cottongrasses grow from the bog-moss carpet, and drier areas support Heather and Deergrass.

In the cool, wet, northern and western uplands, whole landscapes are cloaked in peat. Blanket Bog is the most extensive element within these ecosystems, which are termed blanket mires. However, other habitats can also be found. Raised Bog occurs where the terrestrialisation of waterbodies has taken place but the vegetation is similar to that of the surrounding Blanket Bog. Fen vegetation can be found along watercourses and flushes and ladder fens are characterised by transition communities. In the west, where rainfall is sufficient for peat formation on steeper slopes, water movement promotes vegetation more typical of Valley Mire. Peat can also form over calcareous rock if conditions are sufficiently wet.

Similar habitats

Upland Wet Heath supports many of the same species, but occurs where peat is less than half-a-metre deep and the key peat-forming species (bog-mosses and cottongrasses) are not prominent. Raised Bog can be difficult to identify within blanket mires, but lowland examples are distinctive in their form and context.

Origins and development

Most blanket peat development began 5,000–6,000 years ago when the climate became warmer and wetter. In many areas the formation of Blanket Bog may have been at least partly due to forest clearance by humans. Loss of the forest canopy led to waterlogging as water-loss through transpiration decreased, resulting in conditions unsuitable for tree growth. However, in the wettest, coolest places such as the Flow Country and the Northern Isles, Blanket Bog developed naturally, forming a kind of oceanic

Distribution and extent

Widespread in the north and west of Britain and western Ireland. Eng: 280,000 ha; Sco: 1,759,000 ha; Wal: 56,200 ha; NI: 140,000 ha; Ire: 228,700 ha (ANN I REP). Britain and Ireland hold over 20% of the world's Blanket Bog.

BELOW LEFT: **Quinag, Sutherland** – blanket mires smother the landscape from high mountain slopes down to the sea in both Sutherland and Connemara; note the cut peat face.

BELOW: **Inish Boffin, Connemara** – domestic peat cutting on a patch of Atlantic Blanket Bog just a few metres above sea level.

FACING PAGE – TOP: **Strath Dionard, Foinaven, Sutherland** – Blanket Bog occupies the flat valley floor, grading into Heather – Bilberry Upland Dry Heath then acidic Scree on the steeper sides. Greenshank breed in this bog.

tundra. The relative roles of both anthropogenic and natural forces on the historical and current extent of Blanket Bog is not yet fully understood.

The tradition of burning bogs to encourage palatable young growth dates back to at least the 17th century, but promotes grassy growth at the expense of peat-forming species and kills invertebrates. Drainage and sheep-grazing have also degraded extensive areas, causing peat to dry out, oxidise and erode. Thousands of hectares were lost to afforestation in the second half of the 20th century, encouraged through scandalous tax breaks. Commercial peat cutting for power production, domestic briquettes and horticulture has destroyed extensive areas.

The Flow Country in Caithness and Sutherland is a huge expanse of habitat thought to be entirely natural and unparalleled in the rest of Britain and Ireland. Nearly 5% of the world's Blanket Bog occurs here. Surface patterning is particularly well-developed.

How to recognise

Treeless and sodden with water, blanket bogs can be wild and desolate places. Often rainy or shrouded in cloud, their bleak beauty lies in the wide open spaces and huge skies and the strangely intimate landscape of hummocks and hollows formed of spongy, green, golden and red-coloured bog-mosses. These are often dotted with intriguing insectivorous plants and in the empty landscape, elusive waders betray their presence with distinctive, haunting calls.

On the deepest peat on level or undulating ground small lochans and pools make for treacherous walking. On slopes, small islands and cliffs of peat created through erosion (and known as peat hags) confound the unwary walker.

Many blanket bogs have been drained, burned and cut-over for peat, and this is seen in the more uniform vegetation dominated by sedges and Heather. In the best (and often most remote) sites, the water-table remains high throughout the year, and the different growth forms of bog-mosses result in striking, repeated patterns.

When to visit

Late spring–summer for breeding birds, summer–autumn for flowering plants, year-round for bog-mosses if conditions allow.

Conservation

It is unclear how Blanket Bog will respond to climate change, and the conservation priority is therefore to restore degraded bogs to increase their resilience. Models based on predicted rainfall suggest that Blanket Bog may become restricted to the north-west of Britain. However, this does not take account of biotic factors, particularly changes in the relative abundance of bog-mosses. Hummock mosses are likely to proliferate, but as they decompose more slowly, peat may build more rapidly and help maintain waterlogging. Blocking drainage channels is particularly important in areas where the number of rainfall days make blanket peat formation marginal, leading to drying and erosion. Allowing woodland to regenerate naturally on slopes at the margins of Blanket Bog may be beneficial where marginal erosion and instability on slopes is an issue. Efforts to curtail commercial peat cutting and the demand for horticultural peat are ongoing.

What to look for

Blanket Bog, poor in nutrients and lacking large-scale structural diversity, supports low densities of vertebrates. Look out for tundra-breeding waders such as Golden Plover, Dunlin and (in Scotland) Greenshank, joined in the far north by Arctic Skua. Golden Eagle, Hen Harrier and Short-eared Owl hunt over blanket bogs, and Otters sometimes make their way up gullies from rivers and lochs. Blanket Bog also provides seclusion for Red-throated Diver and Common Scoter breeding on lochans, and is rich in both aquatic and terrestrial invertebrates.

While the core plant species of Blanket Bog remain fairly constant throughout its range, look out for the local influence of climate and topography. Bog-myrtle, White Beak-sedge and Atlantic bryophytes such as Purple Spoonwort are typical on more oceanic western bogs, where Purple Moor-grass can dominate on steeper slopes if there is a degree of lateral flushing. Black Bog-rush is particularly common in western Ireland under the influence of wind-blown marine salts. Higher, drier eastern bogs support more Hare's-tail Cottongrass and dwarf-shrubs, with Bearberry, Mountain Crowberry, Bog Bilberry and reindeer lichens characterising high-altitude Blanket Bog in the Cairngorms. In the north and west (particularly the Hebrides), Woolly Hair-moss co-dominates with bog-mosses. In the south Pennines and Southern Uplands swards of Hare's-foot Cottongrass cover large areas where bogs have been degraded through burning, drainage, atmospheric pollution and grazing.

BELOW: **Rannoch Moor, Highlands** – pine stumps are often exposed in peat hags in bogs that developed on forested land. Woodland has probably developed and retreated on the margins of bogs over millennia, and in other countries is still found on drier mineral ridges within and around bog systems.

BOTTOM LEFT: The distinctive surface patterning found particularly in the north and west is created by the varying growth forms of different bog-mosses. Hollows and pools can be aligned in distinctive repeating patterns that change according to climate and topography.

BOTTOM RIGHT: **Diamond Hill, Connemara** – erosion features such as peat hags and gullies are often found on plateaux and watershed bogs but are not fully understood; they may be natural or due to overgrazing and burning.

TOP LEFT: From July to September look out for the dainty **Black Darter**, which breeds in bog pools and drainage ditches. In the Highlands the scarce Azure Hawker can be seen settling briefly by pools during June and July. TOP RIGHT: **Golden Plover** breeds in Blanket Bog and other moorland habitats, feeding on craneflies and other invertebrates. A wary species, it is often heard rather than seen, despite its striking summer plumage.

LEFT: Nutrient-poor conditions favour carnivorous plant species such as sundews, butterworts and **bladderworts**. Bladderworts take just a fraction of a second to catch prey in a highly sophisticated bladder trap where they are digested and absorbed. INSET BELOW: **Oblong-leaved Sundew** – a species typical of wet hollows.

Did you know?

Peat in Blanket Bogs can reach a depth of over five metres, and accumulates at roughly half-a-millimetre per year.

***Cahersiveen, Iveragh** – cottongrass-dominated Blanket Bog near the summit of Bentee.*

RAISED BOG

Classic lowland Raised Bog is generally found in plains and on valley floors where the topography impedes natural drainage. The dome of the bog is composed of water held in place between particles of peat and covered with a living skin of vegetation, beneath which peat formation is ongoing. Bog-mosses act as a sponge, holding water gained through precipitation. This water is gradually lost through evapo-transpiration, by seepage through the sides of the dome, and in some cases by streams originating within the bog. However, in some bogs a lens of water remains under the vegetative crust, creating Quaking Bog (see *page 164*).The central dome has a slightly steeper margin (the rand), which may be bordered by a lagg. The lagg forms where the bog water-table meets the water-table of the surrounding mineral soil and can support fen or Transition Mire vegetation (see *page 164*). However, most laggs have been drained and intact examples are rare throughout Europe. The wettest area is generally the relatively flat top of the domed bog, which supports similar plant communities to those of other acidic mires. Mosses include Magellanic, Papillose, Red, Feathery and Soft Bog-mosses. Cottongrasses, Deergrass, Heather and Cross-leaved Heath are common, together with Bog Asphodel and Round-leaved Sundew.

Several rare invertebrate species are found on Raised Bog, but often from just one or two sites (*e.g.* Mire Pill Beetle, Bog Bush-cricket, Bilberry Pug (a moth) and Bog Sun-jumper Spider), and it is probable that there are species still to be recorded. Remaining bogs are concentrated in the Central Belt of Scotland, the Solway region, north-west England and central Ireland.

Similar habitats

Raised Bog supports similar species to Blanket Bog and within blanket mire complexes in wetter uplands unconfined Raised Bog can spill over onto the surrounding peatland. Erosion features typical of Blanket Bog are generally absent from Raised Bog and pools are less common (except in Ireland).

Origins and development

Raised Bog originates in shallow glacial lakes and hollows. These fill with the un-decayed remains of marginal vegetation and in-washed sediment, forming fen peat and cutting off the nutrient supply from the lake margins. The surface is colonised by bog-mosses able to flourish in the wet and nutrient-poor conditions, and bog peat begins to develop. The peat raises the vegetation above the original surface of the lake, isolating it from the groundwater, until it becomes entirely dependent on rainfall for nutrients.

Raised Bog has fared particularly badly in the last 100 years or so with only 6% of British and less than 1% of Irish bogs persisting in a relatively

Distribution and extent

Widespread with notable local concentrations. Eng: 17,400 ha; Sco: 8,000 ha; Wal: 2,200 ha; NI: 8,900 ha; Ire: 49,900 ha (ANN I REP). Extremely rare globally but widely distributed in Europe, with a significant proportion in Britain and particularly Ireland.

BELOW LEFT: Peat cuttings in the **Carhar River basin, Iveragh** – of the original 310,000 ha of Raised Bog in Ireland, only 1% remains as active bog, although it is estimated that restoration may be possible on a further 15%.

BELOW RIGHT AND FACING PAGE: **Flanders Moss, Stirlingshire** – one of the biggest (and best) raised bogs in the UK. Drier areas are often invaded by trees such as Downy Birch, which are removed where possible to prevent them from drying out the bog further. However, marginal scrub is important for invertebrates.

ABOVE LEFT: **Bog-mosses** intertwined with **Cranberry** (ABOVE RIGHT) at Carsegowan Moss, Galloway, a remnant of the once extensive Solway peatlands that formed over estuarine clays. BELOW RIGHT **Hare's-tail Cottongrass** can be particularly abundant on degraded bog.

How to recognise

Raised bogs are usually discrete entities in the landscape and, unlike blanket bogs, are often individually named. They are formed of a dome of peat that can rise up several metres above the surrounding agricultural land, although this can be hard to appreciate on the ground. Wet terrain makes Raised Bogs tricky to explore and it is often difficult to get a feel for a whole site unless there is a view from a nearby hill.

On pristine bogs, colourful carpets of bog-mosses patterned with hollows and hummocks are interspersed with sedges and heathers. Many sites are now degraded, having been drained or cut over for peat. These are more heathery and sometimes support an open canopy of birch, pine and Rhododendron woodland. Most Raised Bog is found in the lowlands, but upland examples in blanket mire occur.

undisturbed condition. Many have been drained or stripped for agricultural use, or afforested. Remaining bogs are often too degraded to qualify for protection under wildlife legislation. In Ireland in particular, commercial peat stripping for fuel and horticultural use is carried out on an industrial scale. Atmospheric pollution is affecting the relative proportions of different bog-mosses.

Conservation

The conservation status of Raised Bog is poor, and ongoing effort is needed to halt its destruction and deterioration. On remaining bogs, conservation management centres on raising the water-table by blocking perimeter and internal drains, creating hydrological buffer zones at the margins and removing trees. Scrub encroachment is common on bogs, particularly those drying out as a consequence of drainage or water abstraction from underlying aquifers. However, peat-forming species can re-colonise cut surfaces, and there is plenty of potential for the restoration of active peat-forming systems.

What to look for

Unsurprisingly, bogs are good for Common Toad and Common Frog, but Common Lizard and Adder may also be seen. Many specialist invertebrates are extremely rare, but Large Heath and Small Pearl-bordered Fritillary may be encountered. Characteristic plants include Cranberry, Bog-rosemary and Round-leaved Sundew, but look out also for more generalist species such as the Lesser Butterfly-orchid.

When to visit

June–August for drier conditions, flora and invertebrates (including midges and mosquitoes!). A hard frost can make walking easier in winter, which is a good time to look out for raptors hunting over the bog.

Flanders Moss, Stirlingshire

Upland Spring and Flush

Wherever the water-table is high and water cannot percolate into the substrate, water is forced to the surface, either bubbling out from an obvious springhead or seeping through the vegetation. If the substrate remains impermeable down-slope or is saturated with water, the water flows over the surface in rills or more diffusely in flushes. The vegetation is strongly influenced by the mineral content of the rock through which the water flows, and also the temperature of the water.

Spring water from calcareous rocks is rich in dissolved calcium carbonate, which precipitates out on contact with the air and leaves a crunchy yellowish deposit of calcium (tufa) behind that can help build up low mounds of mosses such as the soft orange-brown Curled Hook-moss. Base-rich flushes and small-sedge fens retain a well-developed bryophyte layer, usually of brown mosses (see *page 164*). These are joined by small sedges such as Flea Sedge and Carnation Sedge, and Common Butterwort, Bird's-eye Primrose and Grass-of-Parnassus may be present. Taller swards can include Angelica, Meadowsweet, Marsh-marigold, Globeflower and Ragged-Robin.

The bright green Fountain Apple-moss often marks out springs on acid rocks, sometimes with the golden-green Marsh Forklet-moss and the dark green or purple liverwort Water Earwort. In acid flushes, a green layer of bog-mosses is sometimes joined by Upland Wet Heath species, and sedges can include Bottle Sedge and Star Sedge.

In the montane zone, Spring and Flush vegetation is enriched with arctic-alpines. It is also found associated with ice-cold springs and channels of meltwater in late-lying snow-beds (see High Montane Heath and Snow-bed, *page 140*). In the warmer oceanic regions of south-west England and Wales, small, well-defined stands of Round-leaved Crowfoot and Blinks emerge from running water in rills and small streams.

Springs and Flushes form permanent wetland features in the landscape and so are important for insects, spiders and other invertebrates with an annual life-cycle. Craneflies feed among mosses, and emerge in great numbers in the summer, providing food for upland wader and grouse chicks, Ring Ouzels, Wheatears and other upland birds.

Similar habitats

Upland Springs and Flushes can be diffuse, gradually merging into the surrounding vegetation (usually upland heathland or grassland). On lower hillsides, flushed gullies support Sharp-flowered and Soft Rushes in Upland Acid Grassland and Upland Rush Pasture.

Distribution and extent

Widely distributed throughout the uplands. Extent unknown, individual features can be very small.

BELOW LEFT: **Balnakiel, Sutherland** – a calcareous flush with brown mosses and Carnation Sedge almost at sea level on Durness limestone.
BELOW RIGHT: **Alpine Silverwort** growing with Lindberg's Bog-moss.
FACING PAGE – TOP LEFT: **Creag Meagaidh, Central Highlands** – Springs and Flushes are most common in the uplands where the water-table is constantly topped up by rain, mist and snow.
FACING PAGE – TOP CENTRE: **Whernside, Yorkshire Dales** – this acid spring below the summit feeds a nearby tarn. FACING PAGE – BOTTOM LEFT: **Starry Saxifrage** can be found in wet flushes up to 1,000 m. FACING PAGE – BOTTOM CENTRE: **Common Butterwort** is a characteristic species of base-rich flushes, and obtains nutrients from small flies caught in its sticky leaf rosette.

How to recognise

Small and richly coloured patches of vegetation that catch the eye amongst duller upland swards indicate the presence of springs and flushes. Springs are often surrounded by plush cushions and mats of mosses and liverworts that are saturated with water, and the sound of flowing water is never far away. Where the water seeps diffusely over the surface in flushes, the ground can be open and stony, or support thick vegetation comprising small sedges, rushes and herbs. These upland jewels are always worth investigating and can support beautiful plants, many of which are uncommon or rare.

Origins and development

Spring and Flush vegetation in the montane zone is natural, maintained by the harsh climate, but at lower altitudes within moorland and upland grassland it is generally grazed. Grazing can help maintain species-richness by removing tall rushes and grasses and keeping the surface open for small flowers and sedges; however, these small features are vulnerable to trampling damage, particularly where there are tufa formations. Bryophytes are particularly susceptible to air-borne pollutants but the 'critical load' beyond which habitat deterioration will occur is not known. Changes in the extent and duration of snow cover will affect high-altitude Springs and Flushes.

Conservation

Upland springs and flushes are typically very small, and are therefore usually subject to management decisions made about wider areas. Greater awareness of their presence and sensitivities would help ensure that management is not harmful. Under less intense grazing regimes some calcareous flushes would probably support montane willows and tall herbs or woodland.

What to look for

Curled Hook-moss growing with Hooked Scorpion-moss and Yellow Starry Feather-moss is a good indicator of species-rich flushes. At medium and high altitudes, look out for Yellow Saxifrage and Russet Sedge.

When to visit

Year-round for bryophytes (conditions permitting); summer for flowering plants.

Coire an Lochain, Cairngorms – an acidic flush rich in bog-mosses and other bryophytes.

Lowland Fen

Lowland Fen is found where the ground remains waterlogged for most of the year or is periodically inundated in floodplains. It occurs in shallow valleys and adjoining open water and is fed by surface and groundwater, as well as rainwater. Conditions are variable, and can be neutral to base-rich and nutrient-poor to fertile. This is reflected in the vegetation, which also varies according to past management. Grazing, mowing, draining and peat-digging all interact with hydrological factors to shape the flora and the structure of vegetation. The small-sedge fens of Anglesey and Ireland are found in alkaline conditions with low nutrient levels. The classic tall-herb and sedge fens of The Norfolk and Suffolk Broads are found on peat of nearly neutral pH in more fertile conditions.

Lowland Fen can be a particularly species-rich habitat, although many of these species are not wetland specialists, and their presence is a reflection of the diversity of conditions found. The fenland fauna includes particularly large numbers of species of flies, beetles and moths. The diversity of invertebrates is reliant upon structural variety: bare areas, tussocks, deep litter, shaded areas, pools and transitions to swamp, carr woodland and Fen Meadow are all important.

Similar habitats

Reedbed is similar to Lowland Fen but can be both wetter and taller, and is almost exclusively dominated by Common Reed. Grazed areas of Lowland Fen supporting Fen Meadow vegetation in northern England can be transitional to Northern Hay-meadows, with Globeflower and Marsh Hawk's-beard. Transitions to Wet Woodland are common.

Origins and development

Lowland Fen develops where landscape features prevent drainage and create waterlogged conditions (*e.g.* the floodplain fens of The Norfolk and Suffolk Broads and basin fens of central Ireland) or where there is a constant flow of water (*e.g.* the spring-fed fens of Anglesey). Lowland Fen is a transitional habitat that would, over time, succeed to Wet Woodland or, where the development of peat isolates the vegetation from the groundwater, to Raised Bog. Various land-use practices including mowing, grazing and

Distribution and extent

Scattered across lowland Britain and Ireland; extensive areas are now confined to East Anglia, Anglesey and Lough Erne. Eng: 8,000 ha; Sco: 8,600 ha; Wal: 6,200 ha; NI: 2,950 ha; Ire: n/k. Generally rare in Europe.

BELOW LEFT: **Redgrave and Lopham Fen, Suffolk** – swamp vegetation is found on the margins of fens and lining dykes where is colonises open water, sometimes forming floating rafts of vegetation (called hover) over water, liquid peat or older rafts. BELOW RIGHT: **Upton Fen, Norfolk** – Marsh Fern is a characteristic component of Common Reed and Saw-sedge fen.

peat digging have arrested this successional process, helping to retain wet conditions by removing plant litter, exposing springs and preventing the establishment of woody species. The decline of such practices since the mid-20th century has seen a deterioration in the quality of many fens, although some are still cut for thatch or marsh hay or for conservation purposes. Fens are also very vulnerable to river engineering that modifies flooding regimes. Vast areas that once supported Lowland Fen have been drained and used for agriculture, and most Lowland Fen is now confined to protected sites.

Conservation

The area of Lowland Fen has declined significantly over the last century across Europe, and Britain and Ireland hold a large proportion of that which remains. However, in Ireland, Lowland Fen is often threatened by polluted groundwater and in Britain by nearby water extraction or lack of flooding due to river engineering. Paradoxically, it can also be threatened if it remains part of intact floodplain systems due to the effects of river-borne nutrients. Attempts to maintain high water levels have included the installation of impermeable liners (*e.g.* at Wicken Fen) and irrigation (*e.g.* at Redgrave and Lopham Fen). Landscape-scale conservation is particularly important for wetland sites, and initiatives such as the Great Fen project in East Anglia are looking to link and buffer existing sites with re-created wetlands.

Did you know?

The Fen Raft Spider is a prodigious hunter, able to take dragonflies and sticklebacks. First discovered in 1956 at Redgrave and Lopham Fen, it is known from only a small handful of sites, and young spiders reared in captivity have been released to try and safeguard the species from extinction in Britain.

How to recognise

Lowland Fen supports tall, dense swards of reeds, large sedges and rushes or a shorter, tussocky sward of rushes and small sedges. It is often rich in other flowering plants, including many conspicuous and attractive species.

Many sites are small and isolated, set within drained farmland, but more extensive areas are still found where wetland landscapes have escaped conversion to agriculture.

The water-table is rarely far below the surface making Lowland Fen hard to explore, particularly where it is dissected by deep dykes or dotted with pools and swampy hollows. At many sites, particularly in East Anglia, the limited access routes are clearly defined by mown trails, raised paths or boardwalks. These can add structural diversity, and are good places to watch for flying insects such as the iconic Broadland species, Swallowtail and Norfolk Hawker. However, some fens are only accessible by boat.

When to visit

Summer for insects and plants.

Thelnetham Fen, Suffolk – a spring-fed valley fen comprising Fen Meadow, Saw-sedge fen and small-sedge fen.

What to look for

On Anglesey, in the shallow East Anglian valleys and on the Carboniferous limestone of Ireland look out for small-sedge fens. They occur near seepages and springs where the summer water-table is close to the surface and are characterised by Black Bog-rush and Blunt-flowered Rush. Look for small sedges and herbs in damp runnels between tussocks and more acid-loving species such as Tormentil and Bog Asphodel on tussock tops. Uncommon and rare species include Narrow-leaved Marsh-orchid, Grass-of-Parnassus and Slender Tufted-sedge.

In the classic tall-herb fens of The Norfolk and Suffolk Broads and Wicken Fen look out for Milk-parsley and Marsh Pea in swards of Common Reed or Reed Sweet-grass, together with bulky herbs such as Yellow Loosestrife, Purple-loosestrife, Meadowsweet, Yellow Iris, Common Valerian, Hemp-agrimony and Wild Angelica. Particularly species-rich swards can be found where cutting followed by grazing creates Fen Meadow communities (see Purple Moor-grass and Rush Pasture, *page 116*).

In East Anglia, keep an eye out for the strangely tusked Chinese Water Deer, an introduced species that favours swampy vegetation (Britain now holds one tenth of its world population). Other fenland mammals include Harvest Mouse, Water Shrew and Water Vole, although they are typically hard to see. Listen out for Grasshopper Warbler, Sedge Warbler and Reed Warbler (favoured by Cuckoo as a host) and, in Britain, Barn Owl is a frequent sight quartering marshes.

TOP LEFT: **Saw-sedge** forms distinctive stands that were traditionally cut in the summer to provide tough thatch for roof ridges. Species-rich examples of Saw-sedge fen (which are of European importance) can include plants such as Fen Orchid, Marsh Helleborine, Lesser Tussock-sedge and Slender Sedge.
TOP RIGHT: **Southern Marsh-orchid** – A diversity of orchids can be found in fens, including this species, Early Marsh-orchid, Common Spotted-orchid, Marsh Helleborine, and the rare Narrow-leaved Marsh-orchid and Fen Orchid.
BOTTOM RIGHT: **Yellow Iris** – a common component of tall-herb fens.

ABOVE: **Swallowtail** – the iconic Swallowtail is now limited to The Norfolk and Suffolk Broads, where it can be seen on various reserves. It lays its eggs on tall plants of Milk-parsley on which the caterpillar (*left*) feeds. Look for the butterfly (*right*) on a windless day in the early morning between late May and mid-July. In some years there is a second brood in mid-August–September. RIGHT: **Grass-of-Parnassus** is a delicate plant that flowers from July to September. It can be found in small-sedge fens and fen meadows or along rides cut in tall-herb fens; it is also typical of upland flushes.

How Hill, Norfolk – much of what is traditionally considered as fen in The Norfolk and Suffolk Broads is dominated by Common Reed and has been created through centuries of reed cutting.

VALLEY MIRE

Valley Mire is best known from lowland heathlands, but also occurs as a component of upland blanket mire. Variation in Valley Mire vegetation is generally due to hydrological factors. The water percolating through the underlying sands and gravels is mostly acid and nutrient-poor. However, in any one valley it may come from a variety of sources, and seepages and springs often introduce more base-rich water, increasing the complexity and diversity of the vegetation. The lateral movement of water contributes to the zonation seen in many larger mires where nutrients tend to accumulate along the central axis. As the ground gets wetter, vegetation dominated by heathers gives way to an open community of bog-mosses with a scattering of vascular plants such as Bog Asphodel and Round-leaved Sundew. Towards the centre of the mire this can be replaced with Black Bog-rush along soakways, the wettest of which may support Marsh St. John's-wort and Bog Pondweed. Birch or willow-dominated woodland can sometimes develop in the centre of mires. Dense patches of Purple Moor-grass may be associated with areas where the water is well-oxygenated, or in valley bottoms where nutrients accumulate. Valley Mire generally shows some surface patterning, with hollows, hummocks and bog pools. In some places, such as Hartland Moor in Dorset, buoyant rafts of vegetation can form over liquid peat (see Transition Mire and Quaking Bog, *page 164*).

Similar habitats

Lowland fens within valleys tend to be larger, usually within agricultural landscapes, and support tall herbs and large sedges characteristic of more alkaline conditions. Lowland Wet Heath shares many species with Valley Mire, but bog-mosses are confined to the small and neat Compact and Soft Bog-mosses, often only present as discrete cushions. Where it occurs within blanket mire in the uplands, Valley Mire can support more Purple Moor-grass, Bog Asphodel, Bog-myrtle and Oblong-leaved Sundew than the surrounding vegetation.

Origins and development

In the warm and dry southern lowlands mires can only form in hollows or shallow valleys where water is held back by topographical features or vegetation. Valley Mire peat is rarely very deep, usually no more than 1·5 m, sometimes only 20 cm or so, but there is evidence at some sites to suggest that mire vegetation has been constantly present over thousands of years. Mires have been affected by peat cutting in the past, and some floating rafts of vegetation are found over what may be re-flooded turbaries (peat diggings). Although usually dependent on natural

Distribution and extent

Map shows lowland Valley Mire only; in the uplands it is widespread in areas supporting blanket mire. Extent unknown. Over half the European resource is thought to be in Britain.

BELOW LEFT: **Stoborough Heath, Dorset** – in summer the mossy-green wetland species in the shallow valley stand out against the heathery background of Lowland Dry Heath.
BELOW RIGHT: **Hartland Moor, Dorset** – in winter the pale litter of Purple Moor-grass and tussocks of Black Bog-rush highlight the curving mire in the shallow valley bottom, with willows in the centre.

topographic features, Valley Mire is also found in ball-clay mines on the Dorset Heaths and tin workings on Dartmoor.

Drainage has affected many mires, either directly or through water extraction/drainage on nearby sites lowering the water-table. Drier mires are also more vulnerable to burning. Recreational disturbance has possibly had a role in the declines of breeding waders (*e.g.* in the New Forest).

Conservation

Valley Mire conservation centres around maintaining (or recreating) suitable hydrological conditions. For example, in the New Forest attempts have been made to slow the loss of water from mires by modifying drainage systems. On the Dorset Heaths, extensive grazing has been reintroduced to prevent coarse vegetation from gradually building up and creating drier conditions, and to maintain an open sward suitable for bog-mosses and small perennials such as sundews.

Did you know?
The New Forest contains 75% of the lowland Valley Mire of north-west Europe

How to recognise

In the lowlands, Valley Mire stands out as a distinctive element in the landscape. Soft, jewel-bright patches of bog-mosses line small channels where the water trickles almost imperceptibly. Dark bog pools are spiked with Common Cottongrass and White Beak-sedge, and in summer the brown, peaty water is warm to the touch. The mires are busy with insects, although even damselflies can be caught by the sticky, insectivorous sundews that speckle the bog-mosses.

Some mires squelch underfoot, others quake treacherously over an unknown depth of liquid peat. In places, tall tussocks of Purple Moor-grass and spicy-scented Bog-myrtle make walking all but impossible. In the uplands, Valley Mire is less striking since where it occurs it forms part of the overall landscape of blanket peat.

When to visit

Valley Mire is slow to come alive in the spring (but listen out for Snipe drumming); it looks best in late summer when most characteristic species are still in flower.

Morden Bog, Dorset – Common Cottongrass stands out when in flower in June.

What to look for

Many species of dragonfly and damselfly are associated with bog pools and runnels, including Small Red Damselfly, Keeled Skimmer and Black Darter. The conical nests of the endangered Black Bog Ant can be found at the transition between Valley Mire and Wet Heath, and the velvety, striped Raft Spider can be seen on the surface of pools. Characteristic breeding birds to look out for include Snipe and Curlew, and Hen Harrier can roost in some mires in winter.

A distinctive habitat of European significance to look out for in Valley Mire is peaty depressions dominated by White Beak-sedge. Found next to bog pools, on flushed areas on the sides of Valley Mire and disturbed areas such as tracks, it can support scarce species such as Brown Beak-sedge, Marsh Clubmoss and Bog Orchid. Only about 400 ha of this habitat remains in and associated with Valley Mire, but it is also found on Blanket Bog and Raised Bog in western Britain and the west and midlands of Ireland.

In soakways, water tracks and shallow pools look for a distinctive community with Marsh St. John's-wort, Bog Pondweed and Cow-horn Bog-moss. It is found in clear, still or only gently moving waters where the water-table fluctuates, so that it is above water during the summer months. It can occasionally include an unusual creeping fern, Pillwort, which also grows at the margins of heathland ponds where there is some clay in the soil and where there has been a long tradition of heavy grazing.

ABOVE LEFT: Bog pools and wet hollows are a key component of Valley Mire, and can support floating mats or spongy carpets of bog-mosses, including **Golden Bog-moss** (hummocks) and **Feathery Bog-moss** (hollows) seen here. Vascular plants include **White Beak-sedge** and Common Cottongrass, with Bog-bean, Lesser Bladderwort and Bog Pondweed in deeper water. ABOVE RIGHT: **Raft Spiders** can be seen from May to August resting on the surface of bog pools and use their legs to sense vibrations in the surface of the water that might indicate the approach of potential prey. BELOW LEFT: **Godlingston Heath, Dorset** – a Valley Mire sward dominated by Bog Asphodel. BELOW RIGHT: **Stoborough Heath, Dorset** – Black Bog-rush growing along a central water track, with Bog Asphodel, White Beak-sedge and Cross-leaved Heath growing among Bog-myrtle to the side.

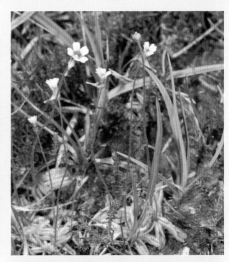

ABOVE LEFT: **Bog Asphodel** – a classic bog species that flowers from July to September. ABOVE CENTRE: **Bog Orchid** is threatened throughout its European range; it favours areas with some water movement, and is found growing both on bog-moss lawns on the edge of runnels and deeper within rushy swards towards the centre of mires. ABOVE RIGHT: **Pale Butterwort** is a perennial species that flowers from June to October and forms large, long-lived seed banks from which it regenerates readily following disturbance. Insectivorous plants such as butterworts and sundews are widespread in Valley Mire, reflecting the limited availability of nutrients. RIGHT: **Keeled Skimmer** – the larvae inhabit debris at the bottom of runnels and pools for two years before emerging. Males often perch nearby and can be locally abundant from June to September.

Hartland Moor, Dorset – White Beak-sedge flowers in July and August and is more widespread than the scarce Brown Beak-sedge which flowers in June–July. Brown Beak-sedge (INSET) can be identified by its broader, yellower leaves, and chestnut spikelets with a projecting bract. In autumn, the fruits of White Beak-sedge also turn brown, and the two species can be confused at first glance.

183

Reedbed

Reedbed is essentially swamp dominated by Common Reed. It is found in a wide range of conditions in the lowlands on permanently waterlogged or seasonally dry situations of differing nutrient status, although it is typical of more nutrient-enriched waters. Common Reed has a vigorous rhizomatous growth form and is adapted to waterlogged conditions (the previous year's stems remain standing for several seasons, helping to aerate the rhizomes), allowing to it maintain its dominance in extensive stands.

Reedbed is a transitional habitat found between water and land. Where it fringes open water, it can give way to floating or submerged aquatics where the water becomes deeper. On the landward margin it can be replaced by Saw-sedge (in nutrient-poor, base-rich waters) or Greater Tussock-sedge and other swamp species (where there are more nutrients). Where conditions are drier, it may grade directly into tall-herb fen, although intact sequences are quite rare due to drainage. The diversity of habitat structure provided by different successional stages, including open wet areas, pools, reed fringes and stands of different ages, is important for wildlife.

In north-west England and Scotland, Reedbed tends to be less extensive and is restricted to more nutrient-rich areas in lakes (*e.g.* the deltas of inflowing streams where Common Reed often forms a patchwork with Bottle Sedge or Bladder-sedge).

Similar habitats

Reedbed forms transitions with tall-herb and sedge Lowland Fen, often in a complex patchwork resulting from varied management. It can be differentiated from tall-herb fen and other swamp communities by the overwhelming dominance of Common Reed.

Origins and development

Common Reed is an active coloniser of open water, and can persist for a long time in areas that are regularly flooded (including tidal areas) – some clones have been aged at over 1,000 years. Elsewhere, the formation of peat and build up of litter leads to the development of Lowland Fen and then Wet Woodand (carr). In the past this process was often set back indefinitely

Distribution and extent

Widespread throughout the lowlands.
Eng: 7,000 ha; Sco: 1,100 ha; Wal: 500 ha;
NI: 3,200 ha; Ire: n/k.

Ant Broads and Marshes, Norfolk. The margins of reedbeds provide habitat for nesting wildfowl and for invertebrates and fishes. Bitterns hunt for fish, amphibians, birds and mammals along the reed/water interface where the water depth is about 15–30 cm; sites with a high ratio of reedbed edge to area support the highest densities of Bittern.

Deben Estuary, Suffolk – Common Reed can tolerate moderately saline water, and is common in brackish estuaries and dykes.

How to recognise

Common Reed can be found fringing still or slow-moving open water, or forming impenetrable expanses in floodplains.

In summer the thick blue-green stands are quite monotonous, although in drier areas they can be laced with sprawling Bittersweet or Hedge Bindweed, and tall-herbs such as Yellow Iris and Great Willowherb add the occasional patch of colour. In winter the reed drops its leaves, and the rustling stands of bleached, brittle stems are quietly atmospheric.

Often growing in standing water, or through thick litter of indeterminate firmness, reedbeds are hard to explore, and are most easily appreciated from their margins or where board-walks have been constructed. Hides are usually the best places to go to catch a glimpse of Bittern skulking through poolside reeds, but Bearded Tits are easier to see as they flit over reed heads.

by winter-only cropping of the upright, bare stems (mainly for thatch), which helped to perpetuate dense, single-species stands.

Reedbeds were once extensive, particularly in the fens of eastern England, but were lost to agriculture once large-scale drainage schemes started in the 17th century. A decline in reed-cutting throughout the 20th century, together with nutrient enrichment from fertilizer run-off, caused a decline in the quality of the remaining sites, often with the loss of key species.

When to visit

Winter for raptors and Starling roosts; spring for breeding birds.

Radipole, Dorset – this Reedbed in the centre of Weymouth supports Bearded Tit and Bittern.

Did you know?

Common Reed can grow in water that is over a metre deep and can produce over 200 shoots per square metre.

Conservation

Of the 900 or so reedbeds in the UK, only about 50 are greater than 20 ha (the minimum size required for breeding Bittern). Conservation effort has focussed on expanding and re-creating reedbeds on inland sites to compensate for expected losses through coastal flooding. Recent projects have addressed issues around setting back succession and creating variation in structure in ways that support the reed-cutting industry and use of cut reed for biofuel and composting. Livestock grazing, used more widely in continental Europe, is also being explored, and may have a role in creating habitat mosaics on larger sites.

What to look for

Reedbed is highly valued for the characteristic suite of birds it can support, some of which only breed in this habitat. Listen out for the distinctive booming of Bittern at dawn and dusk between March and June. Other species to look out for include Bearded Tit, Marsh Harrier, Reed Warbler, Water Rail and Reed Bunting. In coastal areas of southern England and Wales, the robust, explosive song of Cetti's Warbler is an increasingly familiar sound around scrubby Reedbed margins. Reedbed also provides late-summer roost sites for large flocks of migrant Swallow and Sand Martin, and in the winter is used by roosting raptors and Starling. Huge flocks of Starling create an astonishing spectacle, swirling overhead in constantly changing formations. There are also a number of very rare birds associated with Reedbed, such as Little Bittern and Savi's Warbler.

ABOVE LEFT: Reed cutting results in an immediate reduction in breeding birds. Ideally cutting should be carried out on a rotational basis. The interface between mosaics of differently aged patches of reed are favoured by several species. ABOVE: After suffering heavily from habitat loss and illegal persecution, **Marsh Harrier** numbers increased in the late 20th century and it is once again a regular sight flying over Reedbed in some parts of the country.

BELOW: **Reed Leopard** is a local and scarce moth, occurring in East Anglia and Dorset. The larvae feed inside Common Reed stems.
BOTTOM: **Bearded Tit** is a reedbed specialist that lives off reed aphids in the summer and reed seeds in the winter.

ABOVE: **Hickling, Norfolk** contains one of the largest reedbeds in England. Bittern was first photographed by ornithologist Emma Turner here after its return to Britain as a breeding species in the early 20th century. Its subsequent decline prompted a programme of Reedbed restoration projects.

In Britain, Grass Snake may be seen swimming in open water or basking in dry areas. Keep an eye open for Water Vole – Reedbed provides this species with an important refuge from Mink. Fishes, such as Rudd and Eel, are also an important component of ecosystems in which Reedbed is found. At least 25 species of invertebrates are dependent on Reedbed, and up to 700 species have been recorded. A complete transition from open water to fen provides the greatest number of niches, with older, drier parts having the highest invertebrate density. Rare species of conservation importance include the White-mantled Wainscot moth.

Reedbed is intrinsically poor in plants species. Look for Water Mint and Marsh Bedstraw where the reed cover is quite open in shallow water and in denser swards Cowbane, Greater Spearwort and Water Dock. The more nutrient-poor reedbeds of lakes in the north and west can support Bogbean, Marsh Cinquefoil, Bottle Sedge and Water Horsetail.

Westwood Marshes, Walberswick, Suffolk – *this 18th century mill was used to drain the surrounding land for agricultural use before the area was re-flooded as part of Second World War defence works.*

ABOVE LEFT: **Cley Marshes, Norfolk** – many coastal reedbeds, such as those at Cley, are threatened by sea-level rise. In north Norfolk new wetlands are being created on farmland farther inland to compensate for the habitat that is likely to be lost.

ABOVE: **Bittern** – the British population dipped to just 11 booming males at seven sites in 1997 but has since recovered (mainly as a result of habitat creation projects) and over 100 booming males were recorded in 2011.

FRESHWATERS

ORIGINS

Freshwaters encompass a wide range of habitats from high mountain tarns to large sluggish rivers in the lowlands. Nowhere in Britain or Ireland is very far from the sea so very large rivers are absent, but the generally high level of precipitation means that rivers and streams form a key component of most landscapes. River water is derived from precipitation via surface run-off, springs or snow-melt, and usually collects in a drainage basin from which it flows downhill in a channel eroded by the river. In the uplands, fast-flowing rivers can erode 'V'-shaped valleys. As the water flow slows in the middle reaches, the valley becomes shallower and broader and the river starts to meander over the valley bottom floodplain. Upland rivers can also follow 'U'-shaped valleys gouged out by glaciers. Most natural lakes owe their origins to glacial deposits creating dams, or to glaciers over-deepening valleys. England was less heavily glaciated than the rest of Britain and Ireland and, in the lowlands, natural lakes with glacial origins (such as the Shropshire and Cheshire meres) are rare and limited in distribution. There are some natural lakes around the coast where coastal sediment has trapped freshwater (such as Slapton Ley in Devon). However, most lowland lakes are artificial, created through mineral extraction, as drinking water reservoirs, ornamental lakes, moats or canal feeder reservoirs. Ponds and pools across the lowlands are often legacies of small-scale mineral workings or were dug to stock fish or to provide water for livestock; the Norfolk and Suffolk Broads are flooded medieval peat diggings. On a geological time-scale, lakes are temporary features in the landscape, as they gradually trap sediment brought in by rivers and the process of hydrosere succession starts (see Wetlands *page 160*).

Freshwater habitats in two contrasting parts of Britain (both maps are at the same scale). The **Frome and Piddle river valleys** in Dorset (LEFT IMAGE AND MAP) contain Floodplain Grazing Marsh and Ditch systems. There are small areas of standing water in this un-glaciated landscape and the porous chalk geology means that there are relatively few tributaries. In contrast, in upland landscapes (RIGHT IMAGE AND MAP), the hard bedrock means that there is a much higher density of streams and rivers and there are large areas of standing water of glacial origin (such as **Loch Maree** in Wester Ross, shown here).

HABITAT	DESCRIPTION
STANDING WATER	
Nutrient-rich (Eutrophic) Lake *page 196*	Nutrient rich and often alkaline, found in the lowlands. Some naturally mesotrophic lakes are now eutrophic due to pollution.
Upland Lake, Loch and Tarn *page 198*	Nutrient poor, acidic waterbodies found in the uplands.
Peat-stained (Dystrophic) Water *page 200*	Very acidic and nutrient-poor pools found within peatlands.
Turlough and Fluctuating Mere *page 202*	Aquifer-fed waterbodies that fluctuate with the water-table and may dry out completely.
Other Lake Types *pages 204–205*	Mesotrophic Lake, Marl Lake, Lowland Nutrient-poor Lake and Brackish Lake.
Pond *page 206*	Small (< 2 ha), widespread and usually isolated waterbodies.
Ditch *page 208*	Shallow and linear artificial boundary or drainage features.
Canal *page 210*	Shallow, linear waterbodies that join river catchments and were constructed for transport purposes.
FLOWING WATER	
Fast-flowing River and Stream *page 212*	Actively eroding natural watercourses, usually in the uplands, with fast-flowing and clear water.
Sluggish River and Stream *page 214*	River systems with slow-flowing and cloudy water that deposit fine sediment on the river bed, usually in the lowlands. Most have been modified.
Chalk River and Stream *page 216*	Lowland fast-flowing rivers and streams with clear water derived from chalk aquifers, typically supporting water-crowfoot vegetation communities.

TYPES OF FRESHWATER HABITAT

The character of all freshwaters is shaped by the landscape in which they are found. The underlying geology of the catchment influences the water chemistry and physical characteristics such as size, depth or flow. Upland lakes, rivers and streams tend to be low in dissolved nutrients ('oligotrophic'), while in the lowlands glacial deposits create naturally productive, nutrient-rich waters ('eutrophic'). These are simple extremes and a wide variety of intermediate types exist. Humans have had a substantial impact by raising nutrient levels and acidifying waters.

Standing Waters

Standing waters include open waters that lack a unidirectional flow, and can be permanent or seasonal. They have traditionally been classified as oligotrophic or eutrophic according to their nutrient status. Alkalinity (the amount of dissolved calcium carbonate) and pH (the ratio of hydrogen to hydroxyl ions) also influence the overall character of waterbodies. In general, oligotrophic lakes tend to be acidic and eutrophic lakes more alkaline. Oligotrophic waters are most common in the uplands where acidic rocks dominate and the deepest lakes are found. Alkaline waters occur mainly in the lowlands of England and Ireland where rivers and streams drain limestone, and are often eutrophic. Mesotrophic waters are intermediate in their productivity and alkalinity and are generally found in the north and west. Changes in plant and animal communities according to water nutrient status are shown in the chart on *page 191*.

Besides the three main trophic levels, there are other types of standing water where the water chemistry is particularly distinctive: dystrophic waters are peat-stained, highly acidic and poor in nutrients; marl lakes are very alkaline; and brackish waters are partially saline and fluctuate with the tide. Alkalinity, depth, colour, area, altitude, substrate and shape of water bodies all contribute to differences in the plant and animal communities present. Of the 24 aquatic vegetation communities described in the British National Vegetation Classification (NVC), 21 can be found in standing waters. In practice, individual sites are not always easy to categorise and detailed analysis has resulted in various approaches that identify up to 11 types of lake. Seven types of standing water are described in detail in this book, and a summary is provided of four more unusual types.

Flowing Waters

Flowing waters are often shallower than standing waters and are linear. Their character is influenced by flow rate (which is linked to topography), in addition to both

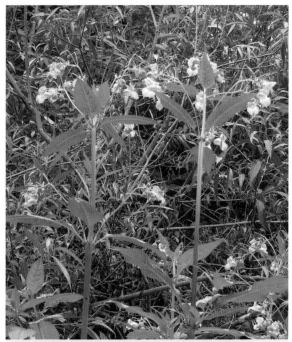

Himalayan Balsam is a garden escape that has rapidly colonised river banks. Like Japanese Knotweed, another invasive non-native, it smothers other vegetation and leaves banks bare and vulnerable to erosion in the winter.

land-use and geology within the catchment (which affect water chemistry). Flow characteristics have a strong influence on the plant and animal communities present, as fast-flowing water presents a fundamental challenge for many aquatic life forms, and here we separate streams and rivers according to flow rate (*i.e.* fast-flowing, eroding watercourses and sluggish streams and rivers that deposit sediment). The dividing line is an arbitrary one, reflecting an essentially upland/lowland split. A single watercourse can include both types and water chemistry may vary along its length, but there is often a change in species and character when it crosses from the uplands into the arable zone. Chalk streams and rivers are described separately, as they are both distinctive and rare. The difference between rivers and streams is again arbitrary. Ordnance Survey maps at a scale of 1:25,000 indicate watercourses that are wider than 8·25 metres with two blue lines (as opposed to one) and this width is often taken as the threshold beyond which a watercourse is considered as a river.

River plant communities are harder to classify than those of standing waters due to the variations in water chemistry within single watercourses. Aquatic plants (macrophytes) occur in both lakes and rivers but in flowing water phytoplankton are not a key part of the flora as they are washed away. Fourteen NVC communities occur in flowing water. As with standing waters, detailed analysis has revealed the complexity of flowing waters, and 10 types have been identified.

THREATS AND ISSUES

Most freshwater habitats are intricately linked to the landscape around them. For rivers and streams and the lakes they feed, those links extend to the entire catchment upstream and consequently human impacts are not limited to those directly affecting the waterbody, but extend into the catchment. Afforestation affects water flow and results in acidification; soil management and overgrazing influence the amount of sediment; artificial fertilizers and pesticides affect water quality; and water abstraction reduces water levels. These factors, combined with run-off from roads and urban areas and sewage effluents, means that few waters are unpolluted. Changes in phosphorous levels started nearly two centuries ago – sediment cores from some lakes in the Lake District indicate changes in the diatom assemblage dating back to the mid-1800s, corresponding to increases in the local human population and tourist use. Nutrient enrichment is now thought to be affecting 80% of UK lakes, and studies of streams have suggested that once agriculture exceeds 30–50% of the catchment area, their condition deteriorates. The impacts of nutrient enrichment are different for each kind of waterbody, but typically result in a loss of key species. Solutions to all these issues are limited and complex, particularly for large waterbodies.

Modification and drainage also affect many watercourses. Channels that have been straightened, embanked or canalised within hard walls are a common sight, and few rivers now have natural braids or are unconstrained within their floodplains; only 11% of the total length of all rivers and streams in England and Wales is thought to be unmodified and near-natural.

A further factor impacting on the ecology of waterbodies is the scale of colonisation by invasive non-native species. The connectivity of waterbodies means that plants and animals can spread quickly. For example, Canadian Pondweed is thought to have been introduced to Ireland from Canada in around 1836. By 1880 it had spread to England and Scotland and was hindering navigation in many watercourses. Now it is widespread but seldom abundant. Himalayan Balsam is the most common non-native bankside plant, particularly along larger rivers. It forms dense stands that out-compete other plants and substantially reduces the abundance of invertebrates associated with the vegetation. Countless introductions of non-native fish (often for angling) have also impacted on other wildlife (*e.g.* Zander suppress other fish populations, carp increase turbidity and remove aquatic macrophytes, and farmed fish reduce genetic diversity within natural fish stocks). American Mink and Signal Crayfish have been associated with the decline of some native species such as Water Vole and White-clawed Crayfish.

The abundance of different groups of plants and animals varies with the nutrient status of the water. This table shows the notional abundance of different groups within different standing water habitats.

	Dystrophic	Oligotrophic	Mesotrophic	Eutrophic	Hypereutrophic
Phytoplankton					
Submerged aquatic plants					
Benthic animals					
Cyprinid fish (Chubb, Dace, Roach, Rudd *etc.*)					
Whitefish (Vendace, Powan, Pollan)					

SOLVING WATER-QUALITY ISSUES: Lessons learned from the Norfolk Broads

The Norfolk Broads were dominated by diverse submerged plant communities until around the middle of the 20th century when most were lost as a consequence of increases in nutrient levels that resulted in dense phytoplankton growth. In the early 1980s, Cockshoot Broad was dammed off from the adjacent River Bure in order to isolate it from the source of further nutrient enrichment, and phosphorus-rich sediment was removed to a depth of almost one metre in an attempt to restore the plant communities. Although submerged plants began to recolonise soon after phosphorous levels dropped, the main area of the Broad was slow to be colonised and, by the mid-1980s, plants began to decline and phytoplankton levels started rising again. It appeared that the fish population had increased and the fish were eating the zooplankton (which control the level of phytoplankton). In 1989 virtually all the fish (nearly 100,000) were removed from the Broad, allowing zooplankton to increase again, and aquatic plants began to recolonise the main part of the Broad. However, the process has been slow, and this has been attributed to waterfowl damage to plants and the arrival of a predatory shrimp (that preys on zooplankton). Levels of aquatic macrophytes have fluctuated markedly since the original fish removal, but on the whole the approach seems to have been successful. This example highlights the complexities and difficulties involved in resolving water quality issues in large waterbodies.

Rivers and streams are particularly sensitive to climate change as water temperature tends to track air temperature closely. Most river organisms are cold-blooded and therefore sensitive to temperature changes. Temperature also affects water chemistry, including oxygen concentration. Water temperature in streams and rivers has already increased by around 1–3°C over the last three decades. Changes in rainfall due to climate change will also affect river flow, which will impact on the distribution and abundance of many river animals. Any reductions in water flow are likely to be exacerbated by high levels of water abstraction in many areas.

CULTURAL IMPORTANCE

Freshwaters have played a key part in determining where people live. Access to freshwater, the importance of water for transport, the presence of crossing points and flood risk have all influenced the location of settlements. Rivers lie at the heart of many cities such as London (the Thames) and Dublin (the Liffey) and have often been used as boundaries (such as the Wye, on the border between England and Wales). Freshwaters provide drinking water (for people and their livestock) and power (now generally hydroelectricity, but water-powered mills were essential to rural life in the past). Rivers and canals have been important transport routes, and freshwaters have provided important food sources (fish and wildfowl). Today in the UK, every person uses around 150 litres of water per day and demand is increasing. Around two-thirds of the UK's water comes from surface sources rather than groundwater.

People are often drawn to water, and many waterbodies are used extensively for recreational pursuits including the use of various watercraft and for angling and bankside walks. Many myths, legends and stories also include water as a key element, often with some kind of mystery attached (such as the Loch Ness monster, or the Waters of Avalon in the legends of King Arthur). Freshwaters are portrayed in many artforms, including books such as Kenneth Grahame's childrens' story *Wind in the Willows*.

CONSERVATION IMPORTANCE AND PROTECTION

Freshwater and wetland habitats together occupy just 3% of the UK's land surface but support around 10% of its species, including around 4,000 invertebrate taxa. Freshwater habitats are protected through a range of legislation. For example, in England there are 28,693 ha of open water within the SSSI network, of which 20,458 ha are standing waters and 7,881 ha are rivers and streams. There are 44 English rivers that, at least in part, are designated as SSSI. Nine freshwater Annex I habitat types are present in Britain and Ireland, two of which are

TOP: Fish ponds were widespread in the Middle Ages and were an important food source. Fishing is a popular modern pastime and many freshwaters are artificially stocked. MIDDLR: Many gravel pits and reservoirs now fulfil a range of roles, including recreation, education and nature conservation. BOTTOM: Otters disappeared from most of England in the latter part of the 20th century due to pollution and habitat destruction, but can once again be found across Britain and Ireland thanks to conservation efforts. Otters use all parts of the catchment, including ditches and small streams – they can even occasionally be seen in Blanket Bog.

Priority Habitats and one (rivers with floating vegetation often dominated by water-crowfoot) for which the UK has a special responsibility (see *page 23*). The European Water Framework Directive required the development of catchment-scale management plans detailing actions needed to maintain and improve the ecological status (among other requirements) of waterbodies up to 2027.

Key Freshwater Areas

1	Wessex Chalk Streams
2	New Forest ponds and streams
3	The Lizard
4	Lake District
5	Turloughs
6	Lough Corrib
7	River Shannon
8	Upper Lough Erne
9	Lough Neagh
10	Uist Machair
11	Lewis Peatlands
12	The Flow Country
13	River Spey
14	Highland lochs
15	Loch Lomond
16	West Midlands Meres
17	River Severn
18	Norfolk & Suffolk Broads
19	River Thames
20	Norfolk & Suffolk Broads
21	Suffolk Coast

The map shows all freshwater habitats (major rivers and lakes only). Ireland holds a number of large lakes, with Lough Neagh (388 km²) and Lough Corrib (200 km²) being far larger than any British site. Scotland holds the deepest waters. and some large sites such as Loch Lomond (71 km²), and 90% of the UK's standing water is in Scotland. The Shannon (386 km) is the longest river in Britain and Ireland, followed by the Severn (354 km) and the Thames (346 km).

Some key locations are labelled on the map; this selection is not intended to be exhaustive but highlights a few of the most important areas.

KEY ELEMENTS

Margins

Sites with a complete hydrosere (see *page 166*) from open water to Wet Woodland have the potential to support the widest range of species. A key part of this is the marginal zone of bank and shallow water, which can be especially diverse, particularly where there is a gently sloping transition rather than an abrupt change. It provides habitat for plants and animals that require both aquatic and terrestrial conditions, and can be particularly rich in invertebrates. Look for a range of shallow water and marginal plant species and invertebrates such as dragonflies, mayflies and craneflies.

Exposed Riverine Sediments

Exposed riverine sediments are shoals of bare sand and shingle that can form spits, bars and islands. They are dynamic, temporary features that are reshaped by every flood and are widespread and common – around 47% of the total length of rivers in England and Wales contains un-vegetated bars. Often a mix of substrates will be present as successive floods deposit different sizes of sediment. They lack continuous vegetative cover, but a suite of specialist invertebrates, including ground beetles, rove beetles, flies and spiders, occupy a range of microhabitats provided by the transition from stonier sediments on the upstream end to the finer sediments at the tail-end. Where vegetation is present, it can be varied and may include heathland species and sometimes montane species washed down from the uplands. Both Common Sandpiper and Little Ringed Plover breed on exposed riverine sediments.

Many of the rare species of the New Forest live at the grazed margins of shallow, vegetation-filled waterbodies. The rare Southern Damselfly breeds on this slow-flowing stream.

Eroding Banks and River Cliffs

Where rivers are able to move naturally across floodplains, faster-flowing water on the outside of meanders erodes the banks and can create cliffs and exposed areas that gradually shift over time. The un-vegetated, loose material can be important for a range of specialist invertebrates, and the cliffs provide nesting sites for Kingfisher and Sand Martin.

*This meander on the **River Wye in Gloucestershire** shows some of the key features found in flowing waters.*

River cliff

Exposed riverine sediment (shingle)

Backwater

This mid-channel bar in the River Avon on the Dorset / Hampshire border is composed of fine shingle. It is re-shaped when the river floods, but in the summer supports sparse ruderal vegetation.

Woody Debris and Log Jams

Although often removed from rivers to allow water to flow easily, whole trees, limbs or branches that fall into waterbodies create an important range of microhabitats. Large pieces of debris add complexity and can modify flows, create pools and catch sediment. They provide shelter, shade and spawning sites for fish, and a variety of conditions for invertebrates and algae, while the smaller organic debris that collects around it provides nutrients. Protruding debris helps the terrestrial adult stage of river flies (mayflies, stoneflies, caddisflies) and dragonflies to emerge from the water, and can provide resting places for mammals and birds. Woody debris is most commonly found in steep-sided, woodland headwater streams, where its role in flood alleviation is increasingly recognised, as it slows the water flow. It also reduces bank erosion and stabilises the stream bed. Its scarcity elsewhere is due the lack of riverine woodland as well as river management practices. However, 're-snagging', the introduction of woody debris, is now a recognised river rehabilitation technique.

FURTHER INFORMATION

Freshwater Habitats Trust: www.freshwaterhabitats.org.uk/
Freshwater Biological Association: www.fba.org.uk/
Rivers by Holmes & Raven (Collins New Naturalist, 2014)

TYPES OF AQUATIC PLANTS

Aquatic plant species have a range of growth forms. **Emergent aquatics** have their roots underwater but their leaves and flowers above (*e.g.* Arrowhead, Flowering-rush and Greater Spearwort). Some have leaves floating on the surface (*e.g.* White Water-lily). **Submerged aquatics,** such as most pondweeds, have all their leaves submerged in the water. Water-crowfoots have both submerged leaves and floating leaves. There are also some species that are entirely **free-floating**, such as Water-soldier, Frogbit and duckweeds.

A range of dragonflies is associated with flowing water. **White-legged Damselfly** (TOP) prefer slow-flows and muddy sediment; **Beautiful Demoiselle** (MIDDLE) and **Golden-ringed Dragonfly** (BOTTOM) are associated with gravelly streams.

Nutrient-rich (Eutrophic) Lake

Naturally nutrient-rich (eutrophic) lakes typically occur in areas with sedimentary rocks or drift deposits from which the nutrients are derived. They are often located within the hard water areas of the un-glaciated southern and eastern lowlands of Britain, and in Ireland they are mainly found in the midlands and the north-east. The bottom sediment is derived from decayed organic matter and, where aerobic conditions develop as a result of bacterial activity, only a specialist fauna (*e.g.* nematode worms) will occur. The relatively high levels of dissolved nutrients in the water support abundant planktonic algae, and these in turn provide the foundation of a complex food web of zooplankton (*e.g.* cyclops and water fleas), larger invertebrates (including snails, dragonflies and water beetles) and fishes (predominantly Cyprinids such as Roach, Rudd and Tench, as well as Perch and Pike). The fish in turn support breeding bird species such as Great Crested Grebe. Amphibians, including Great Crested Newt, are often present. Where algae is dense, it may limit submerged aquatic plants to the shallow water where light can still penetrate, but a rich flora including pondweeds, water-milfoils and Yellow Water-lily is found at the best sites. In many waterbodies the nutrient levels are artificially high as a consequence of agricultural run-off or sewage effluent and the flora and fauna are impoverished.

Similar habitats

Pond and Canal can hold eutrophic water, as can Turlough and Fluctuating Mere, which differs in its hydrology and is also largely restricted to Breckland and western Ireland. Other types of waterbody generally have clearer water and often a rocky shoreline.

Origins and development

Most nutrient-rich lakes are artificial, having been created deliberately for a variety of functions. Many are the remnants of extraction, such as gravel pits, or the special case of the Norfolk and Suffolk Broads, which were created when medieval peat diggings were subsequently flooded. A scattering (*e.g.* the Shropshire and Cheshire Meres) have natural origins, having been created by glacial action. Historically, many sites have been lost through drainage – much of Fenland would once have been covered by shallow, eutrophic lakes – and the remainder have been degraded by pollution. Elevated levels of nutrients (in particular phosphorus) lead to the dominance of algae, turning the water dark green and excluding macrophytes and impoverishing fish communities.

Distribution and extent

Widely scattered. Eng: 17,900 ha; Sco: 7,300 ha; Wal: 700 ha; NI: 14,800 ha; Ire: 41,100 ha (ANN I REP). Uncommon in Europe due to Pollution.

BOTTOM LEFT: **How Hill, Norfolk** – open water with Yellow Water-lily is backed by swamp vegetation of Common Reed and Bulrush with Hemp-agrimony. BELOW: **Small Red-eyed Damselfly** – a recent colonist that can be seen on marginal vegetation and floating vegetation in July and August. BOTTOM RIGHT: Densities of **Great Crested Grebe** are highest on the most nutrient-rich sites.

ABOVE LEFT: Nutrient-rich waters can support high densities of a range of fishes such as **Rudd** (shown), Roach, Tench and Pike. ABOVE RIGHT: Once believed extinct in Britain, **Medicinal Leech** inhabits warm, shallow water with plenty of vegetation. Amphibians, birds and fish are its main prey. RIGHT: Spiked Water-milfoil can tolerate nutrient-rich waters and is widespread.

Conservation

The restoration of nutrient-rich lakes is complex and expensive, but is worth attempting provided the input of pollutants can be stopped. Successful projects have involved phosphate stripping at sewage works discharging into upstream rivers and the removal of nutrient-enriched mud from lake beds. Other threats to nutrient-rich lakes include recreational use (boats increase the turbidity of the water) and invasion by non-native species. Management of the immediate surroundings is integral to the management of the waterbody as many aquatic species (*e.g.* amphibians and invertebrates) spend part of their life-cycles in the adjacent terrestrial habitats.

What to look for

The presence of various pondweeds and stoneworts is a good indication of unpolluted water. Large numbers of waterfowl may be seen in winter.

*Hoveton Great Broad, Norfolk, has lost much of its aquatic flora due to over-enrichment. **Water fleas** (INSET) and other zooplankton form a rich 'soup' visible to the naked eye that in turn supports a range of larger invertebrates.*

Nutrient-rich Lake includes any waterbody between a small pool and a large lake that has a high level of nutrients. Found in the lowlands, some are natural waters (*e.g.* Slapton Ley in Devon, Upper Loch Erne in Fermanagh and Loch Leven in Kinross); others are artificial waterbodies such as flooded gravel pits, ornamental lakes and moats.

The high nutrient level can often be deduced from the greenish water and abundant vegetation. The water clarity varies, but by summer is often quite murky with a distinctive swampy smell. The bottom, which is not often visible, is muddy, deep in rich organic sediment. In the lowlands, robust fringing vegetation and muddy margins can make it hard to reach the shore, and it is often difficult to see the whole extent of a lake. On some sites, a succession from open water through submerged and emergent communities to Reedbed, Lowland Fen and Wet Woodland can be observed, especially from out on the water looking towards the shore.

When to visit

Mid-winter is the peak time to see wildfowl, ideally at dawn or dusk. Visit in the summer to see many of the invertebrates and plants.

UPLAND LAKE, LOCH AND TARN

Upland waterbodies have low levels of nutrients (they are 'oligotrophic') and are not productive. The water is usually very clear because the low nutrient levels limit the growth of phytoplankton, although the leaching of humic substances from the catchment may cause some brown colouration. A variable community of unrelated but distinctive plants called 'isoetids' is associated with oligotrophic lakes. These plants, which absorb carbon dioxide through their roots, have shuttlecock-like rosettes of narrow leaves and include Shoreweed, Quillwort, Water Lobelia, Awlwort and, mainly in western Ireland and the Hebrides, Pipewort. The clear water allows good light penetration and some plants will grow down to a depth of eight metres, although most grow in shallower water. In shallow waters, Bog Pondweed, water-starworts and Floating Bur-reed may be present, while Bottle Sedge and Common Club-rush fringe sheltered bays. With relatively little plant life, there are correspondingly small numbers of plant-eating invertebrates; however, caddisflies, water beetles and water-boatmen are typically present, and River Limpet and freshwater shrimps may be seen around the shoreline. Some deep-water invertebrates and zooplankton only found in oligotrophic lakes may be glacial relics. Brown Trout, Arctic Charr and whitefish are found in lochs up to about 500 m. At higher altitudes, newts may be the top predator in the food chain. Black-throated Diver, Common Scoter, Goldeneye and Red-breasted Merganser breed on upland lochs, which can be some of the least disturbed aquatic habitats in Britain and Ireland.

Similar habitats

The water of Mesotrophic Lake is also clear, but contains lush fringing and aquatic vegetation (some of the Lake District waters are mesotrophic), while the organic shoreline of Nutrient-rich Lake is often fringed with swamp and fen vegetation. Peat-stained (Dystrophic) Waters are typically dark brown.

Origins and development

Upland lake, loch and tarn basins were formed as a result of glacial scour in hard rock landscapes. Tarns (or lochans) are often found in corries, among glacial moraine and in kettle-holes, while larger, deeper lochs and lakes are in 'U'-shaped valleys. Although some smaller examples have been lost through drainage, the number of larger oligotrophic waterbodies has remained stable. However, many have been degraded by inputs of nutrients from agricultural run-off and small domestic point sources. Non-native species are a problem at some sites, in particular fish (*e.g.* Ruffe, which feed on Powan eggs and fry) and plants (*e.g.* New Zealand Pigmyweed).

Distribution and extent

Widespread in the uplands, but extent unknown.

BELOW: **Loch Maree, Wester Ross**, is a large relatively pristine loch where Otter and **Black-throated Diver** (BELOW LEFT) feed on Atlantic Salmon and Brown Trout. Submersion within its waters was once considered a cure for lunacy.

LEFT: **Pipewort** (*top left and centre of image*) is found on peaty substrates, and is seen growing here with Least Bur-reed (*bottom right*). RIGHT: **Water Lobelia** is one of the more distinctive 'isoetids' when in flower during July and August.

Conservation

Conservation measures involve ensuring stable nutrient levels and good water quality, and appropriate land management within the catchment is vital. Diffuse pollution from agriculture is an ongoing problem, and drainage of surrounding peatlands can also be an issue. Atmospheric pollution remains a threat for high altitude lochs, while those near the coast may be affected by salinity due to changes in sea level.

What to look for

In the summer, look out for Floating Water-plantain and the elusive Slender Naiad, also exposed populations of Shoreweed or Bog Hairgrass and Marsh Clubmoss on dry shores. Breeding Black-throated Diver, Common Scoter and Goldeneye may also be present in the summer, and Otter can be seen year-round.

Did you know?

Loch Morar, the deepest in the UK, reaches a depth of 310 m, while Loch Ness holds more water than all the lakes in England and Wales put together.

Upland Lake, Loch and Tarn includes the biggest and deepest waterbodies in Britain and Ireland, such as great lochs of Loch Ness and Loch Maree, and many of the lakes of the Lake District and Snowdonia. Their stony, wave-washed shores and deep, cold water can look forbidding on a bleak day, but in the sunshine the glittering water and often stunning scenery have a more accessible beauty, and they are some of the best-loved features in our landscape.

This habitat type also includes smaller, shallower tarns and lochans, many of which are unnamed. Found high up in mountain corries or on the fells, they are beautiful, solitary places, with just a thin scattering of plants. They often freeze over completely in the winter.

When to visit

Summer for breeding birds and aquatic plants.

Coire an Lochain, Cairngorms – one of the highest waterbodies in Britain and Ireland, this corrie lake freezes over for most of the winter and holds a very limited fauna. CENTRE RIGHT: Coire an Lochain seen from above.

Peat-stained (Dystrophic) Waters

Dystrophic waters are highly acidic and poor in nutrients. They contain dissolved humic acid derived from peat, which also stains the water a dark brown. The colouration makes for poor light penetration, and this, together with the low nutrient content, means that relatively few plant species are able to thrive. Common Cottongrass, Lesser Bladderwort, Bogbean and Bog Pondweed are characteristic, and bog-mosses sometimes dominate, for example in many of the dubh (black) lochans of north-west Scotland. The fringing vegetation is not generally distinctive but tends to reflect that of the surrounding land. Invertebrates include water beetles, caddisfly larvae, water-boatmen and some scarce dragonflies. In small pools, the invertebrate population includes a high proportion of carnivorous species which prey mostly on terrestrial invertebrates that drop into the water. The lack of suitable food means that mayflies and stoneflies (which are largely herbivorous) are mostly absent and many pools are too acidic to support fish. Although individual pools are species-poor, the degree of variation between them means that, at a landscape level, the habitat has greater diversity. Lowland dystrophic pools can be more species-rich than those in the uplands as a result of additional nutrient input from the adjacent land.

Similar habitats

Dystrophic waters occur within mire systems and are linked to Blanket Bog, Raised Bog and Valley Mire. Some oligotrophic waters can also be brown-coloured and the two can be difficult to separate.

Origins and development

Most dystrophic waters are found within blanket mire in the uplands (particularly north-west Scotland and western Ireland). Examples are also found farther south, such as in the mosses of the West Midlands where kettle-holes have developed into basin mires. In southern Britain a few are found over Tertiary sands between Surrey and Dorset, but in most of the mire systems in this area there is little open water; Woolmer Pond in Hampshire is thought to be an ancient peat cutting. Dystrophic waters have been lost from areas such as the Irish Midlands through drainage, peat extraction and forestry.

Distribution and extent

Mostly confined to the north and west of Britain and the Atlantic fringe of Ireland; rare in the lowlands. Eng: 200 ha; Sco: n/k; Wal: 30 ha; NI: 80 ha; Ire: 1,830,000 ha (ANN I REP).

BELOW LEFT: **Lake District** – many small, unnamed peaty pools are found in the uplands.
BELOW: **Abernethy, Speyside** – a dystrophic pool created by damming a stream; pools such as this provide habitat for the rare Northern Damselfly.

ABOVE LEFT: **Northern Damselfly** is restricted to only about 30 sites in central Scotland. ABOVE RIGHT: **Flow Country, Sutherland** – patterning of dubh lochans.

These are the dark, peaty pools and lakes found scattered across our remotest uplands. They are also found in Raised Bog and Valley Mire in the lowlands, but most are an intrinsic part of Blanket Bog where, even on the dullest day, they catch the light and add a sparkle to the otherwise sombre landscape. They are generally small and can occur in isolation or dispersed among knolls and hollows where their prevalence makes it hard to pick a straight route through the bog.

In north-west Scotland, they form ordered linear or concentric patterns. Sometimes they are capped with a quaking mat of mosses and vascular plants (which cannot necessarily take a person's weight).

Larger dystrophic lakes with sandy or gravelly shores are also (rarely) found. Lowland pools tend to be deeper than their upland counterparts.

Conservation

Given their often remote nature, many peaty pools are relatively unaffected by the nutrient enrichment that impacts on other standing waterbodies, and there is little need for conservation intervention beyond that needed for the surrounding habitat. Blanket Bog restoration projects involve restoring the natural hydrology of sites and allowing new pools to form.

What to look for

Look in dystrophic pools for insectivorous plants such as bladderworts. In Scotland, look for Azure Hawker, White-faced Darter and Black Darter, which is also found on southern sites with Emerald Damselfly and, in England and Wales, Small Red Damselfly. In the Shetlands, Orkney and Hebrides, listen out for the strange repetitive call of breeding Red-throated Diver.

When to visit

June for Bogbean and Common Cottongrass in flower and various dragonfly species.

*A dubh lochan on **Rannoch Moor** with **Bog Bean** (INSET) flowering in the foreground. The pools of Rannoch Moor include an unusual diversity of size, depth and shoreline types.*

TURLOUGH AND FLUCTUATING MERE

Turloughs and Fluctuating Meres occur in depressions in Carboniferous limestone and chalk respectively. Springs, swallow holes and openings into underground drainage systems allow limestone basins to fill with groundwater and empty again, while the porous nature of chalk means that water can percolate through it. The variation in water level may be up to six metres, and often follows a seasonal pattern. Turloughs tend to fill around mid-autumn, and empty the following spring. In contrast, fluctuating meres may become fuller in the summer in a delayed response to high winter groundwater levels. They can also dry out altogether for prolonged periods; the process by which they fluctuate is not fully understood.

Plant communities are determined by the period of inundation and the water level. The lowest parts of the basin can be marshy and support Common Sedge, or muddy in which case species such as Knotgrass, Amphibious Bistort and Water-purslane readily grow. Silverweed is particularly characteristic, and can be found across the damper centre and some way up the sides of the basin, usually giving way to a springy turf of Carnation Sedge and wet-meadow species in turloughs, or a band of Reed Canary-grass in fluctuating meres. The aquatic flora is better developed in fluctuating meres than turloughs, and can include pondweeds and stoneworts. Both habitats support a range of invertebrates, usually species adapted to temporary waterbodies. Some are highly mobile (*e.g.* dragonflies), whilst others have forms that can withstand periods of dessiccation (*e.g.* water fleas and Fairy Shrimp, which can flourish in the warm, fish-free water during wet periods). Each site tends to have a different invertebrate fauna according to factors such as water depth and grazing. The waterbodies also provide spawning sites for amphibians, and Great Crested Newt is found in some fluctuating meres. During the winter, turloughs provide important winter feeding grounds for waterfowl, and water-filled fluctuating meres can support breeding wildfowl.

Distribution and extent

Turloughs are largely restricted to the central western lowlands of Ireland; fluctuating meres are only found in the East Anglian Breckland. Eng: 10 ha; Wal: 1 ha; NI: 20 ha; Ire: 6,900 ha. Unique to Britain and Ireland.

Similar habitats

Turloughs and fluctuating meres are similar to lakes when the water levels are high, but unlike lakes can support fen or grassland communities when the water levels drop. Temporary ponds are smaller.

Origins and development

Turloughs form where glacial drift is thin or absent over depressions in grey calcarenite, a type of limestone through which water is able to flow particularly easily. The origins of Breckland's fluctuating meres are unknown, but they also depend on geomorphological features. The absence of a water inlet means that Turloughs and Fluctuating Meres

BELOW LEFT: **Shrubby Cinquefoil** can be found flowering in June and July at the high water mark of turloughs. BELOW RIGHT: **Langmere, East Wretham, Norfolk** – During dry phases the muddy bottom supports ruderal species including Common Nettle. Breckland holds six fluctuating meres and another six smaller fluctuating pools.

FACING PAGE, RIGHT: **Scarce Emerald Damselfly**, sometimes called the Turlough Spreadwing in Ireland, is particularly associated with turloughs.

are not prone to silting up, and may be ancient, although many turloughs contain a layer of marl in the soil profile, suggesting that they were once permanently flooded. Shallow ridges indicate where turloughs were used for cultivation when the human population density was higher, and fluctuating meres have also very occasionally been cropped during dry spells. Grazing systems are integral to the management and diversity of turloughs and larger turloughs are usually commons.

Conservation

While 79 of the 300 turloughs in Ireland are designated as SACs, there is comparatively little in place to ensure their protection, and smaller turloughs may not even be mapped. Lack of awareness and incomplete understanding of their hydrology inhibit long-term conservation planning. Loss of traditional grazing systems linked to the ephemeral nature of turloughs threatens their wildlife interest, as does increased nutrient input through agricultural intensification. Fluctuating meres are more reliably protected, but water abstraction may be prolonging dry periods.

What to look for

Look out for Fen Violet, Water Germander, Shrubby Cinquefoil, Whooper Swan and Scarce Emerald Damselfly in turloughs. Two distinctive mosses, the blackish Smaller Lattice-moss and the large, branched Greater Water-moss, can be seen on the rocks of swallow holes and the bottom of fluctuating meres. When fluctuating meres are water-filled, look for breeding Little Grebe, Tufted Duck, Gadwall and Pochard.

*Water levels in the turloughs of **The Burren, Co. Clare**, seen here in August, respond particularly rapidly to changes in the groundwater level usually linked to rainfall, although Cahergassaun Lough near the coast empties and refills twice daily with the tide in summer. Greater awareness of turloughs is needed to ensure their protection. Many have been lost in the past through drainage, and more recently, suspected turloughs have been lost to development including a bypass and a car salesroom (subsequently abandoned when it flooded!).*

OTHER LAKE TYPES
MESOTROPHIC LAKE

Loch Insh, Speyside – the River Spey flows through this loch and there is an exceptionally fast through-flow of water.

These are neutral to base-rich lakes usually found on the fringes of the uplands, often where calcareous and acidic bedrocks meet. They tend to have hard, rocky bottoms and clear water that allows light to penetrate. With a moderate nutrient status ('mesotrophic'), these lakes can be particularly rich in aquatic plants, unlike the more barren oligotrophic lakes, although most have an upland 'feel'. A range of different aquatic plant communities can occur, depending on the substrate, water depth and exposure. Sheltered areas with a stable water column may hold Alternate Water-milfoil and a variety of pondweeds, while areas with fine sediments (*e.g.* outflows) may support stoneworts. Look out for scarce plants such as Six-stamened Waterwort and Pillwort. Classic sites include Bassenthwaite and Windermere in the Lake District, Loch of the Lowes in Perthshire, and Llyn Eiddwen and Llyn Fannod in Ceredigion.

MARL LAKE

Loch Caladail, near **Durness, Sutherland** – one of a cluster of three marl lakes known for their very clear water.

Marl Lakes occur in limestone areas and have very clear water with a characteristic blue tint. Marl is calcium carbonate that has precipitated out of the water primarily as a result of the removal of carbon dioxide by aquatic plants. This precipitation removes dissolved nutrients from the water and, as a consequence, phytoplankton levels are low. However, macrophytes can obtain nutrients from the marl that forms the bottom sediment and, because of the clarity of the water, can grow at great depths (exceptionally down to 12 m). The flora can be very rich, and stoneworts (large algae that superficially resemble vascular plants and are coated with deposits of calcium carbonate) are a notable feature. The invertebrate fauna is variable, with some lakes supporting a rich diversity of species similar to those found in eutrophic waters, while isolated and upland marl lakes support relatively few invertebrates. Classic sites include the Durness lochs of Sutherland, Malham Tarn (North Yorkshire), Lough Bunny (Co. Clare), Lough Owel (Co. Westmeath) and Lough Carra (Co. Mayo). The Cotswold Water Park is a network of artificial waterbodies including marl lakes that were created through gravel extraction.

LOWLAND NUTRIENT-POOR LAKE

Little Sea, Studland, Dorset is a shallow lake that formed when sea water became landlocked by accreting sand dunes. The water is now fresh and is replenished by acidic, oligotrophic water draining off the adjacent heathland. Much of the aquatic vegetation has disappeared in recent years, probably due to the introduction of Carp.

There are some lowland sites where lakes lie on sandy, acidic substrates and are low in nutrients. Such lakes are similar in their chemistry, and much of their flora to upland oligotrophic lakes, They can support 'isoetid' species such as Water Lobelia, Shoreweed and Quillwort, which may be zoned in single-species lawns. In the UK, these lakes are scarce and occur only at a few heathland and Machair locations; classic sites include Hatchet Pond (New Forest, Hampshire), Little Sea (Studland, Dorset) and Oak Mere (Cheshire) and the South Uist Machair lochs. Ireland is a stronghold for Lowland Nutrient-poor Lakes, with 32 SACs designated for this habitat type, including Lough Corrib, an unusual site with features characteristic of both Marl Lake and Lowland Nutrient-poor Lake in basins in limestone and acidic rocks respectively.

BRACKISH LAKE

Hickling Broad, Norfolk, is connected to the sea by the rivers Thurne and Bure.

Brackish lakes, which can be eutrophic or oligotrophic, are slightly saline, and their water levels show some fluctuation with the tide. In The Broads of East Anglia, Hickling, Horsey and Martham fall into this category. In Scotland there are lochs where sea water can enter at high tide through a narrow inlet. Such sites are rocky and have a gradient from fresh to more saline water along their length; they include Harray and Stenness on Orkney (eutrophic) and Loch an Duin on South Uist (oligotrophic).

POND

Ponds are very diverse and this habitat type supports a correspondingly diverse flora and fauna. Some individual ponds support over 40 aquatic plant species and over 50 large invertebrates. Overall, ponds support a similar number of plant species to lakes, and more large invertebrates than rivers; some two-thirds of freshwater species have been recorded in ponds. Most ponds gradually silt up over time and examination of old maps suggests that many field ponds only last a century or so. However, deeper ponds may be more permanent and some ground ice depressions (sometimes called pingos) have held water for 14,000 years. Many gardens contain ponds, and these can also be rich in wildlife, particularly where they have shallow edges, marginal vegetation and nearby plant cover. Temporary pools that dry out annually are distinctive and, as they tend not to silt up (the dry spells allow organic matter to oxidise), may be a more permanent feature in the landscape than deeper pools. They also lack predatory fish, and so may support different invertebrate communities from those ponds or pools that remain water-filled year-round.

Similar habitats

Ponds are distinctive in being small in size and lacking connectivity. Lakes have a true open-water zone in which algae and submerged plants are dominant. Temporary ponds in heavily grazed grassland are associated with mosaics of acid and neutral grassland and are best seen in the New Forest.

Origins and development

Natural ponds are found in solution hollows, seasonally flooded depressions and pingos dating from the end of the last glaciation. Artificial ponds include those deliberately created as waterbodies such as dew ponds (for watering livestock), decoys (to draw wildfowl for hunting) and pools used for leather and hemp processing. Others were created as a result of the extraction of minerals such as stone (including flint), sand, gravel, clay, brickearth and marl (chalky soil used as a fertilizer). There are also about 5,000 moats that probably date from the 13th century onwards. Many ponds will silt up unless periodically cleared out. Changes in rural practices have often made ponds redundant and so they have been allowed to dry out. Others have been drained or lost to development; 50% of the estimated one million ponds that existed in Britain 100 years ago have vanished.

Distribution and extent

There are around 500,000 ponds in Great Britain plus three million garden ponds, and an unknown number in Ireland and Northern Ireland.

How to recognise

Ponds are small waterbodies (up to 2 ha) that hold water for all or part of the year and are not fed by a stream or river, but depend on rain and groundwater. They are characterised by shallow-water and swamp vegetation, with little deep, open water and can be found in gardens, on village greens, in corners of farmland, deep within woods, and on pastures and heathlands. Ponds are sometimes hidden, lost in overgrown, forgotten tangled thickets.

Unpolluted and not overly shaded ponds can be teeming with wildlife, supporting a wide array of invertebrates and diverse plant species, and providing habitat for amphibians and birds. In some areas they are a characteristic feature of the landscape, such as the 'pingos' of East Anglia, the Cheshire marl pits and the forest and moorland pools of Speyside.

When to visit

Spring for tadpoles; summer for 'bug-hunting' and aquatic and marginal plants; winter for Fairy Shrimp.

LEFT: Village pond, **Redgrave, Suffolk**. Ponds often form a focal point in villages and historically would have fulfilled a range of roles, including water for animals and fish for food.

Conservation

Ponds are vulnerable to pollution (mainly nutrient enrichment from agricultural run-off) and neglect. Temporary ponds are particularly threatened as the small water volume means that they are more vulnerable to drainage and pollution. Some old ponds may benefit from careful restoration, and there are ambitious targets to re-create ponds – the Freshwater Habitats Trust aims to ensure that by 2050 there are once again one million ponds in the UK. New ponds are an effective way of creating new freshwater habitat that is relatively easy to protect from nutrient-enrichment.

What to look for

Search the drying edges of temporary pools for Pennyroyal (in the New Forest), Pigmy Rush (on The Lizard) and Yellow Centaury (south-west England and Ireland). Keep an eye open for Fairy Shrimp when pools refill. Look for Great Crested Newt in permanent ponds with a water depth of over 50 cm and abundant aquatic plants, the much less widespread Natterjack Toad in temporary pools in Sand Dune and lowland heathland. Pond-dipping can reveal a great diversity of invertebrates, including water beetles, diving beetles, water fleas, pond snails, caddisfly larvae and dragonfly nymphs.

BELOW LEFT: A temporary pool on a **New Forest** lawn. Ponds only need to hold water for a few months each year to support a suite of aquatic species. BELOW: **Pennyroyal** flowers during August and September and is associated with temporary pools on heavily grazed village greens. It experienced a drastic decline in the 20th century as habitat was destroyed, or changed as grazing decreased.

Oxwich, Gower – a permanent pond at the back of a sand dune system.

DITCH

In areas that were once extensive wetlands, ditches are the remnant of wetland habitats that have long since disappeared, and provide a continuous link with those habitats. These ditches can be centuries old, and are particularly rich in aquatic plants and invertebrates. Since most ditches are nutrient-rich, differences in vegetation composition are determined by salinity, water depth and flow, substrate type and management. The diversity of the fauna depends on the structural variety within a ditch, and is greatest where there is a mixture of marginal vegetation of different heights, open water, shallow trampled edges and different bank profiles – steep sides are favourable for Water Vole but gentle, shallow edges are preferred by many invertebrate species. Ditches in coastal grazing marshes often contain brackish water, and this adds another suite of specialist species (although influxes of strongly saline water into freshwater ditches can result in low species diversity). Shaded ditches and those colonised by invasive non-native plant species (see Canal, *page 210*) are less diverse. Ditches where some form of management takes place are generally richer in plant and invertebrate species and have a greater abundance of amphibians and visiting birds.

Similar habitats

Ditches can be confused with heavily engineered small streams and may be similar to canals, although the latter are generally wider.

Origins and development

Most ditches were dug to drain land and make it suitable for cultivation or grazing animals, although some were created to transport materials (such as peat or reeds) or to form livestock barriers (known as wet fences). In some grazing marshes, ditches were used to help maintain high water levels in the summer to encourage grass growth, and in places where wetland habitats are being restored, ditches are once again used to bring water onto the site rather than to drain it. Threats include major fluctuations in water level, pollution, invasive non-native species and inappropriate management (either over-management or a lack of management, resulting in the loss of open water).

Conservation

Regular cutting of aquatic and bankside vegetation and the occasional removal of silt is usually necessary to keep ditches open, and is best staggered over time, with stretches left uncut to ensure a wide range of conditions and provide a refuge for species likely to be lost during ditch clearance. Maintaining good water quality is a challenge in areas with intensive farming where nutrient run-off frequently pollutes ditches. Current large-scale wetland restoration projects should benefit ditches.

Distribution and extent

Ubiquitous in the lowlands, in total around 600,000 km in Great Britain.

BOTTOM LEFT: **Loch Gruinart, Islay** – an extensive ditch network in coastal grazing marsh.
BOTTOM RIGHT: **Insh Marshes, Speyside** – this site has a very complex hydrology. The wide ditch was constructed in the 19th Century for drainage purposes. BELOW: **Norfolk Hawker** – distinguished by its brown body, clear wings and green eyes, is an iconic species of the Norfolk Broads where its return from near-extinction signifies the success of conservation projects.

LEFT: **Arne Moors, Dorset** – a relatively nutrient-poor ditch in acid peat. RIGHT: **Frome Valley, Dorset** – a recently cleared ditch. Ditches in this valley support a range of uncommon plants such as Red Pondweed and Lesser Water-plantain.

What to look for

Key plant species include Frogbit, Tubular Water-dropwort, Sharp-leaved Pondweed and Water-soldier, and some ditch systems support stoneworts (look in recently cleared areas). Look for Sea Club-rush, Brackish Water-crowfoot, Spiral Tasselweed and Beaked Tasselweed in brackish ditches. Rare invertebrates include Great Silver Water Beetle and Norfolk Hawker, but more widespread species such as Ruddy Darter and Hairy Dragonfly are easier to see.

*How Hill, Norfolk – a species-rich ditch supporting a range of aquatic plants including **Frogbit** and **Water-soldier** (INSET).*

How to recognise

Ditches are generally a feature of flat land close to sea level and are typically found in Coastal and Floodplain Grazing Marsh, Lowland Fen or farmland, although they extend into the uplands too. They are artificial features that are usually straight and often follow field boundaries. Generally constructed for the purpose of draining the adjacent land, ditches range in size from a spade's width to wide agricultural drains.

The best ditches provide a refuge for wetland species that were once more widespread in the landscape. Rare plants can be found among the marginal and aquatic vegetation, which can support a diverse array of invertebrates including numerous rare water beetles and other scarce and threatened species. Ditches in arable land only rarely support such rich assemblages.

When to visit

Mid-summer (July) is a good time for flowering plants. June is the best time to see dragonflies such as Norfolk Hawker.

CANAL

Canals lack strongly flowing water, and the resulting absence of currents and bank erosion means that they have more ecological similarity with standing water and ponds than rivers. Canals vary markedly in their character, generally depending on water characteristics, the amount of boat traffic and how banksides are managed. For example, the canals of southern England and the English Midlands are eutrophic; those in north-west England receive their water from the Pennines and are mesotrophic, while the Caledonian Canal, which runs through the Great Glen, is oligotrophic.

Aquatic macrophytes can include Rigid Hornwort, Spiked Water-milfoil, pondweeds, duckweeds and Yellow Water-lily, while rare species include Grass-wrack Pondweed and Floating Water-plantain. Invertebrates can include a diversity of dragonflies, beetles, bugs and molluscs, and submerged infrastructure can support freshwater sponges. Where boat traffic is limited, fishes such as Perch, Tench, Rudd and Pike may inhabit the canal. The wildlife interest is not limited to the water; the Greywell Tunnel on the Basingstoke Canal is one of the largest winter bat roosts in the UK.

Canals are often accompanied by linear strips and pockets of other habitat (*e.g.* woodland, scrub, and grassland) which, together with the marginal and aquatic communities of the canal itself, provide corridors of semi-natural habitat linking otherwise isolated sites within agricultural or urban landscapes. Canals can also link autonomous river catchments.

Similar habitats

Canals can be separated from ditches by their width and function. Rivers 'canalised' for transport purposes or in urban settings can look similar, but have a visible flow of water.

Origins and development

The Romans were the first to build canals in Britain, but they did not become widespread until the Industrial Revolution. Most were constructed between 1750 and 1870 to extend water transport for the large-scale movement of materials and goods for which trains of packhorses on poorly surfaced roads were inadequate. Canals made a dramatic impact on the landscape, to which there was often opposition. They started to fall into decline with the advent of rail transport and later, road haulage, and many were closed. However, from the 1960s recreational interest in canals was sufficient to stop further closures, and canals that were already closed began to be restored by groups of enthusiasts. There are plans to build new canals to enhance existing networks for recreational purposes.

Distribution and extent

Widespread, particularly in lowland England.
Eng: 3,300 km; Sco: 200 km; Wal: 200 km;
NI: 110 km; Ire: 300 km.

ABOVE: **Kingfisher** is a widespread species that is often encountered on canals where water quality has been improved.
LEFT: **Wey and Arun Canal, West Sussex** – abandoned in 1871, this 37 km stretch of canal linked two rivers. It shows how, without maintenance and regular boat traffic, open water is gradually colonised by swamp vegetation.

ABOVE: **The Basingstoke Canal, Hampshire**, is nationally important for its large range of aquatic plants and invertebrates. Heavily shaded sections tend to be less species-rich. BELOW RIGHT: **Floating Water-plantain** can carpet stretches of little-used canals in England and Wales, which provide a substitute for its former habitat of slow-moving, mesotrophic rivers; the UK holds a significant proportion of the world population of this plant (which is also found pools and lakes).

Conservation

The wildlife interest of canals is threatened by poor water quality and excessive siltation leading to the loss of open water in derelict canals, and by bank erosion and high water turbidity caused by recreational boat traffic in navigable canals. Canals often run through densely populated areas where urban pressures are high. Non-native invasive species (*e.g.* Mink, Signal Crayfish, New Zealand Pigmyweed and Parrot's-feather) can disperse readily along canal networks. Today, management has to balance heritage, recreation and nature conservation interests, and obtaining the often considerable funding necessary to maintain canals can be challenging.

What to look for

Look out for Water Vole and also Kingfisher, which can be seen even in urban environments. Canals are often good places to see a wide range of dragonflies associated with standing water.

Did you know?

In England and Wales 18 canals are designated as SSSIs, and three (the Cannock Extension Canal, Rochdale Canal and the Montgomery Canal) are SACs, designated for their populations of Floating Water-plantain.

*Canal boats moored on the **Kennet and Avon canal** at Devizes, Wiltshire.*

FAST-FLOWING RIVER AND STREAM

Fast-flowing, turbulent waters are a challenging environment for plants and animals. They occur in areas with high rainfall, steep slopes and impervious substrates, and most show marked variations in water flow. When rivers are in spate, the erosive power of the water increases dramatically. The strength of the current is fundamental in determining the species likely to be present. Water chemistry is less important – most Fast-flowing Rivers and Streams are nutrient-poor. Where the bottom is composed of shifting and unstable stones, the only vegetation present is algae coating some stones, though mosses and liverworts can be found where the sediment is more stable. When streams converge to form rivers the current still causes erosion but the water loses speed and finer sands and gravels may accumulate. However, the substrates are often still too mobile for plants to take hold. Marginal aquatic vegetation is scarce but may include Alternate Water-milfoil and Bulbous Rush.

Turbulent water is rich in oxygen, and suits animals that have a high oxygen demand and strategies that enable them to cope with fast flows. Atlantic Salmon and Brown Trout (salmonids) are strong swimmers and lay their eggs in carefully constructed redds (depressions on the river bed) to prevent them from being washed away, although when the eggs hatch the young head downstream where more food is available. Freshwater Pearl Mussel lives buried or partly buried in coarse sand and fine gravel and has a larval phase that attaches to the gills of juvenile salmonids; it is a good indicator of pollution-free water but is declining severely. Other invertebrates, such as stoneflies, mayflies and caddisflies, use gaps between coarse sediment particles to shelter from the current, and some caddisfly larvae attach themselves to rocks within silk cocoons.

Similar habitats

Some watercourses, such as those on the seaward sides of mountains in Ireland and western Scotland, are fast-flowing for their whole length, while others may be fast-flowing in their headwaters and then gradually slow down. Slow-flowing watercourses can be differentiated by their silty substrate and meandering form (unless modified) and they generally hold more in-stream and marginal vegetation.

Origins and development

Fast-flowing River and Stream is a habitat of upland environments where multitudinous small flushes, rills and runnels gradually merge, firstly into small streams, then into larger tributary streams, before finally forming rivers. Such rivers and streams are essentially eroding systems that carry fine particles, pebbles and boulders with them as they flow downstream.

Distribution and extent

Widespread in the uplands. Extent unknown.

BELOW LEFT: **The River Feshie, Speyside** is one of Britain's most dynamic rivers systems. Its 'flashy' flow regime, soft banks and the abundance of loose sediment result in a continually evolving braided channel.
BELOW: **Creag Meagaidh, Central Highlands** – upland streams are often relatively straight due to the fast-flowing water. This stream is fed by snow-melt that collects in a tarn in the corrie (just out of view). FACING PAGE, INSET: **Dippers** are characteristic of fast-flowing and well-oxygenated streams and rivers, usually in the uplands.

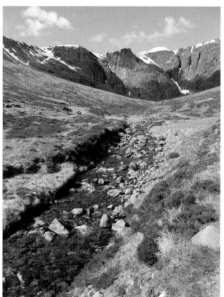

Increases in both nutrients and sediment, together with artificial changes in water flow (*e.g.* through abstraction or damming for reservoirs), have led to increased plant growth and a shift in invertebrate and fish communities in some upland rivers and streams. Acidification through atmospheric pollution and catchment afforestation is widespread.

Conservation

Recent improvements seen in lowland rivers, particularly in urban areas, have not been reflected in the uplands. Conservation measures need to address catchment management, including issues surrounding afforestation, heather-burning, overgrazing and, at lower altitudes, agricultural pollution. Impacts on Fast-flowing River and Stream have cumulative implications for water quality and flow farther downstream, potentially affecting a range of other habitats including Sluggish River and Stream.

What to look for

Particularly characteristic birds of fast-flowing streams include Dipper and Grey Wagtail, which are joined by Red-breasted Merganser and Common Sandpiper in broader reaches. Brown Trout, Grayling and Bullhead can be present, and during the 'salmon run', look out for Atlantic Salmon leaping waterfalls. Near waterfalls, it is worth searching shaded, constantly damp streamside boulders for tiny filmy-ferns.

River Grudie, Wester Ross. The large boulders reveal the strength and variation in the water flow. Cobbles trap detritus and organic matter, which are exploited by detritivore invertebrates.

How to recognise

Fast-flowing River and Stream is characteristic of the uplands, where turbulent water tumbles down steep hillsides in a series of riffles, waterfalls and pools. In their upper reaches, watercourses are often incised into the underlying bedrock. Lower down, where streams flatten out and widen into rivers, boulders, pebbles and gravel start to accumulate but the flow remains relatively fast, and species diversity is low compared to that of slow-flowing lowland rivers.

Loud and exhilarating after rain, fast-flowing rivers and streams can dry rapidly in droughty conditions, exposing spongy cushions of aquatic mosses on boulders and stranding Brown Trout in shrinking pools. Dippers bob on waterside boulders regardless of the water flow, occasionally diving for mayfly nymphs and caddisfly larvae, while in the spring Red-breasted Merganser might be seen around islets and promontories.

When to visit

Year-round for Dipper and bryophytes, autumn after rain for the salmon run. Access can be difficult after heavy rain.

SLUGGISH RIVER AND STREAM

As rivers broaden out and the water flow slows down, the temperature and the amount of sediment on the river bed increase, resulting in a different suite of species from those in the faster-flowing headwaters. Phytoplankton, which is washed away in fast-flowing watercourses, can develop sizeable populations, particularly in backwaters and, together with suspended sediment, makes the water cloudy. In-stream vegetation of pondweeds, water-starworts, water-milfoils and the submerged cabbage-like leaves of Yellow Water-lily can be sufficiently abundant to slow the water flow further, promoting the deposition of sediments and detritus and providing shelter for aquatic fauna. Invertebrates (which include filter-feeders, detritivores, grazers and predators) also shelter in snagged debris and in the bottom sediment, or can be found on the surface film. Insects are the most abundant group, although molluscs are also present. Fishes include Bream, Roach, Dace, Perch, Eel and Pike (a powerful predator), and Brown Trout and Atlantic Salmon may pass through. Marginal vegetation is abundant where the bottom sediment facilitates rooting, and includes robust plants such as Common Reed, Reed Sweet-grass, Bulrush, Hemp-agrimony and water-parsnips, with smaller herbs such as Water Mint, bur-marigolds and Brooklime on shallow edges. In their lower reaches, rivers are influenced by salt water and tides and, where they merge into estuaries, marine species such as mullet, Sea Bass and Flounder may be present.

Distribution and extent
Widespread in the lowlands. Extent unknown.

Similar habitats

Transitional zones intermediate between Fast-flowing and Sluggish River and Stream are found, and there is also overlap between the vegetation of Sluggish River and Stream and Nutrient-rich (Eutrophic) Lake.

Origins and development

Naturally dynamic, slow-flowing rivers and streams shape the surrounding landscape. They gradually migrate across the floodplain as sediment is eroded from the outside of a bend and deposited on the inside. Additional meanders can form on existing loops, and ox-bow lakes develop where meanders are cut off from the main channel. Slow-flowing backwaters are found where the river divides into more than one channel. All these features add to the diversity of species present.

A desire to use flat, fertile floodplains for agriculture and development has meant that extensive stretches of lowland rivers have been engineered and contained. Our rivers are no longer wild; they are often confined to a single channel, prevented from flooding and, in urban areas, diverted into tunnels. As a result they are commonly perceived as a linear entity within a valley, rather than an integral part of a wider wetland system. The character and conservation interest of many rivers has also been severely affected by pollution and water abstraction. However, over the last few decades efforts to clean up pollution and 're-naturalise' rivers have resulted in a return of macrophytes, fish and invertebrates.

TOP: **Mill Lawn Brook, New Forest** – New Forest streams originating in semi-natural habitat are unpolluted and varied in character and support a range of invertebrates. MIDDLE: **The River Shannon** is the longest river in Britain and Ireland and flows through 11 counties with an average flow rate of over 200 m³ per second. BOTTOM: **The River Wampool**, near **Angerton, Cumbria** meanders through agriculturally improved pasture as it approaches the Solway, where the pasture grades into Saltmarsh. FACING PAGE (INSET): **Banded Demoiselle** – one of the most attractive damselflies and a species that is typical of sluggish rivers and streams.

RIGHT: **River Waveney, Suffolk/Norfolk** border. Several surviving fens and marshes hint at the extensive wetland habitat that would once have lined the river valley, including Redgrave and Lopham, the largest remaining river valley fen in England.

Conservation

River restoration projects seek to find the balance between protecting human use of riparian environments and allowing rivers to function naturally. Flood risk can be reduced by setting back embankments and reinstating flood meadows, washlands and grazing marshes. Diffuse pollution from agriculture remains an issue, and can usually only be addressed through catchment-scale changes in land management practices. At a more local scale, the management of river banks to provide a diverse range of vegetation structures is important.

*A backwater of the **River Nene, Earls Barton, Northamptonshire**.*

How to recognise

Sluggish rivers and streams meander slowly through the lowland countryside, depositing fine sediments and organic detritus as they flow seawards. In their natural state, they curve sinuously through their floodplain and include looped meanders, shallow and deep pools, backwaters and mid-channel bars. However, the rivers of Britain and Ireland have largely been tamed and confined, and these dynamic elements are often no longer formed.

Unpolluted waters can still be rich in wildlife. Thick marginal vegetation of 'reedy' species and robust herbs gives way to usually rather cloudy open water with both submerged and emergent aquatic plants. and there can be a host of invertebrate species. Large, pollarded willows often line the river banks, and in some places the floodplains still support Floodplain Grazing Marsh or Lowland Meadow and Pasture, habitats that, together with wetlands and floodplain woodlands, would once have formed an integral part of lowland river systems.

When to visit

Early–mid-summer for flowering plants and invertebrates.

CHALK RIVER AND STREAM

Chalk rivers and streams always originate in chalk springs but they do not necessarily flow over chalk for their entire length. Water is steadily released from the aquifer, although upper reaches show gentle seasonal fluctuations and some headwater sections include winterbournes that run dry in late summer (and support their own distinctive species including Pond Water-crowfoot and rare river flies). Having percolated through the chalk the water is very pure and rich in minerals, and its temperature remains fairly constant throughout the year. These factors combine to allow Chalk River and Stream to support characteristic aquatic plant communities that can be very species-rich – 50 species per kilometre have been recorded from two classic chalk rivers in Hampshire, the Test and the Itchen. Water-cress and Lesser Water-parsnip are common along shallow edges, while the channel holds Stream Water-crowfoot and water-starworts, with River Water-crowfoot more common in downstream reaches. These in-stream plants slow the water flow in the summer and trap sediment, as well as provide food and shelter for invertebrates and fishes. Where there are clean gravels, fishes such as Bullhead, Brook Lamprey and Atlantic Salmon breed; some rivers are also stocked with Brown Trout and Rainbow Trout. The highest diversity and abundance of invertebrates is found on stretches of river bordered by wetland habitats with a range of vegetation structures present.

Similar habitats

Chalk River and Stream is distinguished from other lowland waters by the clarity of the water.

Origins and development

Natural channel geomorphology can no longer be seen on chalk rivers – they have been modified by people over millennia for a variety of activities including transport, milling, fishing, irrigation, drainage and Water-cress beds. Some also have strong links with nearby cities, for example, the Avon (Salisbury), the Itchen (Winchester) and the Wensum (Norwich), and where they occur in densely populated parts of the country impacts relating to recreational pressure and water extraction are correspondingly high. Chalk catchments also include a particularly high proportion of arable land.

Conservation

Some rivers are virtually dry in the summer and over-abstraction of water is a major threat that needs to be addressed. Other issues are the physical modification of banks and channels, pollution from agricultural fertilizers and pesticides, increased amounts of sediment from eroded soil, and intensive fisheries management (such as regular weed cutting, stabilisation of banks and stocking with farm-reared fish). However, there are a number of chalk river conservation projects that aim to maintain a mosaic of habitats in the catchment to restore aquifers and to protect the water from nutrient enrichment, and also to raise the profile of the habitat. The spread of non-native species (*e.g.* Japanese Knotweed and Himalayan Balsam) along banksides is an increasing challenge.

TOP: **Mayflies** spend most of their life underwater as a nymph, then emerge synchronously over a few days in late May when they mate and lay their eggs before dying, all in a matter of a few hours. MIDDLE: **Tributary of the River Itchen** with water-crowfoot beds clearly visible mid-channel. White-clawed Crayfish, once very common in hard waters but declining rapidly, is still found in the Itchen. BOTTOM: **The River Avon** on the Hampshire/Dorset border as winter flood waters retreat. The Avon is the longest chalk river in Europe.

Distribution and extent

There are 200 chalk rivers in the world, of which 85% (3,900 km) are in England. Map shows lowland rivers, with Chalk River in dark blue.

BELOW LEFT: The bed of chalk rivers and streams is usually composed of gravel from flint deposits within the chalk, and fine sediment is limited to slow-flowing outer bends in the river. BELOW RIGHT: A tributary of the **River Piddle, Dorset** – chalk streams probably once arose in willow and Alder carr (although this is rarely the case today) and the water-crowfoot beds that are considered to be a characteristic feature of this habitat type would have been limited to stretches where there were gaps in the tree canopy.

What to look for

Aquatic vegetation is often eye-catching and can include five species of water-crowfoot. Fishes include Brown Trout, Brook Lamprey and Grayling, and Bullhead can sometime be seen under stones. Birds to look out for include Kingfisher and Reed Bunting, and adjacent grazing marsh may support breeding waders.

River Itchen, near Ovington, Hampshire – The Itchen is famous for trout fishing and its designation as an SAC reflects the presence of other species such as Bullhead, Atlantic Salmon and Brook Lamprey.

How to recognise

Chalk Rivers and Streams are some of our most iconic freshwater sites. They can be particularly serene and equable watercourses, where mats of white-flowered water-crowfoots float in the shallow, crystal-clear water that flows swiftly over a gravelly bed. Low banks are fringed with Water-cress and Water Forget-me-not, backed by lush reed-grasses and colourful tall-herbs.

In May, thousands of mayflies emerge together and dance over the water's surface. Swallows swoop down to catch the flying adults and an occasional splash and circle of ripples shows where a Brown Trout has risen to the surface.

Old mills are a common sight, and some rivers have historic structures relating to old irrigation systems. Famous for fly-fishing, some chalk rivers have river keepers and are managed very carefully for angling, while commercial Water-cress beds are associated with some headwaters.

When to visit

Late spring–early summer for water-crowfoots in flower. The last week in May and first week in June is the peak time for mayfly emergence and is known in the trout-fishing world as 'duffer's fortnight' as even incompetent anglers can apparently make a catch!

COASTAL HABITATS

At around 31,000 km, the UK has one of the longest national coastlines in Europe, whilst that of Ireland extends to 6,000 km. Found along these coasts are some of our most important and unique habitats. The coastline is hugely variable and encompasses towering sea stacks; cliffs of black basalt, white chalk and red sandstone; shifting sand dunes; shingle ridges; saltmarshes and mudflats. Some of our oldest shores are composed of rocks that are three billion years old, while shingle and dune systems are dynamic habitats that can be seen to have changed with each visit. Natural features such as Fingal's Cave, the Giant's Causeway, the Cliffs of Moher, the Old Man of Hoy and Durdle Door draw visitors from far and wide, while the islands of Bardsey, Lindisfarne and Iona have both spiritual and cultural importance.

ORIGINS

Many factors have played a part in creating the coastline that we see today: geology, glaciation, sea-level change, sediment supply, wind, wave, tide and human activities all play a role. Britain and Ireland are unusual in having a large tidal range and stormy conditions, and as a consequence the coast is particularly dynamic. Tidal range is highest in the Severn Estuary and varies around the coast; wave energy is greatest on western coasts exposed to the north Atlantic, while the Irish Sea and North Sea are relatively sheltered.

Geology, and in particular rock strength, plays a fundamental role in dictating the shape of the coastline. Rocks that are easily eroded allow bays to develop while more resistant rocks form headlands. Soft rocks generally form sloping cliffs, whereas erosion-resistant rocks are more likely to form vertical cliffs. Geology also determines the character of beaches that develop where eroded sediment from cliffs or from offshore sandbanks is washed ashore by the waves and current. Sand is composed of silica derived from quartz, which is highly resistant to weathering, and can be mixed with shell fragments that raise the pH. Shingle is composed of flints and glacial deposits. Soft shorelines can also form on less exposed coasts where silty material washed down in rivers is deposited and builds up over time to form mudflats and saltmarshes. Soft shorelines are therefore closely linked to areas where the sediment originates, and are influenced by any changes that occur in these places.

Changes in sea levels over time have had dramatic impacts on the coastline. Sea levels rose rapidly when the ice retreated some 11,500 years ago. Added to this, as northern areas lost the weight of ice, the crust sprang upwards, and a see-saw effect ('isostatic rebound') is still causing parts of southern Britain to sink.

Blakeney Point, Norfolk is a four-mile-long shingle spit. Barrier beaches and spits occur in areas with a low tidal range such as East Anglia. Wave action is focused on a narrower band and can have a particularly strong influence.

Raised beaches on **Mull** (looking east from Tostary towards Tràigh na Cille and Ben More) are a dramatic testament to changes in sea level over the past 500,000 years.

The landbridge linking eastern England to the continent disappeared around 7,500 years ago. Seabed surveys show that this area was once a rolling plain with over a thousand kilometres of rivers, 24 lakes and extensive marshes and forests. Peat and pieces of tree trunk visible along the beaches of north Norfolk are a legacy of this lost landscape. Evidence of rising sea waters can be seen elsewhere along the coast. On the beach at Borth in North Wales, the roots of the forest that once filled Cardigan Bay can be seen at low tide, and human footprints from 8,000 years ago have been found in silt deposits exposed in the Severn Estuary. Some shingle beaches, such as Blakeney Point in Norfolk and Chesil in Dorset, have their origins in offshore gravel, pushed to shore by sea levels that rose as ice melted around 7,000 years ago. Individual storms and surges can also have long-lasting affects. Layers of sand overlying clay soils on raised beaches on the east coast of Scotland are thought to have their origins in tsunamis some 7,000 years ago.

TYPES OF COASTAL HABITAT

Coastal habitats are all found at the interface between land and sea, but vary in the degree to which they extend into the intertidal zone (which is regularly inundated

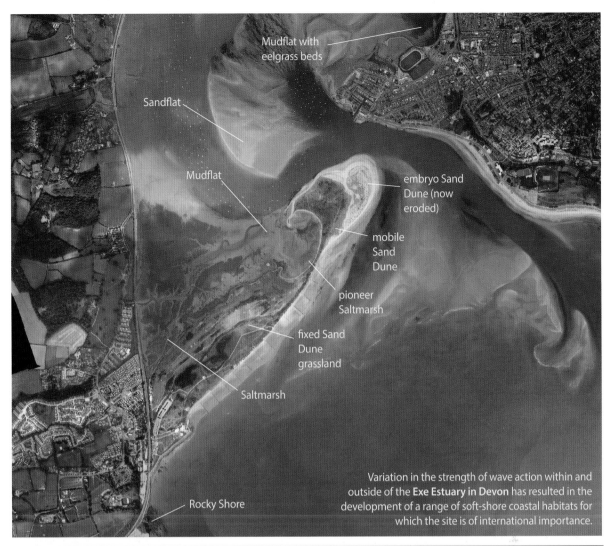

Mudflat with eelgrass beds

Sandflat

Mudflat

embryo Sand Dune (now eroded)

mobile Sand Dune

pioneer Saltmarsh

fixed Sand Dune grassland

Saltmarsh

Rocky Shore

Variation in the strength of wave action within and outside of the **Exe Estuary in Devon** has resulted in the development of a range of soft-shore coastal habitats for which the site is of international importance.

HABITAT	DESCRIPTION
Mudflat and Sandflat *page 224*	Bare expanses of open sand or mud in the intertidal zone.
Saltmarsh *page 226*	Low vegetation growing on the landward edge of mudflats in sheltered bays and estuaries.
Sand Dune *page 228*	Mobile and stable ridges and hollows created when sand from the intertidal zone is blown inland. Supports a succession of vegetation communities.
Machair *page 232*	A cultural landscape comprising a mosaic of dune grassland, wetlands and cultivated land (only found on the northern Atlantic fringe).
Coastal Vegetated Shingle *page 234*	Shingle ridges shaped by currents, tides and storm surges that have become stable enough to supporting a range of vegetation.
Saline Lagoon *page 238*	Coastal lagoons holding salt water but often with no direct connection to the sea.
Rocky Shore *page 240*	Boulders and jumbled rocks extending into the intertidal zone, rich in seaweeds.
Soft Cliff *page 242*	Unstable, sloping cliffs of soft rock often supporting a range of vegetation types.
Hard Cliff and Cliff Slope *page 244*	Sheer rocky cliffs and associated cliff slope vegetation.

but exposed at low tides), or above the limit of extreme high tides. Beyond the high tide mark is a zone that is still strongly affected by the sea through wind-blown salt spray and sand. The maritime influence extends even farther inland due to the effects of high winds, small temperature ranges and high atmospheric humidity.

Coastal habitats can be conveniently divided into eroding and accreting systems, which are linked through the transfer of sediment from one to the other. In many areas the sea erodes the land to form cliffs, which may be formed of hard or soft rock. Hard cliffs are sheer and support only crevice vegetation; many have caves near their base. They are battered by waves particularly during storms, and salt spray influences the cliff slope vegetation. Rocky shores are made up of rocks, boulders and pools within, and just above, the intertidal zone and are found at the base of hard cliffs and shorelines. Soft cliffs are composed of less resistant rock and are often slumped. Their more gentle slopes and terraces can support a range of other habitats. Sediment that is eroded from cliffs enters the water and, depending on tides and currents, is later re-deposited on the shore.

Accreting coastal habitats are formed where eroded sediment carried by currents, tides and waves is deposited on or near the shore in shallow water. Mudflat and Sandflat are almost level areas of fine sediment that are exposed at low tide and are devoid of vascular plants, although they can be rich in invertebrates. Where mud accumulates in sheltered bays and estuaries, it can be colonised by a distinctive suite of vascular plants and the process of succession leads to the formation of Saltmarsh. Not all Saltmarsh plants are restricted to the coastal zone as in rare circumstances some can occur inland – there is a natural salt spring with inland Saltmarsh vegetation in Staffordshire. Beaches are found where coarse sediments accumulate along the shoreline, including within bays between headlands on hard coasts. The intertidal area can be quite dynamic, but on the landward side of the beach, Coastal Vegetated Shingle

THE DYNAMIC COASTLINE

Coastal habitats are naturally dynamic, constantly changing as tides, currents and storms erode or build shorelines. The balance between land and sea in the coastal zone is one that humans have long sought to control. Sea defences were built from Roman times onwards, both as part of land claim and to protect farmland, settlements and industrial sites from flooding. Modern day sea defences include embankments and hard sea walls, and groynes and other beach structures designed to trap sediment and slow its movement. However, on some coasts, too much sediment is a problem and it is removed. Material dredged from shipping channels is often deposited offshore or used to build up eroding beaches.

or Sand Dune can develop and stabilise the sediment, again leading to a succession of plant communities. Soft shorelines can erode if the supply of sediment is disrupted or through storm damage.

On the north-west coast of Ireland and north-west Scotland (especially the Outer Hebrides), the extreme winds give rise to a unique sandy plain known as Machair. Lagoons of salt water trapped by a rocky sill are also found in the Hebrides, while in East Anglia, such lagoons are often associated with shingle areas.

THREATS AND ISSUES

Sea defences restrict the natural dynamism of coastal habitats by interfering with both erosion and accretion and preventing the coastline from shifting in response to changing conditions. In the last 10,000 years, the sea has risen by around 30 m and is currently rising at an estimated 2 mm per year. Coastal habitats are increasingly squeezed as they are eroded at the seaward edge but are unable to roll inland because of the presence of sea defences. Sea-level rise affects all coastal habitats, but coastal squeeze is a particular issue

Calshot, Hampshire. Beach huts and wooden sea defences, including groynes installed to trap the shingle. Trampling is limiting the vegetation growth on the stabilised shingle.

Snettisham, Norfolk. This section of beach supported a healthy population of Ringed Plover before hard sea defences were constructed at the end of the 20th century.

for accreting systems. Many of the UK's soft shores are eroding rather than accreting due insufficient sediment supplies linked to hard sea defences. Climate change is likely to quicken coastal erosion.

Many coastal areas, particularly within bays and along estuaries, support high human populations. Ports, docks, industry and all of our nuclear power stations are found on the coast. Added to this, nowhere in Britain is farther than 110 km from the sea (the distance is even less in Ireland), making the shore easily accessible by a high proportion of the population. The pressure on coastal habitats is often substantial. Excessive trampling, and in some cases wear from vehicles, can damage Sand Dune (particularly foredunes), Saltmarsh, Coastal Vegetated Shingle and Rocky Shore. Disturbance is an issue for breeding and wintering birds, and seals on both hard and soft shores. The impacts of recreation are exacerbated where habitats are constrained and limited in extent.

CULTURAL IMPORTANCE

The coast has always been of great cultural importance in Britain and Ireland. It has provided access to a range of resources including food, transport opportunities and often flat and fertile terrain for agriculture, but nowadays many people choose to live by the coast for aesthetic

Caraun Point, Co. Mayo. Shifting sand can reveal middens and other archaeological features either in vertical sand faces or in the bottom of blow-outs. Middens, the rubbish dumps of our ancestors, can date back 7,000 years and contain abundant winkle and oyster shells.

The rare **Sea Stock** is found on young dunes, which are particularly vulnerable to trampling (Port Eynon, Gower).

Kite surfing and other forms of recreation are popular in **Poole Harbour, Dorset**. In Britain and Ireland, many important sites for nature conservation are also a focus for recreation, whereas in many other parts of the world the two are often separated; it is in coastal habitats that the issues associated with recreation and nature conservation are perhaps most apparent.

Managed realignment at **Paull Holme Strays, on the Humber** – image taken in 2013, ten years after the defences were breached.

reasons and for the recreational opportunities our coastlines offer. However, the coast can be a hostile place to live. In 1953, 326 people died along the east coast of England and Scotland when a combination of high tides, strong winds and low pressure pushed water levels over five metres above mean sea level in some places. In 2014, several storms wreaked havoc along the coasts of Britain and Ireland, with substantial damage to properties and transport infrastructure, in addition to changes to much-loved landmarks, some of which vanished under the waves. Coastal communities have always been vulnerable. Skara Brae in Orkney is the best-preserved prehistoric village in northern Europe. It was engulfed in sand by a storm around 4,500 years ago and remained buried until another storm revealed it in the 1800s. Along the Suffolk coast the coastline has moved 1·5 km inland since Roman times. In the 12th and 13th centuries, the prosperous city of Dunwich was one of the biggest ports in Suffolk. The harbour is now silted up and a tiny village is all that remains. Along the same coast, Orford was an important commercial and naval port, located just by the mouth of the River Alde in the 16th century. Now the mouth of the estuary is some 9 km downriver. As we reassess the wisdom of defending undeveloped land along our shores, change may become a more accepted element of the coastal landscape.

CONSERVATION IMPORTANCE AND PROTECTION

Twenty-two Annex I habitats (see *page 23*) are associated with the coastal habitats covered in this book, and of these the UK and/or Ireland has special responsibility for estuaries, coastal shingle vegetation, vegetated sea cliffs, several dune grassland types, humid dune slacks and machair. England has over half of Europe's chalk coasts and Britain holds some of the most important shingle and coastal lagoon sites in Europe. Machair is unique to Britain and Ireland. Our coastal habitats are important in a global context for a range of species including breeding seabirds, waders, and Grey Seal.

The most complex and difficult decisions regarding coastal habitats often revolve around sea defences. Over 45% of England's coastline is fortified, although the figure is much less in Ireland at about 8%. These

Near **Ballyconneely, Connemara**. Heavily sheep-grazed Machair with four-wheel drive tracks. Not all coastal sites are protected nature reserves.

structures can be costly and difficult to maintain, yet the economic, political and social implications of letting them go are substantial. There are conservation implications too, as important freshwater habitats may occur just inland of sea defences. Coastal habitats such as Saltmarsh can act as natural flood defences, as they dissipate wave energy, but this function is compromised by coastal squeeze. In 'managed realignment' the sea defences are deliberately breached to allow new areas of habitat, particularly Saltmarsh, to form farther inland; for example at Freiston in Lincolnshire and Tollesbury in Essex. Local erosion may also reinvigorate accretion elsewhere. Cost benefit analyses indicate that 'managed realignment' is economically viable in the long-term, with the value of lost farmland or other habitats offset by the costs saved in maintaining flood defences. For nature conservation, it means that some areas of coastal habitats are able to function dynamically once more, although space must be found farther inland for displaced semi-natural habitats previously found just inside the sea wall.

Most coastal habitats need little land management to maintain their conservation interest, as the influence of the sea is the overriding factor shaping the plant and animal communities present. Grazing can be important in maintaining species-diversity on heathland and grassland found on cliff slopes and in sand dune systems, and also on Saltmarsh sites with a long history of grazing. However, grazing regimes can be difficult to maintain where the habitat may be unproductive and challenging for livestock and where recreational access levels are high.

Machair is unique among coastal habitats in being dependent on traditional crofting.

Balancing recreation and nature conservation is a challenge, particularly in popular tourist destinations or areas with high local populations. Measures relating to resolving access impacts, such as wardening, education, interpretation, boardwalks, seasonal no-access zones and dog control orders are in place at many sites.

Where the natural dynamism of habitats has been restricted, options to ensure the full range of communities is present are often limited. Bulldozers have been used to shift dunes in South Wales in a last-ditch attempt to save Fen Orchid and dune slack vegetation communities. Terns and breeding waders such as Ringed Plover are – around most of England's coastline – now restricted to small fenced exclosures that keep people, dogs and predators such as foxes out. Colonies expand inside the fences but the relatively high concentration of birds can draw predators such as Kestrel, owls and Hedgehog (which are difficult to exclude), and they are more vulnerable to chance events.

KEY ELEMENTS

Zonation
The influence of the sea is all-important, and a sequence of zones with decreasing proximity and exposure to waves and spray is found in all coastal habitats. Different zones are worth searching for, as each can support distinctive species within the habitat. On steep hard shores these zones are vertical, while on soft shores they are more horizontal.

Transience
Transient features are key elements to look for. Slumps and landslips on Soft Cliff create a variety of microhabitats for invertebrates and plants; sand bars and new areas of dune habitat are used by nesting birds; and temporary pools in dune slacks are sometimes home to Natterjack Toad.

Exposure
Headlands are the most maritime element of coasts, particularly where they face the prevailing wind. Look here for plant communities maintained by natural exposure, and in autumn and spring for migrant birds.

FURTHER INFORMATION
Sand Dune and Shingle Network (Liverpool Hope University) http://coast.hope.ac.uk/
British Trust for Ornithology (publications and data relating to birds and coastal sites, especially estuaries) www.bto.org/
Common Seaweeds, Lichens of Rocky Shores and Rock Shore Communities (Field Studies Council laminated guides)
Collins Pocket Guide to the Sea Shore of Britain and Europe by Hayward et al. (Collins, 1996)

Kynance, Cornwall, at low tide. At high tide the sand is under water. The middle shore (thick brown lower band), upper shore (black stripe) and splash zone are discernable. Cliff slope grassland at the top of the cliffs is still within reach of the spray in strong winds and storms.

Durl Head, Devon – these cliff slopes are famed amongst botanists for a suite of rare and scarce plant including **Small Restharrow** (BELOW).

Mudflat and Sandflat

This habitat incorporates all intertidal areas of sand and mud. The main factor influencing the structure and composition of Mudflat and Sandflat communities is exposure to wave action, although salinity and length of tidal immersion also play a role. In sheltered areas where silt is deposited, the substrate has a high organic content and is highly productive. Mudflat can be teeming with polychaete worms, bivalves and mud snails. The number of species is low, but the density of individuals can be very high. Sandy substrates have a low organic content and can dry out when exposed. They are inhabited by far fewer invertebrates but can support amphipod crustaceans such as sandhoppers, polychaetes, bivalves such as cockles, and burrowing echinoderms. Muddy sands with intermediate characteristics can be found on the landward side of barrier islands and in estuary mouths and can support Mussel beds where there is some stone or shell to which the mussels can attach. The surface of intertidal flats usually appears bare, although mats of microalgae can be present on mud, binding the surface together. Beds of Dwarf Eelgrass may occur in sheltered locations.

The abundant invertebrates in Mudflat provide an important food source for a wide range of waders and wildfowl including Knot, Dunlin, Oystercatcher and Shelduck, while Brent Goose and Wigeon feed on eelgrasses. Over one and a half million waterfowl spend the winter in Britain and Ireland, drawn by the abundant food and relatively mild winters.

Similar habitats

Tidal Saline Lagoon includes Mudflat, which can also grade into Saltmarsh. Sandflat is a prerequisite for the formation of Sand Dune and Machair.

Origins and development

Mudflat and Sandflat is an entirely natural habitat that forms as a result of waterborne particles settling on the sea or estuary bed. The underlying geology and topography of a coastline determines its basic shape and its potential to accumulate and hold sediment. Sandflat is found on open coasts, beaches and bays where vigorous wave action prevents the deposition of silt, Mudflat occurs in sheltered areas such as estuaries where much finer particles (<0·125 mm) of clay and silt derived from rivers accrete in less energetic waters. In many places the habitat has been reduced by land claim.

Distribution and extent

Dots indicate sites (SPAs) designated for water bird assemblages. Habitat widespread on soft shorelines, particularly the North Sea coast. Eng: 180,000 ha; Sco: 77,400 ha; Wal: 41,700 ha; NI: 9,600 ha; Ire: 63,800 ha (ANN I REP).

BELOW LEFT: **Holme, Norfolk** – extensive Sandflat extends for hundreds of metres at low tide. Near the shore, it has accumulated on top of a layer of peat that was formed before melting glacial ice filled the North Sea basin.

BELOW: **Knot** at Snettisham on The Wash. Over 80% of all the Knot that breed in high-arctic Canada and Greenland spend the winter on just 15 British estuaries. The Wash holds the largest number of wintering waterbirds of any site in Britain and Ireland, with counts in some years of over 400,000 birds.

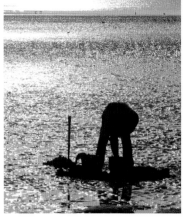

ABOVE LEFT: Mats of **Sea Lettuce** in Poole Harbour, Dorset. Algal mats such as this tend to be most visible in the summer and indicate high nutrient inputs.

ABOVE RIGHT: Bait-diggers are a common sight on many intertidal flats, searching for **Lugworm** (cast shown INSET BELOW RIGHT) and Ragworm, which they use for angling.

Conservation

Pollution from agricultural, industrial and domestic effluents is an issue in some areas. Many harbours and estuaries require dredging to maintain shipping access, and this can reduce the quantity of sediment available within the wider area, affect sediment quality, and release heavy metals or other toxins from below the surface. Fishing, bait digging, commercial shellfish harvesting and recreation bring further pressures and can cause significant disturbance to birds. Mudflat and Sandflat plays a vital role in coastal protection, dissipating wave energy and reducing the likelihood of coastal erosion, damage to sea defences or flooding. However, where fixed sea defences are present, intertidal flats may be lost through coastal squeeze (*i.e.* when the rate of relative sea-level rise is greater than the rate of accretion).

What to look for

A wide range of waders and wildfowl can occur on Mudflat, and Common and Grey Seal can be seen basking on Sandflat. Common Shore Crab is often seen on both.

How to recognise

Intertidal flats are wide, open spaces where land, sea and sky seem to merge. They are governed by the tide and currents in a shifting and changing realm that seems to lie beyond everyday human influence. Sandflat is found in exposed locations where silt cannot settle, and appears bare and pale from a distance. Mudflat is typical of estuaries and sheltered bays, and retains a watery sheen even at low tide. In some places it is relatively firm underfoot and can be crossed; in others it is soft and treacherous. Sandflat is generally firmer to walk on than Mudflat.

On both Sandflat and Mudflat the incoming tide can outstrip a running person, and local knowledge and a tide table are needed before venturing out. One of the most characteristic features of intertidal flats is best seen from slightly higher land on the shore – the spectacular numbers of waders and wildfowl that can be present in the autumn and winter.

When to visit

September–March for waders and wildfowl.

Did you know?
One cubic metre of Mudflat may contain well over 1,000 worms.

Medway, Kent – the meandering central channel gives an indication of the depth of the mud and the tidal reach in this creek.

SALTMARSH

Saltmarsh supports a series of communities of salt-tolerant plants that can be seen in a successional sequence (known as the halosere) from open Mudflat to mature marsh. This sequence is determined by the frequency and period of inundation and can be seen running parallel to the shore, reflecting the development of the saltmarsh. It can also be found in disturbed areas of the upper marsh and within depressions known as pans.

Areas of open mud that are still regularly inundated by the tide support a sparse cover of pioneer plant species. These slow the water, allowing more sediment to accumulate. As the surface of the mud becomes raised up, other species are able to become established, until at the landward side of the marsh species that can only tolerate occasional immersion are found. Erosion also takes place, mainly on meanders in estuaries and along the creeks that form as depressions are scoured out by water draining away on the ebb tide.

There is substantial variation in Saltmarsh across Britain and Ireland. This variation is due to differences in climate, past and present management (including land claim and grazing), and the relative rates of erosion and accretion. At many sites in the south, pioneer marsh is being eroded as sea levels rise.

Nearly 300 species of invertebrate are associated with Saltmarsh, of which around 150 are exclusive to the habitat. In the winter, Saltmarsh provides important feeding and roosting opportunities for birds, notably for seedeaters such as Twite and for wildfowl and waders. Saltmarsh also holds around half of the UK's population of breeding Redshank, and creeks can be important nursery sites for several species of fish.

Similar habitats

Mudflat and Saltmarsh are similar and the transition between them can be continuous. However, Mudflat is typically unvegetated, lower and more homogenous in profile. Saltmarsh can also occur in transitions with Coastal and Floodplain Grazing Marsh, Sand Dune and Vegetated Shingle.

Origins and development

Saltmarsh develops on Mudflat on sheltered coasts where the accumulating mud becomes sufficiently raised above the water level for Saltmarsh plants to become established. The plants stabilise the substrate and help capture more particles suspended in the sea water – and the marsh keeps building so long as it is subject to tidal inundation. Saltmarsh can also form on different habitats if coastal geomorphological processes change. For example, some Saltmarsh in the Hebrides was formerly Machair, and there is a unique type of Saltmarsh on the west coast of Ireland that formed on Blanket Bog following sea-level rise 2,000–4,000 years ago. Some Saltmarsh is of much more recent origin. Common Cord-grass was planted to help stabilise Mudflat and has spread rapidly around the coast,

Distribution and extent

Found in large, sheltered estuaries around Britain and Ireland. Eng: 23,600 ha; Sco: 6,000 ha; Wal: 5,800 ha; NI: 200 ha; Ire: 5,300 ha. Also occurs on Atlantic coasts in western Europe.

BELOW LEFT AND CENTRE: **Glassworts** are plants of pioneer Saltmarsh, where they help slow the flow of water and encourage ongoing silt deposition. Known collectively as samphire, glassworts are harvested as a delicacy in some areas. BELOW RIGHT: **Poole Harbour, Dorset** – an aerial view of Saltmarsh showing a network of creeks that drains into the harbour towards the left of the image. Creeks are not permanent features, and can change course over time, collapse or become treacherously overgrown by the surrounding vegetation.

ABOVE LEFT: Higher up the marsh, species typically include Sea Purslane, **Common Sea-lavender** (INSET BELOW), Sea Aster and Common Saltmarsh-grass.
ABOVE RIGHT: Chenier banks are occasionally found on Saltmarsh where wave action is sufficient to throw shells up onto the marsh where they form distinctive banks, sometimes supporting strandline species (*e.g.* Grass-leaved Orache).

How to recognise

Saltmarsh forms a soft fringe of low vegetation on sheltered coasts where the land gradually merges into the sea. It is found within bays, natural harbours, the heads of sheltered lochs, estuaries, lagoons and behind shingle bars, and can stretch for miles along the coast in a flat, wide band or can form smaller patches or narrow strips.

Saltmarsh is only completely submerged by spring high tides, but with every tide water creeps rapidly and silently up a branching network of sinuous creeks to flood the lower marsh. As the tide ebbs again, it reveals thick, soft mud in creeks and pans; the unwary walker will soon sink boot or even thigh deep into black, smelly mud below the glossy surface.

In the winter saltmarshes can seem bleak places, bereft of colour and inhabited only by wildfowl and roosting waders. However, in the early summer they are brightened by flowering Thrift and the call of breeding Redshank, and later in the summer marshes in the south can turn purple with sea-lavenders.

although in some places it is now dying back naturally. Over millennia, large areas of Saltmarsh have been claimed for farmland and, as a consequence, upper Saltmarsh communities are under-represented in much of southern and eastern England. Recent losses are thought to have been caused by increased storm activity, increases in tidal range and water velocities caused by land claim and seawalls, and a reduction in sediment supply caused by the prevention of erosion of Soft Cliff.

Conservation

The overall area of Saltmarsh is likely to decrease as sea defences prevent it from moving inland in response to sea-level rise (a process called 'coastal squeeze'). However, the important role that this habitat plays in the accumulation of sediment and in diffusing wave action is now recognised, and area of Saltmarsh may be expanded in places where sea defences are 'realigned'. However, re-created Saltmarsh tends to lack some characteristic perennial plant such as Common Sea-lavender.

What to look for

Look out for rare and scarce sea-lavenders, although these are absent from Scotland. In western Scotland, Saltmarsh Flat-sedge and Slender Spike-rush can be found, while Marsh-mallow inhabits brackish patches in the south of England and Wales. Grazed Saltmarsh can support large flocks of wildfowl.

When to visit

Winter for geese and autumn to spring for high-tide wader roosts; May for Thrift in flower, July/August for Common Sea-lavender in flower.

*Saltmarshes on the west coast of Wales, northern England and Galloway are often grazed and the resulting grassy sward and can support grazing ducks and geese. The **Solway Firth** marshes (shown here) support large numbers of Pink-footed and Barnacle Geese in the winter.*

Did you know?
Cord-grasses can trap and stabilise up 10 cm of sediment a year on Saltmarsh.

Sand Dune

Sand dunes develop in places that are inhospitable to the vast majority of plants, as they are dry, salty, unstable, lack nutrients and are liable to inundation. Yet specialist species are able to colonise the bare sand, and in doing so alter the structure, stability, nutrient content, microclimate and hydrology of the incipient sand dune system, allowing other plants to colonise. The classic succession from strandline vegetation through pioneer and mobile dunes to fixed dune grassland, wet dune slacks and scrub is usually more haphazard than the text books suggest; a consequence of storm damage, erosion by people or quirks in the development of individual sites. In reality, on many sites sea-level rise and recreational pressure mean that strandline and embryonic dunes are often absent, while mobile dunes may have been immobilised by sea defences, or the supply of sand cut off altogether by dredging or by the prevention of erosion elsewhere.

The variation in conditions favours a great variety of plant species. Rarities include dune specialists (*e.g.* Sea Stock and Dune Gentian) as well as those also found in other habitats (*e.g.* Round-leaved Wintergreen, Scottish Primrose and Fen Orchid). Warm, open conditions mean that sand dune systems are rich in invertebrates, including butterflies, moths and burrowing bees and wasps – in the UK over 100 invertebrate species are restricted to dunes, and hundreds more are associated with them.

Similar habitats

The early-successional stages of sand dunes support unique vegetation communities, but the vegetation of fixed dunes and slacks is similar to that of Lowland Dry and Wet Heath, Lowland Fen and acid and calcareous grasslands. Machair is a distinctive coastal habitat related to dunes that is restricted to Scotland and Ireland.

Distribution and extent

Occurs widely around the coastlines of Britain and Ireland. Eng: 10,600 ha; Sco: 50,000 ha; Wal: 8,000 ha; NI: 1,500 ha; Ire: 8,000 ha.

Foredune (Braunton Burrows, Devon). Once sand accretion has started, Sand Couch or Lyme-grass can colonise by seed or rhizome fragments and stabilise the pioneer dune – mainly through horizontal growth.

Sand Dune is a familiar habitat, found wherever sandy beaches are wide enough for sand to dry out and blow inland. In some places, a thin strip of parallel dunes at the top of the beach soon gives way to managed countryside. Elsewhere, a confusing maze of sand hills and hollows extends inland, and requires repeated visits to explore.

Many areas are heavily impacted by humans. Sea defences often form a hard interface with the beach, while networks of sandy paths and huge wind-hollowed 'blow outs' show where the vegetation has been eroded away by thousands of feet. But sand dunes are also some of our wildest places, where natural processes are still paramount despite our best efforts, and where a single winter storm can re-shape the seaward face of a dune system, shifting untold tonnes of sand overnight. On windy days, young dunes can be harsh, challenging places; the sand slips constantly underfoot and stings the eyes, and Marram whips the legs. However, within the lee of dunes the flower-rich grassland is more sheltered, and is particularly pleasant on warm summer evenings on sites where Natterjack Toads croak from dune slack pools.

When to visit

The summer months are most rewarding for wildlife; winter visits can be exhilarating and offer the experience of geomorphological processes in action.

TOP: **Strandline** (Saltfleetby – Theddlethorpe, Lincolnshire). Plants such as oraches are able to colonise the beach along the drift line and, together with any debris, start the process of sand accumulation. It is a transitional habitat, either being washed away or developing into dunes.

MIDDLE: **Mobile (yellow) dune** (Studland Beach, Dorset). Once the dune is beyond the limit of tidal inundation, Marram takes hold. The rapid vertical growth of its shoots (about one metre per year) means that dunes can build quickly. The sand at the surface remains loose, and can be blown from the windward face of the dune and deposited in its lee, causing the dune gradually to roll inland.

BOTTOM: **Fixed dune** (Kilinallen, Islay). As new dunes develop in front of the mobile dune, the supply of sand lessens and Marram becomes less vigorous. Mosses, and then lichens, fine grasses and herbs help stabilise the dune and increase the organic matter in the soil.

Origins and development

Sand dunes form through a combination of natural geomorphological and biological processes. Sand brought to the beach by tides and currents is blown inland when the intertidal zone is exposed and dries out. The sand that is deposited starts to accumulate behind any obstacle that slows the wind (*e.g.* vegetation or debris). Hindshore dunes form in bays or where strong winds and a plentiful supply of sand allow dunes to be pushed some way inland and often include dune slacks (*e.g.* the Sefton Coast in Merseyside). Climbing sand dunes can form where strong winds push sand up over rising ground (*e.g.* Stackpole, Pembrokeshire). Frontshore systems project out into the sea across inlets (*e.g.* the Inch Strand, Co. Kerry), at the mouth of an estuary (*e.g.* the Sands of Forvie, Aberdeenshire), where longshore drift acting in opposing directions comes together or where sediment is particularly abundant (*e.g.* Romney Warren, Kent).

Conservation

Sand dunes are dynamic systems that need space and freedom to move. This is a challenge when they are hemmed in by hard sea defences, agricultural land, golf courses, urban development and coniferous plantations (planted to stabilise the dunes); many dune systems in the UK are in effect over-stabilised, and lack bare sand and early-successional habitats. A strategic approach is needed to tackle issues related to shoreline management, particularly where sea defences prevent dune systems from rolling inland in response to sea-level rise. Recreational pressure is often high, and damage to embryonic dunes, which are particularly vulnerable, affects the functioning of entire systems. Strandline and mobile dune communities are natural, but livestock and/or Rabbit grazing are important in retaining the character of fixed dune grassland and some slacks.

What to look for

Along the strandline look for annual species including Prickly Saltwort, Sea Rocket, Sea Sandwort and oraches, the seeds of which can wash up and germinate at the upper limit of the tidal reach. The strandline community, which is usually discontinuous or scattered, is a good indicator of the functional health of a sand dune system, as it requires a constant supply of sand. It can provide habitat for a number of invertebrates, including the Beachcomber Beetle, which feeds on sandhoppers under large pieces of debris. Oystercatcher and Ringed Plover may sometimes be found nesting near the strandline.

Brighter green swards of Sand Couch or silvery Lyme-grass indicate pioneer dunes, but these species soon give way to Marram as sand accretion increases. Mobile dunes are a challenging environment for most plants, but look for Sea Spurge, Sea Bindweed and Sea-holly among the Marram. Mobile dunes warm up quickly and provide shelter, and can be attractive to invertebrates, although more stable sand is preferred by burrowing bees and digger wasps – look out for miniature spoil heaps. Lizard trails can also be seen in the bare sand of mobile dunes. Sand-hill Screw-moss can play an important role in stabilising the sand surface; its tightly twisted leaves unscrewing remarkably rapidly when it becomes wet. Associated species include the annuals Common Whitlowgrass, Early Hair-grass, Sea Fern-grass and Dune Fescue.

On fixed dunes where conditions become too stable for Marram, look for dune grassland with Red Fescue, Lady's Bedstraw and Cat's-ear. Differences in the substrate type, hydrology, climate and grazing pressure mean that dune grassland is very variable. Calcareous dune grassland is the most species-rich, and typically supports Common Centaury, Kidney Vetch, various clovers, Yellow-wort, Pyramidal Orchid and Carline Thistle. Fixed dunes on the east coast of England can support native stands of Sea-buckthorn, and Common Juniper thickets occur on dunes in the north of Scotland. Mixed Scrub is often widespread where it is not prevented from

TOP LEFT: **Holkham, Norfolk** – in drought-prone systems where the accreting sand is acidic, or where leaching is sufficiently strong to remove the calcareous influence of shell sand, lichens (TOP RIGHT) give the sward a characteristic grey tinge. BELOW: **Dawlish Warren** – Dune scrub develops on stabilised dunes, although historically this was often prevented by grazing livestock. If the substrate becomes particularly leached, or is acid to begin with, dune heath can develop (see Lowland Dry Heath, *page 90*). Here the presence of a golf course interrupts the natural transition to Saltmarsh at the back of the spit.

Did you know?
Some dunes date back at least 5,000–6,000 years (nearer 9,000 years in the Outer Hebrides), while others are just a few hundred years old.

TOP LEFT: **Whiteford Burrows, Gower** – particularly in the south, dune slacks can be rich in orchids, including Western, Southern and Early Marsh-orchids; Green-flowered, Broad-leaved, Dune and Marsh Helleborines; Coralroot Orchid; Fen Orchid and Twayblade.
TOP CENTRE: The diminutive **Fen Orchid** is threatened in every country within its range. It is now very rare in Britain and is found in young dune slacks in South Wales, where conservation measures include digging up areas of dune grassland to create suitable early-successional slacks. A taller form is known from a handful of fenland sites in the Norfolk Broads.
TOP RIGHT: **Rhossili, Gower** – a distinctive type of dune grassland dominated by Bloody Crane's-bill, also found in Northumberland.
ABOVE: The scarce **Dune Tiger Beetle** can be seen in the intertidal and around drift lines, where it hunts for insects.
INSET BELOW RIGHT: **Natterjack Toad** is endangered in Britain and Ireland, although it has been reintroduced to a number of sites. It spawns in shallow pools in dunes (and heaths) where seasonal desiccation reduces the numbers of invertebrate predators.

developing by Rabbit or livestock grazing. It can provide valuable shelter for migratory birds, particularly on foreshore systems.

Dune slacks tend to be found on larger sites, and particularly (but not exclusively) in the wetter north and west. Slack vegetation is also very variable, but often supports ankle to knee-deep Creeping Willow. Calcareous slacks can be species-rich, supporting plant communities similar to those of small-sedge Lowland Fen, while acid slacks can support Lowland Wet Heath vegetation.

Whiteford Burrows, Gower – primary dune slacks form when a new dune cuts off an area of beach and changes its hydrology. Secondary slacks occur where the wind scours away the sand (a blow out) until the water-table (which is domed in sand dune systems) is reached. Slacks are seasonally flooded and remain wet or damp in the summer, apparent here from the greener colour of the vegetation at the base of the slack.

Machair

Machair is essentially calcareous fixed dune grassland found as part of a distinctive cultural landscape on the Atlantic fringe. Strong onshore winds provide a constant top-dressing of calcareous shell sand and fragments of calcareous seaweed, and this prevents the soil becoming leached of nutrients despite the wet climate. The grassland is rich in plant species (up to 45 species per square metre) and can be quite variable as a result of historical and current management, in addition to environmental factors such as the proximity of the water-table to the surface.

The word 'machair' is also sometimes used to refer to the wider mosaic of wet grassland, tussocky marshland and small arable plots within which Machair is found. This patchwork of habitats means that several wader species can be found breeding in close proximity. Lapwing is the most common, with Dunlin, Redshank and Snipe in wetter areas, while Oystercatcher and Ringed Plover nest on dry cultivated ground. Corncrake also nests in Machair hay meadows but is much harder to see. Other birds associated with Machair are Twite, Chough and Corn Bunting. The small-scale variation in habitats favours a wide range of invertebrates, including rare beetles and weevils, and the flower-rich grassland is an abundant source of nectar; both the very rare Great Yellow Bumblebee and the scarce Moss Carder Bumblebee are particularly associated with Machair.

Similar habitats

The unique character and limited distribution of Machair make it easy to differentiate from Sand Dune and grassland habitats.

Origins and development

The beaches and dunes of Machair systems were built up thousands of years ago as broken seashells and glacial sediment (washed into the sea at the end of the last glaciation) were brought ashore by wave action. Powerful winds created dunes at the top of the beach, which were periodically eroded, blowing sand far inland. Humans have played a role in the development of Machair since the Mesolithic period, when the light birch and Hazel scrub that had developed on the thin sandy soils was cleared. By the Bronze Age, Machair plains were being used for agriculture, and a system of light cattle-grazing, hay cutting and low-intensity rotational cropping evolved that shaped the vegetation into a landscape similar to that seen today. However, Machair systems are very vulnerable to the changes in traditional crofting practices that have occurred over the past century.

Conservation

A switch to sheep and year-round grazing, earlier harvesting or conversion to silage, drainage, the increased use of artificial fertilizers and the homogenization of management within Machair systems are all problematic, and ongoing support is needed to help maintain the traditional management on which Machair depends. Climate change may lead to increased inundation by seawater and freshwater flooding, which could further jeopardise traditional management, already barely economically viable. Inappropriate recreational use is a particular issue on some Irish sites.

What to look for

Orchids, including particular varieties of Common Spotted-orchid and Early Marsh-orchid, and the rare Irish Lady's-tresses and Lesser Butterfly-orchid. Listen out for Corncrake.

Distribution and extent

Restricted to the north-west coasts of Scotland (particularly the Outer Hebrides) and Ireland. Sco: 14,500 ha; Ire: 2,900 ha (ANN I REP). Unique to Britain and Ireland.

BELOW LEFT: **Machair Bay, Connemara** – tightly grazed Machair with the Twelve Bens mountain range behind.
BELOW RIGHT: Rotational cultivation is a characteristic of Machair systems.

Machair is a particularly attractive type of exceptionally flower-rich dune grassland. It is found in a unique landscape shaped by the oceanic climate and the traditional crofting practices of the west coasts of Scotland and Ireland.

The flat or gently undulating grassland that extends inland from Atlantic beaches typically includes Red Fescue, Lady's Bedstraw, Common Bird's-foot-trefoil, Daisy, Yarrow, Eyebright and Red Clover. Its colour changes subtly throughout the season as different species become dominant in the sward. In some places it is interspersed with cultivated patches, which can hold eye-catching arable weeds such as Corn Marigold, Sun Spurge, and Wild Pansy. Inland, it is usually backed by lochs surrounded by marshy grassland.

Machair is famous for its breeding waders, and in early summer their distinctive calls can be heard all around, while the rasping "crek crek" of the secretive Corncrake may be heard from deep within iris beds.

When to visit

June–August for Machair flora, April–June for breeding waders and Corncrake.

TOP LEFT: The **Belted Beauty** moth is rare in Britain and Ireland outside of the Machair of Galway, Mayo and the west coast of Scotland. Females are flightless – one suggestion is that they reached offshore islands by floating on driftwood. TOP RIGHT: **Great Yellow Bumblebee** – Hebridean Machair is the key habitat for the remaining populations of this species, which was once found across the UK. BOTTOM LEFT **Corn Bunting** – In the past Hebridean Machair held the highest densities of this species in Britain. Rapid recent declines are linked to a lack of winter grain. BOTTOM RIGHT: **Chough** – Machair is a favourite foraging habitat for Chough along the west coast of Ireland and on Islay and Colonsay.

INSET BELOW RIGHT: Declines in the breeding populations of waders such as **Dunlin** were linked to the introduction of Hedgehog to South Uist in 1974. However, declines in areas without Hedgehog indicate that there are wider issues affecting the birds that relate to changes in agricultural practices and other pressures.

Stadhlaigearraidh, South Uist – Machair grassland is characterised by its rich abundance of flowering plants, although none are unique to the habitat.

Did you know?

Winds are exceptional on Machair sites. On the Outer Hebrides gale force winds are recorded on 50 or more days a year and winds of 6 or more on the Beaufort Scale are recorded for over 20% of the year.

COASTAL VEGETATED SHINGLE

Shingle beaches form on exposed coasts where the wave action is sufficiently forceful to bring ashore sediment between 2 mm and 200 mm in diameter. Only a proportion of the 3,500 km or so of coastal shingle around Britain and Ireland can support vegetation, as shingle features often remain mobile and shift with storms and changing currents. Vegetation is usually best developed on stable spits, barriers, barrier islands and cuspate forelands (rounded protrusions of shingle that develop where longshore drift acting in opposition converges).

On larger shingle sites, an intact succession from strandline vegetation to scrub or stunted woodland of oaks or Holly can be seen. Intermediate stages include communities of perennial shingle specialists, grassland, Shingle Heath with lichens and Heather (or Crowberry and Common Juniper in the north) and, in wet hollows, Lowland Fen or Wet Woodland. In Scotland, complete succession to Caledonian Forest is found in Spey Bay. Some of the vegetation communities present are unique to shingle, while others are rare shingle versions of more terrestrial communities.

MAIN PICTURE: ***Shingle Street, Suffolk.*** *When shingle becomes stable, a sparse cover of large, deep-rooted perennials (e.g. Curled Dock, Yellow Horned-poppy and Sea-kale) develops, interspersed with mats of Sea Campion, Sea Mayweed and Sea Pea.*
INSET: *Near **Lepe, Hampshire.** Strandline vegetation (such as the orache community seen here) is able to take hold in relatively mobile shingle wherever sufficient rotting seaweed is washed up. Sea Beet is also common, replaced by Sea Mayweed, Cleavers and Chickweed on moist, sheltered sites farther north.*

Distribution and extent

The largest shingle structures are in north-east Scotland, East Anglia, and the south coast of England. Eng: 3,600 ha; Sco: 2,000 ha; Wal: 100 ha; NI: 50 ha; Ire: 200 ha (ANN I REP). The UK (together with New Zealand and Japan) is of global importance for shingle.

Similar habitats

Communities transitional to Sand Dune or Saltmarsh develop where shingle is overlain with blown sand, or behind spits where mud collects. Some shingle sites include Saline Lagoon.

Origins and development

Most shingle systems in Britain and Ireland were formed by about 4,000 years ago and have been naturally dynamic ever since. However, shingle communities are inherently fragile and easily damaged, and human pressures have substantially degraded and reduced the area of vegetated shingle. At many sites the vegetation and associated fauna have been destroyed, and the shingle structures themselves immobilised by development (*e.g.* power plants, defence structures and housing estates). Many beaches also suffer from the removal or redistribution of shingle for coastal management purposes, the removal of shingle for construction aggregate, water extraction and/or recreational pressure.

Conservation

Although most Coastal Vegetated Shingle is protected by conservation designations, its prospects are poor and increased storm events and changes in sediment budgets will bring new challenges. Emphasis needs to be put on restoring the mobility of shingle systems and allowing the full range of successional stages to develop. This involves reviewing the reliance on shingle structures for flood defence and the use of groynes and sea walls to prevent shingle features from moving, so that shingle features can migrate in response to changes in sea levels. Recreational pressure also needs to be managed to avoid damage to vegetation and associated fauna, and to minimise disturbance to birds.

TOP: **Bawdsey, Suffolk**. As an increasing amount of organic matter aids water retention and grassland or lichen heath develops, with species such as Red Fescue, Cat's-ear, stonecrops, *Cladonia* lichens and Cypress-leaved Plait-moss. RIGHT: **Dungeness, Kent**. Stabilised shingle supporting Gorse and Blackthorn scrub with open, lichen-rich areas.

How to recognise

Shingle beaches are dynamic places, constantly shifting and changing shape as a result of storms and longer-term wave action. Each of the relatively few key shingle sites has its own unique character, a combination of the formative coastal processes and past and present uses.

Shingle sites often have a curiously ambivalent feel; many have been used for nuclear or military installations, and have hard sea defences imposed on them, evidenced in a scattering of concrete structures and fences and nearby edifices. Yet away from these intrusions they are wild places where the power of the elements is overwhelmingly present. The wildlife is unique and distinctive, typified by elusive Ringed Plovers, large perennial plants such as Sea-kale and Yellow Horned-poppy, and intriguing invertebrates including the Whelk-shell Jumping Spider (which lives in washed up whelk shells) and the Scaly Cricket.

When to visit

April–May for breeding waders and terns, May–August for flowering plants, winter for Snow Bunting and other passerines.

Did you know?

Ness (derived from Old Norse for headland) refers to a rounded promontory, and is often found in place names of shingle sites.

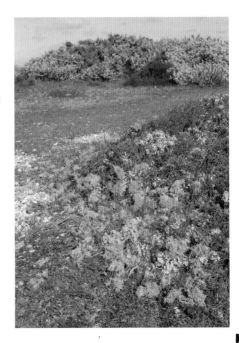

What to look for

Look out for ridges, which indicate areas that have been relatively undamaged by trampling. They are formed when wave-sorting of shingle results in large pebbles lying in the hollows between ridges of smaller pebbles. Shingle with smaller pebbles retains water and organic matter, making it easier for seeds to germinate and causing characteristic stripes of vegetation. On stable shingle look for patches of Shingle Heath, scrub and even stunted woodland. Different sites or stretches of coast are also noted for particular plants, for example Cottonweed (Wexford), Sea Pea (common in East Anglia), Nottingham Catchfly (Dungeness and the Solent), Little-Robin (the Solent) and Oysterplant (Scottish sites). Where Saltmarsh has developed behind a shingle ridge (*e.g.* at sites like Blakeney Point or Chesil) look for a drift-line community dominated by Shrubby Sea-blite.

A range of bees and other nectar feeders can be found on vegetated shingle, including important populations of Shrill and Brown-banded Carder Bees. There is also a range of specialist invertebrates including those that occur below the surface in the shingle matrix, and some exceptionally rare invertebrates, such as the Sussex Emerald moth and the Gilkicker Weevil, are limited to single sites.

Breeding waders are characteristic of undisturbed areas (*e.g.* Ringed Plover and Oystercatcher) while tern and gull colonies are a feature at many sites (such as Cemlyn Bay, Scolt Head, Blakeney Point, Orfordness and Dungeness). Predators such as Stoat, Hedgehog and Fox are often drawn to the breeding bird colonies, and Brown Hare can be seen at some sites such as Orfordness, Dungeness and Snettisham.

Orford Lighthouse, Suffolk – with shingle ridges in the foreground.

Yellow Horned-poppy is a highly toxic plant that is adapted to coastal environments. Its leaves are crumpled and have a waxy coating to help reduce moisture-loss, while silver hairs reflect light.

TOP LEFT: **Sea Pea** is a splash zone specialist with a circumpolar range. Its seeds are dispersed by the sea, and remain viable in salt water for up to five years. TOP RIGHT: **Sea-kale** – another splash zone specialist with buoyant seeds; genetic studies show that there has been a mixing of genes between populations of this plant in France and England, presumably due to dispersal by currents.
BOTTOM LEFT: **Scaly Cricket** – a Mediterranean species found at a few localities along the south coast of England and Wales. It scavenges at night around the upper drift line and during the day can be found by turning over seaweed and pieces of rubbish.
BOTTOM RIGHT: A range of ground-nesting birds occurs on shingle sites. **Ringed Plover** nests between April and August, and is most likely be found on relatively open shingle near to mudflats. Look in areas with low levels of disturbance and listen out for alarm calls that will indicate birds with eggs or chicks.

ORFORD VILLAGE

Coastal grazing marsh

Saltmarsh

Stable vegetated shingle

Splash zone

Saline lagoon
(HAVERGATE ISLAND)

Stable vegetated shingle

Orfordness, Suffolk, looking north. This spit is 16 km long and is formed by longshore drift. Until about 900 years ago the village of Orford faced the open sea.

SALINE LAGOON

Saline Lagoons are very variable in the plants and animals they support, due largely to differences in geomorphology. Isolated lagoons are separated from the sea by a barrier of shingle or sand through which sea water percolates, and can become in-filled over time. Percolation lagoons are ponded water found within depressions in soft sediments, and may rise and fall with the tide. They are often transient, shifting with the substrate. Silled lagoons (found in Scotland) are basins with a rock barrier that retains the water at low tide. Lagoons can also be inlets into which the sea enters with each tide, in some cases through sluices or culverts. The key factor is the salinity of the water, which varies according to the freshwater input, the frequency with which the lagoon is replenished with salt water, and evaporation, and lagoons can be anything from brackish to hypersaline. Only a limited range of plants is found and includes marine species (*e.g.* eelgrasses, wracks and Sugar Kelp), brackish (*e.g.* tassleweeds) and freshwater species (e.g. pondweeds). Invertebrates that are particularly associated with Saline Lagoon include Starlet Sea Anemone, Lagoon Sandworm and Lagoon Sand-shrimp. The muddy and sparsely vegetated margins support a diverse range of beetles and flies, some of which are rare or scarce.

Similar habitats

The fauna and flora of Saline Lagoons are similar to those of estuaries, brackish ditches and some artificial harbours.

Distribution and extent

Uncommon, with concentrations on the east coast of Britain and the Outer Hebrides. Eng: 1,400 ha; Sco: 3,329 ha; Wal: 80 ha; NI: 200 ha; Ire: 2,400 ha (ANN I REP). Scarce in Europe.

LEFT: **Cemlyn Lagoon, Anglesey** supports a diverse range of lagoon species. It is separated from the sea by a shingle ridge. Sea water enters through an inlet with a sluice and by percolation through the shingle. BELOW: **Chesil Fleet from Portland, Dorset** (*right*) and **at Ferrybridge** (*left*) – this 13 km-long tidal lagoon, up to 5 m deep, was formed around 5,000 years ago and runs behind Chesil Beach, which creates a barrier from the sea. There is an inlet at its eastern end. Some 150 species of seaweed, 25 species of fish and 60 species of mollusc have been recorded.

ABOVE LEFT: **Starlet Sea Anemone** occurs in muddy lagoon margins from Dorset round to the Humber. ABOVE RIGHT: An isolated lagoon at **Shingle Street, Suffolk** – lagoons here change frequently as storm events shift huge amounts of shingle, filling in some lagoons and creating new ones. BELOW RIGHT: **Avocet** nests primarily in Saline Lagoon; it recolonised the UK after an absence of about 100 years once sea defences were allowed to breach during the Second World War.

Origins and development

Saline lagoons can be created through natural geomorphological processes, but some have formed as a consequence of the construction of sea defences and can be found on their landward as well as seaward side, for example within Coastal Grazing Marsh and former creeks in Saltmarsh. Saline lagoons around the Solent were used in medieval times for commercial salt production, and some of those in Chichester Harbour were mill ponds.

Conservation

Lagoons are often naturally transient features and habitat continuity can be a problem for some of the resident species if new lagoons are not formed. Threats include sea-level rise, coastal development, and pollution and nutrient enrichment from agricultural run-off and sewage outlets. Unusual tidal incursions or marked changes in the inflow of freshwater can also be damaging as plant and animal communities within individual lagoons are adapted to the specific conditions found there. Lagoons have been successfully created at some sites such as Minsmere in Suffolk.

What to look for

Breeding birds including terns, Ringed Plover and Avocet; wintering wildfowl; specialist invertebrates such as Starlet Sea Anemone; Beaked Tasselweed.

Walberswick, Suffolk – these lagoons support breeding Avocet and Starlet Sea Anemone. They sit behind an artificially created shingle bank.

Saline Lagoons are pools of saline water that are at least partially cut off from the sea by a barrier (often of shingle) that retains water at low tide. They are often shallow and their water level fluctuates little (if at all) with the tide. Those on soft shores can be small and transient, and are a special feature of dynamic sites where natural change is a defining element. Longer-lived lagoons also occur, sometimes in bedrock.

Although lagoons are not species-rich compared to marine habitats, they support specialist invertebrates and plants adapted to the variable conditions, and are always worth investigating. Larger lagoons can support breeding and wintering waders, wildfowl and gulls and terns.

Spring–autumn for invertebrates, year-round for bird interest.

Did you know?

Saline lagoons can be smaller than one hectare, but the largest (Loch of Stenness, Orkney) is 800 ha.

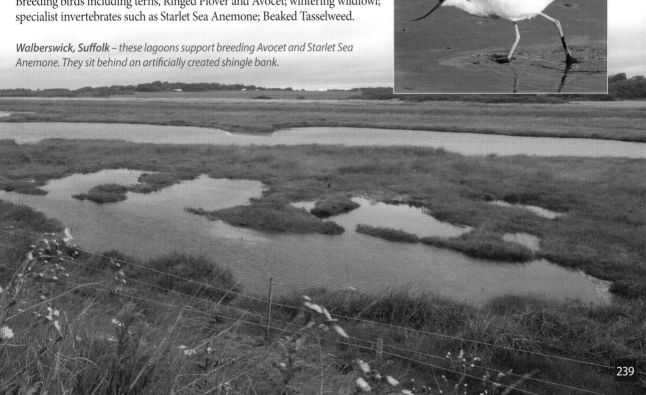

Rocky Shore

Life on the rocky shore is influenced predominantly by the reach of the waves and a series of zones is usually visible on the rocks. The width and character of each zone is variable and is influenced by tidal range, degree of exposure to wave action, slope and aspect. Conditions higher up the shore are more demanding for marine species, and species diversity (and competition between species) generally increases along a gradient down the shore. Plants such as Rock Sea-lavender and Thrift occur on the upper edge of the 'splash zone', the zone above the high tide mark that is not submerged, but is splashed by breaking waves and is dominated by black and orange crustose lichens. Below the splash zone, the 'upper shore zone' is submerged by high tides, but for relatively short periods and not on every tide. Here, green seaweeds can dominate, especially where freshwater runs across the shore. The 'middle shore zone' is submerged for longer and tends to be dominated by tough brown seaweeds (such as Bladder Wrack and Spiral Wrack) that can out-compete seaweeds characteristic of the upper zone. The 'lower shore zone' is submerged most of the time and red seaweeds are common, with large kelps on the extreme lower shore. Exposed shores tend to be less diverse than sheltered shores, as high-energy waves damage seaweeds, but they are still inhabited by sedentary animals that can attach firmly to rocks, including limpets, barnacles and mussels.

Similar habitats

Rocky Shore is often found below Hard Cliff and Cliff Slope, and there is overlap between the splash zone of Rocky Shore and cliff bottoms.

Conservation

In general, conservation management revolves around protection from damaging activities and over-harvesting (commercial harvesting of shellfish and seaweed occurs in some locations). Threats include pollution, both marine (*e.g.* oil spills) and from the land (*e.g.* sewage effluent). There is also some evidence that trampling and harvesting can reduce species diversity. Rocky shores are wonderful places in which to observe a great diversity of species at close quarters and are often visited by school and university field trips. They play an important role in inspiring an interest in ecology and public awareness of the marine environment.

Distribution and extent

Widely distributed around the coasts of Britain and Ireland. Eng: n/k; Sco: 2,400 ha; Wal: n/k; NI: n/k; Ire: n/k.

BELOW LEFT: **Achmelvich, Assynt** – Rock pools can change markedly in temperature, salinity and oxygen content over a relatively short time period. Species that live in them have to be able to tolerate these challenging conditions. Look out for crabs and prawns and fishes such as Butterfish and gobies in larger rock pools.

BELOW RIGHT: **Kimmeridge, Dorset** – a large area of this gently shelving beach is revealed at low tide, exposing intertidal boulders, rock pools, wave-cut platforms and channels. It supports a range of unusual seaweeds including Bushy Rainbow Wrack.

RIGHT, TOP: **Handa, Sutherland** – various zones are visible on this exposed rocky shore.: The **SPLASH ZONE** is just visible in the top of the image; **Twisted Wrack** is a species of the **UPPER SHORE ZONE** while **Dulse** (dark red) and **Oar Weed** (in pool) are **LOWER SHORE ZONE** species.

BELOW, LEFT: **Beadlet anemones** (red and green forms together) – crevices provide shelter from desiccation. BELOW, CENTRE: **Limpets** – found in the middle shore zone, each limpet has a 'home' where its shell forms a tight fit to the rock. The limpets graze on algae and move when submerged (and at night), returning to their home spot as the tide retreats.

FAR RIGHT: **Clifden, Connemara** – on sheltered rocky shores, zones are less obvious and seaweed dominates.

Twisted Wrack

Dulse

Oar Weed

How to recognise

Rocky Shore is a jumble of boulders and ledges of various shapes and sizes, most of which are periodically submerged by sea water. When the tide falls, hollows and channels retain sea water and hold a microcosm of the marine environment, with a great diversity of life-forms including seaweeds, sea sponges, sea anemones, sea urchins, crustaceans, shellfish and small fish. Rock slippery with thick seaweed and speckled with barnacles and limpets is exposed briefly before the tide starts to rise again.

Rocky Shore is a common coastal habitat, found on a range of coasts from exposed Atlantic headlands to the sheltered shores of sea lochs, and is the main coastal habitat of the north and west.

When to visit

Year-round. Check a tide table and try to visit at low tide when the greatest area of shore is exposed – spring tides are best.

What to look for

Rocky Shore life-forms are very diverse. Look out for Sea Slater (a littoral woodlouse) in the splash zone, sandhoppers (tiny shrimp-like crustaceans) under piles of seaweed on the upper shore, Common Hermit Crab inhabiting old Dog Whelk or Common Periwinkle shells, and pipefish camouflaged among weeds. On the lower shore, look out for Sea Lemon (a sea slug), Star Sea Squirt (which grow in jelly-like colonies) and Breadcrumb Sponge and, from the upper shore down, a variety of seaweeds.

Cemlyn, Anglesey – This rocky shore has a good assemblage of seaweeds, including coralline and red encrusting algae in the more exposed rock pools.

Did you know?
Over 500 species of seaweed have been identified in Irish waters. Seaweeds have long been harvested for food and also as a fertilizer. Seaweed was particularly important in areas with poor soil, allowing human settlement and cultivation in areas that would otherwise have been uninhabitable.

Soft Cliff

Soft Cliff is characterised by slumps and landslips caused by the erosion of the cliff base by the sea and by rain and percolating groundwater. These features create a complex environment on a small scale, which is ideal for invertebrates. Twenty-nine species of invertebrate (of which 22 are rare) are, in the UK, limited to Soft Cliff, while another 75 are closely associated with this habitat. The presence of terraced or shallow slopes of different gradients, bare ground, early-successional communities and scrub create a diverse range of vegetation types and structures that influence temperature and soil moisture content and provide suitable conditions for a range of species. For example, dry, friable soils are suitable for burrowing insects while flower-rich vegetation provides nectaring opportunities. Wet areas are used by water beetles, soldier flies and craneflies, and are a source of wet mud used by some solitary bees and wasps for nest building. The warm microclimate of bare areas prolongs the active period of warmth-loving species. This diversity also allows invertebrates to meet the varying requirements of different stages in their life-cycles.

Bare areas of Soft Cliff are colonised by pioneer plants such as Colt's-foot while more stable areas support grassland with Creeping Bent and flowering herbs such as Common Bird's-foot-trefoil and Wild Carrot. Seepages can be rich in orchids. If undisturbed, these communities progress to scrub and eventually woodland.

Similar habitats

Soft Cliff contains small patches of many other habitat types including grassland, wetland, heathland and scrub. The continuity of varied early-successional communities that is characteristic of Soft Cliff is also found on some Brownfield sites, but is otherwise now scarce throughout the countryside.

Origins and development

Soft Cliff is typically formed of soft mudstones, friable sands, shales, glacial deposits, soft chalk or silty limestones that offer little resistance to coastal erosion and weathering. In many places intensive management or development nearby (*e.g.* car parks, caravan parks, agriculture, nearby water abstraction and sea defences) has disrupted the natural processes of erosion and degraded the habitat. Sea-level rise and increasing storminess may lead to increased erosion.

Distribution and extent

Unprotected Soft Cliff is concentrated in England and Wales. Extent unknown. Britain and Ireland hold a significant proportion of the Soft Cliff habitat in north-west Europe.

BELOW LEFT: **Burning Cliff, Dorset** – the vegetated slumped cliff shown here was the site of a fire in 1826 that continued for several years. The fire is believed to have been started by heat generated by the decomposition of pyrite within the shale.

BELOW RIGHT: **Dunwich, Suffolk** – Soft Cliff of Norwich Crag is situated between Coastal Vegetated Shingle and Lowland Dry Heath, creating a continuum of semi-natural habitat.

ABOVE LEFT: **Chapman's Pool, Dorset** – the cliffs in the foreground are composed of Kimmeridge Clay, in the distance Houns-tout is capped with Portland Stone.
ABOVE RIGHT: **Colt's-foot** is a distinctive pioneer species of landslips, Its flowers appearing before the leaves in March.
BELOW RIGHT: **Cliff Tiger Beetle** occurs around wet flushes on Soft Cliff along the south coast of England and can be spotted running over bare ground.

Conservation

Soft cliffs are one of the few habitats in Britain and Ireland where a lack of intervention is crucial. Allowing natural processes to continue is fundamental in ensuring a continuity of varied early-successional habitats. The creation of cliff top buffer strips would allow space for coastal erosion and people. Although recognised for its geomorphological importance, the ecological importance of Soft Cliff has perhaps been rather overlooked in the past.

What to look for

Look in different microhabitats for a range of invertebrates such as mining bees, solitary wasps, rove beetles and butterflies including blues, skippers and the rare Glanville Fritillary. Scrub can hold migrant birds in the spring and autumn and some soft cliffs support Sand Martin colonies. Look out for fossils after cliff falls.

Did you know?

Fossils revealed in Soft Cliff (e.g. at Lyme Regis, Dorset) have helped shape our understanding of evolution and extinction with the discovery of marine reptiles such as ichthyosaurs.

How to recognise

The unstable, soft substrate of Soft Cliff readily slumps and it is rarely sheer like Hard Cliff. The crumbly ground makes access difficult and sometimes dangerous, but the jumbled, untamed wildness of Soft Cliff invites exploration. Heavy rain can cause sections of the cliff to collapse and it can change dramatically and suddenly.

The profile of taller Soft Cliff is often stepped where sections of cliff have slipped, creating flat areas that hold a mix of scrub, grassland, pools, and reedy patches surrounded by open or bare areas. The complex mosaic of a range of microhabitats in a small area make it particularly rich in invertebrates.

When to visit

Summer for invertebrates and safer access.

Eype, Dorset – exposed upper cliff with scrub developing on slumps part-way down the cliff face.

HARD CLIFF AND CLIFF SLOPE

The vegetation of Hard Cliff and Slope varies according to the degree of exposure to wind and salt-spray, the soil type and stability, climate and factors such as grazing. On very exposed or sheer cliffs only lichens grow, although salt-tolerant higher plants such as Rock Samphire or, farther north, Scots Lovage, can be found on ledges and in crevices. The influence of salt-spray can extend inland for 500 m, but drops off rapidly, and grazing and the nature of the soil then become more important. A distinctive maritime form of Red Fescue occupies much of the lower cliff slope, with Thrift and Sea Campion or, on more calcareous soils, Yorkshire-fog and Sea Carrot. Grazing increases the relative abundance of rosette-forming plants such as plantains that are resistant to grazing. Around seabird colonies the soil is nutrient-enriched and supports oraches and Sea Beet in a community that is also found along strandlines. In more sheltered sites, Bluebell can be prominent in the vegetation, often under a canopy of Bracken. Cliff top vegetation can grade into Maritime Heath (see Lowland Dry Heath, *page 90*) or Lowland Calcareous Grassland depending on the substrate. In very exposed positions, 'perched' sand dunes can occur on cliff tops.

Hard Cliff provides disturbance-free nesting locations for raptors such as Peregrine and, in Scotland, White-tailed Eagle, but the most abundant cliff-breeding birds are seabirds. Cliffs are relatively predator-free and easily accessible from the sea, and millions of seabirds breed on them. Seabirds are good indicators of the health of the marine environment, and worrying declines have been linked to a reduction in the quality and quantity of prey species (*e.g.* sandeels) associated with changes in fishing practices and climate change; weather conditions and the impacts of predators have also played a role.

Similar habitats

Hard Cliff and Slope is closely linked to Rocky Shore, Maritime Heath and grassland habitats. Hard Cliff can sometimes be found interspersed with Soft Cliff, which is crumbly and usually has a slumped profile.

Origins and development

Hard Cliff is a natural habitat created by past or present erosion by wind and water of hard rocks. Some cliff slope swards are maintained as grassland through exposure and the thin soils, or by intense physical disturbance from seabirds. Others are maintained through livestock and Rabbit grazing. In other cases, livestock and Rabbit grazing prevents the development of coarser vegetation and scrub. Natural gradations are truncated where cultivated land approaches the cliff top, but in other places cliff slope vegetation grades into inland heathland, grassland or scrub.

Conservation

Disturbance to nesting seabirds from recreational use of the coast can be an issue at more accessible sites – breeding success can be reduced if birds are stressed, and when birds leave their nests, eggs and chicks are susceptible to predation. Rat eradication programmes on some islands (*e.g.* Lundy) have been successful in re-establishing seabird colonies. Invasive, non-native plants such as Hottentot Fig can become dominant in some areas (*e.g.* on The Lizard and at some Irish sites) and the management of these species is difficult in challenging terrain.

Distribution and extent

Dots indicate sites with >10,000 colonially nesting seabirds. Habitat widely distributed, particularly on western and northern coasts and on parts of the east coast of Scotland. Eng: 1,100 km; Sco: 2,400 km; Wal: 500 km; NI: 500 km; Ire: 500 km. England holds a significant proportion of Europe's chalk cliffs.

How to recognise

Hard Cliff and Slope is found in exhilarating and sometimes intimidating locations where more or less sheer faces of granite, sandstone, limestone or basalt are eroded by the sea. Headlands and sites facing the prevailing south-westerly winds tend to be the most maritime in character, pounded by waves and scorched by salt-laden winds.

Cliffs can drop directly into the sea or to a rocky intertidal zone of fallen boulders, and are usually topped with a slope that can be densely or sparsely vegetated.

The sheer rock can be coloured with splashes of lichens and dotted with crevice plants, while cliff slopes often support an eye-catching flora of Sea Campion, Thrift, Kidney Vetch or other plants. Some cliffs support seabird colonies, particularly in more remote locations, and these are unforgettable places with thousands of birds flying around the cliffs and bobbing on the water below.

When to visit

Spring–summer for seabirds and cliff flora.

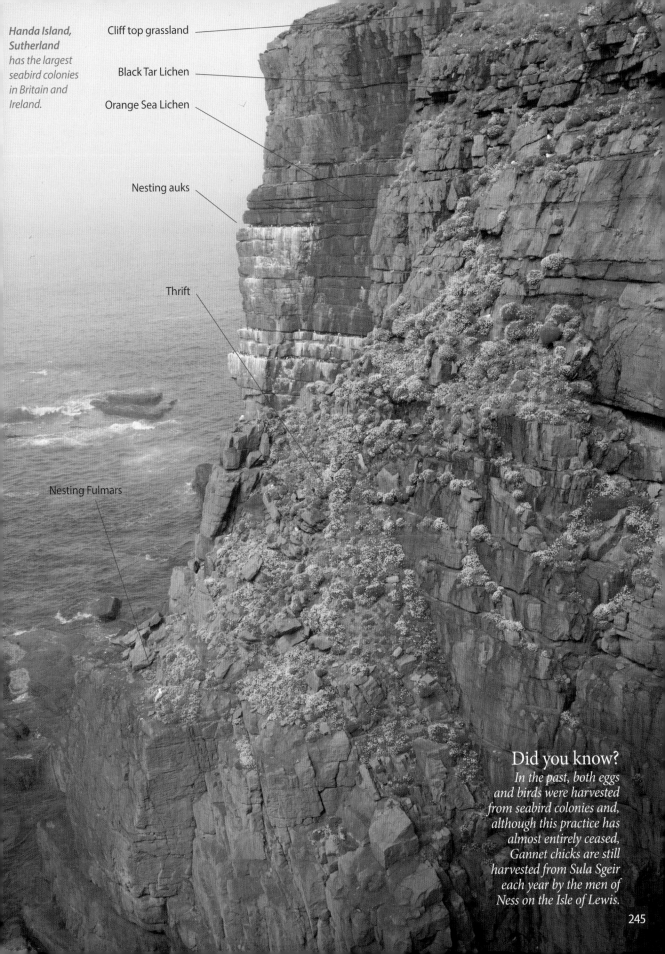

Handa Island, Sutherland has the largest seabird colonies in Britain and Ireland.

Cliff top grassland

Black Tar Lichen

Orange Sea Lichen

Nesting auks

Thrift

Nesting Fulmars

Did you know?
In the past, both eggs and birds were harvested from seabird colonies and, although this practice has almost entirely ceased, Gannet chicks are still harvested from Sula Sgeir each year by the men of Ness on the Isle of Lewis.

245

What to look for

The cliffs of Britain and Ireland hold internationally important colonies of seabirds – 68% of the world's Gannets and 90% of the world's Manx Shearwaters breed here, and in total some eight million seabirds nest around our coastline. From a distance look out for splashes of white guano, that indicate ledges supporting colonies of Guillemot, Razorbill and/or Kittiwake. Search the cliffs for the more scattered nests of Shag, Fulmar, Great Black-backed Gull and Herring Gull. Cormorants also breed at some sites, and build conspicuously large and untidy nests. Where there are no rats (which eat eggs and chicks), Puffin, Manx Shearwater and Leach's Petrel nest on the cliff slopes (the last two species are nocturnal). Manx Shearwaters abandon their chicks at about 10 weeks, and the youngsters are left to find their own way from their burrow out to sea, where they immediately head south to their wintering quarters off South America. Guillemots do not desert their chicks and can be seen below the cliffs on calm evenings in early July, calling to entice their offspring to plunge off the ledges to join them. Gannets mostly breed on remote outcrops and islands – there are 21 gannetries around Britain and Ireland. Black Guillemot (a northern species) nests in rock crevices and under boulders away from seabird colonies, while Chough nests in sea caves on some west coasts sites. Swift and House Martin also breed on coastal cliffs.

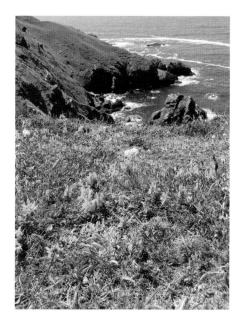

The hard cliffs of the west and south support some specialist invertebrates, including moths such as Thrift Clearwing and Fiery Clearwing (the latter restricted to the chalk cliffs of Kent and Sussex). There is even a water beetle that is restricted to seepages on sandstone cliffs. Relatively few plant species are found on Hard Cliff, but look out for Sea Aster, Rock Samphire, Rock Sea-spurrey, Golden Samphire and, in the north, Scots Lovage and Roseroot. On drought-prone cliff-edge swards look for spring-flowering annuals, together with Spring Squill and, in Scotland, Purple Milk-vetch. A group of rarities particularly associated with The Lizard includes rare clovers, Chives, Hairy Greenweed, Fringed Rupturewort and Autumn Squill).

TOP RIGHT: **The Lizard, Cornwall**. Cliff slope grassland with **Dyer's Greenweed** in the foreground. RIGHT: **Wild Cabbage** flowers between May and August and is found in a localised community on calcareous cliff tops., including at **Ballard Down, Dorset**. Hard chalk cliffs such as these are relatively uncommon and occur predominantly in southern England. BOTTOM RIGHT: **Skomer, Pembrokeshire** – this short, Thrift-dominated sward is maintained by exposure and Rabbit grazing. BELOW LEFT: **Portland, Dorset** – stepped undercliffs such as this can support scrub and stunted woodland, which, in inaccessible areas, may be some of the most natural habitat in lowland Britain and Ireland.

TOP LEFT: **Puffins** typically nest in burrows on the cliff slope, and birds can be seen flying in with beaks full of silvery sandeels once the eggs are hatched. TOP RIGHT: **Razorbills** nest in crevices and among boulders, often near **Guillemots** (TOP CENTRE), which line up along narrow ledges (their large eggs are bottom-heavy so that they roll in circles rather than off the ledge). FAR LEFT: **Orange Sea Lichen** and **Sea Ivory** are distinctive lichens often found on Hard Cliff. LEFT: **Skomer, Pembrokeshire** – Cliff top grassland in spring with Sea Campion, Bluebell and Red Campion. BOTTOM LEFT: **Roseroot** growing in a cliff crevice on Handa Island, Sutherland. The wet climate ameliorates the influence of salt-spray, and allows some species associated with Mountain Ledge to flourish on sheltered maritime cliffs.

Rock Samphire and Thrift growing in crevices near the base of cliffs.

OTHER HABITATS

ORIGINS AND TYPES

This section includes a handful of habitats that do not fit neatly into any one of the other habitat categories: **Arable**, **Brownfield** and **Traditional Orchard**.

The common denominator is that they are all more heavily influenced by humans than other habitats, and are further along the spectrum between semi-natural and artificial. However, this does not mean that they are devoid of wildlife. The best examples can be wonderfully rich in species – for example, Brownfield can contain as many invertebrates as ancient woodland and Arable supports a unique suite of species, many of which are becoming increasingly rare. These habitats do, however, have some major ecological differences. Arable is regularly and frequently disturbed, and supports plant species that are able to regenerate rapidly from the seed bank and complete their life-cycle within a short space of time. Traditional Orchard, on the other hand, supports species such as epiphytic lichens that require long periods of stability. Nevertheless, continuity can be important for both of these habitat types (*e.g.* some arable weeds only occur on sites where they have had a long history). Brownfield is similar to Arable in that it provides bare substrate, but as it remains undisturbed, primary succession is able to take place. Both Arable and Brownfield support large numbers of introduced species, which is unsurprising given how closely linked they are with people, and the opportunities provided for colonisation. For example, around 3,000 non-native species (of which well over half are flowering plants) occur in England (this figure excludes garden plants), and around 11% are species that occur in Brownfield.

Some other habitats that are not semi-natural but can include excellent wildlife habitat are gardens, allotments and churchyards. Gardens occupy over 400,000 ha in the UK and contain around three million ponds and nearly 30 million trees. It is thought that over 12 million UK households actively provide food for birds. Allotments are similar to Arable in that they are regularly disturbed and can support arable weeds. They often include untended patches, scrubby corners, ponds, ditches and hedges that all add to the potential

Intensive farming leaves little room for wildlife.

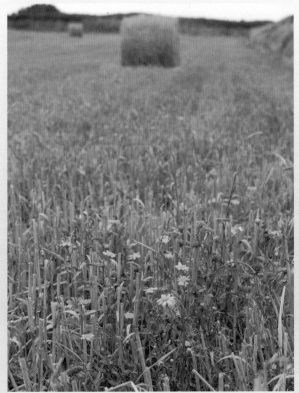

Wild corners often provide opportunities for wildlife, such as this Corn Marigold.

for wildlife. Churchyards can also be rich in wildlife, including species-rich unimproved grassland, hedgerows and veteran trees, and old gravestones may support many species of lichen. Yew trees in particular have an

Key events relating to Arable, Brownfield and Traditional Orchard

Neolithic arable cultivation starts.

Arable cultivation is well established and Arable forms a key part of the landscape.

The Romans arrive into a landscape already de-forested and supporting rotational cropping. Large estates come to dominate the farming system; a demand-led economy develops.

7th century: After the Roman period, towns become depopulated, subsistence agriculture returns and scrub and woodland regenerate.

11th century: The feudal landscape is well established with common grazing land and open field systems.

4500 BC   2000 BC   0   1000   2000

Allotments can be a haven for wildlife. This site in Dorset holds good numbers of Slow-worm and Adder is occasionally seen, while Weasel's-snout is a common weed.

Gardens hold a wealth of wildlife. Jennifer Owens recorded over 2,500 species over a 15 year period of recording in one urban garden in Leicester.

association with old churches – 75% of the ancient Yews in Britain are thought to be within churchyards, many of which are older than the church itself.

CONSERVATION

The species-richness of Arable and Traditional Orchard is highly dependent upon sympathetic management and is particularly susceptible to economic pressures that may either result in intensification (in the case of Arable) or abandonment (in the case of Traditional Orchard). Arable weeds are the most endangered group of plants in Britain, and farmland birds have been identified as the most endangered avian group across Europe; 60% of farmland species are in decline and reversing this trend is proving challenging. A wider uptake of measures such as leaving field margins fallow, reducing pesticide use, and setting aside areas for wildlife would benefit both groups, but require key changes to the European

Common Agricultural Policy. The threats to Brownfield are different, and revolve around planning procedures. Current policy is a presumption in favour of developing brownfield sites provided they are not of high environmental value, the challenge is to ensure their value is identified and recognised through designation as SSSI.

FURTHER INFORMATION

Common Ground – a charity that explores the relationship between nature and culture and works to promote community orchards – www.commonground.org.uk
The Orchard Network – www.orchardnetwork.org.uk
Arable Plants: A Field Guide by Phil Wilson & Miles King (WILD*Guides*, 2004)
Arable Bryophytes by Ron Porley (WILD*Guides*, 2008)
Caring for God's Acre – www.caringforgodsacre.org.uk/
Buglife Brownfield Hub – www.buglife.org.uk/brownfield-hub

14th century: After three centuries of agricultural growth, the Black Death results in the abandonment of much land and sparks changes in the feudal system.

17th–18th century: The Enclosures (of common land) result in a reduction in small-scale, mixed farming.

18th–19th century: The Agricultural Revolution allows sustained population growth; landowners become capitalist farmers.

The Highland Clearances, the arrival of cheap food imports and the Irish potato famine saw the amount of land under arable cultivation drop.

19th century: The Industrial Revolution creates the first brownfield sites and paves the way for future industry.

Britain becomes the world's first urban nation.

20th century: Emphasis turns to increasing self-sufficiency and productivity after the Second World War. New technology, cropping systems, pesticides and artificial fertilizers significantly change agriculture. Many orchards are neglected or destroyed. Brownfield becomes a key haven for wildlife in an increasingly intensively used landscape.

From 1985, agri-environment schemes provided some financial support for wildlife-friendly farming.

Early 21st century: Focus on public services offered by farming (including benefits to wildlife) increases, yet key opportunities to reform CAP are missed and populations of many species continue to decline.

00   1600   1700   1800   1900   2000

Arable

Arable land, cultivated to grow a variety of short-term crops such as cereals, oil-seed rape, sugar beet, beans and potatoes, covers about 25% of Britain and 15% of Ireland. As it is regularly disturbed, it can only support species able to exploit the periodically open conditions created by ploughing and harvesting. A suite of ephemeral plants ('arable weeds') was once widespread across arable land, but has suffered badly from the use of agrochemicals and intensive farming techniques. Arable weeds are mostly annual, and some can produce seeds in as little as six weeks following germination and which can then survive for many years in the soil. Some species, such as Corncockle, have short-lived seed, and are reliant upon the seed being harvested with the crop and re-sown for the next season – an unlikely scenario in modern agriculture. Other species, such as Darnel, are now extinct in the UK but have survived in areas such as the Aran Islands where less intensive farming practices persist.

Weedy strips are important foraging habitat for seed-eating invertebrates and, where flowers occur, a range of nectar-feeding invertebrates may be present. Some invertebrates are associated with disturbed ground, such as the Necklace Ground Beetle and the Set-aside Downy-back Beetle (whose name is a reminder of the set-aside areas intended to decrease arable surpluses in the late 20th century – set-aside strips are now created to benefit wildlife). The bird community of arable land includes a declining suite of species such as Lapwing, Yellow Wagtail, Corn Bunting and Yellowhammer which, together with rare species such as Montagu's Harrier, Stone-curlew, Quail and Cirl Bunting, have suffered from changes in management that have reduced breeding productivity and (for residents) winter survival.

Origins and development

The origins of arable production extend right back to the Neolithic, when an agriculturally based culture gradually expanded across Europe from the Middle East. Many arable weeds are now regarded as ancient introductions that arrived with crop seed, although some were already present in disturbed areas. Together with a range of invertebrates, birds and mammals, they are now closely associated with human agricultural activities. However, modern agriculture, with its efficient seed-cleaning, widespread adoption of pesticides, new crop types, increased fertilizer use, changes in crop rotation, better drainage and switch to winter-sown cereals, has led to severe declines in species.

Distribution and extent

Widespread across Britain and Ireland, particularly abundant in the south and east of England. Arable weed hotspots are concentrated on the chalk of south-east England and also the Atlantic fringes where less intensive farming has persisted. Extent figures are for all arable land – Eng: 4,865,000 ha; Sco: 589,000 ha; Wal: 162,000 ha; NI: 51,600 ha; Ire: 1,160,800 ha.

BELOW LEFT: **Skylark** is the commonest bird to nest in fields but has declined markedly since the 1970s. This decline has been linked to the loss of mixed farming and a switch from spring-sown to autumn-sown cereal crops.
BELOW: **Shepherd's-needle** was once controlled as a pernicious weed, but is now considered to be critically endangered in Britain.

Conservation

The conservation challenge is to reverse the declines in species associated with arable farming across land that is owned by many different individuals and managed commercially. Government funding through agri-environment schemes has provided for a suite of measures such as beetle banks, skylark plots, uncultivated field margins and unsprayed conservation headlands. However, although there is evidence that such measures can be beneficial, the declines are continuing; for example, the farmland bird index (which uses amalgamated trend data for 19 species) continues to decrease. A number of nature reserves, such as Fivehead Arable Fields in Somerset, have been created solely to support populations of rare arable weeds.

What to look for

Check winter stubble for farmland birds and look out for Brown Hare in the spring (Britain only). Look for uncommon arable plants such as Round-leaved Fluellen, Sharp-leaved Fluellen, Small Toadflax and Dwarf Spurge, which may indicate the presence of other rarer plants.

How to recognise

Arable is, by its very nature, primarily managed for food production, and over the last 70 years or so this has usually resulted in large, featureless fields that are treated with pesticides and inorganic fertilizers and hold little natural cover. However, some small areas of arable land are managed less intensively, sometimes with wildlife as well as food production in mind. The best sites are easily spotted in the summer by a splash of colour along field margins where arable weeds are still flourishing, and by the presence of thick hedgerows and unmanaged corners that still hold farmland birds such as Turtle Dove, Yellowhammer and Grey Partridge.

When to visit

July–August for arable weeds; winter for farmland bird flocks.

Did you know?

The word archaeophyte refers to species that were introduced as a consequence of human activity in ancient times. Many arable weeds are archaeophytes.

ABOVE LEFT: With its blunt nose and furry ears, **Harvest Mouse** is distinctive but hard to see. Woven nests above the ground in dense vegetation, such as cereal crops, are the best indication of its presence. ABOVE RIGHT: **Common Poppy** is still widespread in Arable land, but other poppy species such as Prickly Poppy are much scarcer. Some arable weeds have long-lived seed banks, and can reappear in cultivated, uncropped field margins. INSET BELOW RIGHT: A great many of the declining arable weeds such as **Corn Marigold** were once so common and widespread that they were considered to be pests.

BROWNFIELD

Brownfield (technically known as 'open mosaic habitat') has become a refuge for early-successional species that are scarce or absent in the wider urban landscape. The legacy of past industrial use can sometimes be found in piles of fuel ash and other waste products and the thin soils vary markedly in their chemical content and pH, even within a single site. These skeletal soils are crucial in maintaining the habitat in an early-successional stage, an element that is rare in the lowlands. The habitat can be dominated by lichens and mosses, or by tall ruderal herbs such as Rosebay Willowherb, and often includes pools and inundated areas, short open turf, flower-rich grassland and scrub.

The unusual habitat structure and chemical composition of the soil can lead to some unexpected species, and there is also an element of chance in terms of the species that arrive. A range of flowering plants (including non-native species) provides abundant nectar sources for invertebrates, while open bare ground, rubble and exposed concrete provide warm areas for basking, good foraging areas for visual predators and potential sites for burrowing invertebrates. Scrub provides shelter and further structural diversity. Built structures can be colonised too – for example, numbers of Black Redstart peaked in London after the Second World War, when it bred in bomb sites and derelict buildings.

Similar habitats

Brownfield sites can encompass vegetation associated with Lowland Dry Heath, a range of grassland types, scrub and secondary woodland, but are uniquely urban. Calaminarian Grassland (specifically associated with substrates with toxic levels of heavy metals) is also found in post-industrial landscapes.

Distribution and extent

Map shows distribution of urban areas, within which Brownfield is found. Eng: 34,900 ha; Sco: n/k; Wal: n/k; NI: n/k; Ire: n/k.

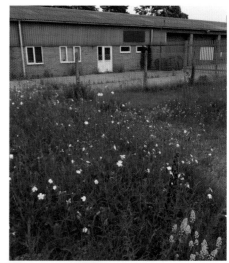

RIGHT: **Brandon, Suffolk** – this 0·1 ha nature reserve in an industrial estate supports a suite of rare species, including Field Wormwood and the Wormwood Moonshiner beetle. Regular soil disturbance is required to maintain the wildlife interest. BELOW LEFT: **West Thurrock Marshes, Essex** was the subject of a long-running legal battle to protect an important brownfield site from development, which was ultimately unsuccessful. The bare ground in the foreground is pulverised fuel ash (waste from a coal power station); this can provide an important substrate for a range of lichens. BELOW RIGHT: **Canvey Wick, Essex** was transformed from coastal grazing marsh in the 1970s to create an oil refinery that was decommissioned in 1973 without ever opening. This was Britain's first Brownfield SSSI and 1,400 invertebrate species have been recorded from this site.

Origins and development

The origins of Brownfield sites are very varied, but all Brownfield sites have been developed and subsequently abandoned. However, they are often threatened, as planners seek to contain development within urban areas rather than extending onto greenfield sites. The importance of Brownfield sites for wildlife is not widely recognised, although open mosaic habitat is a Priority Habitat in the UK.

Conservation

The conservation of Brownfield sites involves raising awareness of the importance of the habitat, undertaking comprehensive survey work of potential sites and ensuring long-term continuity of the habitat. It may be possible for redevelopment proposals to incorporate the wildlife interest by providing new habitat and retaining key features.

What to look for

Brownfield sites can be especially rich in invertebrates, including bees (*e.g.* Brown-banded and Shrill Carder Bees), solitary wasps (including weaver wasps), jumping spiders and a range of beetles. They often provide ideal habitat for reptiles (Slow-worm, Common Lizard, Grass Snake and Adder), and pools can support amphibians (*e.g.* newts and Common Frog). Birds particularly associated with Brownfield include Black Redstart and Little Ringed Plover. Look out for orchids, including Bee Orchid and Fragrant Orchid.

LEFT **Grayling** is a relatively scarce butterfly that is often found on Brownfield sites. RIGHT: Brownfield sites are now key habitats for **Shrill Carder Bee** that requires flower-rich areas and long, tussocky grass in which to nest.

How to recognise

Brownfield is developed land that has become derelict. Generally encountered in urban or industrial settings, it can include corners of industrial estates, abandoned factories, railway sidings, disused power stations, airfields, and even old quarries and brick-pits. Once disused, these sites rapidly take on a wild feel as plants and animals quickly colonise.

Industrial waste, spoil heaps and exposed substrate make for infertile soils and droughty conditions, and as a consequence weeds and species typical of early-successional habitats often dominate, interspersed with scrub, built structures, patches of grassland and bare ground in a higgledy-piggledy mosaic. Part of the attraction of Brownfield is the degree of uncertainty about just what might be found. It is also often the nearest area of habitat for many wildlife lovers.

When to visit

Spring and summer for flowers and invertebrates.

Did you know?

Up to 15% of all the rare and scarce invertebrates in the UK have been recorded on Brownfield sites, and at least 40 invertebrate species are wholly confined to this habitat.

Isle of Grain Power Station, Kent – The Isle of Grain holds a number of Brownfield sites that support rare and endangered invertebrates, and has seen a number battles between conservation organisations and developers with conflicting interests.

TRADITIONAL ORCHARD

The ecological interest of Traditional Orchard (*i.e.* orchard managed in a low-intensity way) is found in the old-growth fruit and nut trees which, together with associated hedgerows, boundary trees, grassland, streams and ponds, can support a large number of plants and animals including rare and scarce species – 1,800 species have been recorded from orchards. Old fruit trees may be retained in Traditional Orchards, and their hollow trunks, rot holes and split bark are good for fungi, lichens, invertebrates and birds such as Lesser Spotted Woodpecker. Fruit trees have a limited life-span (an apple tree has an approximate life of 80–120 years; a plum 50–70 years), and for specialist beetles and lichens to be present, trees must be allowed to age and replacements planted to ensure continuity of old trees.

Trees in Traditional Orchards are often planted at low densities and grown as standards, meaning that their crowns are high enough to allow hay-cutting or grazing. Where orchard grassland has been traditionally managed without artificial fertilizers or pesticides it can hold an interesting flora including species such Green-winged Orchid and Cowslip. Waxcap fungi can sometimes be found if the field layer is kept short.

Orchards can play an important role in contributing to a network of habitats such as Wood Pasture, ancient woodland and Hedgerow, which offer continuity for species requiring stability over time.

Origins and development

Well over 2,000 apple varieties are thought to occur in British and Irish orchards, and DNA evidence indicates that they are descendents of the wild apple of Asia rather than the native Crab Apple. The Romans probably first introduced cultivated apples to Britain, and their fruit-growing skills were perhaps perpetuated in monasteries through the medieval period. By 1700, orchards were a well-established feature of the countryside in key areas, and most farms had their own orchards to provide fruit, and also cider, which was a component of farm workers' wages. From the 1950s, changes in farming practices resulted in the inevitable loss of orchards, cheap supermarket imports reduced the economic viability of commercial orchards, and remaining sites were often neglected. However, there is a resurgence of interest in locally grown varieties, and the social role of orchards is being seen once again in the recent rise of community orchards.

Distribution and extent

Widespread, particularly in the English lowlands, with concentrations in Herefordshire, Worcestershire, Gloucestershire, Somerset and Kent. Eng: 17,000 ha; Sco: n/k; Wal: 1,000 ha; NI: n/k; Ire:: n/k. Map shows inventory undertaken by the People's Trust For Endangered Species for Natural England & Natural Resources Wales.

ABOVE: Veteran tree features such as rot holes are important for invertebrates and can be used by nesting birds and roosting bats.
LEFT: The blossom of fruit trees is a source of nectar for many invertebrates.

ABOVE LEFT: **Mistletoe**, which is semi-parasitic, is commonly found in orchards; six species of invertebrate are associated with this plant, including a moth, a weevil and four bugs. ABOVE RIGHT: Within the UK there are over 2,400 different varieties of apple, 500 varieties of pear and 300 types of plum.

Similar habitats

Traditional Orchards are structurally similar to Wood Pasture, although the tree species are cultivated and managed for fruit production. The grassland can be similar to Lowland Meadow and Pasture.

Conservation

Sympathetic management involves the appropriate pruning of old trees, regenerating orchards through planting new trees, avoiding the use of pesticides and artificial fertilizers and suitable grassland management. Traditional Orchards are usually very small and variable in the species they support, so measures to ensure connectivity between orchards and nearby similar habitat is important in order to support some of the rarer wildlife. The rich heritage of local fruit varieties is maintained by the National Fruit Collection at Brogdale in Kent.

What to look for

Lesser Spotted Woodpecker, Bullfinch and Redstart; a wide range of invertebrates including Noble Chafer and Mistletoe Marble Moth; epiphytic lichens and fungi; Mistletoe.

How to recognise

With their gnarled old fruit trees and long grass rich in flowers, Traditional Orchards seem quintessentially English. Once a ubiquitous feature of the lowland countryside, they can still be found tucked away on the edges of villages and behind farmhouses. They are usually small and may contain a variety of different fruit and nut trees including apple, cherry, pear, plum, damson, quince, walnut and cobnut (a type of hazelnut), many of which may be local varieties.

The trees are widely spaced and scattered over permanent grassland that is often left to grow long in the summer, unlike in modern commercial orchards where dwarf or bush trees grow closely together over mown grass.

When to visit

April/May for blossom; summer for invertebrates and flowering plants; autumn for species drawn to fallen fruit including Fieldfare and Badger.

Did you know?

Over 50% of traditional orchards in England were lost in the second half of the 20th century, but more recently there has been a resurgence of interest in small traditional orchards.

Middlebere Farm, Dorset – A small farmhouse orchard that has been replanted with a variety of traditional apple varieties.

Habitat Correspondence Tables

This table shows how the habitat types described in this book are aligned with commonly used classification systems (see *page 20*), including Annex I habitats, UK BAP priority habitats, British Plant Communities (National Vegetation Classification), the UK Phase 1 Habitat Classification and the Fossitt Habitats of Ireland.

These systems were designed for different purposes, and so do not always correspond neatly. For example, Lowland Mixed Oak and Ash Wood was not identified as being of most need of conservation at a European level, and so is not an Annex I habitat. However, one component of Lowland Mixed Oak and Ash Wood (woodland found in south-east England characterized by oaks and Hornbeam) is an Annex I type (namely '9160 Sub-Atlantic and medio-European oak or oak-hornbeam forests of the *Carpinion betuli*'). Lowland Mixed Oak and Ash Wood is itself only one component of the UK Priority Habitat 'Lowland Mixed Deciduous Woodland', which also includes Lowland Dry Oak and Birch Wood, Wet Woodland and Beech Wood. The Phase 1 category 'A111 Broadleaved woodland - semi-natural' is similarly broad. One Irish habitat falls within Lowland Mixed Oak and Ash Wood ('WN2 Oak – Ash – Hazel woodland') and there is overlap with a second ('WN4 Wet Pedunculate Oak – Ash woodland') although a component of this falls with Wet Woodland. Similarly, vegetation described in two NVC communities (W8 *Fraxinus excelsior – Acer campestre – Mercurialis perennis* woodland and W10 *Quercus robur – Pteridium aquilinum – Rubus fruticosus* woodland) is found in Lowland Mixed Oak and Ash Wood, but some elements of these communities describe vegetation found within Lowland Dry Oak and Birch Wood, Wood Pasture, Atlantic Oak Wood and Upland Mixed Ash Wood. The various relationships can be quite complex, and the following table shows how habitats and communities within each classification either equate to, overlap with or fall within the habitat types described in this book. The National Biodiversity Network (NBN) Habitat Directory available on the NBN gateway website is an interactive resource through which most of the relationships between the other classifications can be more fully explored.

Key

Ann. I: Annex I – habitats considered to be most in need of conservation within Europe for which Special Areas of Conservation (SACs) are designated (habitat descriptions can be found on the Joint Nature Conservation Committee (JNCC) website http://jncc.defra.gov.uk/).

UKPH: UK priority habitats – habitats considered to be under threat in the UK because of their rarity or rate of decline (habitat descriptions can be found via the JNCC website).

NVC: British Plant Communities – plant communities described within the National Vegetation Classification (published by Cambridge University Press in a five-volume series entitled *British Plant Communities* edited by John Rodwell).

P1: Phase 1 – A standardised system for recording semi-natural vegetation and other wildlife habitats in the UK (described in *Handbook for Phase 1 habitat survey - a technique for environmental audit, JNCC, 2010*).

HoI: the Habitat of Ireland – a standard scheme for describing habitats in Ireland (described in *A Guide to Habitats in Ireland* by Julie Fossit, An Chomhairle Oidhreachta /The Heritage Council, 2000).

: contained within classification

: overlaps with classification

: roughly equivalent to classification

: no equivalent classification

Phase 1 habitats are shaded in the tables according to the colour coding used for Phase 1 surveys.

The following list provides the commonly used English names for species that are included in the plant community summary descriptions in the National Vegetation Classification.

Scientific name	Common name
Acer campestre	Field Maple
Agrimonia eupatorium	Agrimony
Agrostis	bent grasses
Agrostis capillaris	Common Bent
Agrostis curtisii	Bristle Bent
Agrostis stolonifera	Creeping Bent
Alchemilla alpina	Alpine Lady's-mantle
Alchemilla glabra	A Lady's-mantle
Alnus glutinosa	Alder
Alopecurus geniculatus	Marsh Foxtail
Alopecurus myosuroides	Black-grass
Alopecurus pratensis	Meadow Foxtail
Ammophila arenaria	Marram Grass
Angelica sylvestris	Wild Angelica
Anthelia julacea	Alpine Silverwort
Anthoxanthum odoratum	Sweet Vernal-grass
Arctostaphylos alpinus	Arctic Bearberry
Arctostaphylos uva-ursi	Bearberry
Armeria maritima	Thrift
Arrhenatherum elatius	False Oat-grass
Artemisia maritima	
[=*Seriphidium maritimum*]	Sea Wormwood
Arthrocnemum perenne	
[=*Sarcocornia perennis*]	Perennial Glasswort
Asplenium ruta-muraria	Wall-rue
Asplenium trichomanes	Maidenhair Spleenwort
Asplenium viride	Green Spleenwort
Aster tripolium	Sea Aster
Athyrium distentifolium	Alpine Lady-fern
Atriplex prostrata	Spear-leaved Orache
Avenula pratensis	
[=*Helictotrichon pratense*]	Meadow Oat-grass
Avenula pubescens	
[=*Helictotrichon pubescens*]	Downy Oat-grass
Beta vulgaris ssp. maritima	Sea Beet
Betula pendula	Silver Birch
Betula pubescens	Downy Birch
Betula spp.	birches
Blysmus rufus	Saltmarsh Flat-sedge
Brachypodium pinnatum	Tor-grass
Brassica oleracea	Wild Cabbage
Bromus erectus	
[=*Bromopsis erecta*]	Upright Brome
Bryum pseudotriquetrum	Marsh Bryum
Cakile maritima	Sea Rocket
Calliergon cuspidatum	
[=*Calliergonella cuspidata*]	Pointed Spear-moss
Calliergon giganteum	Giant Spear-moss
Callitriche stagnalis	Common Water-starwort

Calluna vulgaris	Heather
Caltha palustris	Marsh-marigold
Campylium stellatum	Yellow Starry Feather-moss
Capsella bursa-pastoris	Shepherd's-purse
Carex arenaria	Sand Sedge
Carex bigelowii	Stiff Sedge
Carex curta	White Sedge
Carex dioica	Dioecious Sedge
Carex flacca	Glaucous Sedge
Carex nigra	Common Sedge
Carex panicea	Carnation Sedge
Carex paniculata	Greater Tussock-sedge
Carex riparia	Greater Pond-sedge
Carex rostrata	Bottle Sedge
Carex saxatilis	Russet Sedge
Carex vesicaria	Bladder-sedge
Carex viridula ssp. *oedocarpa*	Common Yellow Sedge
Carlina vulgaris	Carline Thistle
Centaurea nigra	Common Knapweed
Cerastium diffusum ssp. *diffusum*	
[=*Cerastium glomeratum*]	Sticky Mouse-ear
Ceratophyllum demersum	Rigid Hornwort
Ceratophyllum submersum	Soft Hornwort
Chara spp.	stoneworts
Chrysanthemum segetum	Corn Marigold
Cirsium dissectum	Meadow Thistle
Cirsium palustre	Marsh Thistle
Cladium mariscus	Saw Sedge
Cladonia arbuscula	a lichen
Cornicularia aculeata	
[=*Cetraria aculeata*]	a lichen
Corylus avellana	Hazel
Corynephorus canescens	Grey Hair-grass
Crataegus monogyna	Hawthorn
Cratoneuron commutatum	
[=*Palustriella commutata*]	Curled Hook-moss
Crepis paludosa	Marsh Hawk's-beard
Crithmum maritimum	Rock Samphire
Cryptogramma crispa	Parsley Fern
Cynosurus cristatus	Crested Dog's-tail
Cystopteris fragilis	Brittle Bladder-fern
Daucus carota ssp. *gummifer*	Sea Carrot
Deschampsia cespitosa	Tufted Hair-grass
Deschampsia flexuosa	Wavy Hair-grass
Dicranum majus	Greater Fork-moss
Dryas octopetala	Mountain Avens
Eleocharis palustris	Common Spike-rush
Eleocharis uniglumis	Slender Spike-rush
Elodea canadensis	Canadian Waterweed
Elymus farctus ssp. *borealis-atlanticus*	
[=*Elytrigia juncea*]	Sand Couch
Elymus pycnanthus	
[=*Elytrigia atherica*]	Sea Couch
Elymus repens	
[=*Elytrigia repens*]	Common Couch
Empetrum nigrum	Crowberry
Erica ciliaris	Dorset Heath
Erica cinerea	Bell Heather
Erica tetralix	Cross-leaved Heath
Erica vagans	Cornish Heath
Eriophorum angustifolium	Common Cottongrass
Eriophorum vaginatum	Hare's-tail Cottongrass
Eupatorium cannabinum	Hemp-agrimony
Fagus sylvatica	Beech
Festuca ovina	Sheep's-fescue
Festuca rubra	Red Fescue
Filipendula ulmaria	Meadowsweet
Frankenia laevis	Sea-heath
Fraxinus excelsior	Ash
Galium aparine	Cleavers
Galium palustre	Marsh Bedstraw
Galium saxatile	Heath Bedstraw

Galium sterneri	Limestone Bedstraw
Galium verum	Lady's Bedstraw
Geranium sanguineum	Bloody Crane's-bill
Geranium sylvaticum	Wood Crane's-bill
Geum rivale	Water Avens
Glaucium flavum	Yellow Horned-poppy
Glyceria maxima	Reed Sweet-grass
Gymnocarpium robertianum	Limestone Fern
Halimione [=*Atriplex*] *portulacoides*	Sea-purslane
Hedera helix	Ivy
Hieracium pilosella	
[=*Pilosella officinarum*]	Mouse-ear-hawkweed
Hippophae rhamnoides	Sea-buckthorn
Holcus lanatus	Yorkshire-fog
Honckenya peploides	Sea Sandwort
Hyacinthoides non-scripta	Bluebell
Hydrocharis morsus-ranae	Frogbit
Hylocomium splendens	Glittering Wood-moss
Hypericum elodes	Marsh St. John's-wort
Ilex aquifolium	Holly
Inula crithmoides	Golden-samphire
Iris pseudacorus	Yellow Iris
Isoetes lacustris	Quillwort
Isoetes setacea	
[= *Isoetes echinospora*]	Spring Quillwort
Juncus acutiflorus	Sharp-flowered Rush
Juncus bulbosus	Bulbous Rush
Juncus effusus	Soft Rush
Juncus maritimus	Sea Rush
Juncus subnodulosus	Blunt-flowered Rush
Juncus trifidus	Three-leaved Rush
Juniperus communis	
ssp. *communis*	Common Juniper
Juniperus communis ssp. *nana*	Dwarf Juniper
Kiaeria starkei	Starke's Forkmoss
Koenigia islandica	Iceland-purslane
Lemna gibba	Fat Duckweed
Lemna minor	Common Duckweed
Leymus arenarius	Lyme-grass
Ligusticum scoticum	Scots Lovage
Limonium binervosum	Rock Sea-lavender
Littorella uniflora	Shoreweed
Lobelia dortmanna	Water Lobelia
Lolium perenne	Perennial Rye-grass
Luzula sylvatica	Great Wood-rush
Lysimachia nemorum	Yellow Pimpernel
Matricaria maritima	
[=*Tripleurospermum maritimum*]	Sea Mayweed
Matricaria perforata	
[=*Tripleurospermum inodorum*]	
	Scentless Mayweed
Mercurialis perennis	Dog's Mercury
Minuartia verna	Spring Sandwort
Molinia caerulea	Purple Moor-grass
Montia fontana	Blinks
Myriophyllum alterniflorum	Alternate Water-milfoil
Myriophyllum spicatum	Spiked Water-milfoil
Nardus stricta	Mat-grass
Narthecium ossifragum	Bog Asphodel
Nuphar lutea	Yellow Water-lily
Nymphaea alba	White Water-lily
Origanum vulgare	Wild Marjoram
Oxalis acetosella	Wood-sorrel
Papaver rhoeas	Common Poppy
Peucedanum palustre	Milk-parsley
Phalaris arundinacea	Reed Canary-grass
Philonotis fontana	Fountain Apple-moss
Phragmites australis	Common Reed

Pinguicula lusitanica	Pale Butterwort
Pinus sylvestris	Scots Pine
Plantago spp.	plantains
Poa annua	Annual Meadow-grass
Pohlia wahlenbergii var. *glacialis*	
	Mountain Thread-moss
Polygonum amphibium	
[=*Persicaria amphibia*]	Amphibious Bistort
Polytrichum alpinum	
[=*Polytrichastrum alpinum*]	Alpine Haircap
Polytrichum sexangulare	Northern Haircap
Potamogeton natans	Broad-leaved Pondweed
Potamogeton pectinatus	Fennel Pondweed
Potamogeton perfoliatus	Perfoliate Pondweed
Potamogeton polygonifolius	Bog Pondweed
Potentilla anserina	Silverweed
Potentilla erecta	Tormentil
Prunus spinosa	Blackthorn
Pteridium aquilinum	Bracken
Puccinellia distans	Reflexed Saltmarsh-grass
Puccinellia maritima	Common Saltmarsh-grass
Quercus spp.	oaks
Quercus petraea	Sessile Oak
Quercus robur	Pedunculate Oak
Racomitrium heterostichum	Bristly Fringe-moss
Racomitrium lanuginosum	Woolly Fringe-moss
Ranunculus aquatilis	Common Water-crowfoot
Ranunculus fluitans	River Water-crowfoot
Ranunculus omiophyllus	Round-leaved Crowfoot
Ranunculus peltatus	Pond Water-crowfoot
Ranunculus penicillatus	
ssp. *pseudofluitans*	Stream Water-crowfoot
Rhodiola [=*Sedum*] *rosea*	Roseroot
Rubus chamaemorus	Cloudberry
Rubus fruticosus	Bramble
Rumex acetosa	Common Sorrel
Rumex acetosella	Sheep's Sorrel
Rumex crispus	Curled Dock
Sagina maritima	Sea Pearlwort
Sagina nodosa	Knotted Pearlwort
Salicornia	glassworts
Salix cinerea	Grey Willow
Salix herbacea	Dwarf Willow
Salix lapponum	Downy Willow
Salix pentandra	Bay Willow
Salix repens	Creeping Willow
Salix repens ssp. *argentea*	
[=*Salix repens*]	Creeping Willow
Sanguisorba officinalis	Great Burnet
Saxifraga aizoides	Yellow Saxifrage
Saxifraga stellaris	Starry Saxifrage
Scabiosa columbaria	Small Scabious
Schoenus nigricans	Black Bog-rush
Scilla verna	Spring Squill
Scirpus cespitosus	
[=*Trichophorum cespitosum*]	Deergrass
Scirpus lacustris ssp. *lacustris*	
[=*Schoenoplectus lacustris*]	Common Club-rush
Scirpus lacustris ssp. *tabernaemontani*	
[=*Schoenoplectus tabernaemontani*]	
	Grey Club-rush
Scirpus maritimus	
[=*Bolboschoenus maritimus*]	Sea Club-rush
Senecio vulgaris	Groundsel
Sesleria albicans	
[=*Sesleria caerulea*]	Blue Moor-grass
Sibbaldia procumbens	Sibbaldia
Silene acaulis	Moss Campion
Sorbus aucuparia	Rowan
Sparganium erectum	Branched Bur-reed
Spartina	cord-grasses
Spartina alterniflora	Smooth Cord-grass
Spartina anglica	Common Cord-grass
Spartina maritima	Small Cord-grass

Spergula arvensis .... Corn Spurrey
Spergularia marina .... Lesser Sea-spurrey
Spergularia rupicola .... Rock Sea-spurrey
Sphagnum auriculatum
   [=Sphagnum denticulatum] . Cow-horn Bog-moss
Sphagnum capillifolium .... Red Bog-moss
Sphagnum compactum .... Compact Bog-moss
Sphagnum cuspidatum .... Feathery Bog-moss
Sphagnum denticulatum .... Cow-horn Bog-moss
Sphagnum fallax .... Flat-topped Bog-moss
Sphagnum papillosum .... Papillose Bog-moss
Sphagnum russowii .... Russow's Bog-moss
Sphagnum warnstorfii .... Warnstorf's Bog-moss

Spirodela polyrhiza .... Greater Duckweed
Stachys arvensis .... Field Woundwort
Stellaria media .... Common Chickweed
Stratiotes aloides .... Water-soldier
Suaeda maritima .... Annual Sea-blite
Suaeda vera .... Shrubby Sea-blite

Taxus baccata .... Yew
Thymus praecox
   [=Thymus polytrichus] .... Wild Thyme
Thymus pulegioides .... Large Thyme
Triglochin maritima
   [=Triglochin maritimum] .... Sea Arrowgrass

Typha angustifolia .... Lesser Bulrush
Typha latifolia .... Bulrush

Ulex europaeus .... Gorse
Ulex gallii .... Western Gorse
Ulex minor .... Dwarf Gorse
Urtica dioica .... Common Nettle

Vaccinium myrtillus .... Bilberry
Veronica persica .... Common Field-speedwell
Veronica polita .... Grey Field-speedwell
Viola arvensis .... Field Pansy
Viola riviniana .... Common Dog-violet

COASTAL HABITATS   *page 218*

Coastal Vegetated Shingle   *page 234*

P1	H3 Shingle above high tide mark
Ann. I	1210 Annual vegetation of drift lines
	1220 Perennial vegetation of stony banks
UKPH	Coastal vegetated shingle
NVC	SD1 *Rumex crispus – Glaucium flavum* shingle community
	SD2 *Honckenya peploides – Cakile maritima* strandline community
	SD3 *Matricaria maritima – Galium aparine* strandline community
	MC6 *Atriplex prostrata – Beta vulgaris* ssp. *maritima* sea-bird cliff community
Hol	CB1 Shingle and gravel banks
	LS1 Shingle and gravel shores

Hard Cliff and Cliff Slope   *page 244*

P1	H81 Maritime cliff and slope – hard cliff
	H83 Maritime cliff and slope – crevice/ledge vegetation
	H84 Maritime cliff and slope – coastal grassland
	H85 Maritime cliff and slope – coastal heathland
Ann. I	1230 Vegetated sea cliffs of the Atlantic and Baltic coasts
UKPH	Maritime cliff and slope
NVC	MC1 *Crithmum maritimum – Spergularia rupicola* maritime rock-crevice community
	MC2 *Armeria maritima – Ligusticum scoticum* maritime rock-crevice community
	MC3 *Rhodiola rosea – Armeria maritima* maritime cliff-ledge community
	MC4 *Brassica oleracea* maritime cliff-ledge community
	MC5 *Armeria maritima – Cerastium diffusum* ssp. *diffusum* maritime therophyte community
	MC6 *Atriplex prostrata – Beta vulgaris* ssp. *maritima* sea-bird cliff community
	MC7 *Stellaria media – Rumex acetosa* sea-bird cliff community
	MC8 *Festuca rubra – Armeria maritima* maritime grassland
	MC9 *Festuca rubra – Holcus lanatus* maritime grassland
	MC10 *Festuca rubra – Plantago* spp. maritime grassland
	MC11 *Festuca rubra – Daucus carota* ssp. *gummifer* maritime grassland
	MC12 *Festuca rubra – Hyacinthoides non-scripta* maritime bluebell community
	H7 *Calluna vulgaris – Scilla verna* heath
	H8 *Calluna vulgaris – Ulex gallii* heath
	+ overlap with scrub (W21–25) communities
Hol	CS1 Rocky sea cliffs
	CS2 Sea stacks and islets

Machair   *page 232*

P1	H6 Sand dune
Ann. I	21A0 Machairs
UKPH	Machair
NVC	SD8 *Festuca rubra – Galium verum* fixed dune grassland
Hol	CD6 Machair

Mudflat and Sandflat   *page 224*

P1	H11 Intertidal – mud/sand
Ann. I	1130 Estuaries
	1140 Mudflats and sandflats not covered by seawater at low tide
	1160 Large shallow inlets and bays
UKPH	Intertidal mudflats
NVC	
Hol	LS2 Sand shores
	LS3 Muddy sand shores
	LS4 Mud shores
	MW2 Sea inlets and bays
	CW2 Tidal rivers

Rocky Shore   *page 240*

P1	H13 Intertidal – boulders/rocks
Ann. I	8330 Submerged or partially submerged sea caves
	1170 Reefs
UKPH	Intertidal underboulder communities
	Intertidal chalk
NVC	
Hol	LR1 Exposed rocky shores
	LR2 Moderately exposed rocky shores
	LR3 Sheltered rocky shores
	LR5 Sea caves

Saline Lagoon   *page 238*

P1	G16 Standing water – brackish
Ann. I	1150 Coastal lagoons
UKPH	Saline lagoons
NVC	SM19 *Blysmus rufus* salt-marsh community
	SM20 *Eleocharis uniglumis* salt-marsh community
Hol	CW1 Lagoons and saline lakes

Saltmarsh — page 226

P1	**H2 Saltmarsh**
Ann. I	1310 *Salicornia* and other annuals colonising mud and sand 1320 *Spartina* swards (*Spartinion maritimae*) 1330 Atlantic salt meadows (*Glauco-Puccinellietalia maritimae*) 1420 Mediterranean and thermo-Atlantic halophilous scrubs (*Sarcocornetea fruticosi*)
UKPH	Coastal saltmarsh
NVC	SM4 *Spartina maritima* salt-marsh community SM5 *Spartina alterniflora* salt-marsh community SM6 *Spartina anglica* salt-marsh community SM7 *Arthrocnemum perenne* stands SM8 Annual *Salicornia* salt-marsh community SM9 *Suaeda maritima* salt-marsh community SM10 Transitional low marsh vegetation with *Puccinellia maritima*, annual *Salicornia* species and *Suaeda maritima* SM11 *Aster tripolium* var. *discoideus* salt-marsh community SM12 Rayed *Aster tripolium* stands SM13 *Puccinellia maritima* salt-marsh community SM14 *Halimione portulacoides* salt-marsh community SM15 *Juncus maritimus* – *Triglochin maritima* salt-marsh community SM16 *Festuca rubra* salt-marsh community SM17 *Artemisia maritima* salt-marsh community SM18 *Juncus maritimus* salt-marsh community SM19 *Blysmus rufus* salt-marsh community SM20 *Eleocharis uniglumis* salt-marsh community SM21 *Suaeda vera* – *Limonium binervosum* salt-marsh community SM22 *Halimione portulacoides* – *Frankenia laevis* salt-marsh community SM23 *Spergularia marina* – *Puccinellia distans* salt-marsh community SM24 *Elymus pycnanthus* salt-marsh community SM25 *Suaeda vera* drift-line community SM26 *Inula crithmoides* on salt-marshes SM27 Ephemeral salt-marsh vegetation with *Sagina maritima* SM28 *Elymus repens* salt-marsh community
Hol	CM1 Lower salt marsh CM2 Upper salt marsh

Sand Dune — page 228

P1	**H6 Sand dune**
Ann. I	2110 Embryonic shifting dunes 2120 Shifting dunes along the shoreline with *Ammophila arenaria* (`white dunes`) 2131 Fixed dunes with herbaceous vegetation (`grey dunes`) 2140 Decalcified fixed dunes with *Empetrum nigrum* 2150 Atlantic decalcified fixed dunes (*Calluno-Ulicetea*) 2160 Dunes with *Hippophae rhamnoides* 2170 Dunes with *Salix repens* ssp. *argentea* (*Salicion arenariae*) 2190 Humid dune slacks 2250 Coastal dunes with *Juniperus* spp.
UKPH	
NVC	SD2 *Honckenya peploides* – *Cakile maritima* strandline community SD4 *Elymus farctus* ssp. *boreali-atlanticus* foredune community SD5 *Leymus arenarius* mobile dune community SD6 *Ammophila arenaria* mobile dune community SD7 *Ammophila arenaria* – *Festuca rubra* semi-fixed dune community SD8 *Festuca rubra* – *Galium verum* fixed dune grassland SD9 *Ammophila arenaria* – *Arrhenatherum elatius* dune grassland SD11 *Carex arenaria* – *Cornicularia aculeata* dune community SD12 *Carex arenaria* – *Festuca ovina* – *Agrostis capillaris* dune grassland SD13 *Sagina nodosa* – *Bryum pseudotriquetrum* dune-slack community SD14 *Salix repens* – *Campylium stellatum* dune-slack community SD15 *Salix repens* – *Calliergon cuspidatum* dune-slack community SD16 *Salix repens* – *Holcus lanatus* dune-slack community SD17 *Potentilla anserina* – *Carex nigra* dune-slack community
Hol	CD1 Embryonic dunes CD2 Marram dunes CD3 Fixed dunes CD5 Dune slacks

Soft Cliff — page 242

P1	**H82 Maritime cliff and slope – soft cliff**
Ann. I	1230 Vegetated sea cliffs of the Atlantic and Baltic coasts
UKPH	Maritime cliff and slope
NVC	Much of the vegetation does not fit within the NVC, although a range of grassland, scrub and wetland communities may be present
Hol	CS3 Sedimentary sea cliffs

FRESHWATERS — page 188

Chalk River and Stream — page 216

P1	**G22 Running Water – mesotrophic**
Ann. I	H3260 Water courses of plain to montane levels with the *Ranunculion fluitantis* and *Callitricho-Batrachion* vegetation
UKPH	Rivers
NVC	A16 *Callitriche stagnalis* community A17 *Ranunculus penicillatus* ssp. *pseudofluitans* community A19 *Ranunculus aquatilis* community A20 *Ranunculus peltatus* community
Hol	

Fast-flowing River and Stream — page 212

P1	**F2 Marginal and inundation** **G23 Running water – oligotrophic**
Ann. I	H3260 Water courses of plain to montane levels with the *Ranunculion fluitantis* and *Callitricho-Batrachion* vegetation
UKPH	Rivers
NVC	A9 *Potamogeton natans* community A14 *Myriophyllum alterniflorum* community A17 *Ranunculus penicillatus* ssp. *pseudofluitans* community A18 *Ranunculus fluitans* community
Hol	FW1 Eroding/upland rivers

Nutrient-rich (Eutrophic) Lake — page 196

P1	**F2 Marginal and inundation** **G11 Standing water – eutrophic**
Ann. I	3150 Natural eutrophic lakes with *Magnopotamion* or *Hydrocharition*-type vegetation
UKPH	Eutrophic standing waters
NVC	A1 *Lemna gibba* community A2 *Lemna minor* community A3 *Spirodela polyrhiza* – *Hydrocharis morsus-ranae* community A5 *Ceratophyllum demersum* community A6 *Ceratophyllum submersum* community A8 *Nuphar lutea* community A11 *Potamogeton pectinatus* – *Myriophyllum spicatum* community A12 *Potamogeton pectinatus* community A15 *Elodea canadensis* community A19 *Ranunculus aquatilis* community A20 *Ranunculus peltatus* community S3 *Carex paniculata* swamp S4 *Phragmites australis* swamp and reed-beds S5 *Glyceria maxima* swamp S6 *Carex riparia* swamp S8 *Scirpus lacustris* ssp. *lacustris* swamp S12 *Typha latifolia* swamp S13 *Typha angustifolia* swamp S14 *Sparganium erectum* swamp S20 *Scirpus lacustris* ssp. *tabernaemontani* swamp S21 *Scirpus maritimus* swamp S28 *Phalaris arundinacea* tall-herb fen
Hol	FL5 Eutrophic lakes

Other Lake Types — *page 204*

P1	F2 Marginal and inundation
	G12 Standing water – mesotrophic
	G15 Standing water – marl
	G16 Standing water – brackish
Ann. I	3110 Oligotrophic waters containing very few minerals of sandy plains (*Littorelletalia uniflorae*)
	Hard oligo-mesotrophic waters with benthic vegetation of *Chara* spp.
UKPH	Mesotrophic lakes
NVC	A2 *Lemna minor* community A3 *Spirodela polyrhiza – Hydrocharis morsus-ranae* community A4 *Hydrocharis morsus-ranae – Stratiotes aloides* community A8 *Nuphar lutea* community A9 *Potamogeton natans* community A10 *Polygonum amphibium* community A11 *Potamogeton pectinatus – Myriophyllum spicatum* community A13 *Potamogeton perfoliatus – Myriophyllum alterniflorum* community A19 *Ranunculus aquatilis* community A20 *Ranunculus peltatus* community A22 *Littorella uniflora – Lobelia dortmanna* community A23 *Isoetes lacustris/setacea* community
Hol	FL3 Limestone/marl lakes FL4 Mesotrophic lakes

Peat-stained (Dystrophic) Waters — *page 200*

P1	G14 Standing water – dystrophic
Ann. I	3160 Natural dystrophic lakes and ponds
UKPH	Oligotrophic and Dystrophic Lakes
NVC	A24 *Juncus bulbosus* community, often in association with various mire communities (M1–3, M15–21)
Hol	FL1 Dystrophic lakes

Pond, Ditch, Canal — *pages 206–210*

P1	G11 Standing water – eutrophic
	G12 Standing water – mesotrophic
	G13 Standing water – oligotrophic
	G14 Standing water – dystrophic
	F2 Marginal and inundation
Ann. I	H3170 Mediterranean temporary ponds H3110 Oligotrophic waters containing very few minerals of sandy plains (*Littorelletalia uniflorae*) H3130 Oligotrophic to mesotrophic standing waters with vegetation of the *Littorelletea uniflorae* and/or of the *Isoeto-Nanojuncetea* H3140 Hard oligo-mesotrophic waters with benthic vegetation of *Chara* spp. H3150 Natural eutrophic lakes with *Magnopotamion* or *Hydrocharition*-type vegetation H3160 Natural dystrophic lakes and ponds
UKPH	Ponds
NVC	A wide variety of aquatic (A1–12, A15, A16, A20, A21), swamp and fen communities plus vegetation of open habitats (OV28–OV35)
Hol	FL8 Other artificial lakes and ponds FW3 Canals FW4 Drainage ditches

Sluggish River and Stream — *page 214*

P1	F2 Marginal and inundation
	G21 Running water – eutrophic
Ann. I	3270 Rivers with muddy banks with *Chenopodion rubri* and *Bidention* vegetation (Ireland)
UKPH	Rivers
NVC	A5 *Ceratophyllum dermersum* community A7 *Nymphaea alba* community A8 *Nuphar lutea* community A9 *Potamogeton natans* community A10 *Polygonum amphibium* community A11 *Potamogeton pectinatus – Myriophyllum spicatum* community A12 *Potamogeton pectinatus* community A15 *Elodea canadensis* community A16 *Callitriche stagnalis* community
	+ many swamp (S4–9, S11–14, S16–19, S22) and open (OV28–32) communities
Hol	FW2 Depositing/lowland rivers

Turlough and Fluctuating Mere — *page 202*

P1	F2 Marginal and inundation
	G11 Standing water – eutrophic
	G12 Standing water – mesotrophic
Ann. I	3180 Turloughs
UKPH	Aquifer fed naturally fluctuating water bodies
NVC	S11 *Carex vesicaria* swamp S19 *Eleocharis palustris* swamp W3 *Salix pentandra – Carex rostrata* woodland
Hol	FL6 Turloughs

Upland Lake, Loch and Tarn — *page 198*

P1	F2 Marginal and inundation
	G13 Standing water – oligotrophic
Ann. I	3130 Oligotrophic to mesotrophic standing waters with vegetation of the Littorelletea uniflorae and/or of the Isoëto-Nanojuncetea
UKPH	Oligotrophic and Dystrophic Lakes
NVC	A22 *Littorella uniflora – Lobelia dortmanna* community A23 *Isoetes lacustris/setacea* community
Hol	FL2 Acid oligotrophic lakes

Calaminarian Grassland   page 130

P1	I12 Scree I22 Spoil
Ann. I	6130 Calaminarian grasslands of the *Violetalia calaminariae*
UKPH	Calaminarian grassland
NVC	OV37 *Festuca ovina – Minuartia verna* community
Hol	GS1 Dry calcareous and neutral grassland

Coastal and Floodplain Grazing Marsh   page 118

P1	B5 Marsh/marshy grassland
Ann. I	
UKPH	Coastal and floodplain grazing marsh
NVC	MG6 *Lolium perenne – Cynosurus cristatus* grassland MG10 *Holcus lanatus – Juncus effusus* rush-pasture MG11 *Festuca rubra–Agrostis stolonifera – Potentilla anserina* grassland MG13 *Agrostis stolonifera – Alopecurus geniculatus* grassland + overlaps with various other grassland (MG4, 7–9, 12) and swamp (S5–7) and fen (M22–25) communities
Hol	GS4 Wet grassland GA1 Improved agricultural grassland

Lowland Calcareous Grassland   page 108

P1	B3 Calcareous grassland
Ann. I	6210 Semi-natural dry grasslands and scrubland facies: on calcareous substrates (*Festuco-Brometalia*)
UKPH	Lowland calcareous grassland
NVC	CG1 *Festuca ovina – Carlina vulgaris* grassland CG2 *Festuca ovina – Avenula pratensis* grassland CG3 *Bromus erectus* grassland CG4 *Brachypodium pinnatum* grassland CG5 *Bromus erectus – Brachypodium pinnatum* grassland CG6 *Avenula pubescens* grassland CG7 *Festuca ovina – Hieracium pilosella – Thymus praecox/pulegioides* grassland CG8 *Sesleria albicans – Scabiosa columbaria* grassland CG9 *Sesleria albicans – Galium sterneri* grassland
Hol	GS1 Dry calcareous and neutral grassland

Lowland Dry Acid Grassland   page 112

P1	B1 Acid grassland
Ann. I	2330 Inland dunes with open *Corynephorus* and *Agrostis* grasslands
UKPH	Lowland dry acid grassland
NVC	U1 *Festuca ovina – Agrostis capillaris – Rumex acetosella* grassland U2 *Deschampsia flexuosa* grassland U3 *Agrostis curtisii* grassland U4 *Festuca ovina – Agrostis capillaris – Galium saxatile* grassland SD10 *Carex arenaria* dune community SD11 *Carex arenaria – Cornicularia aculeata* dune community
Hol	GS3 Dry-humid acid grassland

Lowland Meadow and Pasture   page 114

P1	B2 Neutral grassland
Ann. I	6510 Lowland hay meadows (*Alopecurus pratensis, Sanguisorba officinalis*)
UKPH	Lowland Meadows
NVC	MG4 *Alopecurus pratensis – Sanguisorba officinalis* grassland MG5 *Cynosurus cristatus – Centaurea nigra* grassland MG8 *Cynosurus cristatus – Caltha palustris* grassland
Hol	GS2 Dry meadows and grassy verges

Northern Hay Meadow   page 124

P1	B2 Neutral grassland
Ann. I	6520 Mountain hay meadows
UKPH	Upland hay meadow
NVC	MG3 *Anthoxanthum odoratum – Geranium sylvaticum* grassland
Hol	

Purple Moor-grass and Rush Pasture   page 116

P1	B5 Marsh/marshy grassland
Ann. I	6410 Purple Moor-grass meadows
UKPH	Purple Moor-grass and rush pasture
NVC	M22 *Juncus subnodulosus – Cirsium palustre* fen-meadow M23 *Juncus effusus/acutiflorus – Galium palustre* rush-pasture M24 *Molinia caerulea – Cirsium dissectum* fen-meadow M25 *Molinia caerulea – Potentilla erecta* mire M26 *Molinia caerulea – Crepis paludosa* mire
Hol	GS4 Wet grassland

Upland Acid Grassland   page 128

P1	B1 Acid grassland
Ann. I	
UKPH	
NVC	U2 *Deschampsia flexuosa* grassland U3 *Agrostis curtisii* grassland U4 *Festuca ovina – Agrostis capillaris – Galium saxatile* grassland U5 *Nardus stricta – Galium saxatile* grassland M25 *Molina caerulea – Potentilla erecta* mire
Hol	GS3 Dry-humid acid grassland

Upland Calcareous Grassland   page 122

P1	B3 Calcareous grassland
Ann. I	6210 Semi-natural dry grasslands and scrubland facies: on calcareous substrates (*Festuco-Brometalia*) 6230 Species-rich *Nardus* grassland, on siliceous substrates in mountain areas (and submountain areas in continental Europe)
UKPH	Upland calcareous grassland
NVC	CG9 *Sesleria albicans – Galium sterneri* grassland CG10 *Festuca ovina – Agrostis capillaris – Thymus praecox* grassland CG11 *Festuca ovina – Agrostis capillaris – Alchemilla alpina* grassland CG13 *Dryas octopetala – Carex flacca* heath U4 *Festuca ovina – Agrostis capillaris – Galium saxatile* grassland U5c *Nardus stricta – Galium saxatile* grassland
Hol	GS1 Dry calcareous and neutral grassland GS3 Dry-humid acid grassland

Upland Rush Pasture   page 126

P1	B5 Marsh/marshy grassland
Ann. I	
UKPH	
NVC	MG10 *Holcus lanatus – Juncus effusus* grassland M23 *Juncus effusus/acutiflorus – Galium palustre* rush-pasture
Hol	GS4 Wet grassland

Lowland Dry Heath — page 86

P1	D1 Dry dwarf shrub heath
	D3 Lichen/bryophyte heath
	H66 Sand-dune – dune heath
	H85 Maritime cliff and slope – coastal heathland
Ann. I	4030 European dry heaths
UKPH	Lowland heathland
NVC	H1 *Calluna vulgaris – Festuca ovina* heath
	H2 *Calluna vulgaris – Ulex minor* heath
	H3 *Ulex minor – Agrostis curtisii* heath
	H4 *Ulex gallii – Agrostis curtisii* heath
	H7 *Calluna vulgaris – Scilla verna* heath
	H8 *Calluna vulgaris – Ulex gallii* heath
	H11 *Calluna vulgaris – Carex arenaria* heath
Hol	HH1 Dry siliceous heath

Lowland Wet Heath — page 92

P1	D2 Wet dwarf shrub heath
Ann. I	4010 Northern Atlantic wet heaths with *Erica tetralix*
	4020 Temperate Atlantic wet heaths with *Erica ciliaris* and *Erica tetralix*
UKPH	Lowland Heathland
NVC	H3 *Ulex minor – Agrostis curtisii* heath
	H4 *Ulex gallii – Agrostis curtisii* heath
	H5 *Erica vagans – Schoenus nigricans* heath
	M16 *Erica tetralix – Sphagnum compactum* wet heath
Hol	HH3 Wet heath

Upland Dry Heath — page 94

P1	D1 Dry dwarf shrub heath
	D5 Dry heath/acid grassland
Ann. I	4030 European dry heaths
UKPH	Upland heathland
NVC	H4 *Ulex gallii – Agrostis curtisii* heath
	H8 *Calluna vulgaris – Ulex gallii* heath
	H9 *Calluna vulgaris – Deschampsia flexuosa* heath
	H10 *Calluna vulgaris – Erica cinerea* heath
	H12 *Calluna vulgaris – Vaccinium myrtillus* heath
	H16 *Calluna vulgaris – Arctostaphylos uva-ursi* heath
	H18 *Vaccinium myrtillus – Deschampsia flexuosa* heath
	H21 *Calluna vulgaris – Vaccinium myrtillus – Sphagnum capillifolium* heath
Hol	HH1 Dry siliceous heath

Upland Wet Heath — page 98

P1	D2 Wet dwarf shrub heath
	D6 Wet heath/acid grassland
Ann. I	4010 Northern Atlantic wet heaths with *Erica tetralix*
UKPH	Upland heathland
NVC	M15 *Scirpus cespitosus – Erica tetralix* wet heath
	M16 *Erica tetralix – Sphagnum compactum* wet heath
Hol	HH3 Wet heath

High Montane Heath and Snow-bed — page 140

P1	D3 Lichen/bryophyte heath
	D4 Montane heath/dwarf herb
	B3 Calcareous grassland
Ann. I	6150 Siliceous alpine and boreal grasslands
	6170 Alpine and subalpine calcareous grasslands
UKPH	
NVC	U7 *Nardus stricta – Carex bigelowii* grass-heath
	U8 *Carex bigelowii – Polytrichum alpinum* sedge-heath
	U9 *Juncus trifidus – Racomitrium lanuginosum* rush-heath
	U10 *Carex bigelowii – Racomitrium lanuginosum* moss-heath
	U11 *Polytrichum sexangulare – Kiaeria starkei* snow-bed
	U12 *Salix herbacea – Racomitrium heterostichum* snow-bed
	U13 *Deschampsia cespitosa – Galium saxatile* grassland
	U14 *Alchemilla alpina – Sibbaldia procumbens* dwarf-herb community
	CG12 *Festuca ovina – Alchemilla alpina – Silene acaulis* dwarf-herb community
Hol	

Montane Dwarf-shrub Heath — page 136

P1	D4 Montane heath/dwarf herb
Ann. I	4060 Alpine and boreal heaths
UKPH	Upland heathland
NVC	H13 *Calluna vulgaris – Cladonia arbuscula* heath
	H14 *Calluna vulgaris – Racomitrium lanuginosum* heath
	H15 *Calluna vulgaris – Juniperus communis* ssp. *nana* heath
	H17 *Calluna vulgaris – Arctostaphylos alpinus* heath
	H19 *Vaccinium myrtillus – Cladonia arbuscula* heath
	H20 *Vaccinium myrtillus – Racomitrium lanuginosum* heath
	H22 *Vaccinium myrtillus – Rubus chamaemorus* heath
Hol	HH4 Montane heath

Montane Scrub — page 146

P1	A2 Scrub
Ann. I	4080 Sub-Arctic *Salix* spp. scrub
UKPH	Inland rock outcrop and scree habitats
NVC	W20 *Salix lapponum – Luzula sylvatica* scrub
Hol	

Mountain Ledge — page 144

P1	C2 Upland species-rich ledges
Ann. I	6430 Hydrophilous tall herb fringe communities of plains and of the montane to alpine levels
UKPH	Inland rock outcrop and scree habitats
NVC	U15 *Saxifraga aizoides – Alchemilla glabra* banks
	U16 *Luzula sylvatica – Vaccinium myrtillus* tall-herb community
	U17 *Luzula sylvatica – Geum rivale* tall-herb community
	CG14 *Dryas octopetala – Silene acaulis* ledge community
Hol	

Arable	*page 250*
P1	**J11 Cultivated/disturbed land – arable**
Ann. I	
UKPH	Cereal field margins
NVC	OV3 *Papaver rhoeas – Viola arvensis* community OV4 *Chrysanthemum segetum – Spergula arvensis* community OV7 *Veronica persica – Veronica polita* community OV8 *Veronica persica – Alopecurus myosuroides* community OV9 *Matricaria perforata – Stellaria media* community OV10 *Poa annua – Senecio vulgaris* community OV11 *Poa annua – Stachys arvensis* community OV13 *Stellaria media – Capsella bursa-pastoris* community
Hol	BC1 Arable crops

Brownfield	*page 252*
P1	**J13 Cultivated/disturbed land – ephemeral/short perennial**
Ann. I	
UKPH	Open mosaic habitats on previously developed land
NVC	Characteristic open communities show a poor fit to NVC communities. There is overlap with grasslands (MG1–2, MG9–11, MG13, CG10, U1–2), scrub (W6, W23) and a variety of aquatic and swamp communities
Hol	ED3 Recolonising bare ground

Traditional Orchard	*page 254*
P1	**A12 Plantation**
Ann. I	
UKPH	Traditional orchards
NVC	MG5 *Cynosurus cristatus – Centaurea nigra* grassland MG6 *Lolium perenne – Cynosurus cristatus* grassland W24 *Rubus fruticosus – Holcus lanatus* underscrub
Hol	WD5 Scattered trees and parkland

Limestone pavement	*page 156*
P1	**I12 Scree**
Ann. I	8240 Limestone pavements
UKPH	Inland rock outcrop and scree habitats
NVC	OV38 *Gymnocarpium robertianum – Arrhenatherum elatius* community OV39 *Asplenium trichomanes – Asplenium ruta-muraria* community OV40 *Asplenium viride – Cystopteris fragilis* community + overlaps with woodland (W9), grassland (CG9, CG10, CG13, M5) and mire (M10, M26, M27) communities
Hol	ER2 Exposed calcareous rock

Rocky Slopes	*page 152*
P1	**I11 Inland cliff**
Ann. I	8220 Siliceous rocky slopes with chasmophytic vegetation 8210 Calcareous rocky slopes with chasmophytic vegetation
UKPH	Inland rock outcrop and scree habitats
NVC	U18 *Cryptogramma crispa – Athyrium distentifolium* snow-bed U21 *Cryptogramma crispa – Deschampsia flexuosa* community OV39 *Asplenium trichomanes – Asplenium ruta-muraria* community OV40 *Asplenium viride – Cystopteris fragilis* community
Hol	ER1 Exposed siliceous rock ER2 Exposed calcareous rock

Scree	*page 154*
P1	**I12 Scree**
Ann. I	8110 Siliceous scree of the montane to snow levels 8120 Calcareous and calcschist screes of the montane to alpine levels
UKPH	Inland rock outcrop and scree habitats
NVC	U18 *Cryptogramma crispa – Athyrium distentifolium* snow-bed U21 *Cryptogramma crispa – Deschampsia flexuosa* community OV38 *Gymnocarpium robertianum – Arrhenatherum elatius* community
Hol	ER3 Siliceous scree and loose rock ER4 Calcareous scree and loose rock

SCRUB	*page 68*

Bracken	*page 78*
P1	**C1 Bracken**
Ann. I	
UKPH	
NVC	W25 *Pteridium aquilinum – Rubus fruticosus* underscrub
Hol	HD1 Dense bracken

Hedgerow	*page 74*
P1	**J2 Hedges**
Ann. I	
UKPH	Hedgerows
NVC	W21 *Crataegus monogyna – Hedera helix* scrub W22 *Prunus spinosa – Rubus fruticosus* scrub W23 *Ulex europaeus – Rubus fruticosus* scrub
Hol	WL1 Hedgerows

Mixed Scrub	*page 72*
P1	**A111 Broadleaved woodland – semi-natural**
Ann. I	
UKPH	
NVC	W21 *Crataegus monogyna – Hedera helix* scrub W22 *Prunus spinosa – Rubus fruticosus* scrub + provisional NVC *Agrimonia eupatoria – Origanum vulgare* community, *Corylus avellana – Geranium sanguineum* community
Hol	WS1 Scrub

Blanket Bog		page 168
P1	**E161 Blanket sphagnum bog**	
	E17 Wet modified bog	
	E18 Dry modified bog	
Ann. I	7130 Blanket bogs	
	7150 Depressions on peat substrates of the Rhynchosporion	
	7140 Transition mires and quaking bogs	
UKPH	Blanket Bog	
NVC	M1 *Sphagnum denticulatum* bog pool community	
	M2 *Sphagnum cuspidatum/fallax* bog pool community	
	M3 *Eriophorum angustifolium* bog pool community	
	M15 *Scirpus cespitosus – Erica tetralix* wet heath	
	M17 *Scirpus cespitosus – Eriophorum vaginatum* blanket mire	
	M18 *Erica tetralix – Sphagnum papillosum* raised and blanket mire	
	M19 *Calluna vulgaris – Eriophorum vaginatum* blanket mire	
	M20 *Eriophorum vaginatum* blanket and raised mire	
	M25 *Molinia caerulea – Potentilla erecta* mire	
Hol	PB2 Upland blanket bog	
	PB3 Lowland blanket bog	
	PB5 Eroding blanket bog	
	PB4 Cutover bog	
	PF3 Transition mire and quaking bog	

Lowland Fen		page 176
P1	**E2 Flush and Spring**	
	E3 Fen	
	F1 Swamp	
Ann. I	7210 Calcareous fens with *Cladium mariscus* and species of the *Caricion davallianae*	
	7230 Alkaline fens	
UKPH	Lowland fens	
NVC	S2 *Cladium mariscus* swamp and sedge beds	
	S24 *Phragmites australis – Peucedanum palustre* tall-herb fen	
	S25 *Phragmites australis – Eupatorium cannabinum* tall-herb fen	
	M9 *Carex rostrata – Calliergon cuspidatum/giganteum* mire	
	M13 *Schoenus nigricans – Juncus subnodulosus* mire	
	M22 *Juncus subnodulosus – Cirsium palustre* fen-meadow	
	M24 *Molinia caerulea – Cirsium dissectum* fen-meadow	
	M25 *Molinia caerulea – Potentilla erecta* mire	
	M27 *Filipendula ulmaria – Angelica sylvestris* mire	
	M28 *Iris pseudacorus – Filipendula ulmaria* mire	
	+ overlap with other swamp (S1–28) communities	
Hol	PF1 Rich fen and flush	
	FS1 Reed and large sedge swamps	
	FS2 Tall-herb swamps	
	GM1 Marsh	

Raised Bog		page 172
P1	**E162 Raised sphagnum bog**	
	E17 Wet modified bog	
	E18 Dry modified bog	
Ann. I	7110 Active raised bogs	
	7120 Degraded raised bogs still capable of natural regeneration	
	7150 Depressions on peat substrates of the Rhynchosporion	
	7140 Transition mires and quaking bogs	
UKPH	Raised Bog	

NVC	M1 *Sphagnum denticulatum* bog pool community
	M2 *Sphagnum cuspidatum/fallax* bog pool community
	M3 *Eriophorum angustifolium* bog pool community
	M15 *Scirpus cespitosus – Erica tetralix* wet heath
	M18 *Erica tetralix – Sphagnum papillosum* raised and blanket mire
	M19 *Calluna vulgaris – Eriophorum vaginatum* blanket mire
	M20 *Eriophorum vaginatum* blanket and raised mire
	W4 *Betula pubescens – Molinia caerulea* woodland
Hol	PB1 Raised bog
	PB4 Cutover bog
	PF3 Transition mire and quaking bog

Reedbed		page 184
P1	**F1 Swamp**	
Ann. I		
UKPH	Reedbed	
NVC	S4 *Phragmites australis* swamp and reed-beds	
	S25 *Phragmites australis – Eupatorium cannabinum* tall-herb fen	
	S26 *Phragmites australis – Urtica dioica* tall-herb fen	
Hol	FS1 Reed and large sedge swamps	

Upland Spring and Flush		page 174
P1	**E2 Flush and Spring**	
	E3 Fen	
Ann. I	7220 Petrifying springs with tufa formation (*Cratoneurion*)	
	7240 Alpine pioneer formations of the *Caricion bicoloris-atrofuscae*	
	7210 Calcareous fens with *Cladium mariscus* and species of the *Caricion davallianae*	
	7140 Transition mires and quaking bogs	
UKPH	Upland flushes, fens and swamps	
NVC	M7 *Carex curta – Sphagnum russowii* mire	
	M8 *Carex rostrata – Sphagnum warnstorfii* mire	
	M9 *Carex rostrata – Calliergon cuspidatum/giganteum* mire	
	M10 *Carex dioica – Pinguicula lusitanica* mire	
	M11 *Carex viridula* ssp. *oedocarpa – Saxifraga aizoides* mire	
	M12 *Carex saxatilis* mire	
	M31 *Anthelia julacea – Sphagnum auriculatum* spring	
	M32 *Philonotis fontana – Saxifraga stellaris* spring	
	M33 *Pohlia wahlenbergii* var. *glacialis* spring	
	M34 *Carex demissa – Koenigia islandica* flush	
	M35 *Ranunculus omiophyllus – Montia fontana* rill	
	M37 *Palustriella commutata – Festuca rubra* spring	
	M38 *Cratoneuron commutatum – Carex nigra* spring	
	+ overlaps with other mire (M4–7, M27–29) and swamp (S9–11, S19, S27) communities	
Hol	FP1 Calcareous springs	
	FP2 Non-calcareous springs	

Valley Mire		page 180
P1	**E31 Fen – valley mire**	
Ann. I	7140 Transition mires and quaking bogs	
	7150 Depressions on peat substrates of the Rhynchosporion	
UKPH	Lowland fens	
NVC	M1 *Sphagnum denticulatum* bog pool community	
	M14 *Schoenus nigricans – Narthecium ossifragum* mire	
	M21 *Narthecium ossifragum – Sphagnum papillosum* valley mire	
	M29 *Hypericum elodes – Potamogeton polygonifolius* soakway	
Hol	PF3 Transition mire and quaking bog	

Atlantic Hazel Wood — *page 62*

P1	A111 Broadleaved woodland – semi-natural
Ann. I	
UKPH	Upland Mixed Ashwoods
NVC	W9 *Fraxinus excelsior – Sorbus aucuparia – Mercurialis perennis* woodland W11 *Quercus petraea – Betula pubescens – Oxalis acetosella* woodland W17 *Quercus petraea – Betula pubescens – Dicranum majus* woodland
Hol	WN2 Oak – Ash – Hazel woodland

Atlantic Oak Wood — *page 52*

P1	A111 Broadleaved woodland – semi-natural
Ann. I	91A0 Old oak woods with *Ilex* and *Blechnum* in the British Isles
UKPH	Upland Oak Woods
NVC	W10 *Quercus robur – Pteridium aquilinum – Rubus fruticosus* woodland W11 *Quercus petraea – Betula pubescens – Oxalis acetosella* woodland W16 *Quercus* spp. – *Betula* spp. – *Deschampsia flexuosa* woodland W17 *Quercus petraea – Betula pubescens – Dicranum majus* woodland
Hol	WN1 Oak – birch – Holly woodland

Beech Wood — *page 40*

P1	A111 Broadleaved woodland – semi-natural
Ann. I	9120 Atlantic acidophilous Beech forests with *Ilex* and sometimes also *Taxus* in the shrublayer 9130 *Asperulo-Fagetum* Beech forests
UKPH	Lowland Beech and Yew Woodland
NVC	W12 *Fagus sylvatica – Mercurialis perennis* woodland W14 *Fagus sylvatica – Rubus fruticosus* woodland W15 *Fagus sylvatica – Deschampsia flexuosa* woodland
Hol	

Caledonian Forest — *page 58*

P1	A131 Mixed woodland – semi-natural
Ann. I	91C0 Caledonian Forest
UKPH	Native pine woods
NVC	W18 *Pinus sylvestris – Hylocomium splendens* woodland W11 *Quercus petraea – Betula pubescens – Oxalis acetosella* woodland W17 *Quercus petraea – Betula pubescens – Dicranum majus* woodland W19 *Juniperus communis* ssp. *communis – Oxalis acetosella* woodland
Hol	

Coniferous Plantation — *page 66*

P1	A122 Coniferous woodland – plantation
Ann. I	
UKPH	
NVC	
Hol	WD4 Conifer plantation

Lowland Dry Oak and Birch Wood — *page 38*

P1	A111 Broadleaved woodland – semi-natural
Ann. I	9190 Old acidophilous oak woods with *Quercus robur* on sandy plains
UKPH	Lowland Mixed Deciduous Woodland
NVC	W10 *Quercus robur – Pteridium aquilinum – Rubus fruticosus* woodland W16 *Quercus* spp. – *Betula* spp. – *Deschampsia flexuosa* woodland
Hol	

Lowland Mixed Oak and Ash Wood — *page 34*

P1	A111 Broadleaved woodland – semi-natural
Ann. I	9160 Sub-Atlantic and medio-European oak or oak – Hornbeam forests of the *Carpinion betuli*
UKPH	Lowland Mixed Deciduous Woodland
NVC	W8 *Fraxinus excelsior – Acer campestre – Mercurialis perennis* woodland W10 *Quercus robur – Pteridium aquilinum – Rubus fruticosus* woodland
Hol	WN2 Oak – Ash – Hazel woodland WN4 Wet Pedunculate Oak – Ash woodland

Upland Birch Wood — *page 64*

P1	A111 Broadleaved woodland – semi-natural
Ann. I	
UKPH	Upland Birchwoods
NVC	W4 *Betula pubescens – Molinia caerulea* woodland W11 *Quercus petraea – Betula pubescens – Oxalis acetosella* woodland W17 *Quercus petraea – Betula pubescens – Dicranum majus* woodland
Hol	WN1 Oak – birch – Holly woodland

Upland Mixed Ash Wood — *page 56*

P1	A111 Broadleaved woodland – semi-natural
Ann. I	9180 *Tilio-Acerion* forests of slopes, screes and ravines 8240 Limestone Pavements
UKPH	Upland Mixed Ashwoods
NVC	W8 *Fraxinus excelsior – Acer campestre – Mercurialis perennis* woodland W9 *Fraxinus excelsior – Sorbus aucuparia – Mercurialis perennis* woodland
Hol	

Wet Woodland — *page 44*

P1	A111 Broadleaved woodland – semi-natural
Ann. I	91E0 Alluvial forests with *Alnus glutinosa* and *Fraxinus excelsior* 91D0 Bog woodlands
UKPH	Wet Woodland
NVC	W1 *Salix cinerea – Galium palustre* woodland W2 *Salix cinerea – Betula pendula – Phragmites australis* woodland W3 *Salix pentandra – Carex rostrata* woodland W5 *Alnus glutinosa – Carex paniculata* woodland W6 *Alnus glutinosa – Urtica dioica* woodland W7 *Alnus glutinosa – Fraxinus excelsior – Lysimachia nemorum* woodland W18 *Pinus sylvestris – Hylocomium splendens* woodland W4 *Betula pubescens – Molinia caerulea* woodland
Hol	WN5 Riparian woodland WN6 Wet willow-alder-ash woodland WN7 Bog woodland WN4 Wet Pedunculate Oak – Ash woodland

Wood Pasture — *page 48*

P1	A31 Parkland and scattered trees – broadleaved
Ann. I	
UKPH	Wood pasture and parkland
NVC	W10 *Quercus robur – Pteridium aquilinum – Rubus fruticosus* woodland W11 *Quercus petraea – Betula pubescens – Oxalis acetosella* woodland W14 *Fagus sylvatica – Rubus fruticosus* woodland W15 *Fagus sylvatica – Deschampsia flexuosa* woodland W16 *Quercus* spp. – *Betula* spp. – *Deschampsia flexuosa* woodland W17 *Quercus petraea – Betula pubescens – Dicranum majus* woodland + various open habitat types
Hol	WD5 Scattered trees and parkland

Yew Wood — *page 42*

P1	A131 Mixed woodland – semi-natural A121 Coniferous woodland – semi-natural
Ann. I	91J0 *Taxus baccata* woods of the British Isles
UKPH	Lowland Beech and Yew Woodland
NVC	W13 *Taxus baccata* woodland
Hol	WN3 Yew woodland

Species referred to in the text

English names have been used wherever possible throughout this book when referring to species, in an attempt to ensure that the text is as accessible as possible for readers who are not familiar with scientific names. English names are in any case most commonly used for groups such as birds, butterflies, mammals and higher plants. For other groups, such as lower plants and some invertebrates, many naturalists are only familiar with the scientific names and although English names have been derived for most, these have only recently started to be used. However, for consistency, and because scientific names may be off-putting, these English names have also been used for the species within these groups. The scientific names for all the species mentioned in the text are listed in this section for the benefit of readers who are only familiar with scientific names or who wish to know what its scientific name is. Details of the sources for the nomenclature used are given on *page 25*.

The following abbreviations are used:

agg. (aggregate) – a group of microspecies that are commonly referred to as a single species.

sens. lat. (*sensu lato*) – the species name is used in the broadest sense.

spp. (species) – use where more than one species of a particular genus is referred to.

ssp. (subspecies) – a taxonomic rank below that of species.

Var. (variety) – a taxonomic rank below that of species used for some plants, algae and fungi.

* Not the common name used by the relevant authority but nonetheless more widely used.

Flowering Plants

Adder's-tongue	*Ophioglossum vulgatum*
Alder	*Alnus glutinosa*
Allseed	*Radiola linoides*
Alpine Bartsia	*Bartsia alpina*
Alpine Bistort	*Persicaria vivipara*
Alpine Blue-sow-thistle	*Cicerbita alpina*
Alpine Catchfly	*Lychnis alpina*
Alpine Cinquefoil	*Potentilla crantzii*
Alpine Clubmoss	*Diphasiastrum alpinum*
Alpine Forget-me-not	*Myosotis alpestris*
Alpine Gentian	*Gentiana nivalis*
Alpine Hair-grass	*Deschampsia cespitosa var. pulchra*
Alpine Lady's-mantle	*Alchemilla alpina*
Alpine Lady-fern	*Athyrium distentifolium*
Alpine Meadow-rue	*Thalictrum alpinum*
Alpine Mouse-ear	*Cerastium alpinum*
Alpine Pearlwort	*Sagina saginoides*
Alpine Pennycress	*Thlaspi caerulescens*
Alpine Saw-wort	*Saussurea alpina*
Alpine Saxifrage	*Saxifraga nivalis*
Alpine Speedwell	*Veronica alpina*
Alpine Woodsia	*Woodsia alpina*
Alternate Water-milfoil	*Myriophyllum alterniflorum*
Amphibious Bistort	*Persicaria amphibia*
Angular Solomon's-seal	*Polygonatum odoratum*
Annual Knawel	*Scleranthus annuus*
Arctic Mouse-ear	*Cerastium arcticum*
Arctic Sandwort	*Arenaria norvegica ssp. norvegica*
Ash	*Fraxinus excelsior*
Aspen	*Populus tremula*
Autumn Lady's-tresses	*Spiranthes spiralis*
Autumn Squill	*Scilla autumnalis*
Awlwort	*Subularia aquatica*
Baneberry	*Actaea spicata*
Barberry	*Berberis vulgaris*
Bastard Balm	*Melittis melissophyllum*
Bastard-toadflax	*Thesium humifusum*
Bay Willow	*Salix pentandra*
Beaked Tasselweed	*Ruppia maritima*
Bearberry	*Arctostaphylos uva-ursi*
Bee Orchid	*Ophrys apifera*
Beech	*Fagus sylvatica*
Beech Fern	*Phegopteris connectilis*
Bell Heather	*Erica cinerea*
Bilberry	*Vaccinium myrtillus*
Bird's-foot Sedge	*Carex ornithopoda*
Bird's-nest Orchid	*Neottia nidus-avis*
Bird's-eye Primrose	*Primula farinosa*
Biting Stonecrop	*Sedum acre*

Bittersweet	*Solanum dulcamara*
Bitter-vetch	*Lathyrus linifolius*
Black Bog-rush	*Schoenus nigricans*
Black Bryony	*Tamus communis*
Black Medick	*Medicago lupulina*
Black-poplar	*Populus nigra ssp. betulifolia*
Blackthorn	*Prunus spinosa*
Bladder Campion	*Silene vulgaris*
Bladder-sedge	*Carex vesicaria*
bladderworts	*Utricularia* spp.
Blinks	*Montia fontana*
Bloody Crane's-bill	*Geranium sanguineum*
Blue Heath	*Phyllodoce caerulea*
Blue Moor-grass	*Sesleria caerulea*
Bluebell	*Hyacinthoides non-scripta*
Blunt-flowered Rush	*Juncus subnodulosus*
Bog Asphodel	*Narthecium ossifragum*
Bog Bilberry	*Vaccinium uliginosum*
Bog Orchid	*Hammarbya paludosa*
Bog Pondweed	*Potamogeton polygonifolius*
Bogbean	*Menyanthes trifoliata*
Bog-myrtle	*Myrica gale*
Bog-rosemary	*Andromeda polifolia*
Bottle Sedge	*Carex rostrata*
Box	*Buxus sempervirens*
Bracken	*Pteridium aquilinum*
Brackish Water-crowfoot	*Ranunculus baudotii*
Bramble	*Rubus fruticosus* agg.
Bristle Bent	*Agrostis setacea*
Brittle Bladder-fern	*Cystopteris fragilis*
Broad Buckler-fern	*Dryopteris dilatata*
Broad-leaved Helleborine	*Epipactis helleborine*
Brooklime	*Veronica beccabunga*
Broom	*Cytisus scoparius*
Brown Beak-sedge	*Rhynchospora fusca*
Buck's-horn Plantain	*Plantago coronopus*
Buckthorn	*Rhamnus cathartica*
Bugle	*Ajuga reptans*
Bulbous Rush	*Juncus bulbosus*
Bulrush	*Typha latifolia*
Bur Medick	*Medicago minima*
Burnet Rose	*Rosa pimpinellifolia*
Burnt-tip Orchid	*Orchis ustulata*
Butcher's-broom	*Ruscus aculeatus*
buttercups	*Ranunculus* spp.
butterworts	*Pinguicula* spp.
Carline Thistle	*Carlina vulgaris*
Carnation Sedge	*Carex panicea*
Cat's-ear	*Hypochaeris radicata*
Cedar-of-Lebanon	*Cedrus libani*
Chaffweed	*Anagallis minima*

Chalk Eyebright	*Euphrasia pseudokerneri*
Chalk Milkwort	*Polygala calcarea*
Chickweed-wintergreen	*Trientalis europaea*
Chives	*Allium schoenoprasum*
Cleavers	*Galium aparine*
Cloudberry	*Rubus chamaemorus*
clovers	*Trifolium* spp.
Clustered Clover	*Trifolium glomeratum*
Cock's-foot	*Dactylis glomerata*
Coltsfoot	*Tussilago farfara*
Common Bent	*Agrostis capillaris*
Common Bird's-foot-trefoil	*Lotus corniculatus*
Common Butterwort	*Pinguicula vulgaris*
Common Centaury	*Centaurium erythraea*
Common Club-rush	*Schoenoplectus lacustris*
Common Cord-grass	*Spartina anglica*
Common Cottongrass	*Eriophorum angustifolium*
Common Cow-wheat	*Melampyrum pratense*
Common Dog-violet	*Viola riviniana*
Common Gorse	*Ulex europaeus*
Common Knapweed	*Centaurea nigra*
Common Milkwort	*Polygala vulgaris*
Common Nettle	*Urtica dioica*
Common Poppy	*Papaver rhoeas*
Common Reed	*Phragmites australis*
Common Rock-rose	*Helianthemum nummularium*
Common Saltmarsh-grass	*Puccinellia maritima*
Common Sea-lavender	*Limonium vulgare*
Common Sedge	*Carex nigra*
Common Sorrel	*Rumex acetosa*
Common Spotted-orchid	*Dactylorhiza fuchsii*
Common Stork's-bill	*Erodium cicutarium* agg.
Common Valerian	*Valeriana officinalis*
Common Water-crowfoot	*Ranunculus aquatilis*
Common Whitlowgrass	*Erophila verna*
Compact Rush	*Juncus conglomeratus*
Coral Necklace	*Illecebrum verticillatum*
Coralroot Orchid	*Corallorhiza trifida*
cord-grasses	*Spartina* spp.
Corn Marigold	*Chrysanthemum segetum*
Corncockle	*Agrostemma githago*
Cornish Heath	*Erica vagans*
Cottonweed	*Otanthus maritimus*
Cow Parsley	*Anthriscus sylvestris*
Cowbane	*Cicuta virosa*
Cowberry	*Vaccinium vitis-idaea*
Cowslip	*Primula veris*
Crab Apple	*Malus sylvestris*
Cranberry	*Vaccinium oxycoccos*
Creeping Bent	*Agrostis stolonifera*
Creeping Buttercup	*Ranunculus repens*
Creeping Lady's-tresses	*Goodyera repens*
Creeping Willow	*Salix repens*
Crested Dog's-tail	*Cynosurus cristatus*
Cross-leaved Heath	*Erica tetralix*
Crowberry	*Empetrum nigrum*
Cuckooflower	*Cardamine pratensis*
Curled Dock	*Rumex crispus*
Curved Wood-rush	*Luzula arcuata*
Cyphel	*Minuartia sedoides*
Daisy	*Bellis perennis*
Dandelions	*Taraxacum* agg.
Dark-leaved Willow	*Salix myrsinifolia*
Dark-red Helleborine	*Epipactis atrorubens*
Darnel	*Lolium temulentum*
Deergrass	*Trichophorum cespitosum*
Dense-flowered Orchid	*Neotinea maculata*
Devil's-bit Scabious	*Succisa pratensis*
Devon Whitebeam	*Sorbus devoniensis*
Diapensia	*Diapensia lapponica*
Divided Sedge	*Carex divisa*
Dogwood	*Cornus sanguinea*
Downy Birch	*Betula pubescens*
Downy Currant	*Ribes spicatum*
Downy Willow	*Salix lapponum*
Drooping Saxifrage	*Saxifraga cernua*
Dropwort	*Filipendula vulgaris*
duckweeds	*Lemnaceae*
Dune Fescue	*Vulpia fasciculata*
Dune Gentian	*Gentianella uliginosa*
Dune Helleborine	*Epipactis dunensis*
Dwarf Birch	*Betula nana*
Dwarf Cornel	*Cornus suecica*
Dwarf Cudweed	*Gnaphalium supinum*
Dwarf Eelgrass	*Zostera noltei*
Dwarf Gorse	*Ulex minor*
Dwarf Juniper	*Juniperus communis* ssp. *nana*
Dwarf Milkwort	*Polygala amarella*
Dwarf Spurge	*Euphorbia exigua*
Dwarf Willow	*Salix herbacea*
Dyer's Greenweed	*Genista tinctoria*
Eared Willow	*Salix aurita*
Early Forget-me-not	*Myosotis ramosissima*
Early Gentian	*Gentianella anglica*
Early Hair-grass	*Aira praecox*
Early Marsh-orchid	*Dactylorhiza incarnata*
Early Spider-orchid	*Ophrys sphegodes*
Early-purple Orchid	*Orchis mascula*
Elder	*Sambucus nigra*
Enchanter's-nightshade	*Circaea lutetiana*
Eyebright	*Euphrasia officinalis* agg.
Fairy Flax	*Linum catharticum*
False Oat-grass	*False Oat-grass*
False Sedge	*Kobresia simpliciuscula*
Fen Orchid	*Liparis loeselii*
Fen Violet	*Viola persicifolia*
Fern-grass	*Catapodium rigidum*
Field Maple	*Acer campestre*
Field Scabious	*Knautia arvensis*
Field Wormwood	*Artemisia campestris*
filmy-ferns	*Hymenophyllum* spp.
Fir Clubmoss	*Huperzia selago*
Flea Sedge	*Carex pulicaris*
Floating Bur-reed	*Sparganium angustifolium*
Floating Sweet-grass	*Glyceria fluitans*
Floating Water-plantain	*Luronium natans*
Fly Orchid	*Ophrys insectifera*
Forked Spleenwort	*Asplenium septentrionale*
Foxglove	*Digitalis purpurea*
Fragrant Orchid	*Gymnadenia conopsea*
Fringed Gentian	*Gentianella ciliata*
Fringed Rupturewort	*Herniaria ciliolata*
Fringed Sandwort	*Arenaria ciliata*
Fritillary	*Fritillaria meleagris*
Fritillary	*Fritillaria meleagris*
Frog Orchid	*Coeloglossum viride*
Frogbit	*Hydrocharis morsus-ranae*
Ghost Orchid	*Epipogium aphyllum*
Giant Bellflower	*Campanula latifolia*
Glaucous Sedge	*Carex flacca*
Globeflower	*Trollius europaeus*
Goat Willow	*Salix caprea*
Golden Samphire	*Limbarda crithmoides*
Goldenrod	*Solidago virgaurea*
Gorse	*Ulex europaeus*
gorse	*Ulex* spp.
Grass-leaved Orache	*Atriplex littoralis*
Grass-of-Parnassus	*Parnassia palustris*
Grass-wrack Pondweed	*Potamogeton compressus*
Great Burnet	*Sanguisorba officinalis*
Great Willowherb	*Epilobium hirsutum*
Great Wood-rush	*Luzula sylvatica*
Greater Bird's-foot-trefoil	*Lotus pedunculatus*
Greater Butterfly-orchid	*Platanthera chlorantha*
Greater Knapweed	*Centaurea scabiosa*
Greater Spearwort	*Ranunculus lingua*
Greater Stitchwort	*Stellaria holostea*
Greater Tussock-sedge	*Carex paniculata*
Green Spleenwort	*Asplenium viride*
Green-flowered Helleborine	*Epipactis phyllanthes*
Green-winged Orchid	*Orchis morio*
Grey Hair-grass	*Corynephorus canescens*
Grey Willow	*Salix cinerea*
Guelder-rose	*Viburnum opulus*
Hair Sedge	*Carex capillaris*
Hairy Bird's-foot-trefoil	*Lotus subbiflorus*
Hairy Greenweed	*Genista pilosa*
Hard Shield-fern	*Polystichum aculeatum*
Hare's-tail Cottongrass	*Eriophorum vaginatum*
Harebell	*Campanula rotundifolia*
Hart's-tongue	*Phyllitis scolopendrium*
Hawthorn	*Crataegus monogyna*

Common name	Scientific name
Hazel	Corylus avellana
Heath Bedstraw	Galium saxatile
Heath Rush	Juncus squarrosus
Heath Spotted-orchid	Dactylorhiza maculata
Heather	Calluna vulgaris
Hedge Bindweed	Calystegia sepium
Hedge Woundwort	Stachys sylvatica
Hemp-agrimony	Eupatorium cannabinum
Herb-Paris	Paris quadrifolia
Highland Cudweed	Gnaphalium norvegicum
Highland Saxifrage	Saxifraga rivularis
Himalayan Balsam* [Indian Balsam]	Impatiens glandulifera
Hoary Rock-rose	Helianthemum oelandicum
Hoary Whitlowgrass	Draba incana
Holly	Ilex aquifolium
Holly-fern	Polystichum lonchitis
Honeysuckle	Lonicera periclymenum
Hornbeam	Carpinus betulus
Horseshoe Vetch	Hippocrepis comosa
Hottentot-fig	Carpobrotus edulis
Intermediate Wintergreen	Pyrola media
Irish Heath	Eirca erigena
Irish Lady's-tresses	Spiranthes romanzoffiana
Ivy	Hedera helix
Ivy-leaved Bellflower	Wahlenbergia hederacea
Garlic Mustard	Alliaria petiolata
Jacob`s-ladder	Polemonium caeruleum
Japanese Knotweed	Fallopia japonica
Jointed Rush	Juncus articulatus
Common Juniper	Juniperus communis ssp. communis
Kidney Vetch	Anthyllis vulneraria
Knotgrass	Polygonum aviculare
Lady Orchid	Orchis purpurea
Lady's Bedstraw	Galium verum
Lady's-mantle	Alchemilla spp.
Large-leaved Lime	Tilia platyphyllos
Lemon-scented Fern	Oreopteris limbosperma
Lesser Bladderwort	Utricularia minor
Lesser Butterfly-orchid	Platanthera bifolia
Lesser Celandine	Ranunculus ficaria
Lesser Pond-sedge	Carex acutiformis
Lesser Skullcap	Scutellaria minor
Lesser Twayblade	Listera cordata
Lesser Water-parsnip	Berula erecta
Lesser Water-plantain	Baldellia ranunculoides
Lily-of-the-valley	Convallaria majalis
Limestone Bedstraw	Galium sterneri
Limestone Fern	Gymnocarpium robertianum
Little Mouse-ear	Cerastium semidecandrum
Little-Robin	Geranium purpureum
Lizard Orchid	Himantoglossum hircinum
Lousewort	Pedicularis sylvatica
Lyme-grass	Leymus arenarius
Mackay's Heath	Erica mackaiana
Maiden Pink	Dianthus deltoides
Maidenhair Fern	Adiantum capillus-veneris
Maidenhair Spleenwort	Asplenium trichomanes
Male-fern	Dryopteris filix-mas
Man Orchid	Aceras anthropophorum
Many-stalked Spike-rush	Eleocharis multicaulis
March Clubmoss	Lycopodiella inundata
Marram	Ammophila arenaria
Marsh Arrowgrass	Triglochin palustre
Marsh Bedstraw	Galium palustre
Marsh Cinquefoil	Potentilla palustris
Marsh Clubmoss	Lycopodiella inundata
Marsh Fern	Thelypteris palustris
Marsh Foxtail	Alopecurus geniculatus
Marsh Gentian	Gentiana pneumonanthe
Marsh Hawk's-beard	Crepis paludosa
Marsh Helleborine	Epipactis palustris
Marsh-mallow	Althaea officinalis
Marsh Pea	Lathyrus palustris
Marsh St. John's-wort	Hypericum elodes
Marsh-marigold	Caltha palustris
Mat-grass	Nardus stricta
Meadow Buttercup	Ranunculus acris
Meadow Crane's-bill	Geranium pratense
Meadow Oat-grass	Helictotrichon pratense
Meadow Saffron	Colchicum autumnale
Meadow Thistle	Cirsium dissectum
Meadowsweet	Filipendula ulmaria
Melancholy Thistle	Cirsium heterophyllum
Military Orchid	Orchis militaris
Milk-parsley	Peucedanum palustre
Mistletoe	Viscum album
Monkey Orchid	Orchis simia
Moonwort	Botrychium lunaria
Moschatel	Adoxa moschatellina
Moss Campion	Silene acaulis
Mossy Stonecrop	Crassula tillaea
Mountain Avens	Dryas octopetala
Mountain Crowberry* [Crowberry]	Empetrum nigrum ssp. hermaphroditum
Mountain Everlasting	Antennaria dioica
Mountain Male-fern	Dryopteris oreades
Mountain Sorrel	Oxyria digyna
Mountain Willow	Salix arbuscula
Mouse-ear-hawkweed	Pilosella officinarum
Mousetail	Myosurus minimus
Mudwort	Limosella aquatica
Musk Orchid	Herminium monorchis
Myrtle-leaved Willow	Salix myrtilloides
Narrow-leaved Helleborine	Cephalanthera longifolia
Narrow-leaved Marsh-orchid	Dactylorhiza traunsteineri
Narrow-leaved Water-dropwort	Oenanthe silaifolia
Narrow-lipped Helleborine	Epipactis leptochila agg.
Net-leaved Willow	Salix reticulata
Nettle-leaved Bellflower	Campanula trachelium
New Zealand Pigmyweed	Crassula helmsii
Northern Rock-cress	Arabis petraea
Norwegian Mugwort	Artemisia norvegica
Nottingham Catchfly	Silene nutans
Oak Fern	Gymnocarpium dryopteris
Oblong Woodsia	Woodsia ilvensis
Oblong-leaved Sundew	Drosera intermedia
One-flowered Wintergreen	Moneses uniflora
Opposite-leaved Golden-saxifrage	Chrysosplenium oppositifolium
oraches	Atriplex spp.
Orpine	Sedum telephium
Oxeye Daisy	Leucanthemum vulgare
Oxlip	Primula elatior
Oysterplant	Mertensia maritima
Pale Butterwort	Pinguicula lusitanica
Parrot's-feather	Myriophyllum aquaticum
Parsley Fern	Cryptogramma crispa
Parsley-piert	Aphanes arvensis agg.
Pasqueflower	Pulsatilla vulgaris
Pedunculate Oak	Quercus robur
Pennyroyal	Mentha pulegium
Pepper-saxifrage	Silaum silaus
Perennial Knawel	Scleranthus perennis
Perennial Rye-grass	Lolium perenne
Petty Whin	Genista anglica
Pigmy Rush	Juncus pygmaeus
Pignut	Conopodium majus
Pill Sedge	Carex pilulifera
Pillwort	Pilularia globulifera
Pipewort	Eriocaulon aquaticum
plantains	Plantago spp.
Plymouth Pear	Pyrus cordata
Pond Water-crowfoot	Ranunculus peltatus
pondweeds	Potamogeton spp.
Portland Spurge	Euphorbia portlandica
Prickly Saltwort	Salsola kali ssp. kali
Primrose	Primula vulgaris
Purple Gromwell	Lithospermum purpurocaeruleum
Purple Milk-vetch	Astragalus danicus
Purple Moor-grass	Molinia caerulea
Purple Ramping-fumitory	Fumaria purpurea
Purple Saxifrage	Saxifraga oppositifolia
Purple-loosestrife	Lythrum salicaria
Purple-stem Cat's-tail	Phleum phleoides
Pyramidal Orchid	Anacamptis pyramidalis
Pyrenean Scurvygrass	Cochlearia pyrenaica
Quaking-grass	Briza media
Quillwort	Isoetes lacustris
Ragged-Robin	Lychnis flos-cuculi
Red Campion	Silene dioica
Red Clover	Trifolium pratense
Red Currant	Ribes rubrum
Red Fescue	Festuca rubra agg.
Red Helleborine	Cephalanthera rubra
Red Pondweed	Potamogeton alpinus
Reed Sweet-grass	Glyceria maxima

Ribwort Plantain	Plantago lanceolata
Rigid Bucker-fern	Dryopteris submontana
Rigid Hornwort	Ceratophyllum demersum
Rock Samphire	Crithmum maritimum
Rock Sea-lavender	Limonium binervosum agg.
Rock Sea-spurrey	Spergularia rupicola
Rhododendron	Rhododendron ponticum
Rosebay Willowherb	Chamerion angustifolium
Roseroot	Sedum rosea
Rough Hawkbit	Leontodon hispidus
Round-headed Rampion	Phyteuma orbiculare
Round-leaved Crowfoot	Ranunculus omiophyllus
Round-leaved Fluellen	Kickxia spuria
Round-leaved Sundew	Drosera rotundifolia
Round-leaved Wintergreen	Pyrola rotundifolia
Rowan	Sorbus aucuparia
Royal Fern	Osmunda regalis
Rustyback	Ceterach officinarum
Salad Burnet	Sanguisorba minor ssp. minor
Saltmarsh Flat-sedge	Blysmus rufus
Saltmarsh Rush	Juncus gerardii
Sand Catchfly	Silene conica
Sand Couch	Elytrigia juncea
Sand Sedge	Carex arenaria
Sanicle	Sanicula europaea
Saw Sedge	Cladium mariscus
Scaly Male-fern	Dryopteris affinis
Scots Lovage	Ligusticum scoticum
Scots Pine	Pinus sylvestris
Scottish Asphodel	Tofieldia pusilla
Scottish Primrose	Primula scotica
Sea Aster	Aster tripolium
Sea Beet	Beta vulgaris ssp. maritima
Sea Bindweed	Calystegia soldanella
Sea Campion	Silene uniflora
Sea Carrot	Daucus carota ssp. gummifer
Sea Clover	Trifolium squamosum
Sea Club-rush	Bolboschoenus maritimus
Sea Fern-grass	Catapodium marinum
Sea Lettuce	Ulva latuca
Sea Mayweed	Tripleurospermum maritimum
Sea Pea	Lathyrus japonicus
Sea Plantain	Plantago maritima
Sea Purslane	Atriplex portulacoides
Sea Rocket	Cakile maritima
Sea Sandwort	Honckenya peploides
Sea Spurge	Euphorbia paralias
Sea Stock	Matthiola sinuata
Sea-buckthorn	Hippophae rhamnoides
Sea-holly	Eryngium maritimum
Sea-kale	Crambe maritima
sea-lavenders	Limonium spp.
Selfheal	Prunella vulgaris
Sessile Oak	Quercus petraea
Shallon	Gaultheria shallon
Sharp-flowered Rush	Juncus acutiflorus
Sharp-Leaved Fluellen	Kickxia elatine
Sharp-leaved Pondweed	Potamogeton acutifolius
Sheep's-fescue	Festuca ovina
Sheep's Sorrel	Rumex acetosella ssp. acetosella
shield-ferns	Polystichum spp.
Shepherd's-needle	Scandix pecten-veneris
Shepherd's Cress	Teesdalia nudicaulis
Shetland Mouse-ear	Cerastium nigrescens
Shoreweed	Littorella uniflora
Shrubby Cinquefoil	Potentilla fruticosa
Shrubby Sea-blite	Suaeda vera
Sibbaldia	Sibbaldia procumbens
Silver Birch	Betula pendula
Silverweed	Potentilla anserina
Six-stamened Waterwort	Elatine hexandra
Slender Hare's-ear	Bupleurum tenuissimum
Slender Naiad	Najas flexillis
Slender Sedge	Carex lasiocarpa
Slender Spike-rush	Eleocharis uniglumis
Slender Tufted-sedge	Carex acuta
Small Cow-wheat	Melampyrum sylvaticum
Small Restharrow	Ononis reclinata
Small Scabious	Scabiosa columbaria
Small Toadflax	Chaenorhinum minus
Small-leaved Lime	Tilia cordata
Small-white Orchid	Pseudorchis albida

Smooth Cat's-ear	Hypochaeris glabra
Smooth Hawk's-beard	Crepis capillaris
Snow Pearlwort	Sagina nivalis
Snowdon Lily	Lloydia serotina
Soft Rush	Juncus effusus
Solomon's-seal	Polygonatum multiflorum
Southern Marsh-orchid	Dactylorhiza praetermissa
Spanish Catchfly	Silene otites
Spiked Speedwell	Veronica spicata
Spiked Water-milfoil	Myriophyllum spicatum
Spindle	Euonymus europaeus
Spiral Tasselweed	Ruppia cirrhosa
Spring Gentian	Gentiana verna
Spring Sandwort	Minuartia verna
Spring Speedwell	Veronica verna
Spring Squill	Scilla verna
Squinancywort	Asperula cynanchica
St. Dabeoc's Heath	Daboecia cantabrica
Star Sedge	Carex echinata
Starry Saxifrage	Saxifraga stellaris
Stemless Thistle	Cirsium acaule
Stiff Sedge	Carex bigelowii
stonecrops	Sedum spp.
Strawberry-tree	Arbutus unedo
Stream Water-crowfoot	Ranunculus penicillatus
Subterranean Clover	Trifolium subterraneum
Suffocated Clover	Trifolium suffocatum
Sun Spurge	Euphorbia helioscopia
sundews	Drosera spp.
Sweet Chestnut	Castanea sativa
Sweet Vernal-grass	Anthoxanthum odoratum
Sycamore	Acer pseudoplatanus
Tea-leaved Willow	Salix phylicifolia
Teesdale Sandwort	Minuartia stricta
Teesdale Violet	Viola rupestris
Three-leaved Rush	Juncus trifidus
Three-lobed Crowfoot	Ranunculus tripartitus
Thrift	Armeria maritima
Thyme-leaved Sandwort	Arenaria serpyllifolia sens. lat.
Tor-grass	Brachypodium pinnatum
Tormentil	Potentilla erecta
Trailing Azalea	Loiseleuria procumbens
Traveller's-joy	Clematis vitalba
Tubular Water-dropwort	Oenanthe fistulosa
Tufted Hair-grass	Deschampsia cespitosa
Tunbridge Filmy-fern	Hymenophyllum tunbrigense
Turkey Oak	Quercus cerris
Twayblade	Listera ovata
Twinflower	Linnaea borealis
Twin-headed Clover	Trifolium bocconei
Violet Helleborine	Epipactis purpurata
Viviparous Fescue	Festuca vivipara
Wall-rue	Asplenium ruta-muraria
Water Avens	Geum rivale
Water Dock	Rumex hydrolapathum
Water Forget-me-not	Myosotis scorpioides
Water Germander	Teucrium scordium
Water Horsetail	Equisetum fluviatile
Water Lobelia	Lobelia dortmanna
Water Mint	Mentha aquatica
Water-cress	Rorippa nasturtium-aquaticum
water-milfoils	Myriophyllum spp.
water-parsnips	Berula spp.
Water-purslane	Lythrum portula
Water-soldier	Stratiotes aloides
water-starworts	Callitriche spp.
Wavy Hair-grass	Deschampsia flexuosa
Wavy St. John's-wort	Hypericum undulatum
Wayfaring-tree	Viburnum lantana
Weasel's-snout	Misopates orontium
Western Gorse	Ulex gallii
Western Marsh-orchid	Dactylorhiza majalis
White Beak-sedge	Rhynchospora alba
White Clover	Trifolium repens
White Helleborine	Cephalanthera damasonium
whitebeams	Sorbus spp.
Whorled Caraway	Carum verticillatum
Wild Angelica	Angelica sylvestris
Wild Cabbage	Brassica oleracea var. oleracea
Wild Carrot	Daucus carota
Wild Cherry	Prunus avium
Ramsons	Allium ursinum

Wild Gladiolus	Gladiolus illyricus
Wild Pansy	Viola tricolor
Wild Privet	Ligustrum vulgare
Wild Service-tree	Sorbus torminalis
Wild Strawberry	Fragaria vesca
Wild Thyme	Thymus polytrichus
Wilson's Filmy-fern	Hymenophyllum wilsonii
Wood Anemone	Anemone nemorosa
Wood Crane's-bill	Geranium sylvaticum
Wood Sage	Teucrium scorodonia
Wood Stitchwort	Stellaria nemorum
Wood-sorrel	Oxalis acetosella
Woolly Willow	Salix lanata
Wych Elm	Ulmus glabra
Yarrow	Achillea millefolium
Yellow Archangel	Lamiastrum galeobdolon
Yellow Bird's-nest	Monotropa hypopitys
Yellow Centuary	Cicendia filiformis
Yellow Horned-poppy	Glaucium flavum
Yellow Iris	Iris pseudacorus
Yellow Loosestrife	Lysimachia vulgaris
Yellow Oxytropis	Oxytropis campestris
Yellow Saxifrage	Saxifraga aizoides
Yellow Water-lily	Nuphar lutea
Yellow Whitlowgrass	Draba aizoides
Yellow-rattle	Rhinanthus minor
Yellow-wort	Blackstonia perfoliata
Yew	Taxus baccata
Yorkshire-fog	Holcus lanatus
Young's Helleborine	Epipactis youngiana

Mosses and Liverworts

Alpine Silverwort	Anthelia julacea
Bird's-foot Earwort	Scapania ornithopodioides
Bristly Fringe-moss	Racomitrium heterostichum
Broom Fork-moss	Dicranum scoparium
Common Hair-cap	Polytrichum commune var. commune
Common Tamarisk-moss	Thuidium Tamariscinum
Compact Bog-moss	Sphagnum compactum
Cow-horn Bog-moss	Sphagnum denticulatum
Curled Hook-moss	Palustriella commutata
Cypress-leaved Plait-moss	Hypnum cupressiforme
Donn's Notchwort	Anastrophyllum donnianum
Dwarf Neckera	Neckera pumila
Feathery Bog-moss	Sphagnum cuspidatum
Fountain Apple-moss	Philonotis fontana
Fox-tail Feather-moss	Thamnobryum alopecurum
Frizzled Crisp-moss	Tortella tortuosa
Glittering Wood-moss	Hylocomium splendens
Golden Bog-moss	Sphagnum pulchrum
Greater Copperwort*	Cephaloziella nicholsonii
Greater Water-moss	Fontinalis antipyretica
Green Shield-moss	Buxbaumia viridis
Hooked Scorpion-moss	Scorpidium scorpioides
Imbricate Bog-moss	Sphagnum affine
Juniper Prongwort	Herbertus aduncus ssp. hutchinsiae
Lindberg's Bog-moss	Sphagnum lindbergii
Magellanic Bog-moss	Sphagnum magellanicum
Marsh Forklet-moss	Dichodontium palustre
Mougeot's Yoke-moss	Amphidium mougeotii
Mountain Thread-moss*	Pohlia wahlenbergii var. glacialis
Neat Feather-moss	Pseudoscleropodium purum
Northern Haircap	Polytrichastrum sexangulare
Papillose Bog-moss	Sphagnum papillosum
Purple Spoonwort	Pleurozia purpurea
Red Bog-moss	Sphagnum capillifolium ssp. rubellum
Red-stemmed Feather-moss	Pleurozium schreberi
River Feather-moss	Brachythecium rivulare
Sand-hill Screw-moss	Syntrichia ruralis ssp. ruraliformis
Smaller Lattice-moss	Cinclidotus fontinaloides
Soft Bog-moss	Sphagnum tenellum
Starke's Forkmoss	Kiaeria starkei
Swan-necked Thyme-moss	Mnium hornum
Water Earwort	Scapania undulata
Wood's Whipwort	Mastigophora woodsii
Woolly Fringe-moss	Racomitrium lanuginosum
Yellow Feather-moss	Homalothecium lutescens
Yellow Starry Feather-moss	Campylium stellatum

Fungi

Hazel Gloves	Hypocreopsis rhododendri
Orange Tooth	Hydnellum aurantiacum
Blue Tooth	Hydnellum caeruleum
Nail Fungus	Poronia punctata
Chicken of the Woods	Laetiporus sulphureus
bracket fungi	Gandoderma spp.
waxcaps	Hygrocybe spp.
fairy clubs	Clavarioids
pinkgills	Entolomatcaeae
earthtongues	Geoglossaceae

Lichens

Black Tar Lichen	Hydropunctaria maura
Common Tree Lungwort	Lobaria pulmonaria
cudbear lichens	Ochrolechia ssp.
Iceland Moss	Cetraria islandica ssp. islandica
Octopus Suckers	Collema conglomeratum
Orange Sea Lichen	Caloplaca marina
reindeer lichens	Cladonia spp.
Sea Ivory	Ramalina siliquosa
Yellow Specklebelly	Pseudocyphellaria crocata

Macro-algae

stoneworts	Chara spp.

Seaweeds

Bladder Wrack	Fucus vesiculosus
Bushy Rainbow Wrack	Cystoseira tamariscifolia
Dulse	Palmaria palmata
kelps	Laminaria spp.
Oar Weed	Laminaria digitata
Sea Lettuce	Ulva lactuca
Spiral Wrack	Fucus spiralis
Sugar Kelp	Saccharina latissima
wracks	Fucaceae

Invertebrates

Adonis Blue	Polyommatus bellargus
Argent and Sable	Rheumaptera hastata
Azure Hawker	Aeshna caerulea
Barberry Carpet	Pareulype berberata
barnacles	Chthamalus spp.
Beachcomber Beetle	Eurynebria complanata
Beadlet Anemone	Actinia equina
Beewolf	Philanthus triangulum
Belted Beauty	Lycia zonaria
Bilberry Bumblebee	Bombus monticola
Bilberry Pug	Pasiphila debiliata
Black Bog Ant	Formica picea
Black Darter	Sympetrum danae
Bog Bush-cricket	Metrioptera brachyptera
Bog Sun-jumper Spider	Heliophanus dampfi
Brown Argus	Aricia agestis
Brown Hairstreak	Thecla betulae
Brown-banded Carder Bee	Bombus humilis
Bumblebee Robberfly	Laphria flava
Chalkhill Blue	Polyommatus coridon
Chequered Skipper	Carterocephalus palaemon
Cliff Tiger Beetle	Cylindera germanica
Common Field Grasshopper	Chorthippus brunneus
Common Shore Crab	Carcinus maenas
craneflies	Tipulidae
Dark Crimson Underwing	Catocala sponsa
Dark-green Fritillary	Argynnis aglaja
Dingy Skipper	Erynnis tages
Dog Whelk	Nucella lapillus
Duke of Burgundy	Hamearis lucina
Dune Tiger Beetle	Cicindela maritima
Emerald Damselfly	Lestes sponsa
Emperor Moth	Saturnia pavonia
Fairy Shrimp	Chirocephalus diaphanus
Field Cricket	Gryllus campestris
Fox Moth	Macrothylacia rubi
freshwater sponges	Porifera
Gilkicker Weevil	Pachytychius haematocephalus
Glanville Fritillary	Melitaea cinxia

Glow-worm	*Lampyris noctiluca*
Grayling	*Hipparchia semele*
Great Silver Water Beetle	*Hydrophilus piceus*
Great Yellow Bumblebee	*Bombus distinguendus*
Green Hairstreak	*Callophrys rubi*
Green Tiger Beetle	*Cicindela campestris*
Grizzled Skipper	*Pyrgus malvae*
Hairy Dragonfly	*Brachytron pratense*
Heath Sand Wasp	*Ammophila pubescens*
Heath Tiger Beetle	*Cicindela sylvatica*
Hermit Crab	*Pagurus bernhardus*
High Brown Fritillary	*Argynnis adippe*
Hornet Robberfly	*Asilus crabroniformis*
Keeled Skimmer	*Orthetrum coerulescens*
Ladybird Spider	*Eresus sandaliatus*
Lagoon Sand-shrimp	*Gammarus insensibilis*
Lagoon Sandworm	*Armandia cirrhosa*
Large Blue	*Phengaris arion*
Large Heath	*Coenonympha tullia*
Large Marsh Grasshopper	*Stethophyma grossum*
limpets	*Patella* ssp.
Lugworm	*Arenicola marina*
Lulworth Skipper	*Thymelicus acteon*
Marbled White	*Melanargia galathea*
Marsh Fritillary	*Euphydryas aurinia*
mayflies	Ephemeroptera
Medicinal Leech	*Hirudo medicinalis*
Mire Pill Beetle	*Curimopsis nigrita*
Mistletoe Marble Moth	*Celypha woodiana*
Moss Carder Bumblebee	*Bombus muscorum*
Mottled Bee-fly	*Thyridanthrax fenestratus*
Mountain Ringlet	*Erebia epiphron*
Mussel	*Mytilus edulis*
Narrow-bordered Bee Hawk-moth	*Hemaris tityus*
Narrow-headed Ant	*Formica exsecta*
Necklace Ground Beetle	*Carabus monilis*
Noble Chafer	*Gnorimus nobilis*
Norfolk Hawker	*Aeshna isoceles*
Northern Brown Argus	*Aricia artaxerxes*
Northern Colletees	*Colletes floralis*
Northern Damselfly	*Coenagrion hastulatum*
Orange-tip	*Anthocharis cardamines*
Pearl-bordered Fritillary	*Boloria euphrosyne*
periwinkles	*Littorina* spp.
Purbeck Mason-wasp	*Pseudepipona herrichii*
Purple Hairstreak	*Neozephyrus quercus*
Raft Spider	*Dolomedes fimbriatus*
Ragworm	*Hediste diversicolor*
Red Admiral	*Vanessa atalanta*
Reed Leopard	*Phragmataecia castaneae*
River Limpet	*Ancylus fluviatilis*
Ruddy Darter	*Sympetrum sanguineum*
Rufous Grasshopper	*Gomphocerippus rufus*
sawflies	Symphyta
Scaly Cricket	*Pseudomogoplistes squamiger*
Scarce Chaser	*Libellula fulva*
Scarce Emerald Damselfly	*Lestes dryas*
Scotch Argus	*Erebia aethiops*
Scotch Burnet	*Zygaena exulans*
sea anemones	Actiniaria
Sea Slater	*Ligia oceanica*
Set-aside Downy-back	*Ophonus laticollis*
Sheep Tick	*Ixodes ricinus*
Shrill Carder Bee	*Bombus sylvarum*
Signal Crayfish	*Pacifastacus leniusculus*
Silver-spotted Skipper	*Hesperia comma*
Silver-studded Blue	*Plebejus argus*
Silver-washed Fritillary	*Argynnis paphia*
Small Blue	*Cupido minimus*
Small Copper	*Lycaena phlaeas*
Small Pearl-bordered Fritillary	*Boloria selene*
Small Red Damselfly	*Ceriagrion tenellum*
Small Red-eyed Damselfly	*Erythromma viridulum*
Small Tortoiseshell	*Aglais urticae*
soldier flies	Stratiomyidae
Southern Damselfly	*Coenagrion mercuriale*
Speckled Wood	*Pararge aegeria*
Stag Beetle	*Lucanus cervus*
Starlet Sea Anemone	*Nematostella vectensis*
stoneflies	Plecoptera
Stripe-winged Grasshopper	*Stenobothrus lineatus*

Sussex Emerald	*Thalera fimbrialis*
Swallowtail	*Papilio machaon*
Triangle Spider	*Hyptiotes paradoxus*
Variable Damselfly	*Coenagrion pulchellum*
Wall Mason Bee	*Osmia parietina*
water-boatmen	Corixidae
Whelk-shell Jumping Spider	*Pseudeuophrys obsoleta*
White Admiral	*Limenitis camilla*
White-clawed Crayfish	*Austropotamobius pallipes*
White-faced Darter	*Leucorrhinia dubia*
White-letter Hairstreak	*Strymonidia w-album*
Wormwood Moonshiner	*Amara fusca*
Yellow Meadow Ant	*Lasius flavus*
Yellow-ringed Combe-horn	*Ctenophora flaveolata*

Fishes

Arctic Charr	*Salvelinus alpinus*
Atlantic Salmon	*Salmo salar*
Bream	*Abramis brama*
Brook Lamprey	*Lampetra planeri*
Brown Trout	*Salmo trutta*
Bullhead	*Cottus gobio*
Butterfish	*Pholis gunnellus*
Dace	*Leuciscus leuciscus*
Eel	*Anguilla anguilla*
Flounder	*Platichthys flesus*
Grayling	*Thymallus thymallus*
mullet	Mugilidae
Perch	*Perca fluviatilis*
Pike	*Esox lucius*
pipefish	Syngnathinae
Powan	*Coregonus clupeoides*
Rainbow Trout	*Oncorhynchus mykiss*
Roach	*Rutilus rutilus*
Rudd	*Scardinius erythropthalmus*
Ruffe	*Gymnocephalus cernua*
sandeels	Ammodytidae
Sea-bass	*Dicentrarchus labrax*
Tench	*Tinca tinca*

Reptiles

Slow-worm	*Anguis fragilis*
Smooth Snake	*Coronella austriaca*
Sand Lizard	*Lacerta agilis*
Grass Snake	*Natrix natrix*
Adder	*Vipera berus*
Common Lizard	*Zootoca vivipara*

Amphibians

Common Toad	*Bufo bufo*
Common Frog	*Rana temporaria*
Great Crested Newt	*Triturus cristatus*
Natterjack Toad	*Epidalea calamita*
newts	Urodeles

Birds

Gill & Donsker (2012) / IOC international English name in square brackets where appropriate.

Arctic Skua [Parasitic Jaeger]	*Stercorarius parasiticus*
Avocet [Pied Avocet]	*Recurvirostra avosetta*
Barn Owl [Western Barn Owl]	*Tyto alba*
Barnacle Goose	*Branta leucopsis*
Bean Goose [Tundra/Taiga Bean Goose]	*Anser fabalis*
Bearded Tit [Bearded Reedling]	*Panurus biarmicus*
Bewick's Swan [Tundra Swan]	*Cygnus columbianus*
Bittern [Eurasian Bittern]	*Botaurus stellaris*
Black Grouse	*Tetrao tetrix*
Black Guillemot	*Cepphus grylle*
Black Redstart	*Phoenicurus ochruros*
Black-tailed Godwit	*Limosa limosa*
Black-throated Diver [Black-throated Loon]	*Gavia arctica*
Brambling	*Fringilla montifringilla*
Brent Goose [Brant Goose]	*Branta bernicla*

Bullfinch [Eurasian Bullfinch]	*Pyrrhula pyrrhula*
Capercaillie [Western Capercaillie]	*Tetrao urogallus*
Chough [Red-billed Chough]	*Pyrrhocorax pyrrhocorax*
Cirl Bunting	*Emberiza cirlus*
Common Crossbill	*Loxia curvirostra*
Common Sandpiper	*Actitis hypoleucos*
Common Scoter	*Melanitta nigra*
Cormorant [Great Cormorant]	*Phalacrocorax carbo*
Corn Bunting	*Emberiza calandra*
Corncrake [Corn Crake]	*Crex crex*
Crane [Common Crane]	*Grus grus*
Crested Tit [European Crested Tit]	*Parus cristatus*
Curlew [Eurasian Curlew]	*Numenius arquata*
Dartford Warbler	*Sylvia undata*
Dipper [White-throated Dipper]	*Cinclus cinclus*
Dotterel [Eurasian Dotterel]	*Charadrius morinellus*
Dunlin	*Calidris alpina*
Dunnock	*Prunella modularis*
White-fronted Goose [Greater White-fronted Goose]	*Anser albifrons*
Fieldfare	*Turdus pilaris*
Firecrest [Common Firecrest]	*Regulus ignicapillus*
Fulmar [Northern Fulmar]	*Fulmarus glacialis*
Gadwall	*Anas strepera*
Gannet [Northern Gannet]	*Sula bassana*
Garden Warbler	*Sylvia borin*
Garganey	*Anas querquedula*
Golden Eagle	*Aquila chrysaetos*
Golden Plover [European Golden Plover]	*Pluvialis apricaria*
Goldeneye [Common Goldeneye]	*Bucephala clangula*
Goshawk [Northern Goshawk]	*Accipiter gentilis*
Grasshopper Warbler [Common Grasshopper Warbler]	*Locustella naevia*
Great Crested Grebe	*Podiceps cristatus*
Green Woodpecker [European Green Woodpecker]	*Picus viridis*
Greenshank [Common Greenshank]	*Tringa nebularia*
Grey Partridge	*Perdix perdix*
Grey Wagtail	*Motacilla cinerea*
Guillemot [Common Murre]	*Uria aalge*
Hen Harrier	*Circus cyaneus*
Herring Gull [European Herring Gull]	*Larus argentatus*
House Martin [Common House Martin]	*Delichon urbica*
Kestrel [Common Kestrel]	*Falco tinnunculus*
Kingfisher [Common Kingfisher]	*Alcedo atthis*
Kittiwake [Black-legged Kittiwake]	*Rissa tridactyla*
Knot [Red Knot]	*Calidris canutus*
Lapwing [Northern Lapwing]	*Vanellus vanellus*
Lesser Whitethroat	*Sylvia curruca*
Lesser Spotted Woodpecker	*Dendrocopos minor*
Linnet [Common Linnet]	*Carduelis cannabina*
Little Bittern	*Ixobrychus minutus*
Little Grebe	*Tachybaptus ruficollis*
Little Owl	*Athene noctua*
Little Ringed Plover	*Charadrius dubius*
Long-eared Owl	*Asio otus*
Marsh Harrier [Western Marsh Harrier]	*Circus aeruginosus*
Marsh Tit	*Parus palustris*
Meadow Pipit	*Anthus pratensis*
Merlin	*Falco columbarius*
Montagu's Harrier	*Circus pygargus*
Nightingale [Common Nightingale]	*Luscinia megarhynchos*
Nightjar [European Nightjar]	*Caprimulgus europaeus*
Osprey [Western Osprey]	*Pandion haliaetus*
Oystercatcher [Eurasian Oystercatcher]	*Haematopus ostralegus*
Parrot Crossbill	*Loxia pytyopsittacus*
Peregrine [Peregrine Falcon]	*Falco peregrinus*
Pied Flycatcher [European Pied Flycatcher]	*Ficedula hypoleuca*
Pink-footed Goose	*Anser brachyrhyncus*
Pochard [Common Pochard]	*Aythya ferina*
Ptarmigan [Rock Ptarmigan]	*Lagopus mutus*
Puffin [Atlantic Puffin]	*Fratercula arctica*
Purple Sandpiper	*Calidris maritima*
Quail [Common Quail]	*Coturnix coturnix*
Raven [Northern Raven]	*Corvus corax*
Razorbill	*Alca torda*
Red Grouse [Willow Ptarmigan]	*Lagopus lagopus*
Red Kite	*Milvus milvus*
Red-breasted Merganser	*Mergus serrator*
Lesser Redpoll [[Common Redpoll]]	*Carduelis cabaret*
Redstart [Common Redstart]	*Phoenicurus phoenicurus*
Red-throated Diver [Red-throated Loon]	*Gavia stellata*
Reed Bunting [Common Reed Bunting]	*Emberiza schoeniclus*
Reed Warbler [Eurasian Reed Warbler]	*Acrocephalus scirpaceus*
Ring Ouzel	*Turdus torquatus*
Ringed Plover [Common Ringed Plover]	*Charadrius hiaticula*
Rock Pipit [Eurasian Rock Pipit]	*Anthus petrosus*
Sand Martin	*Riparia riparia*
Savi's Warbler	*Locustella luscinioides*
Scottish Crossbil	*Loxia scotica*
Sedge Warbler	*Acrocephalus schoenobaenus*
Shag [European Shag]	*Phalacrocorax aristotelis*
Short-eared Owl	*Asio flammeus*
Siskin [Eurasian Siskin]	*Carduelis spinus*
Skylark [Eurasian Skylark]	*Alauda arvensis*
Snipe [Common Snipe]	*Gallinago gallinago*
Snow Bunting	*Plectrophenax nivalis*
Spotted Crake	*Porzana porzana*
Spotted Flycatcher	*Muscicapa striata*
Starling [Common Starling]	*Sturnus vulgaris*
Stone-curlew [Eurasian Stone-curlew]	*Burhinus oedicnemus*
Stonechat [European Stonechat]	*Saxicola torquata*
Swallow [Barn Swallow]	*Hirundo rustica*
Swift [Common Swift]	*Apus apus*
Teal [Eurasian Teal]	*Anas crecca*
Tree Pipit	*Anthus trivialis*
Tree Sparrow [Eurasian Tree Sparrow]	*Passer montanus*
Tufted Duck	*Aythya fuligula*
Turtle Dove [European Turtle Dove]	*Streptopelia turtur*
Twite	*Carduelis flavirostris*
Water Rail	*Rallus aquaticus*
Wheatear [Northern Wheatear]	*Oenanthe oenanthe*
Whinchat	*Saxicola rubetra*
White-tailed Eagle	*Haliaeatus albicilla*
Whitethroat [Common Whitethroat]	*Sylvia communis*
Whooper Swan	*Cygnus cygnus*
Wigeon [Eurasian Wigeon]	*Anas penelope*
Willow Tit	*Parus montanus*
Willow Warbler	*Phylloscopus trochilus*
Wood Warbler	*Phylloscopus sibilatrix*
Woodlark	*Lullula arborea*
Wren [Eurasian Wren]	*Troglodytes troglodytes*
Yellow Wagtail [Western Yellow Wagtail]	*Motacilla flava*
Yellowhammer	*Emberiza citrinella*

Mammals

Badger	*Meles meles*
Bank Vole	*Myodes glareolus*
Barbastelle	*Barbastella barbastellus*
Beaver [Eurasian beaver]	*Castor fiber*
Brown Hare	*Lepus europaeus*
Brown Long-eared Bat	*Plecotus auritus*
Chinese Water Deer	*Hydropotes inermis*
Common Seal	*Phoca vitulina*
Eurasian Lynx	*Lynx lynx*
Fox	*Vulpes vulpes*
Greater Horseshoe Bat	*Rhinolophus ferrumequinum*
Grey Seal	*Halichoerus grypus*
Grey Squirrel	*Sciurus carolinensis*
Harvest Mouse	*Micromys minutus*
Hazel Dormouse	*Muscardinus avellanarius*
Hedgehog [European Hedgehog]	*Erinaceus europaeus*
Irish Hare	*Lepus timidus* ssp. *hibernicus*
Mink [American Mink]	*Neovison vison*
Mountain Hare	*Lepus timidus*
Natterer's Bat	*Myotis nattereri*
Noctule	*Nyctalus noctula*
Otter	*Lutra lutra*
Pine Marten	*Martes martes*
Polecat	*Mustela putorius*
Red Deer	*Cervus elaphus*
Red Squirrel	*Sciurus vulgaris*
Roe Deer	*Capreolus capreolus*
Serotine	*Eptesicus serotinus*
Spotted Hyena	*Crocuta crocuta*
Stoat	*Mustela erminea*
Water Shrew	*Neomys fodiens*
Water Vole	*Arvicola terrestris*
Wild Boar	*Sus scrofa*
Wolf	*Canis lupus*
Woolly Mammoth	*Mammuthus primigenius*
Woolly Rhinocerous	*Coelodonta antiquitatis*

Photographic Credits

The production of this book would not have been possible without the help of the photographers whose images have been reproduced. All photographs apart from those taken by the main authors Sophie Lake or Durwyn Liley are listed here, together with the photographer's initials:

Andy Acton (AA); David Adam (DA); Steve Aylward (SA); Paul Brock (PB); Laurie Campbell/SNH (LC/SNH); Graham Catley, http://gcatley.zenfolio.com/ (GC); Channel Coastal Observatory, www.channelcoast.org (CCO); Sandy Coppins (SC); Greg and Yvonne Dean, WorldWildlifeImages.com (G&YD); Guy Dutson (GD); Dorset County Museum (DCM); Brendan Dunford, www.burrenbeo.com (BD); Butterfly Conservation/Peter Eeles (BC/PE); Rue Ekins (RE); David Evans/Creative Commons (DE/CC); Peter Evans/Creative Commons (PE/CC); Steven Falk (SF); Footprint Ecology (FE); Rob Fuller (RF); Bob Gibbons (BG); Lorne Gill/SNH (LG/SNH); Bill Grayson (BGr); Paul Harris (PH); Hugh Harrop (HH); Hedgelink, www.hedgelink.org.uk (H); Duncan Hull/Creative Commons (DH/CC); Roger Key (RK); Mark Lake (ML); Simon Ledingham/Creative Commons (SL/CC); James Lowen, www.pbase.com/james_lowen (JL); Lutz Lucker/Creative Commons (LL/CC); John MacPherson, www.john-macpherson-photography.com/ (JM); Magnus Manske/Creative Commons (MM/CC); David Mardon (DM); Peter Moore (PM); Steve Moore (SM); Carly C Murphy/Creative Commons (CM/CC); David Newland (DN); Nick Owens (NO); Mike Page (MP); Kristian Peters/Creative Commons (KP/CC); Dave Pickett (DP); Gordon Rothero (GR); Sue Smallshire (SS); Brett Spencer (BS); Richard Starling/The Broads Reed and Sedge Cutters Association (RS); Rob Still (RSt); Andy and Gill Swash, WorldWildlifeImages.com (A&GS); Stewart Taylor (ST); David Tipling (DT); Andy Waddington/Creative Commons (AW/CC); Alan Watson Featherstone, Trees for Life (AWF); Richard Webb/Creative Commons (RW/CC); and Yamatsu/Creative Commons (Y/CC).

Page 190 Himalayan Balsam: (http://commons.wikimedia.org/wiki/File:Smestow_Brook_21_Himalayan_Balsam.JPG?uselang=en-gb)
Page 192 Otter: JL
Page 195 Beautiful Demoiselle: A&GS
Page 195 White-legged Damselfy: A&GS
Page 195 Golden-ringed Dragonfly: A&GS
Page 196 Great-crested Grebe: GC
Page 197 Red-eyed Damselfly: A&GS
Page 197 Spiked Water-milfoil: BG
Page 197 Cyclops: DH/CC (http://www.flickr.com/photos)
Page 197 Rudd: GC
Page 197 Medicinal Leech: RK
Page 198 Black-throated Diver: G&YD
Page 201 Flow Country: SM
Page 201 Northern Damselfly: A&GS
Page 205 Hickling aerial: MP
Page 208 Norfolk Hawker: A&GS
Page 208 Saltmarsh aerial: FE

Page 210 Wey and Arun Canal: (https://flic.kr/p/8xNvoz)
Page 210 Kingfisher: DT
Page 211 Floating Pondweed: KP/CC (http://commons.wikimedia.org/wiki/File:Luronium_natans.jpg)
Page 211 Kennet and Avon Canal: ML
Page 213 Dipper: LG/SNH
Page 214 River Shannon: CM/CC (https://www.flickr.com/photos/nikonfire/2115117016)
Page 214 River Wampool: SL/CC (http://commons.wikimedia.org/wiki/File:RiverWampool(SimonLedingham)Sep2004.jpg)
Page 215 Banded Demoiselle: A&GS
Page 215 River Waveney: RF
Page 217 River Itchen: RSt
Page 218 Raised beaches, Mull: ML
Page 219 Dawlish Aerial: CCO
Page 221 Caraun Point: ML
Page 224 Knot: JL

Page 227 Higher saltmarsh: SA
Page 231 Natterjack Toad: JL
Page 232 Rotational cultivation: JM
Page 233 Chough: A&GS
Page 233 Machair view: BG
Page 233 Dunlin: JL
Page 233 Corn Bunting: JL
Page 233 Belted Beauty: PH
Page 237 Ringed Plover: A&GS
Page 237 Orfordness aerial: MP
Page 239 Avocet: A&GS
Page 247 Guillemot: HH
Page 249 Garden pond: LG/SNH
Page 250 Shepherd's-needle: A&GS
Page 250 Harvest Mouse: JL
Page 250 Skylark: MM/CC (http://commons.wikimedia.org/wiki/File:Skylark_(6886721148).jpg)
Page 252 West Thurrock Marshes: SF
Page 252 Canvey Wick: SF
Page 253 Shrill Carder Bee: JL

Map Credits

One of the key features of this book is the maps that provide an overview of the physical characteristics of Britain and Ireland, and show the distribution of each habitat type. The following information summarises the data sources and relevant copyright details.

Geology data are reproduced with the permission of the British Geological Survey © NERC. All rights Reserved. The data for Ireland are Copyright Government of Ireland/Geological Survey of Ireland.

Climate data (*page 15*) include gridded data from the Met Office. The data are © Crown Copyright (2009). The UK Climate Projections data have been made available by the Department for Environment, Food and Rural Affairs (Defra) and Department for Energy and Climate Change (DECC) under licence from the Met Office, Newcastle University, University of East Anglia and Proudman Oceanographic Laboratory. These organisations accept no responsibility for any inaccuracies or omissions in the data, nor for any loss or damage directly or indirectly caused to any person or body by reason of, or arising out of, any use of these data. Data for Ireland are from the MET ÉIREANN website and are © copyright Met Éireann.

The upland vegetation boundary (*page 14*) is adapted from that in Averis, A., Averis, B., Birks, J., Horsfield, D., Thompson, D. & Yeo, M. (2004). An Illustrated Guide To British Upland Vegetation. JNCC, Peterborough, England.

SAC boundary data (*pages 24* and *180*) are as supplied by the European Environment Agency. The data for the UK is, in part, derived from Ordnance Survey data and contains Ordnance Survey data © Crown copyright and database right (2014). The data contain public sector information licensed under the Open Government Licence v2.0 (full details can be found at http://www.ordnancesurvey.co.uk/docs/licences/os-opendata-licence.pdf).

The combined habitat map (*page 9*), habitat introduction maps (*pages 31, 83, 105, 135, 161*) and individual habitat maps (*pages 66, 72, 74, 78, 86, 92, 94, 98, 108, 112, 126, 128, 184, 224, 226, 228, 244, 250* and *252*) are drawn from CORINE Land Cover (2006), © European Environment Agency (EEA).

Maps on *pages 210, 212, 214* and *216* are derived from OpenStreetMap, © OpenStreetMap contributors. Turloughs (*page 202*) were mapped using the Environmental Protection Agency Ireland Turlough database. The inset maps of rivers on *page 188* contain Ordnance Survey data © Crown copyright and database right (2014).

Traditional Orchards (*page 254*) were mapped using the Traditional Orchards survey data from the People's Trust for Endangered Species. Data were downloaded from the Natural England and Natural Resources Wales websites, © Natural England copyright (2014). This contains Ordnance Survey data © Crown copyright and database right (2014).

Maps on *pages 34, 58* and *64* contain, or are based on, information supplied by Forestry Commission Scotland. They contain Ordnance Survey data © Crown copyright and database right (2014). In the maps on *pages 34* and *64* the data for Ireland is strictly the copyright of The Department of Arts, Heritage and the Gaeltacht. Data on *page 48* is based on information supplied by Natural England, © Natural England copyright (2014); it also contains Ordnance Survey data © Crown copyright and database right (2014).

Natural England Priority Habitat spatial data are used in the maps on *pages 86, 92, 108, 112, 118, 122, 176, 184, 228* and *244*. These are reproduced with the permission of Natural England. The maps contain Ordnance Survey data © Crown copyright and database right (2014).

Landmap data downloaded from the Natural Resources Wales website are used in the maps on *pages 34, 86, 108, 112, 122, 176, 184* and *228*. These contain public sector information licensed under the Open Government Licence v1.0. The data are © Natural Resources Wales. All rights reserved. The maps contain Ordnance Survey Data. Ordnance Survey Licence number 100019741. Crown Copyright and Database Right (2012).

Individual habitat maps that incorporate grid cells (*pages 38, 42, 44, 52, 98, 116, 114, 122, 124, 130, 136, 140, 144, 146, 152, 154, 156, 168, 172, 174, 176, 196, 198, 200, 234, 238* and *244*) are derived from the 3rd Habitats Directive Article 17 Report 2013 at http://cdr.eionet.europa.eu/ie/eu/art17/envubzfmg. UK data from http://jncc.defra.gov.uk/page-6568, accessed July 2014.

Acknowledgements

Many people have helped in the production of this book and our sincere thanks go to them all. For information about habitats and places or access to sites, we thank: Isabel Alonso (Natural England), Steve Aylward (Suffolk Wildlife Trust), Jeremy Biggs (Freshwater Habitats Trust), Sandy Coppins, Alistair Crowle (Natural England), Iain Diack (Natural England), Mark Everard (Environment Agency), Digger and Lauren Jackson, Francisco Laborde, Richard Lindsay (University of East London), James Lowen, Lindsay Maskell (Centre for Ecology and Hydrology), Ed Mountford (Joint Nature Conservation Committee), Kenny Nelson (Scottish Natural Heritage), Colin Newlands (Natural England), Lisa Norton (Centre for Ecology and Hydrology), Matt O'Callaghan (University of Birmingham), Peter Quelch, the Randalls (Goodens Farm, Dorset) and Ken Thompson (University of Sheffield).

A range of people helped us to source GIS data or assisted us in how to best use data and we extend our gratitude to: Lauren Alexander (People's Trust for Endangered Species), Dave Chambers (Joint Nature Conservation Committee), Katie Cruickshanks (Footprint Ecology), Ian Denham (Natural England), David Edwards (Northern Ireland Environment Agency), Crispin Hayes (CW Hayes Associates), Ian Macleod (Forestry Commission), Daniel O'Connell (Ordnance Survey Ireland), Oliver Robertson (Centre for Ecology and Hydrology), Michael O'Neill (Environmental Protection Agency), Antony Myers (British Geological Society), Ray Scanlon (Geological Survey of Ireland), and Phillip Wyndham (Ordnance Survey). Copyright information and sources for map data are given on *page 274*.

We were very fortunate to be able to draw on the expertise and wide experience of a number of people who commented on drafts of the text: Malcolm Ausden (RSPB), Sandy Coppins, Rachel Hoskin (Natural England), Rob McGibbon (Footprint Ecology), Douglas Kite (Natural England), Miles King (Footprint Ecology), Richard Lindsay (University of East London), Helen Read (Corporation of London), Peter Tinsley (Dorset Wildlife Trust) and Jim White (Footprint Ecology). In particular we would like to thank John Underhill-Day (Footprint Ecology) for sharing the great breadth of his knowledge about British and Irish habitats and for his unstinting help and support. Gill Swash read through and commented on all sections of the book, and receives our wholehearted thanks.

We are grateful to the photographers who allowed us to use their lovely images, which have greatly enhanced this book. They are listed on *page 273*. Particular thanks go to Graham Catley, Bob Gibbons, Lorne Gill and the Scottish Natural Heritage image library, Mark Lake and Andy and Gill Swash (WorldWildlifeImages.com). We are grateful to the following who helped us source images: Peter Brash (National Trust), Tom Brereton (MarineLife/Butterfly Conservation), Nigel Bourne (Butterfly Conservation), Keith Dover, Dave Foot, Andy Jukes, Paul Kirkland (Butterfly Conservation), Richard Lindsay (University of East London), Rob McGibbon (Footprint Ecology), Pam Moncur (Scottish Natural Heritage), Caroline Reid (Scottish Natural Heritage), Michael Szebor (RSPB) and Des Thompson (Scottish Natural Heritage).

Others provided help and support in a range of ways. We are grateful to Footprint Ecology for allowing us leave to work on this book and for the use of GIS. Many friends also provided support and encouragement, and our especial thanks go to Victoria Copley, Emma Foulger, Peter Fox, Tania Kaplan, Sarah Honour, Lisa Nicholson and Neil Wiffen.

Finally, a thank you to our families. Judy and Bill Lake were very generous with their time and energy. Mark Lake, Paddy Woodman and Mary Liley helped in an assortment of ways. Willoughby Liley and Tamsin Lake climbed mountains, ventured through bogs, traipsed across hillsides and escaped more or less unhurt from numerous escapades while our attention was elsewhere.

Index

Names in **bold** highlight the habitat types that are afforded a full account.

Bold numbers indicate the page where the main habitat account can be found.

Italicized figures indicate other page(s) where the habitat is mentioned and ***bold italicized*** numbers relate to relevant page in the Habitat Correspondence Tables.

Non-bold, regular figures indicate the main page for those habitats that are not the subject of a full account.